Urban Revolution Now

Henri Lefebvre in Social Research and Architecture

Edited by

Łukasz Stanek
Christian Schmid
and
Ákos Moravánszky

ASHGATE

Published by
Ashgate Publishing Limited
Wey Court East
Union Road
Farnham
Surrey, GU9 7PT
England

Ashgate Publishing Company
110 Cherry Street
Suite 3-1
Burlington, VT 05401-3818
USA

www.ashgate.com

British Library Cataloguing in Publication Data
A catalogue record for this book is available from the British Library

Library of Congress Cataloging-in-Publication Data
Stanek, Lukasz.
  Urban revolution now : Henri Lefebvre in social research and architecture / by Lukasz Stanek, Christian Schmid and Akos Moravanszky.
    pages cm
  Includes bibliographical references and index.
  ISBN 978-1-4094-4293-6 (hardback : alk. paper) -- ISBN 978-1-4094-4292-9 (pbk. : alk. paper) -- ISBN 978-1-4094-4294-3 (ebook) -- ISBN 978-1-4724-0271-4 (epub) 1. Lefebvre, Henri, 1901-1991. 2. Urbanization. 3. Sociology, Urban. 4. Space and time. I. Schmid, Christian. II. Moravanszky, Akos. III. Title.
  HT361.S73 2014
  307.76--dc23

2014019269

ISBN 978-1-4094-4293-6 (hbk)
ISBN 978-1-4094-4292-9 (pbk)
ISBN 978-1-4094-4294-3 (ebk – PDF)
ISBN 978-1-4724-0271-4 (ebk – ePUB)

MIX
Paper from
responsible sources
FSC® C018575

Printed and bound in Great Britain
by MPG PRINTGROUP

Contents

List of Figures *vii*
About the Contributors *xi*

Introduction: Theory, Not Method – Thinking with Lefebvre 1
    Christian Schmid, Łukasz Stanek and Ákos Moravánszky

PART I   ON COMPLETE URBANIZATION

1   The Trouble with Henri: Urban Research and the Theory of
    the Production of Space 27
    Christian Schmid

2   During the Urban Revolution – Conjunctures on the Streets
    of Dhaka 49
    Elisa T. Bertuzzo

3   Where Lefebvre Meets the East: Urbanization in Hong Kong 71
    Wing-Shing Tang

4   Henri Lefebvre and 'Colonization': From Reinterpretation
    to Research 93
    Stefan Kipfer and Kanishka Goonewardena

PART II   CONTRADICTIONS OF ABSTRACT SPACE

5   Plan Puebla Panama: The Violence of Abstract Space 113
    Japhy Wilson

6   'Greater Paris': Urbanization but No Urbanity – How Lefebvre
    Predicted Our Metropolitan Future 133
    Jean-Pierre Garnier

7   The Production of Urban Competitiveness: Modelling
     22@Barcelona   157
     Greig Charnock and Ramon Ribera-Fumaz

8   Reconstructing New Orleans and the Right to the City   173
     M. Christine Boyer

PART III   EVERYDAY ARCHITECTURES

9   Ground Exploration: Producing Everyday Life at the South Bank,
     1948–1951   191
     Nick Beech

10   The Space of the Square: A Lefebvrean Archaeology of
     Budapest   207
     Ákos Moravánszky

11   The Archi-texture of Power: An Inquiry into the Spatial Textures
     of Post-socialist Sarajevo   227
     Mejrema Zatrić

12   For Difference 'in and through' São Paulo: The Regressive-
     Progressive Method   243
     Fraya Frehse

PART IV   URBAN SOCIETY AND ITS PROJECTS

13   Architectural Project and the Agency of Representation: The
     Case of Nowa Huta, Poland   265
     Łukasz Stanek

14   The Debate about Berlin Tempelhof Airport, or: A Lefebvrean
     Critique of Recent Debates about Affect in Geography   283
     Ulrich Best

15   Novi Beograd: Reinventing Utopia   301
     Ljiljana Blagojević

16   Lefebvrean Vaguenesses: Going Beyond Diversion in the
     Production of New Spaces   319
     Jan Lilliendahl Larsen

Index   *341*

List of Figures

Every effort has been made to trace all the copyright holders, but if any have been inadvertently overlooked, the publishers will be pleased to make the necessary arrangement at the first opportunity.

2.1	Urbanization-in-progress. Courtesy of Gunter Nest	50
2.2	Private development to the north of Dhaka: the urban, the industrial, the rural. Courtesy of Gunter Nest	52
2.3	Leaving the old city. Courtesy of Gunter Nest	56
2.4	Emerging urban folk? Courtesy of Gunter Nest	57
2.5	Not climbing the social ladder. Courtesy of Gunter Nest	59
2.6	Encroaching water bodies – everybody's business. Courtesy of Gunter Nest	60
6.1	Greater Paris, 650 sub-projects. Courtesy ateliergrandparis.fr	134
6.2	Greater Paris Express. Courtesy Société du Grand Paris	140
9.1	Royal Festival Hall Progress, London Metropolitan Archive, Special Collection, PHL/02/1016–1022, C41. Courtesy London Metropolitan Archives	198
9.2	Particle Size Distribution, in Leonard Cooling and Alec Skempton, 'A Laboratory Study of London Clay', Journal of the ICE, vol. 17, no. 3 (January 1942), 251–76, 255. Courtesy ICE Publishing	200
10.1	Satellite image of the Oktogon. Courtesy of Google	209
10.2	The Oktogon around 1900. Courtesy Collection of the Ervin Szabó Library, Budapest	211
10.3	Satellite image of the Wekerle garden city. Courtesy of Google	213
10.4	The main square of the Wekerle garden city, today's Kós Károly tér. Courtesy Collection of the Ervin Szabó Library, Budapest	215

10.5   Gate and apartment building on Kós Károly tér. Photograph by
       Ákos Moravánszky   215
10.6   Satellite image of the II. János Pál pápa tér. Courtesy of Google   217
10.7   OTI housing ensemble. Photograph by Tivadar Kozelka, author's archive   218
10.8   Satellite image of Nyugati tér. Courtesy of Google   220

11.1   Historical frontlines and the position of Sarajevo. Drawing by
       Mejrema Zatrić   228
11.2   Sarajevo today: the urban structure and the position of Marijin Dvor.
       Drawing by Mejrema Zatrić   230
11.3   Marijin Dvor: some features of its spatial textures. Drawing by
       Mejrema Zatrić   239

12.1   Southern view of Praça da Sé with the cathedral (February 2012).
       Photograph by Fraya Frehse   248
12.2   Southern bird's-eye view of Praça da Sé (February 2012). Photograph
       by Fábio M. Gonçalves. Courtesy of Fábio M. Gonçalves   249
12.3   Location of some regular furniture and pedestrian types (2007–12).
       Drawing by Jenny Perez and Fraya Frehse   251
12.4   Northern view of the plaza's imperial palm forecourt (April 2011).
       Photograph by Fraya Frehse   253
12.5   Northeastern view of the plaza's shaded rectangle (February 2012).
       Photograph by Fraya Frehse   253
12.6   Southeastern view of the former cathedral (1862). Photograph by
       Militão de Azevedo. Courtesy of Jamil Nassif Abib Collection   255

13.1   'I Live Here': a production in Łaźnia Nowa (2004). Photograph by
       Krescenty Głazik. Courtesy of Łaźnia Nowa   272
13.2   Klub 1949. Photograph by Łukasz Stanek (2008)   273
13.3   Romuald Loegler & team, Centrum E housing complex (1988–95),
       as seen from behind the Lenin monument. Drawing by Romuald
       Loegler. Courtesy of Romuald Loegler   275
13.4   Alley of Roses in the 1950s. Photograph by Henryk Hermanowicz.
       Courtesy Muzeum Historyczne Miasta Krakowa (Nowa Huta)   275
13.5   The Lenin monument in the Alley of Roses, after 1973. Photograph
       by Henryk Hermanowicz. Courtesy Muzeum Historyczne Miasta
       Krakowa (Nowa Huta)   276
13.6   The design of the Alley of Roses (2002) by the architectural office
       Aarcada. Rendering by Piotr Gajewski Architects, Kraków. Courtesy
       of Piotr Gajewski   277
13.7   The Alley of Roses in the 1960s, published in *Głos Tygodnik
       Nowohucki* (no. 35, 2002) as a critique of the realized design.
       Courtesy of *Głos Tygodnik Nowohucki*   278

14.1   Future Tempelhofer Feld. Source: Senatsverwaltung für
       Stadtentwicklung (2008)   291

15.1 Radiant Landscape: Novi Beograd Plan, 1947, by Edvard Ravnikar.
Source: Edvard Ravnikar, 1947. Veliki Beograd, *Obzornik*, 11–12, 455   306
15.2 Urban Landscape: Novi Beograd Outline Plan, 1948, by Nikola
Dobrović. Source: Nikola Dobrović. 1948. Novi Beograd, *Arhitektura*,
III (8–10), 12   306
15.3 Green City: Novi Beograd Master Plan, 1958, by Branko Petričić.
Source: *Novi Beograd*, 1961. Beograd: Direkcija za izgradnju grada, 27   308
15.4 Generic City: background rendering. Illustration by author based on:
2007 'deltacity2-zoom'   309
15.5 Milan Aleksić, 'Buvljak' (Flea Market in Novi Beograd), photograph,
original in colour 122 × 106 cm, 2003   310
15.6 Wolfgang Tschapeller, Centre for the Promotion of Science in
Novi Beograd, winning competition entry, 2010   312
15.7 Hotel 'Jugoslavija' as billboard, 2007, colour photograph by
Milica Lopičić   313

16.1 Wilder's Island with Krøyer's Place in the central part of the harbour
of Copenhagen. Source: Municipality of Copenhagen/Supertanker   323
16.2 Diversion in a space of vacuity. Through simple wood structures
and sand, warehouse B is transformed into an urban meeting place.
Source: Supertanker   324
16.3 'Where the energy was let loose'. Copenhageners participate in
the diverting sand beaches of the quayside on the north side of
Luftkastellet. Source: Supertanker   325
16.4 Sheep grazing on the roof of warehouse B send a diversionary
message to the rest of Copenhagen. Source: Supertanker   325
16.5 The informal atmosphere of Luftkastellet spills into the refurbished
Supertanker workspace in warehouse B. Source: Supertanker   327
16.6 Supertanker translated the informal but politically conscious
atmosphere of the warehouses into strict public processes of
deliberation, for example in staged trials such as *Free Trial!* here at
Copenhagen Town Hall. Source: Alexandra Buhl/Supertanker   327
16.7 From diverted space to tabula rasa. The conventional mode of
producing space clears the practical and semantic traces of diversion.
Source: Supertanker   329

About the Contributors

NICK BEECH

Nick Beech is Lecturer in Architecture at Oxford Brookes University. His PhD (2010), 'Constructing Everyday Life: An Architectural History of the South Bank in Production, 1948–1951', reconsidered Henri Lefebvre's *Critique of Everyday Life* for architectural history, turning to questions raised by the co-transformation of technologies and techniques, state and market forms, and ideologies in processes of post-war reconstruction. His current research is concerned with the history of industrial and professional transformation, as this occurred through the production of the built environment in Britain during and after the Second World War.

ULRICH BEST

Ulrich Best, PhD (Plymouth University), teaches Geography and German Studies as a DAAD visiting professor at York University, Toronto. He has worked on questions of stigmatization and neighbourhood identity in Berlin, the politics of mapping, the history of critical geography in Germany, and the critical geopolitics of Europe. He also studied US–Soviet youth encounters during the Cold War at the Artek holiday camps in Crimea.

ELISA T. BERTUZZO

Elisa T. Bertuzzo is a Berlin-based researcher in cultural and critical urban studies, dealing with survival tactics of the subaltern in South Asia. In her current project 'Archives of movement', she is documenting the everyday life of circular migrants in Bangladesh and India with the focus on the re-definition of the city–country interface and the dominant discourses on 'urbanization'. Her PhD (Technical University Berlin, 2009) focused on the production of space in Dhaka by applying the theories of Henri Lefebvre. She is an active member of the non-profit organisation Habitat Forum Berlin, for which she curates collaborative projects encompassing research, activism and art.

LJILJANA BLAGOJEVIĆ

Ljiljana Blagojević is an architect and associate professor at the Faculty of Architecture, University of Belgrade, Serbia. Her authored books include *Modernism in Serbia: The Elusive Margins of Belgrade Architecture, 1919–1941* (MIT Press 2003) and *Novi Beograd: Osporeni Modernizam* (New Belgrade: Contested Modernism, Zavod za Udžbenike 2007). Her research articles have been published in *StadtBauwelt, Perspecta, The Journal of Architecture, Architektúra&Urbanizmus, Prostor, Český lid, arq-Architectural Research Quarterly.* She held a visiting associate professorship at Yale University School of Architecture in 2009 and 2010. She co-authored the presentation of Serbia at the 11th International Exhibition of Architecture in Venice, 2008.

GREIG CHARNOCK

Greig Charnock teaches international politics at The University of Manchester. He has authored and co-authored several journal articles on the social theory of Henri Lefebvre, and more recently is co-author of *The Limits to Capital in Spain* (Palgrave Macmillan 2014). He is on the editorial board of the journal *Capital & Class.*

M. CHRISTINE BOYER

M. Christine Boyer is the William R. Kenan Jr. professor at the School of Architecture, Princeton University. She is the author of *Le Corbusier: homme de lettres* (Princeton Architectural Press 2011), *CyberCities: Visual Perception in the Age of Electronic Communication* (Princeton Architectural Press 1996), *The City of Collective Memory: Its Historical Imagery and Architectural Entertainments* (MIT Press 1994), *Manhattan Manners: Architecture and Style* 1850–1890 (Rizzoli 1985) and *Dreaming the Rational City: The Myth of City Planning 1890–1945* (MIT Press 1983). She is currently preparing for publication a book entitled *Not Quite Architecture: Writings around Alison and Peter Smithson.*

FRAYA FREHSE

Fraya Frehse is professor of Sociology at Universidade de São Paulo. Her areas of expertise are anthropology and sociology in their interfaces with history, with emphasis on urban studies. She is the author of *Ô da Rua! O Transeunte e o Advento da Modernidade em São Paulo* (Hey You from the Street! The Passer-By and the Onset of Modernity in São Paulo, Edusp 2011), and of *O Tempo das Ruas na São*

Paulo de Fins do Império (Times of the Street in São Paulo at the End of the Empire, Edusp 2005). She recently edited the dossier 'Urban Studies in/on Latin America in the 21st Century: Current State of Play and Future Perspectives' (Iberoamericana 45, 2012).

JEAN-PIERRE GARNIER

Jean-Pierre Garnier is an urban thinker, scholar, educator and political activist with anarcho-autonomous movements, and a collaborator of alternative media. He worked as a planner in France and Cuba, and as an educator and researcher at various French institutions (Toulouse, Paris VIII, Paris I, Ecole Spéciale d'Architecture, CNRS). His research focuses on various aspects of capitalist urbanization: urban politics, practices and representations of the city dwellers, urban violence, transformations of public space, ideological and political function of city planners, architects and urban researchers. He is member of the editorial staff of the journals *Espaces et Sociétés* and *L'Homme et la Société*. His recent book is titled *Une violence éminemment contemporaine* (A Highly Contemporary Violence, Agone 2010).

KANISHKA GOONEWARDENA

Kanishka Goonewardena was trained as an architect in Sri Lanka and now teaches urban design and critical theory at the University of Toronto. He is a co-editor of *Space, Difference, Everyday Life: Reading Henri Lefebvre* (Routledge 2008) and writes on urbanization, colonization and radical theory.

STEFAN KIPFER

Stefan Kipfer teaches politics, planning and urbanization at York University, Toronto. His research focuses on comparative urban politics and social theory. He is co-editor of *Gramsci: Space, Nature, Politics* (Wiley 2013) and *Space, Difference, Everyday Life: Reading Henri Lefebvre* (Routledge 2008).

JAN LILLIENDAHL LARSEN

Jan Lilliendahl Larsen is a researcher, teacher and practicing urbanist. He has studied and participated in urban development and politics in the past two decades. He completed his PhD at Roskilde University in 2008 with a dissertation based primarily on Henri Lefebvre. The empirical study in this work contributed to the creation in 2003 of Supertanker, a Copenhagen-based group of urbanists. Together with Supertanker he organized participatory processes, workshops and conferences. He has authored several essays, reports and articles on the current state of political urbanity, published in Denmark and internationally.

ÁKOS MORAVÁNSZKY

Ákos Moravánszky is Titular Professor of the Theory of Architecture at the Institut gta of ETH Zurich. He studied architecture in Budapest and received his PhD in Vienna. He was a Research Fellow at the Zentralinstitut für Kunstgeschichte in Munich, and the Getty Center in Santa Monica. From 1991 until 1996 he was appointed Visiting Professor at the MIT. The main areas of his research and publication activities are the history of East and Middle European architecture in the nineteenth to twentieth centuries, the history of architectural theory, and the iconology of building materials and constructions. He is the author of several books such as *Competing Visions: Aesthetic Invention and Social Imagination in Central European Architecture* (MIT Press 1998).

RAMON RIBERA-FUMAZ

Ramon Ribera-Fumaz is the director of the 'Urban Transformation in the Society of Knowledge Research Programme' at IN3 and Senior Lecturer at the Economics and Business Department of Open University of Catalonia (UOC), Barcelona. He holds a MA in Economy, Society and Space and a PhD in Geography by The University of Manchester. He joined UOC in 2007 after being postdoctoral fellow in the Institute of Advanced Studies at Lancaster University. His research interests gravitate around the geographies of contemporary urban transformation from a critical perspective focusing on the interaction between technology, culture, economy and politics.

CHRISTIAN SCHMID

Christian Schmid is a geographer and sociologist and teaches at the Department of Architecture, ETH Zurich. His scientific work is on planetary urbanization in international comparison, and on theories of urbanization and of space. He is a founding member of the International Network for Urban Research and Action (INURA). He is the author of *Stadt, Raum und Gesellschaft: Henri Lefebvre und die Theorie der Produktion des Raumes* (Steiner 2005), a critical reconstruction of Henri Lefebvre's theory of the production of space. Together with Swiss architects Roger Diener, Jacques Herzog, Marcel Meili, and Pierre de Meuron he has authored *Switzerland – an Urban Portrait* (Birkhäuser 2006), an analysis of the urbanization process in contemporary Switzerland. He is also co-editor of *Space, Difference, Everyday Life: Reading Henri Lefebvre* (Routledge 2008).

ŁUKASZ STANEK

Łukasz Stanek is Lecturer at the Manchester Architecture Research Centre, The University of Manchester. Stanek authored *Henri Lefebvre on Space: Architecture, Urban Research, and the Production of Theory* (University of Minnesota Press 2011) and edited Lefebvre's unpublished book about architecture, *Toward an Architecture of Enjoyment* (University of Minnesota Press 2014). Stanek also studies the Cold War transfer of architecture from socialist countries to West Africa and the Middle East; on this topic he published the book *Postmodernism Is Almost All Right. Polish Architecture After Socialist Globalization* (Fundacja Bęc-Zmiana 2012) and co-edited a themed issue of *The Journal of Architecture* (2012). Stanek taught at the ETH Zurich and Harvard University Graduate School of Design.

WING-SHING TANG

Wing-Shing Tang is professor at the Department of Geography, Hong Kong Baptist University. His research interests focus on interrogating Lefebvre, Foucault, Harvey and other urban thinkers with socio-historical processes and patterns of urban development in China (including Hong Kong). His research projects focus on land (re)development regime and urban utopianism in Hong Kong and China. This research is substantiated by a comparative project between Chinese and Indian cities.

JAPHY WILSON

Japhy Wilson is a lecturer in International Political Economy at The University of Manchester. His research concerns the relationship between space, power and ideology in the politics of international development. He is the author of *Jeffrey Sachs: The Strange Case of Dr Shock and Mr Aid* (Verso 2014), and co-editor with Erik Swyngedouw of *The Post-Political and Its Discontents: Spaces of Depoliticization, Spectres of Radical Politics* (Edinburgh University Press 2014).

MEJREMA ZATRIĆ

Mejrema Zatrić is doctoral fellow and PhD candidate at the Institut gta of ETH Zurich. She holds degrees in architecture from the University of Sarajevo and the 'Metropolis' Program of the Universitat Politecnica de Catalunya in Barcelona. Informed and inspired by the work of Henri Lefebvre and critical urban theory, her research is focused on the urban transformations of socialist and post-socialist Europe. Her doctoral project examines the theoretical implications and the socio-political underpinnings of the urban research undertaken by pioneering architects in socialist Yugoslavia of the 1950s.

Introduction:
Theory, Not Method – Thinking with Lefebvre

Christian Schmid, Łukasz Stanek and Ákos Moravánszky

In 1970, Henri Lefebvre formulated his thesis on complete urbanization. He understood urbanization as a general transformation of society, fundamentally changing the living conditions in urban and rural areas. Having studied rural life for decades, Lefebvre was well aware of the fundamental transformations of the traditional forms of agrarian societies occurring as a result of urbanization: not only the material structure, the built environment and the urban morphology were changing, but also everyday life. For Lefebvre, urbanization was an encompassing process stretching out in time and space, transforming all aspects of society and having a planetary reach. He described this process in dramatic words: the expanding city attacks the countryside, corrodes and dissolves it. This strange urban life, savage and artificial at the same time, penetrates peasant life, dispossessing it of its traditional features, such as crafts and small centres. The village as a traditional unit of rural life has been absorbed or obliterated by larger entities and has become an integral part of networks of industrial production and consumption. At the same time cities have experienced the dissolution of their social and morphological structure through the extension of financial, commercial and industrial networks accompanied by the dispersion of all sorts of urban fragments: suburbs, residential conglomerations, industrial complexes, tourist resorts, distant urban peripheries and so on.[1]

In a powerful metaphor, borrowed from atomic physics, Lefebvre described the urban process as 'implosion–explosion': 'the tremendous concentration (of people, activities, wealth, goods, objects, instruments, means, and thought) of urban reality and the immense explosion, the projection of numerous, disjunct fragments (peripheries, suburbs, vacation homes, satellite towns)' (Lefebvre 2003 [1970]: 14).

Lefebvre accounted for this process of implosion and explosion, of condensation and dispersion, by introducing the term 'urban fabric' (*le tissu urbain*). He never defined this term precisely: it is not reduced to urban morphology, but encompasses all manifestations of the urban; it forms an economic base and the material support of a more or less intense urban way of life that penetrates ever larger areas. This implies a whole system of material relations but also a system of values. With its varying density, thickness and activity, the urban fabric is more or less tightly woven: it profoundly changes the old urban cores, erodes them and integrates them into a worldwide web; it is differentiated into agglomerations, stretches further out and corrodes the residues of agrarian life. More than a piece of fabric thrown over a territory, this term designates a proliferation allowing larger or smaller areas to escape – thus forming islands of 'ruralism' and islands of 'nature', which nevertheless have their character completely changed in the course of the process.

At the time when Lefebvre put forward this hypothesis, he expressed a tendency rather than an already existing reality. Extending Marx's approach from the methodological chapter of the *Grundrisse* (Marx 1973 [1939]), Lefebvre projected the current tendency into the future in order to allow the future to illuminate the past, the virtual to examine and situate the realized. Thus the hypothesis of complete urbanization served as a point of arrival for existing knowledge and as a point of departure for a new study and a new project. The result of this regressive–progressive procedure leads to a virtual point of convergence: the complete urbanization of society marks a decisive turning point and indicates a possibility – the fundamental transformation of society into an urban society. Urbanization lays the groundwork for this urban society, but in order to be realized, it needs a social upheaval – the urban revolution that unleashes and realizes the potentials that the urbanization process generates.

What is the urban society – or the 'urban' tout court? Lefebvre did not give any specific answer: the current reality presented itself to the observer as a 'blind field', whose properties were still to be detected. The urban society, this virtual object, would reveal itself only as the result of a contradictory historical process full of conflicts and struggles. Curiosity and openness are decisive qualities if we want to understand today's urban trajectories and to reveal their potentials. Urban reality is by necessity unfinished: it is an open horizon; it is the possible, defined by a direction. In this sense, it is a promise, a project and a practice: to bring the impossible into the realm of the possible.

THE URBAN REVOLUTION TODAY

Looking back, it becomes evident that Lefebvre's hypothesis of complete urbanization marked a fundamental turning point in critical urban theory and opened up a new way of thinking 'the urban'.

First, it changed the focus of analysis from urban form to urban process, which has profound consequences for the definition of the urban. For a long time, the urban was defined mainly in respect of a morphological and/or sociospatial form, indicated by the size or density of the population, or by similar characteristics, while approaches that understood the urban as a process of social transformation were relatively rare (see for example, Harvey 1982). Once the urban is conceptualized as process, it becomes obvious that urban form is a floating and ultimately ephemeral phenomenon, as it is a constantly changing, temporary result of an underlying transformation, and is thus shaped according to the trajectory and the rhythms of urbanization, which brings new urban forms constantly to the fore.

Second, Lefebvre understood the urban as totality, and thus proceeded towards a multidimensional analysis of urbanization while criticizing strongly reductive definitions, which often limit urbanization to one single element or a restricted series of factors, such as the growth of cities or the expansion of urban networks. In contrast to those attempts, Lefebvre strove to grasp the concept's complexity and contradictions – which led him to a conception of urbanization as a process that transforms not only physical and socioeconomic structures but also everyday life and lived experience.

Third, Lefebvre not only critically analysed the phenomenon of urbanization and its implications, but at the same time explored and revealed its potentials. His research was among the first studies that theorized the instrumentality of urbanization processes in the reproduction of capitalist relationships, but at the same time he also explored urban space as a place of transgression and alternative social projects. According to Lefebvre, urbanization carries on this projective energy, which he captured in concepts such as 'centrality', 'difference', 'the right to the city' and 'concrete utopia'.

When Lefebvre was writing four decades ago, the urban society appeared as a black box, an unknown continent stretching out in time and space. Today, we are living on this urban continent: urbanization has become a dominant reality in almost all parts of the globe, giving rise to a great variety of urban situations. We can detect a large range of new urbanization processes that has emerged in recent years, going far beyond what Lefebvre could have observed in his time, such as the emergence of urban mega-regions and urban galaxies (Soja and Kanai 2007), the development of new scales of urbanization, the blurring and rearticulation of urban territories through manifold processes of decentralization and recentralization, the disintegration of the 'hinterland', the urbanization of the 'global rural' and the end of the 'wilderness' (see Brenner and Schmid 2011). We still lack a specific and adequate vocabulary to express these complex processes.

At the same time, new representations of the urban are proliferating. Especially in recent years, a range of interventions into the urban field has been advanced in order to grasp today's urban reality, often echoing Lefebvre's fundamental thesis. The twenty-first century was often declared to be the 'urban century'. One of the most widespread and most-often quoted claims is the thesis asserting that the world entered an 'urban age' because, for the first time in history, more than half the world's population now supposedly lives in cities (UN–Habitat 2007, Burdett and Sudjic 2007). However, this thesis is based on a very narrow and limited definition of urbanization – in fact, it focuses merely on the size of 'cities' as they are defined in national statistics, brought together under the auspices of the UN (for a detailed critique of the urban age concept see Brenner and Schmid 2014).

Such empiricist, city-centric conceptualizations give only pale and even distorted accounts of the full dimensions of urbanization. They ignore all the urbanization processes that are transforming the putatively 'non-urban' spaces and thus massively underestimate the whole dimension of urbanization. Far from Lefebvre's call for a careful analysis of the complexity of this process, simple concepts dominate today's scientific as well as political debates on cities and urbanization, thus leading to an undifferentiated and ahistorical understanding of urbanization.

At the same time, and this is the other side of the coin, the 'urban' is sometimes perceived as invested with an almost magical power. In recent years, a new meta-narrative evolved that even declares the 'urban' a superior form of life, thereby establishing a decisively city-centric vision of the world developing towards a 'new metropolitan mainstream' (Schmid 2012b). In a kind of urban triumphalism, cities are presented as places of wealth and progress, as engines of innovation, and as privileged places that make people richer and happier (see for example, Glaeser 2011). In this context, the term 'urban revolution' is even used for the promotion of modernization policies and growth-oriented urban development strategies, as books such as *Welcome to the Urban Revolution* (Brugmann 2009), or *The Metropolitan Revolution* (Katz and Bradley 2013) illustrate – tellingly not mentioning Lefebvre at all.

Against such approaches, a revisiting of Lefebvre's original concepts is crucial: do they keep the promise to guide an encompassing and differentiated analysis of urbanization; to stake out future research on the urban question; and to inspire an alternative project of an urban society? And, decisively, how can this theory be mobilized for fruitful applications in many different fields of urban research and practice? The challenge today is to do empirical research with this theory: to use it, to make sense of it, to realize it and to develop it beyond the formulation of its author.

We must reassess the meaning of the 'urban revolution' today. Taking Lefebvre's thesis as a guideline, we present in this volume scenes from highly contradictory and differentiated contemporary urban development. This book brings together contributions from different fields in a novel collection, engaging in the application of Lefebvre's theory and exploring today's urban realities as they unfold in many different situations and constellations.

EMPIRICAL RESEARCH WITH LEFEBVRE

How should we analyse urbanization and how can we find practical answers and proposals to current problems and challenges posed by the urban question? Lefebvre gives no clear-cut or ready-to-use proposals, but provides us with a series of important concepts that he developed over decades. Crucially, he put the urban question into an overarching context and developed his theory of the production of (urban) space. This theory had already appeared in his work in rural and urban sociology from the 1940s, but its core was formulated in a relatively short period between 1968 ('The Right to the City') and 1974 (*The Production of Space*). It can be seen as a general social theory integrating the fundamental aspects of social reality, the perceived, the conceived and the lived moments, into a three-dimensional conception of the production of space. Space can thus be understood as socially produced in the relationships between material social practices, practices of representing space, and practices of its appropriation in everyday life. At the same time, this theory offers a general theoretical framework integrating the main topics of Lefebvre's research: everyday life, the state, and the urban as intermediary and mediating level. Thus the urban lies in the core of this open-ended social theory (Kipfer et al. 2012, Schmid, Chapter 1 in this volume).

For a long time, Lefebvre's work was mostly seen as purely theoretical. It is therefore decisive to underscore that Lefebvre's theoretical concepts were strongly influenced by his own empirical studies as well as by those of his collaborators and students. As Łukasz Stanek (2011) showed in great detail, the theory of production of space has to be seen as a reinterpretation and development of Marxian categories from within a series of studies on the processes of urbanization of postwar France, which Lefebvre carried out or supervised from the late 1940s to the 1980s. This included his own studies on the Pyrenean communities during the Second World War; his research in rural and urban sociology at the Centre d'études sociologiques from the 1940s until the early 1960s; the interdisciplinary research projects headed by him as professor in Strasbourg (1961–65) and Nanterre (1965–73); and the studies on practices of dwelling carried out by the Institut de sociologie urbaine (ISU), which Lefebvre co-founded in 1962 and over which he presided until 1973. In the course of these studies, but also in response to the most heated political debates of postwar France, and his intense exchanges with architects and planners, Lefebvre's concepts were constantly reinterpreted, which contributed to the engaged, contextual, appropriative and performative character of his writings.

However, applications and mobilizations of Lefebvre's theory for empirical studies came late. For a long time, debates on his work concentrated mainly on theoretical questions. The long and difficult history of Lefebvre interpretation through the conjunctures of neo-Marxist urban theory in the 1970s and postmodern geographies of the 1990s was dominated by one-dimensional readings and marked by conflicting views and claims between different epistemological positions. Only in the 1990s did a 'third wave' of Lefebvre interpretation develop that not only bridged the gap between 'political–economic' and 'cultural' readings, but understood Lefebvre's consistent integration of questions of political economy, state theory, language theory, architecture, everyday life and lived experience in an encompassing materialist and dialectical framework as the decisive advantage of his theory (Kipfer et al. 2008a).

In the last two decades, theoretical debates have thus shed light on many aspects of this complex and ramified theoretical work, and successfully clarified many questions, such as the basic construction of this theory, questions of dialectics, the concept of everyday life, the relationship between urbanization and the urban, the role of space, the spatial triad, the state and the production of nature.[2] By contrast, only rare attempts were made to utilize this theory for concrete research. This situation changed only slowly in the 1990s, when, inspired and propelled by the translation of *The Production of Space* into English (1991), considerably more applications of this theory appeared, testing it in a wide range of topics, conceptual frameworks and places.

Many of these attempts aimed at an operationalization of Lefebvre's three-dimensional concept of the production of space: Shields (1989) applied it in his case study of a shopping mall in Baltimore; Allen and Pryke (1994) studied the production of the abstract space of finance in London, contrasting the everyday lives and spaces of those who work in the financial markets and those who work in the low-income support sector of the financial sector. Fyfe (1996) analysed modernization processes in postwar Glasgow, highlighting the dialectical relationship between representations of space and spaces of representation, and weaving together discourses about the city in planning and poetry. Dierwechter (2002) looked at the formation of modernities and the production of space through an excavation of informality, urban planning and economic survival in post-apartheid Cape Town. Pile (1996) explored the mobilization of psychoanalytical approaches for urban studies and combined Lefebvre's spatial triad with concepts borrowed from Lacan and Kristeva. Interesting further examples for applications of Lefebvre's work include Cartier (1997) on preservation activists who mobilized place-based representations to fight against development plans in Melaka, Malaysia; Hubbard and Sanders (2003) on street prostitution in Birmingham; and Sin (2003) on the political control of ethnic groups in Singapore.

However, many of those first engagements with Lefebvre in empirical research remained isolated contributions in dispersed research fields and disciplinary contexts, and were not further developed into a more elaborated and lasting research perspective. As Kipfer et al. (2012: 121) remind us in a recently published survey on current Lefebvre debates, Lefebvre's analyses need to be translated, actualized and de- and recontextualized. This means fully appropriating his work, enriching and deploying it in constant interaction with specific empirical studies to bring it into a dialogue with other approaches and eventually to develop new concepts and research perspectives (see also Schmid, Chapter 1 in this volume).

Systematic attempts to introduce Lefebvre's thoughts into urban research have been relatively rare – with the remarkable exception of David Harvey, who, since his pathbreaking book *Social Justice and the City* (1973), has been coming back again and again to Lefebvre's concepts. Another important exception is Edward Soja's work on Los Angeles, which until today represents a major attempt to deploy Lefebvre's theory for the analysis of urbanization (Soja 1989, 1996, 2000). While his decidedly postmodern reading of Lefebvre and his reinterpretation and redefinition of the spatial triad have been criticized (Kipfer et al. 2008a, Schmid 2008), his empirical studies reveal a remarkable 'urban imagination' and a sensibility for long-neglected aspects of urbanization – and illustrate the productivity of the combination of the concept of lived space in a political–economic perspective.

From a different epistemological starting point based on German-language critical debates on space and urban dialectics, another strand of urban analysis has evolved, mainly in two research groups in Frankfurt and Zurich, which critically analysed the urban development of these two cities while at the same time making critical interventions in public debates. Both groups developed a similar theoretical approach, integrating Lefebvre's writings on the urban and on space, and especially the spatial triad, with questions of urban struggle, the global city concept, the regulation approach and debates on urbanity and difference (see Hitz et al. 1995). This led to a series of contributions that productively combined Lefebvre's urban epistemology and the triad of production of space by Walter Prigge (1986, 2008 [1991], 1995, 1996) and Christian Schmid (Hartmann et al. 1986, Schmid 1998, 2004, 2006, 2012a).

In a related effort, starting from critical studies on urban development in Toronto, Kanishka Goonewardena and Stefan Kipfer (2004, 2005) created an original approach to urban analysis especially based on, among others, the concept of 'levels of social reality' (Goonewardena 2005) and the concept of 'difference', shedding light on the key distinction between 'minimal' and 'maximal' difference (Kipfer 2008). These efforts were complemented by a long-term project to develop a renewed Lefebvrean approach with a decidedly postcolonial perspective (Kipfer 2007, Kipfer and Goonewardena, Chapter 4 in this volume).

The accelerated globalization and urbanization of recent decades has also changed the scales of urban territories dramatically, creating massive implications for regional development and regional politics. Starting from the widely debated 'scale question', Neil Brenner referred to Lefebvre's insights in order to bring together the scale question and the urban question (Brenner 1997, 2000; for a reply see Kipfer 2009). He consistently widened the scope of analysis on the role of the state in the production of space and developed the concept of 'state spaces' (Brenner 2004), mobilizing Lefebvre's work De l'État (1976–78) that had passed almost without notice for years and has unfortunately not been translated into English (a selection of chapters and essays has been published in Brenner and Elden 2009).

All these engagements in urban research posed the question of social struggle and urban social movements. As early as the 1970s, this field was theoretically defined and structured by Manuel Castells's conception of 'collective consumption' and the related concept of 'urban social movements' (Castells 1977 [1972], 1973, 1983). In contrast to this approach, Lefebvre did not conceptualize urban social movements as such, but understood them always in the context of the dialectical contradiction between urbanization and social struggle. Herein lies the specificity of Lefebvre's perspective on urban movements (see for example, Schmid 1998, Uitermark 2004). From this point of view, Lefebvre's call for the 'right to the city', serving as the title of his first book on urbanization from 1968 (Lefebvre 1996 [1968]), not only marked a political statement and defined a specific urban perspective, but was also the starting point of a debate that is today more vibrant than ever, with or without reference to Lefebvre's theory (see below). An important contribution in this respect was Don Mitchell's book (2003) on the right to the city, public space and social justice, which focused on various struggles in the USA throughout history in order to show that the 'right to the city' is a demand that goes far beyond the provision of decent housing, but includes also the collective creation of urban spaces in response to the needs, desires and pleasures of its inhabitants.[3]

Another important strand of research not yet fully developed until today is the analysis of the urbanization of nature, leading to an urban political ecology that also owes much to Lefebvre's insights, especially to his notion of socially produced nature and his understanding of urbanization as the production of a second nature. Thus political ecology was extended to an analysis of the urban condition, often explicitly referring to Lefebvre's thesis of complete urbanization (see for example Keil 2003). Foundational in this respect was Erik Swyngedouw's (1996) analysis of the urbanization of water, illustrated by the example of the lack of access to potable water in the city of Guayaquil in Ecuador, coming to the conclusion that the social struggle for water was fundamentally a struggle for the right to the city itself. Those ideas were further developed in Swyngedouw and Heynen (2003), Swyngedouw (2004) and Heynen et al. (2006).[4]

If Lefebvre's theory of production of space entered architectural culture only slowly, it was because of the strong association of the discourse on 'architecture as space' with the architectural avant-gardes of the 1920s and 1930s, against which some of the most innovative architects of the second half of the twentieth century rebelled, including Robert Venturi, Denise Scott-Brown and Rem Koolhaas (Scott-Brown and Venturi 2004, Koolhaas 2007, 344). Yet within the debates on the 'spatial turn', or the reassertion of space in social theory that occurred in the course of the 1980s (Soja 1989), Lefebvre's concept of space was contrasted with the discourse of modern architecture and functionalist urbanism, against which Lefebvre had been writing since the 1950s (Stanek 2011). Rather than returning to the modernist definition of 'architecture as space', his concept of space as produced and productive in multiple, heterogeneous and often competing practices was taken up by architectural and urban historians and theorists. Lefebvre's argument that the production of capitalist modernity allows for a retrospective recognition of space as always-already produced offered a new perspective on architecture's instrumentality as perceived individually and collectively, experienced, interpreted, contested and appropriated (Blau 1999, Arnade et al. 2002, Stieber 2006).

This was complemented by discussions in postcolonial and feminist theories focused on the everyday as a place of submission and normalization, transgression and resistance; Lefebvre's work was a key reference here (see for example, Ross 1995, 1997), despite critiques on moments of 'infuriating sexism' in his texts (McLeod 2000). For many scholars, counter-hegemonic practices of everyday space production became sites where the agency of architecture in the reproduction of social relationships could be addressed and, potentially, extended towards architectural innovation. Hence, within a reaffirmed understanding of architecture as production of space, Iain Borden studied skateboarding and argued that it is a particular type of space–time production that offers a 'critical exterior' to architecture and lends itself to rethinking 'architecture's manifold possibilities' (Borden 2001: 1).

Lefebvre's theory of production of space was developed into a number of specific questions, including that of centrality (Devisme 1998) and in a critical account of architectural projects (Milgrom 2002, 2008). In a much wider research perspective, ETH Studio Basel (Diener et al. 2006) was aiming at an encompassing analysis of urban Switzerland based theoretically and methodologically on

Lefebvre's hypothesis of complete urbanization and a reformulated concept of the spatial triad (see Schmid, Chapter 1 in this volume).

The position of Lefebvre's theory for architectural culture was one of the core questions in the work of Łukasz Stanek, who reconstructed Lefebvre's own exchanges with artists, architects and planners of various generations (Stanek 2011), and showed the productivity of Lefebvre's theory in architectural research (Stanek 2012). He studied the position of architectural practices within the division of labour in space production and, in particular, he analysed representations of space and spaces of representation as both products of architectural labour and as intermediaries, tools, instruments, milieus and media of space production (Stanek 2009, 2014).

At the end of the first decade of the twenty-first century the stream of applications and mobilizations of Lefebvre's theory expanded, spreading out into many different fields. Today, contributions informed by Lefebvre's concepts may be found in fields as diverse as geography, sociology, cultural anthropology, urban studies, cultural studies, architecture and urban design, planning, humanities, literature studies, arts, pedagogy, history, and even legal studies. They are operating with many different concepts, often stretch out over several disciplines and thus contribute to the constitution of transdisciplinary fields of research. A short overview of most recent contributions is no longer possible.

In this volume, we present a selection of essays covering a wide variety of applications of Lefebvre's theory in urban research, architecture and urban design, providing several cross-sections through these vast and transdisciplinary fields. The texts gathered in this volume stem mainly from two conferences: 'Rethinking Theory, Space, and Production: Henri Lefebvre Today' (Delft University of Technology, 11–13 November 2008) and 'Urban Research and Architecture: Beyond Henri Lefebvre' (ETH Zurich, 24–26 November 2009).[5] Starting with a section (Part I) gathering contributions that engage with the thesis of complete urbanization and its consequences, we focus in Part II on the very core of the urban question in discussing the power of abstraction, the contradictions of abstract space, the role of difference and the call for the right to the city. The question of everyday architectures and the application of the spatial triad are the subject of Part III, and Part IV, finally, discusses the possibilities of 'concrete utopias' and the contributions of urban projects and strategies to the development of an urban society.

ON COMPLETE URBANIZATION

How to analyse complete urbanization? How to make use of this concept? Part I questions the importance and actuality of Lefebvre's hypothesis of 'complete urbanization', which he posited more than four decades ago. This thesis has been an important inspiration for many accounts of the urban, but it was only rarely examined in detail and applied to concrete empirical analyses of urban territories.[6] This changed in recent years, when a Lefebvre-inspired debate on 'planetary urbanization' evolved (see Brenner and Schmid 2011, Merrifield 2013), starting from the observation that a variegated terrain of urbanized conditions is being produced, extending well beyond the zones of agglomeration that have long monopolized the attention of urban researchers. In a recently edited volume that refers directly to Lefebvre's concept of 'implosion–explosion', Brenner (2014) presents a wide collection of already published as well as new papers on this question.

Under conditions of complete urbanization, the meaning of the urban must itself be fundamentally reimagined both in theory and in practice. This perspective is introduced by Christian Schmid in Chapter 1: 'The Trouble with Henri: Urban Research and the Theory of the Production of Space'. He analyses the difficulties involved in applying Lefebvre's theory to concrete urban research, focusing especially on the analysis of complete urbanization of Switzerland and presenting methodological tools for the analysis of extended processes of urbanization.

To take complete urbanization seriously means looking at all parts of the planet, studying the uneven development of capitalist urbanization and exploring the great differences that are evolving today. This becomes obvious in Chapter 2, by Elisa Bertuzzo, 'During the Urban Revolution – Conjunctures on the Streets of Dhaka'. Starting from a long-term engagement with urbanization in Dhaka by creatively applying the triad of space as structuring concept (Bertuzzo 2009), she provides a reading of the entire city by constantly zooming in and out of various neighbourhoods, thus showing the simultaneity of different urban situations, exploring what urbanization means today and what it involves. Bertuzzo highlights that, within the ongoing urban revolution, the urban takes on many different forms, thereby also amalgamating rural and urban structures in unprecedented ways.

Following this line of argument, Wing-Shing Tang (Chapter 3) analyses the urbanization of Hong Kong with the example of the complex relationships between the urban and the rural in this process. In his chapter, 'Where Lefebvre Meets the East: Urbanization in Hong Kong', he questions Lefebvre's account of the contradictory relationship between city and country and makes clear that we have to be careful with concepts of the urban that are based on Western historical experiences. He invites us to rethink the rural and the urban, and the way they are related to each other, coming to the provocative conclusion that Hong Kong experiences at the same time a ruralization of the city and an urbanization of the countryside. While Lefebvre (as well as Marx and Engels) was well aware of the different relationships between city and country that existed in different parts of the world,[7] this intervention starts an important debate on the very content of the urban and the rural and their mutual relationships in the course of urbanization.

This debate leads directly to the postcolonial critique of Lefebvre's concepts. Based on their longstanding engagement with postcolonial theory, Stefan Kipfer and Kanishka Goonewardena are proposing a reformulation of the concept of colonization, enriched by lectures of Frantz Fanon and based on a rereading of Lefebvre's De l'État (1976–78), going far beyond Lefebvre's original conception and use of this term. In Chapter 4, 'Henri Lefebvre and "Colonization":

From Reinterpretation to Research', they apply this approach by comparing neo-colonial strategies in public housing redevelopment projects in Paris and Toronto.

These contributions raise the question of whether we can apply Lefebvre's concepts directly to all possible situations in the contemporary urbanized world. Does the Western bias of his concepts, strongly (but not exclusively) influenced by his experiences in Paris and the Pyrenees, inevitably limit the explanatory power of his approach? A planetary perspective can only be reached with a multi-polar analysis of knowledge production and political struggle focusing on the differences that shape the urban world today. It is necessary to destabilize well-established Western narratives in urban studies and to take into consideration the wide range and great variety of urban conditions that shape today's world (Robinson 2006, Roy 2009). In this respect, Lefebvre's open-ended conception of the urban could indeed be one (out of several) important starting points for conversations about urbanity and urbanisms across the diversity of contemporary urban situations and their multiple histories (Robinson 2014).

CONTRADICTIONS OF ABSTRACT SPACE

From the debates and contributions on urbanization presented above, a further question emerges: what is the urban in an urbanized society? One of the main theoretical consequences of the thesis of complete urbanization is the need for a new definition of the urban: if the contradiction between city and country no longer serves as the epistemological anchor for the definition of the urban, this new definition must be based on the properties and differentiations developing inside the urban itself. In Lefebvre's dialectical conception the urban is a concrete abstraction, defined by the contradiction between abstract space and differential space (see Stanek 2008). From this epistemological basis Lefebvre developed an understanding of the power of abstraction, which served as a tool for his forceful critique of planning and design concepts. In the perspective of complete urbanization, Lefebvre distilled three terms that structure and define the contradictions of the urban field: 'centrality', 'mediation' and 'difference' (see Schmid 2006, Kipfer et al. 2008b). The urban must be understood as a force field marked by constant debates, controversies and struggles.

One key concept in this respect is 'the right to the city', which Lefebvre formulated in response to the struggles of the late 1960s in large parts of the world, but also reflecting his own experiences in Paris, as well as his historical studies of the Paris Commune of 1871. In recent decades, this term has been employed in a bewildering variety of contexts, in the most diverse adaptations and appropriations. Whether developed with or without explicit reference to Lefebvre's original concept, these debates have been marked by radical as well as reformist positions and strategies. In France, there has long been a split between a position oriented towards Lefebvre the revolutionary (Coornaert and Garnier 1994, Garnier 2010) and a reform-oriented, social-democratic position trying to integrate Lefebvre's call into official politics (Castro 1994). In the middle of the first decade of the 2000s 'the right to the city' has been placed on the official agenda of UN–Habitat.[8] The literature on the different aspects and readings of the right to the city is meanwhile so widespread that it is no longer possible to give a short overview of it.[9]

For Lefebvre, urban struggle was always a decisive reference point for the understanding of the urban. Set into the wider perspective of his theory, it must be clear that his concept of the right to the city is far away from liberal claims for diversity of city life, multicultural tolerance or the concepts of the 'creative city' that have mushroomed in the last decade: it includes resistance to the concretization of globally competitive abstract space, struggle against the reduction of urban differences, and protests against the enclosures of everyday life. The results of these struggles are always open, as is the urban process itself. Part II of this book refers to these concepts and resonates in many ways with Lefebvre's dialectics. It studies various examples of the functionalization, homogenization and commodification of urban space, and explores the struggles involved in the creation of concrete utopias of 'difference', a term that Lefebvre in his later writing substituted for the 'right to the city' (Schmid 2012b).

Chapter 5, 'Plan Puebla Panama: The Violence of Abstract Space', by Japhy Wilson deploys this contradiction between 'abstract' and 'differential' space, and analyses the various struggles against the regional development programme for southern Mexico and Central America, the Plan Puebla Panama. He analyses the effects of this plan on the large-scale restructuring of the whole region and shows that it embodies the structural, symbolic and direct forms of violence inherent in the process of abstraction.

Another instance of abstraction processes in space production is analysed by Jean-Pierre Garnier in Chapter 6, '"Greater Paris": Urbanization but No Urbanity. How Lefebvre Predicted Our Metropolitan Future'. Garnier discusses urban development in contemporary Paris on the tracks of Lefebvre's own critique of planning and urban development so forcefully put forward in *The Right to the City* and *The Urban Revolution* (1996 [1968]). He critically evaluates the recent debates on a fundamental restructuring of the Paris region through the spatial strategy to create a 'Grand Paris', impressively demonstrating that Lefebvre's analytical instruments have lost none of their power.

These contributions are complemented by critiques of urban strategies that are dominated by the ideological concepts of 'global competitiveness' and 'creative cities'. They are analysed by Greig Charnock and Ramon Ribera-Fumaz in Chapter 7, using the example of the urban restructuring of Barcelona ('The Production of Urban Competitiveness: Modelling 22@Barcelona'). This contribution opens the perspective on a wide range of studies referring to Lefebvre's concepts in the critical analysis of strategies of upgrading, gentrification and urban regeneration.[10]

Finally the discussion in Part II comes back to the original question of the right to the city in its most basic notion as the right to stay in one's place and to survive in it. In her contribution, 'Reconstructing New Orleans and the Right to the City', M. Christine Boyer (Chapter 8) carefully analyses the reconstruction of New Orleans after Hurricane Katrina (2005) and shows in detail how the needs and desires of the most vulnerable inhabitants, including their right to return to New Orleans, are denied for a second time.

EVERYDAY ARCHITECTURES

The starting and the end point of any Lefebvrean analysis is everyday life. Urbanization and the changes that come with it are first and foremost visible in the changes in the everyday – the central indicator of the condition of a society. The concept of everyday life was also the first conveyor of Lefebvre's concepts into architectural history and theory in Anglo-American architectural audience in the 1990s. Writing after the translation into English of his major works, Mary McLeod (1997) embraced the concept of the 'everyday', rather than 'space', and argued that it is a resource for an architectural practice opposing the commodification of architecture, both in the 'banality and mediocrity' of the generic built environment and in the star system of the neo-avant-garde. Several other authors bringing Lefebvre to architectural debates at the turn of the century built up a contrast between a 'small-a' architecture of the everyday, ordinary and anonymous; and the 'big-A' Architecture as an individualized, unique and extraordinary object (Upton 2002). The aim was either to challenge the position of the designers by shifting power from the professional expert to the inhabitant, or to refuse to choose one of the sides of this binary opposition and instead advocate for a constant interchange between the ordinary and extraordinary in architectural practice, with the everyday as a productive context for the making, occupation and criticism of architecture (Crawford 1999; Till and Wigglesworth 1998).

The everyday is the guiding line for the chapter 'Ground Exploration: Producing Everyday Life at the South Bank, 1948–1951' (Chapter 9), by Nick Beech, who discusses the dialectical conditioning between the production of space, the production of subjects/bodies, and the production of state and market forms within the emergent welfare state of mid-twentieth-century Britain. Here, Lefebvre's concepts clarify the entanglement of nature, humans and matter within new forms of 'state–space' at various scales.

Beech stresses that his analysis requires a return to Lefebvre's spatial triad. As we have shown above, this triad was applied in many ways in many studies, and it is made operative also in many contributions in this volume. In discussing and applying Lefebvre's concept of space, we should be aware that we can understand space only in relation to time. Indeed, the notion of 'production of space' already implies time, as 'production' is a process that develops in time. A remarkable complement to the spatial triad was Lefebvre's posthumously published *Éléments de Rythmanalyse*; after its translation into English (Lefebvre 2004 [1992]) the concept of rhythmanalysis became one of the topical guidelines for urban research (see especially the wide selection of contributions in Edensor 2012, cf. also Highmore 2005, Meyer 2008, Vogelpohl 2012).

This temporal aspect of triadic space production is a common thread in the chapters by Ákos Moravánszky, Mejrema Zatrić and Fraya Frehse. In Chapter 10, 'The

Space of the Square: A Lefebvrean Archaeology of Budapest', Ákos Moravánszky addresses four urban squares within the *longe durée* of the production of space in Budapest. He comes back to the 'first' spatial turn in the second half of the nineteenth century: the introduction of the concept of 'urban space' (*Stadtraum* in German) into discussions about the city, under the influence of research and theoretical work in the physiology and psychology of visual perception. This historicizing of the concept of urban space allows Moravánszky to question its ideological function, and indeed the possible ideological function of Lefebvre's triad, where the supposed harmony between the perceived, the conceived and the lived obscures the surface-bound realities of real estate, dominating the production of space in post-socialist Budapest.

The role of an architectural object in the production of space is discussed by Mejrema Zatrić in her chapter, 'The Archi-texture of Power: An Inquiry into the Spatial Textures of Post-socialist Sarajevo' (Chapter 11). Zatrić focuses on Marijin Dvor, on the verge of the historic core of Sarajevo, and studies the production of centralities in successive ideological eras, from the erection of a Catholic church in the 1930s, the construction of the Parliament of the Socialist Republic in the 1970s, to a Saudi-based real estate development in the post-Yugoslav period. Inspired by Lefebvre's comments on architecture as 'architexture', Zatrić develops an analysis of architecture as a part of the production of centrality, developing Lefebvre's own analysis of the campus of Paris-Nanterre in May 1968 (Lefebvre 1969 [1968]; for discussion, see Stanek 2011).

Finally, in Chapter 12, 'For Difference 'in and through' São Paulo. The Regressive-Progressive Method', Fraya Frehse offers a creative reading of Lefebvre's triad in an anthropological study of the everyday uses of São Paulo's cathedral square. Lefebvre's spatial triad is translated here into the analysis of the mediating role of space between perceptions, experiences and concepts, and reveals the square as a *different* urban space.

URBAN SOCIETY AND ITS PROJECTS

Part IV of this book questions the very concepts on which it is based: what is an urban society? What is the urban? For Lefebvre, the development towards an urban society is at the same time an analytical hypothesis and a social and political project. As such, it poses the question of urban strategies that could fruitfully exploit the potentials and possibilities that the urban contains.

Key to this question is the concept of representation in its double aspect: as 'space of representation', which Lefebvre described as a space referring to an 'elsewhere' that becomes embodied in the everyday experience; and as 'representations of space'. Architects operate at the intersection of these two aspects of representation, and in Chapter 13, 'Architectural Project and the Agency of Representation: The Case of Nowa Huta, Poland', Łukasz Stanek shows how competing representations intervene into the production of space in the 'first socialist city in Poland'. Lefebvre's strategic decision to theorize practices of representing space as practices of production of space, rather than seeing representations as secondary, was the starting point for the research on Nowa Huta. Instead of confirming or refuting particular representations of this city, Stanek studies specific conjunctures in which representations of space became operative; for example as arguments in municipal investment policies, as conceptual frames for architectural competitions; as operative design concepts, but also as vessels of everyday experiences of urban spaces.

The critique of the mobilization of affective 'lived space' is developed by Ulrich Best with the example of the conflict concerning the defection of an airport in Berlin (Chapter 14: 'The Debate about Berlin Tempelhof Airport, or: A Lefebvrean Critique of Recent Debates about Affect in Geography'). Best argues that the turn towards memory and affect allows redrawing the social and political geography of the city of Berlin. By discussing the 'spatial politics of affect' around the airport he problematizes the space of affect not only as a potential space of freedom but also as a potential space of control.

In 'Novi Beograd: Reinventing Utopia' (Chapter 15) Ljiljana Blagojević addresses the urban problematic of a post-socialist city. Planned and constructed during socialist rule in the former Yugoslavia according to the principles of modern urbanism and the paradigm of the 'functional city', in the post-socialist period the urban space in Novi Beograd was transformed primarily as a result of privatization, commodification and gentrification. Discussed by Lefebvre in the 1980s (Lefebvre et al. 2009), Novi Beograd becomes a privileged example for reassessing the concepts of the right to the city and urban citizenship in today's post-socialist condition.

In Chapter 16, 'Lefebvrean Vaguenesses: Going Beyond Diversion in the Production of New Spaces', Jan Lilliendahl Larsen shows the experience of Supertanker, a network of architects, sociologists and geographers in the informal and creative diversions of industrial wastelands in the harbour of Copenhagen. Larsen shows how the activities of Supertanker revealed some of the potentials in Lefebvrean concepts such as the lived, the urban, the moment, the possible, self-management, appropriation and, in particular, diverted space. The author suggests 'vagueness' as an essential conceptualization of the potentials and perils of diverted spaces, connoting openness towards lived experiences and thus varying conditions of possibility for participation in and appropriation of an unevenly developed social space through the different moments of association.

A remarkable contribution to this discussion is made by the newly found manuscript 'Toward an Architecture of Enjoyment', edited by Łukasz Stanek. In this book, written in 1973 and never published, Lefebvre argues for architectural ways of thinking about habitation, and sketches a vision of architecture as a 'pedagogy of space' that is not a disciplinary practice but a development of the senses (Lefebvre 2014).

THEORY, NOT METHOD

What is the result of the current conjuncture of engagement with Lefebvre's approach? As the chapters in this book clearly show, Lefebvre's theory has proved its capacity to guide research, to be an important source of inspiration and to invite researchers to further develop their ideas by exchanges between theoretical experimentation and empirical research. It is possible to treat a wide range of different questions in urban research with this approach in a sincere and sophisticated way. In relation to earlier waves of Lefebvre interpretation, the current engagement is marked by great rigour in theoretical conceptualization; it uses the theory not to search for catchphrases to decorate a text, but as an instrument of analysis and research. Furthermore, many contributions successfully combine Lefebvre's theory with other approaches, as well as develop original interpretations and appropriations.

As this book shows, there are many ways to understand Lefebvre's theory and to make use of it. The chapters that follow cover many aspects, but they all share certain characteristics.[11]

First of all, they appear as decisively *transdisciplinary*, encompassing the work of sociologists, geographers, architects and planners, but also historians of architecture and the city. Lefebvre's concepts, such as everyday life, complete urbanization, the perceived, conceived, lived space, the concept of rhythms, and the 'right to the city', are mobilized not as the lowest common denominators of the various disciplines involved, but as research perspectives stressing the heterogeneity of social practices of the production of space. Thus a convergence of perspectives that appears through these different engagements not only reveals shared points of interest, but also establishes a transdisciplinary field of urban research.

Second, most of the contributions are characterized by an ambition to link the analysis of a specific case study to an account of the *urban society as a whole*. This ambition – or the bet on the possibility of such a research perspective – is what distinguishes these contributions from much of today's scientific production on urbanization processes. While highlighting a specific aspect or exploring a well-defined problematique, they bypass the common scheme of exemplification of general processes and phenomena, such as 'gentrification' or 'urban social movements'. What brings these different accounts together is their shared understanding that urban society is becoming 'planetary'. Thus, reading these chapters, an overall picture emerges – however uneven, fractured and contradictory – of a planetary urban society.

Third, most of these contributions develop Lefebvre's understanding of *production of space* as a dialectical process irreducible to one original contradiction. The three 'moments' of space production, as theorized by Lefebvre, do not form a synthesis but rather exist in interaction, in conflict or in alliance with each other. What is crucial in this respect is not to apply this triad in a schematic way, but to develop it in view of each case study according to its specificity and complexity.

A fourth characteristic is that many authors treat Lefebvre's theory more as a *general orientation* than as a solid and codified corpus of knowledge. This relates directly to Lefebvre's specific approach to introducing concepts by drawing complex networks of relationships between them rather than defining them in an essentialist and isolated manner. In this way, they become structuring elements of his attempt to theorize space as part of a general social theory.

This points finally to the Marxist core of Lefebvre's theory, which he developed in a persistent dialogue with the writings of Marx while, in many cases, opposing their dominant readings (Stanek 2011). Lefebvre constantly stressed the *non-reductionist character* of the thinking of Marx and aimed at thinking the social whole without reducing the underlying heterogeneity of its phenomena and processes.

What becomes clear is that Lefebvre's concepts are not technical, well-defined and ready-to-hand tools to be instantly implemented. In that sense, doing research 'with' Lefebvre goes far beyond a simple application of concepts and ideas. It is not possible to apply them using a unified method, not even with a standardized set of methods. As this book clearly shows, a wide range of methods came into operation for performing a methodological multiplicity.

Theory, not method: this is Lefebvre's legacy in urban research, to which this volume subscribes. Even in those few contexts in which he characterized his own work by means of a 'method', he did not prescribe a systematic research formula. Rather, he preferred the term '*démarche*' (procedure) to indicate the openness of his research. He aimed at a confrontation of a variety of methods from within a shared theoretical framework, which allows outlining long-term research projects and, in turn, offers criteria for choosing specific case studies from within a historical conjuncture. These two sides of Lefebvre's work – the theoretical guidelines that form a persistent structure throughout his texts, and the experience of their operationalization in response to urgent questions – constitute the essential dynamics of his writings and one that can be fruitfully learned from and developed today. Taking Lefebvre as a starting point for research and design is thus still an endeavour and an adventure, and an expedition into unknown fields.

NOTES

1   See here, and in the following paragraphs: Lefebvre (1996 [1968]: 71ff,119,123), Lefebvre (2003 [1970]: 3f, 16f, 23, 166f).

2   For an overview see especially Gottdiener (1985), Schmidt (1990), Kofman and Lebas (1996), Shields (1999), Gardiner (2000), Elden (2004), Schmid (2005), Merrifield (2006), Roberts (2006), Goonewardena et al. (2008), Brenner and Elden (2009), Ajzenberg et al. (2011), Stanek (2011), Goonewardena (2011), Loftus (2012).

3   Other important contributions to this debate from the early 2000s can be found for example, in Staeheli et al. (2002); see also Purcell (2003).

4   See also Whitehead et al. (2006), Whitehead (2009), Angelo and Wachsmuth (2014).

5   For full programs of the conferences, see: www.henrilefebvre.org.

6   For exceptions see Diener et al. (2006), and Monte-Mór (2014 [1995]).

7   Cf. for example, Lefebvre (2003 [1970]: 119).

8   A critical analysis of the use of the concept 'the right to the city' in the policies of UN agencies is presented in Kuymulu (2013).

9   For a discussion of the basic concept see Schmid (2012b); for an overview of the debate in relation to urban social movements see Mayer (2012). The question of citizenship is approached, among others, in Gilbert and Dikeç (2008). In a wider context see also David Harvey's (2012) discussion of this conception.

10   See for example, Wilson and Wouters (2004) on Chicago, Davidson (2007) on London, and Dörfler (2010, 2011) on Berlin and Hamburg. Phillips (2002) analysed gentrification processes in two villages in south-east England. For two different Lefebvrean analyses of the political mobilizations around the demolitions of the Star Ferry pier and the Queen's pier in Hong Kong, see Ng et al. (2010) and Ku (2012).

11   This is based largely on Stanek and Schmid (2011).

REFERENCES

Ajzenberg, A., Lethierry, H. and Bazinek, L. (eds) 2011. *Maintenant Henri Lefebvre: Renaissance de la pensée critique*. Paris: L'Harmattan.

Allen, J. and Pryke, M. 1994. 'The Production of Service Space', *Environment and Planning D: Society and Space* 12(4): 453–75.

Angelo, H. and Wachsmuth, D. 2014. 'Urbanizing Urban Political Ecology: A Critique of Methodological Cityism', *International Journal of Urban and Regional Research*, forthcoming.

Arnade, P., Howell, M. and Simons, W. 2002. 'Fertile Spaces: The Productivity of Urban Space in Northern Europe', *Journal of Interdisciplinary History* 4: 515–48.

Bertuzzo, E. 2009. *Fragmented Dhaka: Analysing Everyday Life with Henri Lefebvre's Theory of Production of Space*. Stuttgart: Franz Steiner Verlag.

Blau, E. 1999. *The Architecture of Red Vienna, 1919–1934*. Cambridge, MA: MIT Press.

Borden, I. 2001. *Skateboarding, Space and the City: Architecture and the Body*. Oxford: Berg.

Brenner, N. 1997. 'Global, Fragmented, Hierarchical: Henri Lefebvre's Geographies of Globalization', *Public Culture* 10(1): 135–67.

Brenner, N. 2000. 'The Urban Question as a Scale Question: Reflections on Henri Lefebvre, Urban Theory and the Politics of Scale', *International Journal for Urban and Regional Research* 24(2): 361–78.

Brenner, N. 2004. *New State Spaces: Urban Governance and the Rescaling of Statehood*. Oxford: Oxford University Press.

Brenner, N. (ed.) 2014. *Implosions /Explosions: Towards a Study of Planetary Urbanization*. Berlin: Jovis.

Brenner, N. and Schmid, C. 2011. 'Planetary Urbanization', in *Urban Constellations*, edited by M. Gandy. Berlin: Jovis Verlag, 10–13.

Brenner, N. and Schmid, C. 2014. 'The "Urban Age" in Question', *International Journal of Urban and Regional Research* 38(3): 731–55.

Brugmann, J. 2009. *Welcome to the Urban Revolution: How Cities Are Changing the World*. New York: Bloomsbury.

Burdett, R. and Sudjic, D. (eds) 2007. *The Endless City*. London: Phaidon.

Cartier, C.L. 1997. 'The Dead, Place/Space, and Social Activism: Constructing the Nationscape in Historic Melaka', *Environment and Planning D: Society and Space* 15(5): 555–86.

Castells, M. 1973. *Luttes urbaines et pouvoir politique*. Paris: Maspero.

Castells, M. 1977 [1972]. *The Urban Question: A Marxist Approach*. London: Edward Arnold.

Castells, M. 1983. *The City and the Grassroots: A Coss-Cultural Theory of Urban Social Movements*. Berkeley and Los Angeles, CA: University of California Press.

Castro, R. 1994. *Civilisation Urbaine ou Barbarie*. Paris: Pion.

Coornaert, M. and Garnier, J.-P. 1994. 'Présentation: Actualités de Henri Lefebvre', *Espaces et Sociétés* 76: 5–11.

Crawford, M. 1999. 'Introduction', in *Everyday Urbanism*, edited by J. Chase, M. Crawford and J. Kaliski. New York: Monacelli Press, 8–15.

Davidson, M. 2007. 'Gentrification as Global Habitat: A Process of Class Formation or Corporate Creation?', *Transactions of the Institute of British Geographers* 32: 490–506.

Devisme, L. 1998. *Actualité de la pensée d'Henri Lefebvre à propos de l'urbain: la question de la centralité*, Tours: Maison des sciences de la ville.

Diener, R., Herzog, J., Meili, M., de Meuron, P. and Schmid, C. 2006. *Switzerland – An Urban Portrait*. Basel: Birkhäuser.

Dierwechter, Y. 2002. 'Lefebvre's Modernities: Informality, Planning and Space in Cape Town', in *Planning in a Global Era*, edited by A. Thornley and Y. Rydin. Aldershot: Ashgate, 189–210.

Dörfler, T. 2010. *Gentrification in Prenzlauer Berg? Milieuwandel eines Berliner Sozialraums seit 1989*. Berlin: Transcript Verlag.

Dörfler, T. 2011. 'Antinomien des (neuen) Urbanismus: Henri Lefebvre, die HafenCity Hamburg und die Produktion des posturbanen Raumes', *Raumforschung und Raumordnung* 69: 91–104.

Edensor, T. (ed.) 2012. *Geographies of Rhythm: Nature Place Mobilities and Bodies*. Aldershot: Ashgate.

Elden, S. 2004. *Understanding Henri Lefebvre*. New York: Continuum.

Fyfe, N.R. 1996. 'Contested Visions of a Modern City: Planning and Poetry in Postwar Glasgow', *Environment and Planning D: Society and Space* 28(3): 387–403.

Gardiner M.E. 2000. *Critiques of Everyday Life*. New York: Routledge.

Garnier, J.-P. 2010. *Une violence eminemment contemporaine*. Paris: Agone.

Gilbert, L. and Dikeç, M., 2008. 'Right to the City: Politics of Citizenships', in *Space, Difference, Everyday Life: Reading Henri Lefebvre*, edited by K. Goonewardena, S. Kipfer, R. Milgrom and C. Schmid. New York: Routledge, 250–63.

Glaeser, E. 2011. *Triumph of the City: How Our Greatest Invention Makes Us Richer, Smarter, Greener, Healthier, and Happier*. New York: The Penguin Press.

Goonewardena, K. 2005. 'The Urban Sensorium: Space, Ideology and the Aestheticization of Politics'. *Antipode* 37(1): 46–71.

Goonewardena K. 2011. 'Henri Lefebvre', in *The Wiley-Blackwell Companion to Major Social Theorists. Volume 2: Contemporary Social Theorists*, edited by G. Ritzer and J. Stepnisk. Chichester: Wiley-Blackwell, 44–64.

Goonewardena, K. and Kipfer, S. 2004. 'Creole City: Culture, Class and Capital in Toronto', in *The Contested Metropolis. Six Cities at the Beginning of the 21ˢᵗ Century*, edited by INURA and R. Paloscia. Basel: Birkhäuser, 225–30.

Goonewardena, K. and Kipfer, S. 2005. 'Spaces of Difference: Reflections from Toronto on Multiculturalism, Bourgeois Urbanism and the Possibility of Radical Urban Politics', *International Journal of Urban and Regional Research* 29(3): 670–78.

Goonewardena, K., Kipfer, S., Milgrom R. and Schmid, C. (eds) 2008. *Space, Difference, Everyday Life: Reading Henri Lefebvre*. London: Routledge.

Gottdiener, M. 1985. *The Social Production of Urban Space*. Austin, TX: University of Texas Press.

Hartmann, R., Hitz, H., Schmid, C. and Wolff, R. 1986. *Theorien zur Stadtentwicklung*. Oldenburg: Geographische Hochschulmanuskripte (GHM).

Harvey, D. 1973. *Social Justice and the City*. London: Edward Arnold.

Harvey, D. 1982. *The Limits to Capital*. Oxford: Blackwell.

Harvey, D. 2012. *Rebel Cities: From the Right to the City to the Urban Revolution*. London: Verso.

Heynen N., Kaika M. and Swyngedouw E. (eds) 2006. *In the Nature of Cities. Urban Political Ecology and the Politics of Urban Metabolism*. New York: Routledge.

Highmore, B. 2005. *Cityscapes: Cultural Readings in the Material and Symbolic City*. New York: Palgrave.

Hitz, H., Keil, R., Lehrer, U., Ronneberger, K., Schmid C. and Wolff, R. (eds) 1995. *Capitales Fatales: Urbanisierung und Politik in den Finanzmetropolen Frankfurt und Zürich*. Zürich: Rotpunktverlag.

Hubbard, P. and Sanders, T. 2003. 'Making Space for Sex Work: Female Street Prostitution and the Production of Urban Space', *International Journal of Urban and Regional Research* 27(1): 75–89.

Katz, B. and Bradley, J. 2013. *The Metropolitan Revolution: How Cities and Metros Are Fixing Our Broken Politics and Fragile Economy*. Washington, DC: The Brookings Institution.

Keil, R. 2003. 'Progress Report: Urban Political Ecology', *Urban Geography* 24(8): 723–38.

Kipfer, S. 2007. 'Fanon and Space: Colonization, Urbanization, and Liberation from the Colonial to the Global City', *Environment and Planning D: Society and Space* 25(4): 701–26.

Kipfer, S. 2008. 'Hegemony, Everyday Life, and Difference: How Lefebvre Urbanized Gramsci', in *Space, Difference, Everyday Life: Reading Henri Lefebvre*, edited by K. Goonewardena, S. Kipfer, R. Milgrom and C. Schmid. New York: Routledge, 193–211.

Kipfer, S. 2009. 'Why the Urban Question Still Matters: Reflections on Rescaling and the Promise of the Urban', in *Leviathan Undone*, edited by R. Keil R and R. Mahon. Vancouver: UBC Press, 67–86.

Kipfer, S., Goonewardena, K., Schmid, C. and Milgrom, R. 2008a. 'On the Production of Henri Lefebvre', in *Space, Difference, Everyday Life: Reading Henri Lefebvre*, edited by K. Goonewardena, S. Kipfer, R. Milgrom and C. Schmid. New York: Routledge, 1–23.

Kipfer, S., Schmid, C., Goonewardena, K. and Milgrom, R. 2008b. 'Globalizing Lefebvre?', in *Space, Difference, Everyday Life: Reading Henri Lefebvre*, edited by K. Goonewardena, S. Kipfer, R. Milgrom and C. Schmid. New York: Routledge, 285–305.

Kipfer, S., Saberi, P. and Wieditz, T. 2012. 'Henri Lefebvre: Debates and Controversies', *Progress in Human Geography* 37(1): 115–34.

Kofman, E. and Lebas, E. 1996. 'Lost in Transposition: Time, Space and the City', in *Writings on Cities* by Henri Lefebvre, edited by E. Kofman and E. Lebas. Oxford: Blackwell, 3–60.

Koolhaas, R., 2007. 'Navigating the Local: Conversation with Sang Lee', in *The Domestic and the Foreign in Architecture*, edited by S. Lee and R. Baumeister. Rotterdam: 010 Publishers, 340–50.

Ku, A.S. 2012. 'Remaking Places and Fashioning an Opposition Discourse: Struggle over the Star Ferry Pier and the Queen's Pier in Hong Kong', *Environment and Planning D: Society and Space* 30: 5–22.

Kuymulu, M.B. 2013. 'The Vortex of Rights: "Right to the City" at a Crossroads', *International Journal of Urban and Regional Research* 37(3): 923–40.

Lefebvre, H. 1969 [1968]. *The Explosion: Marxism and the French Revolution*. New York: Monthly Review Press.

Lefebvre, H. 1976–78, *De l'État*. Paris: UGE, 4 vols.

Lefebvre, H. 1991 [1974]. *The Production of Space*. London: Blackwell.

Lefebvre, H. 1996 [1968]., 'The Right to the City', in *Writings on Cities* by Henri Lefebvre, edited by E. Kofman and E. Lebas. Oxford: Blackwell, 63–182.

Lefebvre, H. 2003 [1970]. *The Urban Revolution*. Minneapolis, MN: University of Minnesota Press.

Lefebvre, H. 2004 [1992]. *Rhythmanalysis: Space, Time, and Everyday Life*. London: Continuum.

Lefebvre, H. 2009. *State, Space, World: Selected Essays*, edited by N. Brenner and S. Elden. Minneapolis, MN: University of Minnesota Press.

Lefebvre, H. 2014. *Toward an Architecture of Enjoyment*. Minneapolis, MN: University of Minnesota Press.

Lefebvre, H., Guilbaud, P. and Renaudie, S. 2009. 'International Competition for the New Belgrade Urban Structure Improvement', in *Autogestion, or Henri Lefebvre in New Belgrade*, edited by S. Bitter and H. Weber. Berlin: Sternberg Press, 1–71.

Loftus, A. 2012. *Everyday Environmentalism: Creating an Urban Political Ecology*. Minneapolis, MN: University of Minnesota Press.

Marx, K. 1973 [1939]. *Grundrisse: Foundations of the Critique of Political Economy*. Harmondsworth: Penguin.

Mayer, M. 2012. 'The "Right to the City" in Urban Social Movements', in *Cities for People, Not for Profit: Critical Urban Theory and the Right to the City*, edited by N. Brenner, P. Marcuse and M. Mayer. New York: Routledge, 63–85.

McLeod, M. 1997. 'Henri Lefebvre's Critique of Everyday Life: An Introduction', in *Architecture of the Everyday*, edited by D. Burke and S. Harris. New York: Princeton Architectural Press, 9–29.

McLeod, M. 2000. 'Everyday and "Other" Spaces', in *Gender Space Architecture: An Interdisciplinary Introduction*, edited by J. Rendell, B. Penner, and I. Borden. London: Spon, 182–202.

Meyer, K. 2008. 'Rhythms, Streets, Cities', in *Space, Difference, Everyday Life: Reading Henri Lefebvre*, edited by K. Goonewardena, S. Kipfer, R. Milgrom and C. Schmid. New York: Routledge, 147–60.

Merrifield, A. 2006. *Henri Lefebvre: A Critical Introduction*. New York: Routledge.

Merrifield, A. 2013. 'The Urban Question under Planetary Urbanization', *International Journal of Urban and Regional Research* 37(3): 909–22.

Milgrom, R. 2002. 'Realizing Differential Space? Design Processes and Everyday Life in the Architecture of Lucien Kroll', *Capitalism Nature Socialism* 13(2): 75–95.

Milgrom, R. 2008. 'Lucien Kroll: Design, Difference, Everyday Life', in *Space, Difference, Everyday Life: Reading Henri Lefebvre*, edited by K. Goonewardena, S. Kipfer, R. Milgrom and C. Schmid. New York: Routledge, 264–82.

Mitchell, D. 2003. *The Right to the City: Social Justice and the Fight for Public Space*. New York: Guilford Press.

Monte-Mór, R.L. 2014 [1995]. 'Extended Urbanization and Settlement Patterns in Brazil: An Environmental Approach' in *Implosions /Explosions: Towards a Study of Planetary Urbanization*, edited by N. Brenner. Berlin: Jovis 109–21.

Ng, M.K., Tang, W.S., Lee, J. and Leung, D. 2010. 'Spatial Practice, Conceived Space and Lived Space: Hong Kong's "Piers Saga" Through the Lefebvrian Lens', *Planning Perspectives* 25(4): 411–31.

Phillips, M. 2002. 'The Production, Symbolization and Socialization of Gentrification: Impressions from Two Berkshire Villages', *Transactions of the Institute of British Geographers* 27: 282–308.

Pile, S. 1996. *The Body and the City: Psychoanalysis, Space and Subjectivity*. London: Routledge.

Prigge, W. 1986. *Zeit, Raum und Architektur: Zur Geschichte der Räume*. Stuttgart: Dt. Gemeindeverlag.

Prigge, W. 1995. 'Urbi et orbi – zur Epistemologie des Städtischen', in *Capitales Fatales: Urbanisierung und Politik in den Finanzmetropolen Frankfurt und Zürich*, edited by H. Hitz et al. Zürich: Rotpunktverlag.

Prigge, W. 1996. *Urbanität und Intellektualität im 20. Jahrhundert: Wien 1900, Frankfurt 1930, Paris 1960*. Frankfurt/M.: Campus Verlag.

Prigge, W. 2008 [1991]. 'Reading the Urban Revolution: Space and Representation', in *Space, Difference, Everyday Life: Reading Henri Lefebvre*, edited by K. Goonewardena, S. Kipfer, R. Milgrom and C. Schmid. New York: Routledge, 46–61.

Purcell, M. 2003. 'Citizenship and the Right to the Global City', *International Journal of Urban and Regional Research* 27(3): 564–90.

Roberts, J. 2006. *Philosophizing the Everyday*. London: Pluto Press.

Robinson, J. 2006. *Ordinary Cities: Between Modernity and Development*. London: Routledge.

Robinson, J. 2014. 'New Geographies of Theorising the Urban: Putting Comparison to Work for Global Urban Studies', in *A Routledge Handbook on Cities of the Global South*, edited by S. Parnell and S. Oldfield. London: Routledge, 57–70.

Ross, K. 1995. *Fast Cars, Clean Bodies: Decolonization and the Reordering of French Culture*. Cambridge, MA: The MIT Press.

Ross, K. 1997. 'French Quotidian', in *The Art of the Everyday: The Quotidian in Postwar French Culture*, edited by L. Gumpert. New York: New York University Press, 19–30.

Roy, A. 2009. 'The 21st Century Metropolis: New Geographies of Theory', *Regional Studies* 43(6): 819–30.

Schmid, C. 1998. 'The Dialectics of Urbanisation in Zurich: Global City Formation and Urban Social Movements', in *Possible Urban Worlds: Urban Strategies at the End of the 20th Century*, edited by INURA. Basel: Birkhäuser, 216–25.

Schmid, C. 2004. 'A New Paradigm of Urban Development for Zurich', in *The Contested Metropolis. Six Cities at the Beginning of the 21st Century*, edited by INURA and R. Paloscia. Basel: Birkhäuser, 237–46.

Schmid, C. 2005. *Stadt, Raum und Gesellschaft: Henri Lefebvre und die Theorie der Produktion des Raumes*. Stuttgart: Franz Steiner Verlag.

Schmid, C. 2006. 'Theory', in *Switzerland – an Urban Portrait*, edited by R. Diener, J. Herzog, M. Meili, P. de Meuron and C. Schmid. Basel: Birkhäuser, 163–223.

Schmid, C. 2008. 'Henri Lefebvre's Theory of the Production of Space: Towards a Three-dimensional Dialectic', in *Space, Difference, Everyday Life: Reading Henri Lefebvre*, edited by K. Goonewardena, S. Kipfer, R. Milgrom and C. Schmid. New York: Routledge, 27–45.

Schmid, C. 2012a. 'Travelling Warrior and Complete Urbanization in Switzerland: Landscape as Lived Space', in *Landscript 1: Landscape, Vision, Motion*, edited by C. Girot and F. Truniger. Berlin: Jovis, 138–55.

Schmid, C. 2012b. 'Henri Lefebvre, the Right to the City, and the New Metropolitan Mainstream', in *Cities for People, Not for Profit: Critical Urban Theory and the Right to the City*, edited by N. Brenner, P. Marcuse and M. Mayer. New York: Routledge, 42–62.

Schmidt, H. 1990. *Sozialphilosophie des Krieges. Staats- und subjeckttheoretische Untersuchungen zu Henri Lefebvre und Georges Bataille*. Essen: Klartext Verlag.

Scott-Brown, D. and Venturi, R. 2004. *Architecture as Signs and Systems: For a Mannerist Time*. Cambridge, MA: Harvard University Press.

Shields, R. 1989. 'Social Spatialization and the Built Environment: the West Edmonton Mall', *Environment and Planning D: Society and Space* 7(2): 147–64.

Shields, R. 1999. *Lefebvre, Love and Struggle. Spatial Dialectics*. London: Routledge.

Sin, C. H. 2003. 'The Politics of Ethnic Integration in Singapore: Malay "Regrouping" as an Ideological Construct', *International Journal of Urban and Regional Research* 27(3): 527–44.

Soja, E.W. 1989. *Postmodern Geographies: The Reassertion of Space in Critical Social Theory*. London: Verso.

Soja, E.W. 1996. *Thirdspace. Journeys to Los Angeles and Other Real-and-Imagined Places*. Oxford: Blackwell.

Soja, E.W. 2000. *Postmetropolis. Critical Studies of Cities and Regions*. Oxford: Blackwell.

Soja, E.W. and Kanai, M. 2007. 'The Urbanisation of the World', in *The Endless City*, edited by R. Burdett and D. Sudjic. New York: Phaidon Press, 54–69.

Staeheli, L.A., Dowler, L. and Wastl-Walter, D. (eds) 2002. 'Social Transformation, Citizenship and the Right to the City', *GeoJournal* 58(2–3).

Stanek, Ł. 2008. 'Space as Concrete Abstraction: Hegel, Marx and Modern Urbanism in Henri Lefebvre', in *Space, Difference, Everyday Life: Reading Henri Lefebvre*, edited by K. Goonewardena, S. Kipfer, R. Milgrom and C. Schmid. New York: Routledge, 62–79.

Stanek, Ł. 2009. 'Die Produktion des städtischen Raums durch massenmediale Erzählpraktiken: Der Fall Nowa Huta', in *Sozialistische Städte zwischen Herrschaft und Selbstbehauptung: Kommunalpolitik, Stadtplanung und Alltag in der DDR*, edited by H. Reif and C. Bernhardt. Stuttgart: Franz Steiner Verlag, 275–98.

Stanek, Ł. 2011. *Henri Lefebvre on Space: Architecture, Urban Research and the Production of Theory*. Minneapolis, MN: University of Minnesota Press.

Stanek, Ł. 2012. 'Architecture as Space, Again? Notes on the "Spatial Turn"', *Spéciale'Z* (Paris), No. 4: 48–53.

Stanek, Ł. 2014. 'A Manuscript Found in Saragossa. Toward an Architecture', Introduction to *Toward an Architecture of Enjoyment* by Henri Lefebvre, edited by Ł. Stanek. Minneapolis, MN: University of Minnesota Press, xi–lxi.

Stanek, Ł. and Schmid, C. 2011. 'Teoría, no método: Henri Lefebvre, investigación y diseño urbanos en la actualidad', *Urban* 02: 59–66.

Stieber, N., 2006. 'Space, Time, and Architectural History', in *Rethinking Architectural Historiography*, edited by D. Arnold, E.A. Ergut and B.T. Özkaya. New York: Routledge, 171–82.

Swyngedouw, E. 1996. 'The City as a Hybrid: On Nature, Society and Cyborg Urbanization', *Capitalism Nature Socialism* 7(2): 65–80.

Swyngedouw, E. 2004. *Social Power and the Urbanization of Water: Flows of Power*. Oxford: Oxford University Press.

Swyngedouw, E. and Heynen, N.C. 2003. 'Urban Political Ecology, Justice and the Politics of Scale', *Antipode* 35(5): 898–918.

Till, J. and Wigglesworth, S. 1998. 'The Everyday and Architecture', *Architectural Design* 68(7/8): 7–9.

Uitermark, J. 2004. 'Looking Forward by Looking Back: May Day Protests in London and the Strategic Significance of the Urban', *Antipode* 36: 706–27.

UN–Habitat (United Nations Human Settlement Programme) 2007. *The State of the World's Cities Report 2006/2007: 30 Years of Shaping the Habitat Agenda*. London: Earthscan for UN–Habitat.

Upton, D. 2002. 'Architecture in Everyday Life', *New Literary History* 33(4): 707–23.

Vogelpohl, A. 2012. *Urbanes Alltagsleben: Zum Paradox von Differenzierung und Homogenisierung in Stadtquartieren*. Wiesbaden: Springer VS.

Whitehead, M. 2009. 'The Wood for the Trees: Ordinary Environmental Injustice and the Everyday Right to Urban Nature', *International Journal of Urban and Regional Research* 33(3): 662–81.

Whitehead, M., Jones, M. and Jones, R. 2006. 'Spatializing the Ecological Leviathan: Territorial Strategies and the Production of Regional Natures', *Geografiska Annaler: Series B, Human Geography* 88(1): 49–65.

Wilson, D. and Wouters, J. 2004. 'Successful Protect-community Discourse: Spatiality and Politics in Chicago's Pilsen Neighborhood', *Environment and Planning A* 36: 1173–90.

PART I
On Complete Urbanization

1

The Trouble with Henri: Urban Research and the Theory of the Production of Space

Christian Schmid

Translated by Christopher Findlay

Henri Lefebvre's theory of the production of (urban) space, which he developed over a short period from the mid-1960s to the mid-1970s, is today widely quoted and the subject of intense debates. Just two decades ago, this theory was regarded as almost inaccessible, extremely difficult to apply and was consequently rarely used for empirical research. Since then, it has experienced widespread reception and application, both in the field of urban studies as well as in architecture and urban design.

This process of appropriation and application of Lefebvre's theory has not been untroubled. Time and again, all sorts of confusions and problems have arisen. While these initially concerned mainly questions of interpretation and theoretical construction, more recent discussions have primarily focused on the question of how this theory can be successfully introduced into empirical analysis. Engaging with Lefebvre's theory is indeed a remarkable experience: as in one of Hitchcock's funniest movies, where the corpse of poor Harry suddenly disappears and then reappears in the most unexpected places, this theory creates all kinds of unforeseen trouble.[1] As soon as it seems that one problem is solved, another appears.

The following text sheds light on some of these problems and identifies possible paths towards creative applications of the theory of the production of space. It begins with the current state of reception, explains the fundamental structure of this theory, lays out Lefebvre's epistemological strategy, and analyses his understanding of the relationship between theory and empirical research. These points are then illustrated with examples of concrete research on the urbanization of Switzerland, on planetary urbanization and on the urban development of Havana.

ON THE THIRD WAVE OF LEFEBVRE INTERPRETATION

In the past few years, the debate on the theory of the production of space has entered a new phase. While mainly reductionist and one-sided interpretations were dominant in the 1970s and 1980s, especially in the English- and French-speaking debates, a new and more open appropriation of this theory has asserted itself in recent years (see Kipfer et al. 2008, Kipfer et al. 2012).

In that first phase, Lefebvre's texts on urbanization and on space had an ambivalent reception: in France during the early 1970s, Lefebvre was pushed to the margins of intellectual life, mainly by the strong influence of Manuel Castells' vehement critique of his broad and far-reaching conception of the urban revolution (Castells 1977 [1972]).[2] This critique also influenced Lefebvre's reception in the English-speaking world, where his work was almost absent from the debates of new urban sociology, radical geography or urban political economy – an important exception being David Harvey, who was especially inspired by Lefebvre's rigorous analysis of the relationship between urbanization and the dynamics of capital accumulation (see notably Harvey 1973 and 1982).[3] However, both theorists finally pursued very different projects: while Harvey developed a relatively restricted theory of the political economy of space, Lefebvre had the much broader vision of a comprehensive theory of the production of space. But this project did not arouse much interest for quite some time.

This situation changed fundamentally in the 1990s, when, under the influence of the spatial and the cultural turn, the theory of the production of space was 'rediscovered' and finally received with great interest and even enthusiasm (for example, Soja 1989, 1996, Gregory 1994, Dear 2000). Accordingly, this second phase of Lefebvre reception was strongly influenced by postmodern and poststructuralist thought, which also manifested often a reductionist tendency in presenting Lefebvre as a precursor of postmodernism and in trying to narrow his complex and dynamic theory of the *production* of space to a kind of a spatial ontology (see especially Soja 1989). However, it is very difficult to reconcile a postmodernist or poststructuralist approach with Lefebvre's decidedly historical, materialist and dialectical epistemology (cf. Kipfer et al. 2008, Schmid 2008).

For a few years now, a new and different form of access to Lefebvre's work can be observed, which we may consider as the third wave of Lefebvre interpretation (cf. Schmid 2005, Kipfer et al. 2008). It is marked first of all by the fact that it relates in a fundamentally different way to Lefebvre's heterodox and open-ended materialism than earlier interpretations. It no longer tries to demarcate its position from Lefebvre's epistemology, or conversely to functionalize his work for a specific theoretical approach, but rather to have an independent and open debate on his thinking.

Second, an informed and intense discussion of the epistemological and historical context of his theory was initiated, together with careful analysis of a wide range of aspects of his complex work.[4] This development was much favoured by the translation of some of his most important texts into English,[5] which made many aspects of his theory accessible to a broader audience – the lack of translations had long posed almost insurmountable obstacles to the English-language interpretation of his work. Thus, in recent years, it has been possible to clarify many open questions that had caused considerable confusion, especially concerning the construction of his theory. Furthermore, after the dominant Lefebvre interpretation had long focused mainly on the question of space, topics such as urbanization and the urban, the state and everyday life found a new or renewed interest.

Third, this reception is characterized by curiosity and an open-minded approach to Lefebvre's work. An increasing number of texts take Lefebvre's theory as a point of departure, place it in a contemporary context, and thus make it fruitful for further reflections and analysis. Among these are efforts to combine Lefebvre's with other approaches and thus to open up new perspectives.

Fourth, there has been an increasing number of empirical applications. More and more studies are being published that not only cite Lefebvre's work – such citations having become almost routine in certain fields of research – but integrate his theory into the very heart of the investigation itself. The present book is evidence of the breadth and creativity of these efforts.

In this way, the third wave of Lefebvre interpretation has brought about an important expansion of our horizon: it is rooted in an undogmatic reading, uses Lefebvre's work as a point of departure for further reflection, and is at the same time more precise and more open than previous phases of reception.

A GENERAL HISTORICAL–MATERIALIST THEORY OF SOCIETY

Discussion of Lefebvre's work has acquired a new quality in recent years. Key elements of his theory that had long been sources of considerable confusion have been clarified, and the main lines of his thinking can be laid open today. The reconstruction of his theory requires a twofold analysis: first of all, a historical reading that reconstructs the sequence of questions and fields arising in his work and that reveals how they have unfolded in the course of historical development. Second, it requires a synchronic reading that is capable of identifying the overall structure of Lefebvre's theory and of positioning the various aspects in a general theoretical framework.

The Historical Production of Social Realities and Theoretical Concepts

A fundamental aspect of understanding Lefebvre's thinking arises from the fact that he always developed and advanced his theoretical concepts through a thorough engagement with the social reality of his times. Thus a range of new questions came to the fore in the course of his intellectual trajectory. His point of departure was a critical engagement with the philosophical debates of the 1920s and also with the avant-garde and artistic movements of his time – Dada and Surrealism, and later the Situationists. He had not only helped to introduce Hegel and the early works of Marx into the French debate, but continuously developed his own heterodox materialism through critical engagement with phenomenology, existentialism and structuralism. In this regard, the 'German Dialectic' based on the works of Hegel, Marx and Nietzsche played a crucial role, and would become a formative constant in his work. From those quite diverse sources he developed his very specific approach of a heterodox, revolutionary, materialist and dialectical thinking.

This epistemological basis had an immediate effect on his theoretical and empirical analyses, in which a key topic gained prominence even before the Second World War: 'everyday life'. This problematic, which was a very unusual subject for scientific research at the time, marked the consequent application of his strong critique of contemporary philosophical thought, his related claim to wrest philosophy away from pure contemplation, to make it practical and thus also to bring it down to earth – hence his attempts to grasp social reality through concrete investigations. Interestingly, Lefebvre began his empirical work in the countryside, in the Pyrenees, and soon extended it to an analysis of social reality in postwar France.[6] The topic of everyday life remained a recurring theme of his work until the end of his life. He returned to it again and again and illuminated it from various angles. It is also reflected in his philosophical work, which in the 1960s dealt with questions of metaphilosophy, modernization and modernity, and – even before the linguistic turn in social sciences – with language theory.[7]

In the course of Lefebvre's explorations of everyday life, a new phenomenon gradually emerged, indicating a fundamental historic transformation: urbanization. Once more based on his investigations in the Pyrenees, where Lefebvre had observed and analysed the construction of a new town, this new phenomenon gained prominence and soon became a dominant subject of his work.[8] The urban question also proved to be a key aspect of the emerging social protest that culminated in the revolts of the late 1960s and particularly in the events of May 1968 in Paris that marked a decisive experience for Lefebvre.[9] His theoretical and practical explorations of the urban phenomenon led him to the identification of two decisive and interrelated aspects: on the one hand, he analysed the process of urbanization and placed it in the context of industrialization and modernization. On the other, he studied the conditions of the emergence of a (possible, virtual) urban society as a concrete utopia. He finally found and developed the central term signifying the epistemological shift from urbanization to urban society: difference.[10]

Soon after these pioneering works, which marked the beginning of critical urban studies in social science, Lefebvre dedicated himself to a further related question that initially won but little attention, yet was later considered his most important contribution by many scholars: the question of space and its social production.[11] This work, which is as comprehensive as it is challenging and difficult to access, anticipated not only the spatial turn, but in some respects also the cultural turn in social science, thus providing the decisive point of reference for postmodern and poststructuralist interpretations. It is also in this work that Lefebvre fully developed and employed his three-dimensional dialectic.

Just two years later, Lefebvre's intellectual trajectory once more took an unexpected turn when, at the very beginning of globalization, he provided a comprehensive discussion of the questions of the state and of *mondialisation*, before he returned to the question of everyday life and expanded it with an analysis of rhythms.[12]

In this impressive sequence of topics and research fields, a determining aspect of Lefebvre's overall *œuvre* becomes visible: it follows the process of historic development, explores new aspects of social reality and identifies a whole range of new processes. This implies, for any appropriation and application of Lefebvre's thinking, conceptualizing social reality as well as the production of theory as a historical process, analytically and empirically following the course of social dynamics and, therefore, consistently advancing his concepts.

A General Theory of Society in Space and Time

The apparently loose sequence of topics and questions emerging through the course of Lefebvre's intellectual trajectory is thus not the incidental result of a cruise through the *Zeitgeist*, but the findings of a careful study of the unfolding of social reality that can be embedded in an overall historical and theoretical context. A systematic reading reveals that Lefebvre's theoretical construction displays great rigour and coherence on the one hand, but also offers a flexible framework that facilitates the continuous adoption of new developments and allows them to be integrated into the theory. Accordingly, the second, systematic reading reveals a very different depiction of Lefebvre's theoretical concepts. Here, three core analytical categories may be distinguished: levels, dimensions and fields.[13]

The category of 'space-time levels' of social reality refers to the social context of the production of space. Here, Lefebvre identifies first of all a general level or distant order; second, a private level or near order; and third, an intermediate and mediating level, the genuine level of the urban (cf. also Goonewardena 2005). Within this category, the four central topics that dominate Lefebvre's later work can be related to each other and placed in a general scheme: 'everyday life', the 'urban', the 'state' and 'space'. In this framework, 'space' is to be understood as the comprehensive category, while the other categories refer to specific space-time levels of space. One might also say that what is referenced here is the spatial component of social life, and thus also the patterns of spatial development at their various scales.

The category of 'space-time dimensions' in social reality refers to the fundamental aspects of any social practice: the perceived, the conceived, and the lived (*le perçu, le conçu, le vécu*). Lefebvre superimposes upon these three phenomenological terms three corresponding terms derived from linguistics and semiotics: spatial practice, the representation of space, and space as representation. The production of space may therefore be grasped analytically as the totality of three dialectically interlinked production processes that mutually imply each other: the production of material goods, the production of knowledge, and the production of meanings. On a more general level, one might state that there are various ways of accessing social reality: it can be perceived (that is, observed using the five senses); it can be conceived and constructed; and it can also be experienced. From this point of view, the three dimensions constitute a contradictory, three-dimensional or triadic unity (cf. Schmid 2008).

The category of 'space-time fields' of social reality relates to the historicity and temporality of the production of space. Lefebvre refers to these fields in various ways: at the level of the urban, he identifies a succession of the rural, the industrial and the urban field. At the general level, he sees a historical development from absolute to abstract and finally to differential space. These fields refer to specific ways of production of space that are relatively stable over time. One might also say that reference is made here to the trajectories and pathways, but also to the rhythms of social development (see also Bertuzzo and Tang, Chapters 2 and 3 in this volume).

In these diverse theoretical elements, we find nothing less than a general theory of society that integrates space and time as constitutive aspects into its basic structure. Such a theory offers decisive advantages in several respects: first of all, it can be applied at all scales – it allows general analyses of planetary urbanization as well as studies of a concrete urban situation on a street corner. Second, this theory opens up a broad range of applications ranging from the social sciences to architecture and urban design, and it provides productive links to many of the existing assets of urban theory and research that have been developed in the past decades. This volume gives evidence of the great variety of possible fields and questions that can be addressed and productively supported by Lefebvre's theory. Third, the famous 'turns' in the social sciences of recent decades, from the linguistic and the spatial to the cultural turn, are already included in this theory. For instance, questions of language and semiotics, but also questions of symbolisms and everyday experiences, are integrated as constitutive elements into this social theory. Long before concepts of the actor-network theory were introduced into urban research, Lefebvre had already explicitly integrated the materiality of the urban and of space into his theory and had opened it up to applications in the field of political ecology. Furthermore, his theory also bridges the divide between economic and cultural studies that was largely responsible for the rifts between political economy and postmodern and poststructuralist approaches. Fourth, not the least of its advantages is that it constitutes a general theory of society in its spatial and temporal conditions. As such, it not only offers some heuristic principles and guidelines, but also enables the embedding of a vide variety of questions in an encompassing theoretical framework.

However, these advantages have a price: certain specificities of this theory must be accepted that resist any easy and fast appropriation and application.

ON LEFEBVRE'S EPISTEMOLOGY

Even though the basic construction of Lefebvre's theory has in the meantime gained visible contours, considerable difficulties remain in the appropriation of his theory. This is largely due to the fact that the epistemological base of Lefebvre's thinking exhibits certain characteristics that are not widely appreciated in today's strongly empirically oriented and often theoretically shallow debates.

A Three-Dimensional Dialectic

One of the fundamental characteristics is the dialectical construction of Lefebvre's concepts, which entails that they are not easily accessible and comprehensible. The question of dialectics has repeatedly caused a great deal of confusion. Even today, it often remains little understood and continues to create significant problems. Another difficulty is the unusual version of this dialectic, which Lefebvre himself explained only at a late stage. Unlike the dialectics of Hegel and Marx, Lefebvre's version is three-dimensional; that is, it relates three terms to each other. This is a basic principle that appears already in his early texts and develops gradually in the course of his writings (cf. e.g. Lefebvre 2002 [1962], 1966), until it finally unfolds to achieve its full scope in *The Production of Space*, where it becomes the cornerstone of the three-dimensional social theory.

This dialectic has a tremendous potential, but it also makes comprehension of the related concepts difficult. For the dialectical movement of the concepts must be comprehended in its entirety and cannot be reduced to singular quotes – a frequent problem in the interpretation of Lefebvre's texts. Often, scholars and researchers try to circumvent this dialectic and apply only selected aspects of the concepts. However, if Lefebvre's concepts are used in a non-dialectical way, they get detached from their underlying 'deep' structure and thus lose a significant part of their analytical power and effectiveness.

Concrete Abstraction

Directly related to this dialectic is the principle of 'concrete abstraction', Lefebvre's 'key to the real' (Lefebvre 1977: 63). In his understanding, it is necessary not only to construct concepts, but also to free them from their ontological seclusion and to comprehend them in the context of the concrete social reality itself. Therefore he aims to trace the genesis of the concepts in the historical process and in the dialectic of mental abstraction and concrete reality. By way of exemplary explanation, Lefebvre refers to the ambiguous concept of the 'commodity' as developed by Marx at the beginning of the first volume of *Capital*: the commodity has an exchange value that is, however, always based on its use value. The use value is the material support of the exchange value, which in turn constitutes the social form of wealth in capitalist societies. The use value is absorbed in the social abstraction of exchange, but it can be realized only in use, in consumption. The commodity is therefore abstract, but at the same time always concrete and imbued with certain properties and qualities. Thus the commodity has a general, abstract aspect (its exchange value) as well as a concrete, material aspect (its use value). It is necessary to advance from the abstract to the concrete in order to apprehend the contradictory nature of the social world (see also Stanek 2008).

In Lefebvre's view, therefore, abstraction is the result of a historical process and is generated by social reality. Key terms such as 'everyday life', 'the urban' or 'state' are conceived as concrete abstractions (Lefebvre 2003 [1970]: 87, Lefebvre 1991 [1974]: 341). The application of this principle to space brought Lefebvre to his concept of 'abstract space', which is simultaneously homogeneous and fragmented: it is homogeneous and abstract because it is part of the global dominance of the commodity and because its existence is achieved only through the convertibility of all its constituent parts; at the same time it is concrete and fragmented because, as such, it is a part of the material social reality and therefore always localized (Lefebvre 1991 [1974]: 341–42).

Strategy of Knowledge

Based on these insights, Lefebvre also pursues a specific strategy of knowledge (Lefebvre 2000 [1972]: 28). He frequently introduces his terms as approximations, or 'strategic hypotheses', whose scope and range of applicability he explores in the course of his investigation. Accordingly, his terminology is also continuously shifting dialectically – it might be said that it is marked by a fluctuating underlying structure.

In Lefebvre's understanding, terms emerge under certain historical conditions, both in social reality and in theoretical thought (Lefebvre 1980: 15–16, 61). This is why terms must always be embedded in their historical context of emergence and understood historically. At the same time, these terms express not only a 'truth', but have also an 'effectiveness': they elucidate reality and simultaneously animate the future. Developing a concept therefore means situating it, consolidating it, and also detecting its limitations until it can finally be used as an instrument of analysis and critique. Lefebvre's theoretical and empirical procedure (démarche) consists of carrying out precisely this process in the course of an analysis, which is also reflected in his books: he usually sets out by offering a tentative definition of a concept in order subsequently to develop it. As he explains, the 'truth' of a concept does not make itself known until the end of a book as the result of a process of enquiry that reveals the dynamic nature of the concept (Lefebvre 1980: 16). It is of course evident that this process will not stop at the end of a book – thus the concept will continue to evolve further in theoretical debates as well as in practice. However, this being the case, the theory as a whole must also be continuously developed; it must never stand still.

Thus Lefebvre's theory not only serves as an analytical framework, but might even become a generating force: it invites us to investigate certain questions that otherwise would have remained unconsidered, and it leads to certain logical conclusions, whether we like them or not – this is the very practical value of such a theory. The point is therefore to reduce this theory not to a nice bouquet of quotations that may be used to decorate one's empirical studies, but as an instrument of analysis and as a tool for practical application.

ON THE RELATIONSHIP BETWEEN THEORY AND EMPIRICAL RESEARCH

How then can these complex theoretical concepts be used empirically? This brings us to the next source of possible trouble: while his theory has gradually found better understanding in recent years, and many of his concepts have been debated and clarified, the question of empirical application has long remained opaque. Lefebvre did not really offer clarification here, as his books remain elusive when it comes to this question, and the examples he gives are often more illustrative in character than exact in presenting detailed results of concrete field research. In his recent book *Henri Lefebvre on Space*, Łukasz Stanek (2011) closed this lacuna. He meticulously traces how Lefebvre developed his theories on the basis of concrete empirical studies, and how he repeatedly also participated in the elaboration of concrete architectural and urbanistic projects (see also Bittner and Weber 2009). It is necessary in this context to clearly contest and rectify certain myths that have been spread time and again and are still used as arguments against empirical research on the basis of his theory: Lefebvre's theory has an empirical background and is designed for empirical application.

However, Lefebvre did not develop any sophisticated methodology. He and his colleagues and assistants used the existing methods that were available at the time, based mainly on qualitative methodologies. It follows that there are no simple recipes or models that would allow us to apply his concepts. Many of those cannot be transferred directly, or only with a considerable effort. This is a problem in particular because working with Lefebvre's theory is not simply about applying an existing repertoire of concepts, but about the necessity of continuously advancing the theory as part of an engagement with current developments in society. This is largely due to the specific dialectical relationship between theory and empirical research in Lefebvre's understanding.

Transdisciplinarity

Lefebvre's metaphilosophical point of departure is his comprehensive analysis of social processes. Accordingly he attempts to grasp the totality of social reality and he does not respect disciplinary boundaries, but on the contrary attempts to transcend and abolish them. Thus he fiercely criticizes the prevalent division of labour in academia frequently and repeatedly states explicitly his opposition to the specialization, the parcelling and the resulting disciplining of knowledge. He understands the splitting up of knowledge into individual disciplines as seriously limiting the possibility of generating new insights (Lefebvre 1980: 37).

As Lefebvre stated in *The Urban Revolution*, grasping the problematic of urbanization in its entire breadth would justify the foundation of a university bringing together a wide range of disciplines; but it would also require the convergence of those disciplines (Lefebvre 2003 [1970]: 54, 56). Thus his approach consists of rigorous transdisciplinarity: the point is not to split up knowledge and to reduce research questions to isolated aspects; instead, one should strive to comprehend the totality of a phenomenon. However, such an aspiration is a frequent cause of conflicts with the narrow institutional boundaries of the various disciplines.

Transduction

A second important aspect of Lefebvre's research is transduction. His own metaphilosophical epistemology prevented him from attempting to systematize terms on the basis of a (new or old) speculative principle. Instead, his goal was to explore the meaning, the content, the boundaries and ultimately the conditions of the social validity of his concepts, which meant applying a double-edged procedure: a critique of the concepts through practice; and a critique of practice through the concepts. This means that (abstract) concepts must always be related to a concrete reality, and thus exposed to a real confrontation. Lefebvre's ambition was to use his concepts as guidelines in order to understand society, by provoking a confrontation of the philosophical concepts with the non-philosophical world (Lefebvre 2000 [1965]: 50, 114; Lefebvre 2000 [1972]: 28).

Thus Lefebvre develops his concepts in mutual interaction with empirical research. His empirical approach is neither induction nor deduction, but dialectical transduction (Lefebvre 2002 [1962]: 118; 2003 [1972]: 5). He regards this process as a dialectical movement: the first (dialectical) moment is the comprehension of concrete social practice; the second moment aims to approach lived experience without destroying it; the third and final moment consists of developing the concept that will simultaneously permit comprehension of the (historical) social process, a critique of the present, and a prospective illumination of the horizon of the future (Lefebvre 1980: 37). Lefebvre's theoretical concepts can therefore not simply be 'applied', that is, used as a theoretical framework for analysing and explaining various empirical case studies. Rather, the purpose is to confront these concepts with reality, or to immerse them in reality and thus make them productive.

Critique and Project

In order to understand this confrontation it is imperative to have a clear understanding of what Lefebvre's project really was: in a universal sense, no less than a project for the emancipation of humankind (Lefebvre 2000 [1965]: 106). Lefebvre's goal was thus not, as is so often the case in academia, to solve puzzles, but to achieve a change in society and to apply the analysis as an instrument of transformation. Such an analysis is always both a critique and a project (see Stanek 2011). In this sense, the critique constitutes a theoretical act and thus an intervention into a social field.

This is what Lefebvre referred to as 'metaphilosophy': the philosophy becomes 'realized', part of the 'world'. This means, however, that it has to give up its status as philosophy and become a project that realizes itself in the world and, through this very realization, negates itself in the process of (dialectical) sublation (Lefebvre 2000 [1965]: 63). Thus the starting point has to be a radical critique of the present situation, which finally opens up the possibility of practical (and radical) change.

One cannot therefore adopt Lefebvre's theory 'as it is', but must advance it conceptually in constant interaction with social reality. This is why the theory must also constantly be further developed: what is needed is an open and creative way of handling it. This will be explained in the following sections by several concrete examples.

THE THREE-DIMENSIONAL ANALYSIS OF THE PRODUCTION OF SPACE

Nowhere are both the problems and the potentialities of Lefebvre's theory more evident than in his famous three-dimensional conception of the production of space, the key epistemological element of this theory. As outlined above, what this conception refers to is not a set of three independent dimensions, but an ensemble of three contradictions and thus interdependencies between three poles. Therefore the goal cannot be to use the three dimensions like drawers to be filled with corresponding empirical examples or as a scaffold that serves to order the abundance of social reality. Rather, it should be understood as an instrument that can be used to actively advance the analysis. Therefore there are the dialectical relationships between the three poles that are of primary interest. The aim must be to regard such relationships as active elements and not to study them independently, but rather to analyse the dialectical interplay of the dimensions. As Lefebvre emphasized again and again, the three dimensions or moments should be neither conflated nor separated (see for example, Lefebvre 1991 [1974]: 12, 413).

Thus there are many analyses that work with a three-dimensional outline, but few that fully apply it and make it fruitful. This is due not least to the complexity of this theory: empirical studies that fully operate with this three-dimensionality require a huge effort, as they must first analyse spatial practice, that is, the material processes related to the production of space; second, examine the representations of space, that is, discourses, concepts, plans and so on; and finally also integrate into the analysis the spaces of representation and thus lived experience. That means applying a whole range of often demanding and laborious, mainly qualitative, methods. Additionally, the dialectical interdependencies between the three dimensions must be analysed, which is again not an easy task. Nevertheless, it is possible to carry out such analyses, and they can be very fruitful (see for example, Stanek, Chapter 13 in this volume, Bertuzzo 2009, Schmid 2012).

Networks, Borders, Differences

In order to allow a broader application, it is often useful to narrow the research question or to develop a more accessible analytical framework. This is what we did in the project *Switzerland – An Urban Portrait* at ETH Studio Basel (Diener et al. 2006). This project, which involved architects Roger Diener, Jacques Herzog, Marcel Meili and Pierre de Meuron, about 150 students of architecture and about 20 research assistants, aimed at developing a novel analysis of the urbanization of Switzerland. In order to allow the involvement of students in the empirical research, we developed a simplified theoretical concept or 'field kit' based on Lefebvre's triad that is easy to comprehend and can be applied in the field, but at the same time is solidly anchored in theory. As a result we found a series of three terms that could guide and inspire our investigation: networks, borders and differences.

These three terms relate directly to the three basic concepts of Lefebvre's triad (cf. Schmid 2006): first of all, spatial practice can be operationalized using the concept of *networks*. Urban space is a space of exchange, meeting and interaction. It is permeated by all sorts of networks that can be analysed in order to identify various urban constellations on different scales. Second, urban spaces are always permeated by manifold political, social and cultural *borders*: one may understand these as indicators of the urban condition of a territory and therefore use them as the basis of a critical investigation of various definitions of urban space. The methodological assignment here was always to frame the map in such a way that the borders are in the centre: in this way, the existing representations of space were decentred, while the borders between various areas became visible. It is often the case that maps are left with white spaces beyond the borders, as nothing is shown there, and thus they might conceal key elements of spatial development. An analysis of the 'white realms' of a map can therefore be particularly illuminating. Third, we used a term that often creates difficulties, but that is crucial for any analysis of urban spaces following Lefebvre's approach: *difference*, which denotes a specific aspect of lived space. Our goal here was on the one hand to discover various forms of difference, and, on the other, to investigate differences as constitutive elements of urban territories. These three terms enabled a dynamic definition and analysis of urban areas and the development of a typology of different urbanization processes.

ON THE ANALYSIS OF URBAN TERRITORIES

In order to apply this set of tools empirically, we followed Lefebvre's classic procedure by taking his famous thesis of complete urbanization as the starting point of our analysis. This thesis had already proven to be very fruitful on many occasions. The first time that we, as students, had applied this thesis to Switzerland (Hartmann et al. 1986), it was a real provocation: we met with vigorous opposition from all sides – the thesis simply flew in the face of everyday observation and of the prevalent rural image of Switzerland, notwithstanding the fact that Switzerland had already become largely industrialized and urbanized in the nineteenth century. Even years later, this thesis continued to evoke objections. However, in Switzerland (as in many other countries), agriculture has become a modern industry applying digital technology and is heavily subsidized by the government. At the same time, the so-called 'rural' areas are far removed from idyllic ideas of village communities: they have long become integrated into manifold urban networks; their territory is covered with all kinds of urban symbols and signals; standards of living and lifestyles have largely become similar to those of urban regions; and everyday life is oriented towards the needs of an urban population. No doubt there are still cows on Swiss meadows – but they are not rural cows, they are urban cows.

The contradiction between 'city' and 'countryside' has been fundamentally transformed and can no longer serve as a fruitful starting point of an analysis. This means that the analysis should no longer focus on the differences between 'urban' and 'rural' areas, but examine the differences developing within the urban. It would be completely misleading to start from the assumption that the thesis of complete urbanization implies a homogenization of all territories. On the contrary, urbanization is a process that is constantly bringing forth new urban situations and thus also creating new differences. This also means not reducing urbanization to the production of the built environment, but understanding it as a comprehensive social process and developing a much broader definition of the urban, while also including other aspects in the analysis: the transformation of everyday life; the development of (different) urban lifestyles; the changing patterns of communications and mobility; the manifold interdependencies and linkages of social and economic life and so on.

Complete Urbanization in Switzerland

In the project *Switzerland – An Urban Portrait* we finally took the thesis of complete urbanization as the basis for a systematic analysis of the urban conditions in Switzerland. The challenge was to proceed with a comprehensive analysis of urbanization for the entire territory, including so-called 'rural' areas, and to find a methodological design that allowed us to detect various forms of urbanization. We developed a methodological procedure that combined methods of social sciences and of architecture and also attributed great epistemological significance to the design process. Maps were finally the main instruments of this analysis; the texts were ultimately only commentaries on the maps – it was a cartographical analysis in the proper sense of the term. For this empirical enquiry, we applied a multi-step approach. First, we came up with the three theoretical categories – networks, borders and differences – that would guide our investigation. Second, we developed a set of empirical methods that we called 'drills': a specific combination of classic field research methods such as interviews, participant observation and document research with which we explored the urban conditions in various places in Switzerland. Third, based on this empirical material, we used a specific form of mapping to construct and design the urban spaces of Switzerland, essentially following two methodological guidelines: on the one hand, we superimposed a wide range of indicators in order to grasp urbanization as a multilayered phenomenon, while, on the other, we avoided drawing sharp delineations of the various urban spaces in order to emphasize the blurriness and the processual nature of urbanization. Fourth, based on this cartographic analysis, we developed a typology of urbanized territories. The fifth and final phase saw the validation of this analysis through interviews and conversations with experts. This is particularly important in such a case, since the point is to test and consolidate these representations of space, benefiting from the wealth of implicit knowledge that local experts have, which is often much more substantial than statistical analyses.

The result of this work was a new image of Switzerland that avoided the term 'rural' altogether. We identified five different types of urbanized territories: *metropolitan regions, networks of cities, quiet zones, Alpine resort,* and *Alpine fallow lands.* We thus succeeded in shedding light on urbanization processes that are not usually within the scope of an urban analysis, especially various forms of peripheral urbanization.

On Planetary Urbanization

If we take this analysis one step further, it has manifold implications far beyond Switzerland. Urbanization today is a process that involves the entire territory of the planet and not only certain areas. There is no longer an 'outside' of the urban condition. A concept with further reach is therefore required, capable of comprehending, depicting and analysing the wide variety of urbanization processes that take place outside of the areas hitherto regarded as 'urban'. This is grasped with the concept of 'planetary urbanization' (Brenner and Schmid 2011, 2014, Merrifield 2013) that is also based on Lefebvre's thesis of complete urbanization.

Lefebvre captured this observation in the powerful metaphor of 'implosion–explosion': the tremendous concentration of people, activities, wealth, goods, objects, instruments, means and thought, and, at the same time, the immense explosion, the projection of numerous, disjunct fragments into space (Lefebvre 2003 [1972]: 14). Based on these considerations, Neil Brenner and I developed a novel conception that understands urbanization as a dialectical relationship of 'concentrated' and 'extended' urbanization. It is designed not only to focus on processes of agglomeration alone, but also to take into account the concomitant wide expansion of urban networks, infrastructural arrangements and sociometabolic processes (Brenner and Schmid 2014).

REPRESENTATIONS OF SPACE AND 'FORGOTTEN' SPACES

In Lefebvrean terms, we can understand such new images and definitions of urban areas, as discussed above, as 'representations of space'. As Nietzsche has stated, we cannot see something without giving it a name (Lefebvre 1980: 39). Accordingly, we are not able to act within a space without having developed an idea of what that space looks like. In order to communicate this idea, we require terms, concepts, images and maps that delimit and denote this space. Thus representations of space are defined in a twofold manner – as (conceived) ideas and as (communicated) concepts.[14] They signify something, they prescribe something, they guide our actions and give them a direction. As Lefebvre tells us, such representations are never innocent: they are always associated with power.

What effects do such representations of space have? They privilege certain aspects and suppress others. This raises the question of what is present and what is absent, what is illuminated and what is hidden – what is not shown is often more important than what is shown. It was for good reason that Lefebvre called these phenomena 'representations of space', although they are close to ideologies. However, in his later work, Lefebvre preferred to develop a theory of representation instead of further employing the term 'ideology' (Lefebvre 1980: 27; see also Goonewardena 2005, Wachsmuth 2014). For representations of space have an operational quality: their purpose is to denote something, to illuminate something, to change something. Thus proposing a different representation of space constitutes an intervention in the debate. Lefebvre's theory is self-reflexive at this point and shows how the researcher himself becomes an actor in the process of the production of space. This directly poses the question of the responsibility of the researcher: as Lefebvre notes, the author has to take a personal responsibility in such operations and incurs risks, including the risk of error (Lefebvre 2000 [1972]: 28).

The Project: A New Representation of Switzerland

This nexus can be illustrated particularly well in *Switzerland – An Urban Portrait*, which was conceived from the beginning not only as an analysis, but also as a project: its declared purpose was to create a new image of Switzerland, and to substitute it for the old image. This meant advancing the analysis to the point where it effectively turned into a project. Initially, frequent criticism was voiced that this portrait contained no concrete proposals – the notion of architects 'only' analysing without proposing a project was unacceptable to many. They overlooked the fact that this analysis simultaneously constituted a project. Primarily, it comprised a detailed critique of the existing representations of Switzerland, especially of the concept of 'decentralized concentration' that had been developed in the 1930s and been reissued and refined repeatedly ever since. This concept, which portrayed Switzerland as a compromise between 'urban' and 'rural' areas, called for a decentralized settlement of the country, which, however, ultimately constituted one of the key conditions for the complete urbanization of Switzerland. The image of Switzerland in the *Urban Portrait*, on the other hand, was diametrically opposed to such idyllic and outdated conceptions and revealed what many did not like to recognize: the presence of large-scale sociospatial inequalities, different speeds of development and varying qualities of urbanization. Our maps thus revealed what many earlier studies – in particular those operating with statistical analyses – had carefully concealed: the unequal development of the territory. Thus, for instance, the category of 'rural areas' as shown in many statistics comprises two completely different types of areas: on the one hand, areas experiencing strong pressure of urbanization (we called them 'quiet zones'), and on the other hand, areas marked by a continuous loss of social energy and activities (which we called *Alpine Brachen* or 'Alpine fallow lands'). This second type in particular gave rise to intense public debate and strong criticism. The long-cultivated image of Switzerland as a decentralized, but well-organized, carefully balanced and regionally equilibrated country had developed cracks and fissures, which were clearly addressed and exposed in our new representation of space.

In this context, it was interesting to note other reactions, for example: 'What you're showing is nothing new – we've known that for years.' In reality, however, we have found no publication that depicted Switzerland in a similar way before the *Urban Portrait* was published. Thus our representation was seen as so plausible that some regarded it as a statement of well-known facts. This observation, in turn, takes us back to the triadic analysis: it is impossible to perceive a space without previously having conceived it, and space cannot be conceived without having been experienced. In order to be effective, the depiction must therefore be based on experience; it must re-present something that is rooted in a concrete reality.

Interestingly, the new image of Switzerland we proposed has largely established itself in the meantime. It marked the beginning of a paradigm shift in Swiss planning history and has left a significant mark on it, up to the point where it was even used as the starting point for a new official planning concept for the spatial development of Switzerland (Bundesamt für Raumentwicklung 2012).

Havana Profunda: 'Forgotten' Space and Alternative Project

The approach of the *Urban Portrait* was also adopted in another project, in order to elaborate an analysis for the future urban development of Havana (Peña Díaz and Schmid 2008). This analysis had obviously to cope with completely different conditions and to apply other means than those used in the *Urban Portrait*, mainly because of a blatant scarcity of statistics, data and information. We therefore organized a series of workshops with experts from academia and urban planning to elaborate a new conception of Havana's urban structure.[15] Here, too, the identification and analysis of urban configurations revealed an urban structure that was completely different from the hitherto dominant representation of this urban space, which is basically defined in strictly geographical terms: the prevailing planning concept, which has been applied for many years, subdivided the entire urban area of Havana into three zones – a central, a peripheral and an intermediary zone. In contrast to this representation, two major urban configurations emerged from our analysis: the *Blue Strip* and *Deep Havana*.

The *Blue Strip* is our term for a heterogeneous strip of varying breadth along the coast in which the important institutions, facilities, restaurants and hotels are concentrated. It is the area that continues to determine the image of Havana today – where the image of a tropical, urban Eldorado, reproduced for decades in cinema, literature and advertisements, finds its world-famous iconography. Accordingly, the *Blue Strip* is also the part of Havana that draws the greatest international attention, as well as the crowds of tourists and visitors and the influx of investments. International architectural and research projects also focus almost exclusively on this area. By contrast, the south of the city features a large area that is also quite heterogeneous and comprises very diverse neighbourhoods. While it is located right in the geographical centre of Havana, it forms in many respects a remote, forgotten, neglected and disregarded part of the Caribbean metropolis, which is overshadowed by the famous neighbourhoods along the coast and is far away from the flows of visitors and capital. It also became clear that there are hardly any academic studies on this area. We called this area *Deep Havana*.

In this case, too, the elaboration of an 'other' representation of space was the key to addressing the issue of social and sociospatial inequalities that have developed in Havana. Although the full analysis has yet to be published, the two terms we coined have already entered the local debate on planning and urban development.

As these examples show, the full reach of the three-dimensional analysis unfolds here: what representations of space reveal, illuminate, make explicit, are just as significant as what they leave in the dark and conceal. This allows us to identify 'forgotten' spaces, underappreciated spaces, disregarded spaces.

The mere exposure already has an effect in this context: it is important to disclose another reality and to draw a different map. The analysis reveals something and brings it to the surface; the point is to make something visible, to show a reality that was always present, but is not depicted, expressed and exposed in dominant representations and is therefore absent from discourse and not subject to debate. Addressing this reality and thus making it accessible to experience is one of the decisive moments of analysis and marks the beginning of a possible alternative project.

BEYOND LEFEBVRE[16]

How should the theory of the production of space be handled? These examples show only a few of the possibilities for mobilizing and applying this theory in a productive way. This book presents further examples, and of course there are many other possible ways for engaging with this theory. However, based on the reflections presented above, I can nevertheless sketch a few elements of a possible research strategy.

First of all, Lefebvre's theory must be taken seriously if it is to deploy its full potential. It should not be regarded as a *quantité négligeable*; nor should it be used as a quarry of ideas and concepts. Rather, its principles of construction should be illuminated and the full potential of its effectiveness should be exhausted.

Second, it is crucial to remember that the most important texts on the theory of the production of space were written more than four decades ago, which means that their further development is unavoidable. We live in a completely different world today: new developments have arisen, and we require new concepts to be able to understand the world. It is therefore essential that Lefebvre's work not be canonized, but continuously expanded in engagement with reality. Additionally, theoretical advances that have since been achieved should also be acknowledged and taken into account.

Finally and most importantly, employing Lefebvre's concepts means applying them, which implies following the core of Lefebvre's procedure: always confronting the theory with concrete experiences, experimenting, continuously engaging with concrete practice in order to develop the theory further, immersing the theory in reality and making it fruitful – and thus ultimately also going beyond Lefebvre.

NOTES

1   *The Trouble with Harry* (dir. Alfred Hitchcock, 1955).

2   Cf. also Coornaert and Garnier 1994. Castells later revised his view on Lefebvre's theory considerably: cf. Castells 1983.

3   One of the few other scholars who positively received Lefebvre's theory was Gottdiener (1985).

4   The list of important publications on Lefebvre's work has become very long in the meantime. To quote just a few: Hess 1988, Kofman and Lebas 1996, Shields 1999, Elden 2004, Schmid 2005, Merrifield 2006, Goonewardena et al. 2008, Brenner and Elden 2009, Stanek 2011, Ajzenberg et al. 2011.

5   Since the English translation of *La Production de l'espace* in 1991, a whole series of further translations of books and articles on the city and urbanization, on everyday life and modernity and also on the state has been published.

6   Lefebvre 2008 [1947, 1958]; 2000 [1972]; cf. Stanek 2011.

7   Lefebvre 2000 [1965], 1995 [1962], 1966.

8   Lefebvre 1996 [1968], 2003 [1972].

9   Lefebvre 1969 [1968].

10   Lefebvre 1970. Cf. Schmid 2005, Kipfer 2008.

11   Lefebvre 1991 [1974].

12   Lefebvre 1976a, 1976b, 1977, 1978, 2006 [1981], 2004 [1992], Brenner and Elden 2009.

13   The theory of the production of space is reconstructed in detail in Schmid 2005.

14   Lefebvre (1980: 8) refers here to the German terms *Vorstellung* and *Darstellung*.

15   This was a participative process involving around 50 experts in varying compositions; see also Peña Díaz and Schmid 2008.

16   This title refers to the conference 'Urban Research and Architecture: Beyond Henri Lefebvre' (ETH Zurich, 24–26 November 2009, see: www.henrilefebvre.org).

REFERENCES

Ajzenberg, A., Lethierry, H. and Bazinek, L. (eds) 2011. *Maintenant Henri Lefebvre: Renaissance de la pensée critique*. Paris: L'Harmattan.

Bertuzzo, E. 2009. *Fragmented Dhaka: Analysing Everyday Life With Henri Lefebvre's Theory of Production of Space*. Stuttgart: Franz Steiner Verlag.

Bitter, S. and Weber, H. 2009. *Autogestion, or Henri Lefebvre in New Belgrade*. Berlin: Sternberg Press.

Brenner, N. and Schmid, C. 2011. 'Planetary Urbanization', in *Urban Constellations*, edited by M. Gandy. Berlin: Jovis Verlag, 10–13.

Brenner, N. and Schmid, C. 2014. 'The "Urban Age" in Question'. *International Journal for Urban and Regional Research* 38(3): 731–55.

Bundesamt für Raumentwicklung, 2012. *Raumkonzept Schweiz*. Bern: are.

Castells, M. 1977 [1972]. *The Urban Question: A Marxist Approach*. London: Edward Arnold.

Castells, M. 1983. *The City and the Grassroots: A Cross-Cultural Theory of Urban Social Movements*. Berkeley and Los Angeles, CA: University of California Press.

Coornaert M. and Garnier, J.-P. 1994. 'Présentation: Actualités de Henri Lefebvre'. *Espaces et Sociétés* 76: 5–11.

Dear, M. 2000. *The Postmodern Urban Condition*. Oxford: Blackwell.

Diener, R., Herzog, J., Meili, M., de Meuron, P. and Schmid, C. 2006. *Switzerland – An Urban Portrait*. Basel: Birkhäuser.

Elden, S. 2004. *Understanding Henri Lefebvre*. New York: Continuum.

Goonewardena, K. 2005. 'The Urban Sensorium: Space, Ideology and the Aestheticization of Politics'. *Antipode* 37(1): 46–71.

Goonewardena, K. Kipfer, S., Milgrom R. and Schmid, C. (eds) 2008. *Space, Difference, Everyday Life: Reading Henri Lefebvre*. London: Routledge.

Gottdiener, M. 1985. *The Social Production of Urban Space*. Austin, TX: University of Texas Press.

Gregory, D. 1994. *Geographical Imaginations*. Oxford: Blackwell.

Hartmann, R., Hitz, H., Schmid, S. and Wolff, R. 1986. 'Die urbane Revolution – Thesen zur Stadtentwicklung Zürichs', in *Zürich ohne Grenzen*, edited by T. Ginsburg, H. Hitz, C. Schmid and R. Wolff. Zürich: Pendo, 150–65.

Harvey, D. 1973. *Social Justice and the City*. London: Edward Arnold.

Harvey, D. 1982. *The Limits to Capital*. Oxford: Blackwell.

Hess, R. 1988. *Henri Lefebvre et l'aventure du siècle*. Paris: Éditions A.M. Métailié.

Kipfer, S. 2008. 'Hegemony, Everyday Life, and Difference: How Lefebvre Urbanized Gramsci', in *Space, Difference, Everyday Life: Reading Henri Lefebvre*, edited by K. Goonewardena, S. Kipfer, R. Milgrom and C. Schmid. New York: Routledge, 193–211.

Kipfer, S., Goonewardena, K., Schmid, C. and Milgrom, R. 2008. 'On the Production of Henri Lefebvre', in *Space, Difference, Everyday Life: Reading Henri Lefebvre*, edited by K. Goonewardena, S. Kipfer, R. Milgrom and C. Schmid. New York: Routledge, 1–23.

Kipfer, S., Saberi, P. and Wieditz, T. 2012. 'Henri Lefebvre: Debates and Controversies'. *Progress in Human Geography* 37(1): 115–34.

Kofman, E. and Lebas, E. 1996. 'Lost in Transposition: Time, Space and the City', in *Writings on Cities: Henri Lefebvre*, edited by E. Kofman and E. Lebas. Oxford: Blackwell, 3–60.

Lefebvre, H. 1966. *Le langage et la société*. Paris: Gallimard.

Lefebvre, H. 1969 [1968]. *The Explosion: Marxism and the French Upheaval*. New York and London: Monthly Review Press.

Lefebvre, H. 1970. *Le manifeste différentialiste*. Paris: Gallimard.

Lefebvre, H. 1976a. *De l'État. Tome 1: L'État dans le monde moderne*. Paris: Union Générale d'Éditions.

Lefebvre, H. 1976b. *De l'État. Tome 2: Théorie Marxiste de l'État de Hegel à Mao*. Paris: Union Générale d'Éditions.

Lefebvre, H. 1977. *De l'État. Tome 3: Le mode de production étatique*. Paris: Union Générale d'Éditions.

Lefebvre, H. 1978. *De l'État. Tome 4: Les contradictions de l'État moderne*. Paris: Union Générale d'Éditions.

Lefebvre, H. 1980. *La présence et l'absence. Contribution à la théorie des représentations*. Paris: Casterman.

Lefebvre, H. 1986. *Le retour de la dialectique. 12 mots clefs pour le monde moderne*. Paris: Messidor/Éditions sociales.

Lefebvre, H. 1991 [1974]. *The Production of Space*. Oxford: Blackwell.

Lefebvre, H. 1995 [1962]. *Introduction to Modernity: Twelve Preludes*. New York: Verso.

Lefebvre, H. 1996 [1968]. 'The Right to the City', in *Writings on Cities* by Henri Lefebvre, edited by E. Kofman and E. Lebas. Oxford: Blackwell, 63–182.

Lefebvre, H. 2000 [1965]: *Métaphilosophie*. Paris: Éditions Syllepse.

Lefebvre, H. 2000 [1972]. *Everyday Life in the Modern World*. New York: Continuum.

Lefebvre, H. 2002 [1962]. *Critique of Everyday Life Volume 2. Foundations for a Sociology of the Everyday*. New York: Verso.

Lefebvre, H. 2003 [1970]. *The Urban Revolution*. Minneapolis, MN: University of Minnesota Press.

Lefebvre, H. 2004 [1992]. *Rhythmanalysis: Space, Time and Everyday Life*. New York: Continuum.

Lefebvre, H. 2006 [1981]. *Critique of Everyday Life Volume 3. From Modernity to Modernism*. New York: Verso.

Lefebvre, H. 2008 [1947, 1958]. *Critique of Everyday Life Volume 1: Introduction*. New York: Verso.

Lefebvre, H. 2009. *State, Space, World: Selected Essays*, edited by N. Brenner and S. Elden. Minneapolis, MN: University of Minnesota Press.

Merrifield, A. 2006. *Henri Lefebvre: A Critical Introduction*. New York: Routledge.

Merrifield, A. 2013. 'The Urban Question under Planetary Urbanization'. *International Journal of Urban and Regional Research* 37(3): 909–22.

Peña Díaz, J. and Schmid, C. 2008. 'Deep Havana', in *Havana Lessons,* edited by H. Gugger and H. Spoerl. Lausanne: Lapa, ENAC, EPF Lausanne, 156–67.

Schmid, C. 2005. *Stadt, Raum und Gesellschaft: Henri Lefebvre und die Theorie der Produktion des Raumes*. Stuttgart: Franz Steiner Verlag.

Schmid, C. 2006. 'Theory', in *Switzerland – An Urban Portrait,* edited by R. Diener, J. Herzog, M. Meili, P. de Meuron and C. Schmid. Basel: Birkhäuser, 163–223.

Schmid, C. 2008. 'Henri Lefebvre's Theory of the Production of Space: Towards a Three-dimensional Dialectic', in *Space, Difference, Everyday Life: Reading Henri Lefebvre*, edited by K. Goonewardena, S. Kipfer, R. Milgrom and C. Schmid. New York: Routledge, 27–45.

Schmid, C. 2012. 'Travelling Warrior and Complete Urbanization in Switzerland: Landscape as Lived Space', in *Landscript 1: Landscape, Vision, Motion*, edited by C. Girot and F. Truniger. Berlin: Jovis, 138–55.

Schmid, C. 2013. 'Patterns and Pathways of Global Urbanization: Towards Comparative Analysis', in *Globalization of Urbanity*, edited by J. Acebillo, J. Lévy and C. Schmid. Barcelona: Actar, 51–77.

Shields, R. 1999. *Lefebvre, Love and Struggle. Spatial Dialectics*. London: Routledge.

Soja, E.W. 1989. *Postmodern Geographies: The Reassertion of Space in Critical Social Theory*. London: Verso.

Soja, E.W. 1996. *Thirdspace. Journeys to Los Angeles and Other Real-and-Imagined Places*. Oxford: Blackwell.

Stanek, Ł. 2008. 'Space as Concrete Abstraction: Hegel, Marx and Modern Urbanism in Henri Lefebvre', in *Space, Difference, Everyday Life: Reading Henri Lefebvre*, edited by K. Goonewardena, S. Kipfer, R. Milgrom and C. Schmid. New York: Routledge, 62–79.

Stanek, Ł. 2011. *Henri Lefebvre on Space: Architecture, Urban Research and the Production of Space*. Minneapolis, MN: University of Minnesota Press.

Swyngedouw, E. and Heynen, N.C. 2003. 'Urban Political Ecology, Justice and the Politics of Scale'. *Antipode* 35(5): 898–918.

Wachsmuth, D. 2014. 'City as Ideology: Reconciling the Explosion of the City Form with the Tenacity of the City Concept'. *Environment and Planning D: Society and Space* 32(1): 75–90.

2

During the Urban Revolution – Conjunctures on the Streets of Dhaka

Elisa T. Bertuzzo

Branches of canals, still the biotope of water plants and lotus flowers, making their way through construction sites where greyish concrete slabs wait to be mounted on high-rise buildings; privately developed residential blocks awaiting the official provision of electricity and water and then the arrival of middle-class families, while the ever-growing settlements of the poor conduct a life of their own. The signs of accelerated urbanization are easy to detect in Dhaka, corrugated-iron capital city of Bangladesh. Its streets attest to the highly diverse lifestyles of millions of inhabitants, many of them immigrants from all over the country, each pursuing individual, and not always reciprocally compatible, dreams, visions and expectations.

In the following, I shall conceptualize these inhabitants as the producers of *differential time*. I shall show how the latter should become the actual object of urbanization studies in an age in which the old formula 'the city is the conflation of diversity' is of little or no help in grasping an urban process that, evolving beyond Western contexts, confronts us with new challenges. Pointing to conceptual as well as practical problems of the 'stylization' of urbanization on the basis of Europe's and North America's experience, I elaborate an alternative approach based on Lefebvre's regressive–progressive procedure. This endeavour aims in parallel at a discussion of Lefebvre's understanding of space and time, rather than at solely applying a 'method' inspired by his writings.[1] In the final section, I delineate the advantages of thinking that, in spite of fashionable discourses treating the world's 'complete urbanization' as a *fait accompli*, we haven't yet reached but the middle of the urban revolution.

ON DIFFERENTIAL TIME

What should we understand by differential time? I borrow this term from Lefebvre's differential space, about which he wrote (1991 [1974]: 52): 'inasmuch as abstract

Fig. 2.1
Urbanization-
in-progress

space tends towards homogeneity, towards the elimination of existing differences or peculiarities, a new space cannot be born (produced) unless it accentuates differences'. On this basis, it is possible to conceive of differential time as the time that originates from the contradicting perceptions of, for example, farmers thinking about the approaching harvest season while pulling a cycle-rickshaw through the rush hour's traffic jam, of female garment-workers learning to claim better conditions at work but obeying the same old patriarchal rules at home, of college students miming Bollywood stars and dreaming of an MBA admission in the US or in Canada, of rural workers displaying cattle and goats on the roadsides before the Eid[2] celebrations, when the city resembles a huge haat (rural market), of housemaids and waiters spending half their day in the air-conditioned rooms of luxurious apartments and five-star hotels to return at night to their barely electrified homes. The list could go on, yet the above should suffice to evidence how, in a city like Dhaka, individuals' everyday life is embedded in contemporary but diverse temporalities, as well as in contiguous but distinguished spaces: pre-modern, modern and postmodern at once; village, industrializing city and urbanized 'megacity' at one and the same time.[3]

Such a conflation of diversities is not fully understood by just asserting that the city is a 'convergence of diversity'. With its focus on, obviously diversified, people and practices that gather in social space, this long-known formula lacks a temporal perspective and thus misses the point. When not only people and practices, but also the historically given modes of production and the temporally forged perceptions of everyday spaces are as varied as in Dhaka, we need to tackle a twofold challenge: first to develop a definition of the city that comprehends non-European settings in a twenty-first-century, often postcolonial, context, in which the meaning of 'rural', 'industrial' and 'urban' may strongly differ from Western understandings. Second, since that formula not only coincided with the concept of urbanity but also legitimized a particular social model (that of classic European democratic systems, with state intervention balancing capitalist growth), it concerns the question whether the 'urban', as a social model inspiring policy and planning, is still a viable option. Clearly, this is far too complex a challenge to be resolved in a single chapter. I rather elaborate a series of 'preparatory' thoughts, starting from the term Lefebvre used with regard to exactly such conflation: space-time. Therewith he indicated that, when differential time and differential space are considered together, one must overcome the traditional distinction between spatial analysis (as practised for example in geography, urban design or architecture) and temporal analysis (as for example in history, anthropology or psychology).[4]

COMPLETE URBANIZATION?

In *La révolution urbaine*, Lefebvre (2003a [1970]: 32) pointed out that certain countries are simultaneously undergoing the rural, the industrial and the urban phase. His insight does not seem to be taken into much consideration by works of recent decades, which treat the urban as the ultimate dimension of social life in cities. A gross misunderstanding of the hypothesis of 'complete urbanization of society' is thereby apparent and goes along with a not always careful use of some of Lefebvre's key concepts, for example differential space, (space as) process and, not least, revolution. Thus, social contexts that actually display the rural, the industrial and the urban at once – such as the fast-growing cities in the so-called developing world – are often treated as if they were just waiting for industrialization to progress and the 'complete urban' to succeed it.[5] Moreover, analyses on urbanization generally cover solely cities and so-called urban regions (or, at most, urbanizing regions), whereas the transformations of so-called rural areas are usually confined to discussions on rural development in spite of the fact that they are also transformed by urbanization, as Lefebvre put it.

What are the reasons for such a tendency to interpret the urban as if it were an exclusive feature of cities? The answer partly relates to the fact that the production of concepts, until today, occurs mainly in academic institutions of the West. There, urbanization went hand in hand with infrastructural interventions that, over at least 200 years, changed both the cities, in which cement and permanent buildings replaced ephemeral structures and nature was brought under human

Fig. 2.2 Private
development
to the north of
Dhaka: the urban,
the industrial,
the rural

Fig. 2.2 Private development to the north of Dhaka: the urban, the industrial, the rural

control, and the landscape, increasingly demarcated by cities' 'hard edges'. From such a perspective, industrialization appears to play the role of mediator, if not medium, of urbanization. In many Western countries, culture, lifestyles and the everyday in cities became relatively homogeneous since the late twentieth century due to the erasure of agricultural labour and the decline of industry; the figures defining 60 per cent to 70 per cent of today's population as urban, problematic as they are, ultimately mirror such homogeneity.[6] However, many researchers overlook the fact that urbanization has other manifestations in countries in which, after the end of colonial dominance, phenomena linked to economic globalization created completely new frameworks for the growth of cities.[7] Let's think for example of contexts such as India or Brazil, whose progress depends mostly on the development of the tertiary, and not secondary, sector: the consequences for their cities, mainly described as 'contradictory' or 'hybrid', are rarely analysed in connection with the 'otherness' of the respective production modes. When it comes to Bangladesh, an obsession with the features a city 'should' display to meet Western representations is responsible for Dhaka being defined the 'world's most ruralized city' by Bangladeshi social scientists.[8] Other than the oxymoron 'rural city', which, with its counterpart 'urban village', may be legitimately used to point to special trends of urban development, this paradoxical assertion mirrors the difficulty of grasping Bangladesh's own process of urbanization by means of the traditional axioms of urban studies.

'ZOOMING IN AND OUT' TO MAKE CONJUNCTURES EMERGE.

In his preoccupation with everyday life in modern society, Lefebvre forged a perspective that I like to call a 'radically materialist gaze' and that finds one realization in the regressive–progressive procedure. It is well known that Lefebvre preferred the term 'procedure' (*démarche*) to 'method' to describe his empirical research. In 'La méthode d'Henri Lefebvre', Rémi Hess (2004) traces this attitude back to Surrealism, the movement that influenced another thinker of space and time, Walter Benjamin, and, later, some of the Situationists. My rendering of Dhaka, exposed in the next section, results from a 'gaze' developed from within such an imaginary triangle: Henri Lefebvre, Walter Benjamin, Situationist dérive.

For Lefebvre, as a Marxist thinker, it was important to make the present the reference point of social analysis. He occupied himself with the temporal made-ness of the present, with historicity. This specification is central to understand the 'gaze', which is not just about studying history and time, but about deconstructing them in order to ease their critical analysis. In other words, Lefebvre concentrated his attention on the discontinuities of production, whereby he detached himself from historical materialism's focus on the issue of the class-determined production of social order. I am convinced that precisely this move in Lefebvre's thought brought about the regressive–progressive procedure. It consists of three steps: (1) consider attentively and describe what exists; (2) bring to light its historical determinants; and (3) create a different narration, via these determinants, of the present.[9] In Hess's reading, Lefebvre essentially aimed via these steps at unravelling in the present the possibilities, the virtualities, obliterated by history.[10] A similarity to Benjamin's concept of the resurrection of the past in the present is perceptible here,[11] as also the clear emergence of the procedure's ultimate goal: to bring temporal and spatial thinking into a new relation, thereby highlighting ruptures, exceptions, and 'holes' in the production process. The regressive–progressive procedure is rooted in this understanding of history as detectable and redeemable in the present – and, more concretely: of revolution as enactable in the present from within the past. This allows for Lefebvre's thought to be revolutionary even under today's changed social conditions, as gazing in a radically materialist manner can in fact represent a poietic act, able to generate analytical and conceptual approaches to revolutionary urbanization most needed today, as disillusion, disorientation and 'aesthetic critique' (Boltanski and Chiapello 2005) have replaced utopia to an extent that in the revolutionary years around 1968 would have been difficult to foresee. Hence the procedure's radicality.

Time (and its inherent difference) was not Lefebvre's only concern: his interest in the present brought space and spatial analysis to the fore. Whence, the various attempts to conceive of space-time, the sum of differential space and time. In my application, the effort to think time and space together translates in a recollection of walks on Dhaka's streets. This means that, in something of a re-enactment of Benjamin's *flânerie* and the Situationists' *dérive*, I 'dig' in time to gather and recompose various walks taken over recent years, thereby looking at Dhaka and its urbanization photographically, capturing instants rather than sequences in spaces. What does photography have to do with the regressive–progressive procedure? As explained above, the procedure sets out with a descriptive moment that is spatial–sociological. In the second moment, details are progressively brought to light; the observed is inspected more closely and time plays an increasingly important role. In the third, the repetitions as well as ruptures of time become evident by placing impression next to impression. It is not difficult to detect the similarity of the first moment to the act of photographing; of the second, the search for historical developments, to the work in a darkroom, and of the third, the interplay of observations developed in the previous moment and impressions, to the combined effect of various chemical agents on the photographic image.

Lefebvre himself often applied optical metaphors in his writings. In one such metaphor, he drew attention to the peculiarity of the optical apparatus, based on a void, the pupil, and an impregnable tissue, the retina.[12] Following his clue, a first basic rule of the regressive–progressive procedure could go as follows: 'in order to see [that is, abandoning the metaphor, to attain a radically materialist gaze at urbanization], we must first make the centre of our vision void of the usual representations'. 'Representations' indicates the dominant Western images of, for example, urbanity, rurality, ways of life, social systems and so on, which usually direct our gaze onto space. Before these representations is the essential performance of the pupil, dilating or contracting. The blank or dark moment (Lefebvre 2003a: 26) implied by global urbanization not only requires better illumination, but actually compels us to change our perspective, interchanging temporal references 'now' and 'then' (regressive–progressive), and scales of observation: the local, the urban, the global.[13] I formulate, on this basis, a second rule: 'in order to grasp urbanization and its direction toward "some other thing" [Lefebvre 2003a: 67], we must use different lenses and, from time to time, also reverse the images'. Repeated zooming in and out in relation to the object, urbanization, forges a perspective on space and spatial processes that goes beyond traditional understandings (both finalistic and teleological) of the present. The present can thus emerge as the result, itself multifaceted, of multiple production relations; as economically, historically, geographically as well as culturally determined; and in spite of its high specificity, as the product of a globally detectable process.

Summarizing, the application that follows must fulfil a twofold task. On the one hand, it must create an awareness of differential time. Inasmuch as spatial relations always contain residues of history, time – meaning the time of the body, of daily routines, but also recomposed in memory – essentially differs in space. Understanding this difference could help to acknowledge the possibility for dominant time and space relations to be subverted. On the other hand, it should allow for conjunctures to emerge. In Lefebvre's view, conjunctures occur when, in the analysis of space, the conflation of 'horizontal' complexities such as organization, structure and everyday life and 'vertical' complexities, such as historical events, developments and genealogies,[14] creates the opportunity for an unexpected recognition. Conjunctural moments cannot be planned: they unify an observer's perception, knowledge and intuition.[15]

ZOOM OUT: FROM THE STREET TO THE WORLD, FROM THE PAST TO THE FUTURE

The application, starting from the particular and progressively zooming outwards, begins in the segregated bazar[16] of puran dhaka (Old Dhaka), where artisans and customers of innumerable retail outlets and workshops chat from one veranda to another along the narrow roads. Since many former house-owners shifted to the airy new developed outskirts and were promptly substituted by inflowing immigrants, the old town experienced a high fluctuation of population in the last three decades.[17] The kutti, old Dhaka's traditional dwellers, 'wearing white shirt and white lungi',[18] are meanwhile reduced to legendary figures rather than controlling the bazar, now dominated by the proliferating newcomers. So too are the old shell-engravers, gold- and silversmiths, papermakers and bookbinders witnessing the extinction of their century-long crafts vis-à-vis the mechanization of production and the expansion of imports of cheap items from South East Asia and China. Their sons opt for different jobs, although they may not leave their houses in the bazar, which is becoming more crowded and less characteristic. The observer searching for traces of resistance to such dissolution of traditional production and social forms considers with hope the collective funds to which the residents of each bazar still contribute. Administrated by respective committees, they cover the expenditures for public events such as the Eid rally and various puja,[19] for example to put up stands, pay invited musicians or to clean the streets after the celebrations, but are also distributed to families in need. In Lefebvre's terms, the committees could be regarded as intermediate phenomena linking the particular – for example individual and family issues in specific households – to the general – for example the broader spatial and social organization of each neighbourhood. Physical qualities, primarily the narrowness and segregatedness of the bazar with its traditional architectural features, such as the tiny lanes facilitating communication and the inner courtyards where women usually interact, thus play an important role. The same observer, *vis-à-vis* today's pressure to construct,[20] may complain about the high-rise residential and commercial buildings, progressively erasing Old Dhaka's traditional house forms and posing a threat to self-organization in the neighbourhoods. But would such complaint be legitimate? Are the committees really a means to cope with overall economic uncertainty and the authorities' neglect? Here, the sociologist or the development worker finds terrain on which to test, for example, the hypothesis that social exclusion enhances social cohesion. Or are the committees, rather, evidence of persistent segregation and rigid power as well as strict gender hierarchies within the bazar? We should consult the anthropologist or the heritage conservationist to get answers to that question. What is certain is that not only the committees' future, but also puran Dhaka's present-day situation, is inscrutable. Who are Old Dhaka's inhabitants: the kutti, exponents of a pre-industrial time, or the migrants embodying a twenty-first century's urbanization *à la* 'arrival city'?[21] Where is its industrial, where its urban phase? Are the transformations of Old Dhaka witnessing an urban revolution that occurred without anyone noticing it? How to speak of one urbanization vis-à-vis these multifaceted developments?

Slightly zooming out, we pass from the micro-sphere of the neighbourhood to a more urban level by gazing at streets that, to every Bangladeshi, symbolize the country's cultural and national identity. Flanked by majestic trees, colonial buildings as well as recent constructions evidencing a strong legacy of classic

Fig. 2.3   Leaving
the old city

রিক্সা প্রবেশ নিষেধ

modern architecture,[22] the campus of Dhaka University is vibrant with groups
of students, the omnipresent cycle-rickshaws and street hawkers selling sweets
and colourful jewellery. People from all over Dhaka love to gather in the area
and in the adjacent Ramna Park, which regularly hosts cultural celebrations. Wall
paintings, cartoons and monuments commemorating the Bangladeshis' fight for
independence, which was mostly carried out in this part of the city, merge with
the not at all museum-like overall scene. Since 1952, students and intellectuals
from Dhaka University animated the 'Language Movement' and brought it to a
dramatic peak in 1970–71, when the 'Liberation War' against what was then West
Pakistan led to the declaration of independence.[23] Decades later, during the
dictatorship of General Ershad (1983–90), the campus again became the stage of
political fights for democracy; and, still today, strikes, rallies and demonstration
such as the 2013 Shahbag Movement[24] began in this area. Does history repeat
itself in the campus? Since *Le droit à la ville*,[25] we should rather acknowledge the
fact that people, at certain moments in history, seek, in urban spaces evocative of
historical events, inspiration, strength and/or unity.

Leaving the local and intermediate level, we approach, via a further zoom
out, the general sphere of planning and the state. We compare an urban
improvement project from the mid-1950s, the residential neighbourhood of
Dhanmondi, with the type of development fostered in the 1980s in another
residential neighbourhood, Gulshan. The first, designed by a trust offering
advantageous purchasing conditions on a 99-year lease basis, is meanwhile
a mixed-use district with local and international cultural institutions, English
and Bengali intermediate schools, private hospitals, clinics, clubs, boutiques,
cafés and snack bars, galleries and shopping centres. Over three decades since
Liberation, its inhabitants, the educated middle- to higher-income group, carried
on a progressive transformation of social practices that made Dhanmondi a

Fig. 2.4   Emerging urban folk?

synonym for civilized, culture- and art-loving urbanity.[26] Also in Dhanmondi, the neoliberal developments of the last decade caused real-estate speculation, environmental degradation and higher rental prices. These are in turn boosting protests against illegal construction and public demonstrations demanding consistent environmental preservation and protection from encroachment, unseen in other areas of the city.

For Dhanmondi residents, the new downtown for international companies and diplomatic staff to Dhaka's north-east, Gulshan, lacks historical and cultural meaning as well as sociability. Indeed, its main feature is an accumulation of security guards and watchmen protecting one does not understand what. The origins of this area trace back to 1961, when the above-mentioned improvement trust approved the development of a further residential model town for the upper classes to the north of Dhaka. This was to be followed by the western model town, Banani, approved in 1964, and the north-eastern model town, Baridhara, approved in 1972, which now are part of the Gulshan thana (sub-district). However, due to both economic and political instability in the East Pakistan phase, construction in all three neighbourhoods was slow until the late 1980s, when a new class of businessmen and high-status local and foreign functionaries started to settle in the young capital city. The delayed boom caused later subdivisions of the housing blocks by new owners, attested by the lack of house and even street numbers within the neighbourhoods' grid pattern, and an overall clumsy development, with a particularly high number of small, medium and large squatter settlements that kept emerging as construction workers and other labourers working in the area took possession of vacant plots. While high-rise buildings are taking the place of private villas, the contrasting plans and visions for Gulshan often have a central place in news and public debates. How to integrate the wishes of the community of owners reunited in the Gulshan Society, demanding the preservation of green areas, improvement of roads and leisure facilities as well as (further) eviction of illegal occupants, the urban poor's claims for their right to stay in what have become their neighbourhoods and homes, and the administration's constant struggle for available land?

This first series of observations started at the street level and zoomed out, thereby moving from the present to the past, posing questions about the future. Now, the gaze will be redirected from the general/global to the particular, or private. The scene is that provided by globalization of economic networks and communication, parallel to worldwide migration from peripheries to centres.[27]

ZOOMING IN: FROM THE GLOBAL TO THE PARTICULAR, FROM THE PRESENT TO THE PAST

Dhaka, Bangladesh, beginning of the twenty-first century. Here they arrive and spread out, compelled by capitalist production and its constitutive crises – the employees of European, US, Japanese or Korean firms that shifted 'low-skilled' sectors such as manufacturing and especially textile, garments and clothing from their homelands to countries providing cheap labour. Those seeking business opportunities in Bangladesh stand on a privileged course at the airport's visa-issuing post. The textile and garment sector accounts for 70 to 75 per cent of Bangladesh's total exports and employs about 3.5 million workers, with about 2 million of these in factories based in Dhaka. The city looks back on a century-long textile manufacturing tradition that started with the Mughals and was further expanded by the British. After Liberation in 1971, the textile sector experienced Bangladesh's major industrial development, first under state direction, then on the basis of private investment. Thanks to an 'open-door policy' implemented to attract foreign investment, since the 1980s this textile industry has been supplemented by an export-oriented garment industry. Private-sector-friendly laws also helped local firms grow, and these in time became the suppliers, via a chain of mediators, of multinationals.

Dhaka was the main site of this progress, as, owing to its long-term regional primacy, it offered already-developed infrastructural and logistical conditions that favoured the establishment of industries.[28] Initially, the factories were based in Tejgaon, a manufacturing area set up by the British along the railway track in the nineteenth century, in what was then then city's northern outskirts. Its development into a modern industrial site had been envisioned in the 1950s, but industrialization did not start up at that point. When it finally took off, some 30 years later, Dhaka had expanded further north and the originally destined Tejgaon had to compete with the cheaper, new fringe areas. With the urban authorities lacking the power (or the interest) to implement the 1959 master plan prescriptions,[29] industrial development was progressively attracted away from the city core and, for the second time, Dhaka missed the chance to establish a proper industrial zone.

Expatriated Bangladeshis investing their savings in firms, land and apartment buildings are important agents of a construction boom steered by both local and

Fig. 2.5   Not climbing the social ladder

international developers and builders. Yet the inflow of capital as well as of foreign organizations and diplomatic institutions only aggravates the state's habit of concentrating public efforts in Dhaka. Since the 1980s, residential and administrative buildings, cinemas, shopping centres, cultural and financial institutions were built at a breathtaking pace with major benefits for the construction and, once these premises became operational, the tertiary sectors. The needed decentralization programmes failed, and the discrepancy between Dhaka and secondary cities, but especially between Dhaka and the rural areas with their precarious socioeconomic situation, was further aggravated (Bertuzzo 2009: 11–14). With immigration as a direct consequence of unbalanced growth, its population grew from 1 to 10 million within three decades.[30]

We now zoom in on the 'urban level'. As early as in the mid-1950s, the Dhaka Improvement Trust[31] tackled urban growth by offering advantageous leasing programmes that made residential ownership possible. The upper-middle-income class (composed of higher public officers, teachers and professionals) started settling for example in Dhanmondi, while to its north, similar schemes fostered the development of middle- and lower-middle-class residential areas. Particularly since the 1990s, however, such programmes lost their attractiveness for the state, whose answer to the challenge of housing today is just to ignore it. The task is thus transferred to the private real-estate sector, or to cost-efficient public–private partnerships.[32] In such conditions, urban development proceeds in segments, with plots often being built up before the provision of water, canalization and road networks, which remain the domain of public authorities. In spite of the clear northwards expansion of the city, the comparatively 'old' Dhanmondi, with its well-laid roads and basic services, but even the congested Old Dhaka, have not lost their attractiveness for real-estate business. There, the owners of residential premises

Fig. 2.6
Encroaching
water bodies
– everybody's
business

increasingly allow the development of six-, eight- or even 20-storey buildings on their plots in exchange for ownership of two or three new flats – a popular way to secure long-term income, as a social pension programme is still absent in Bangladesh. Lack of planning and high degrees of illegality concerning both the sale of plots in ecologically relevant areas and the approval of irregular building typologies characterize the described processes.[33] Parallel to influential citizens' illegal construction of commercial as well as residential buildings on public space, the poorer inhabitants have been increasingly squatting on land because of lack of accommodation as well as occupying the pavements as street vendors.[34]

How does this affect space? To answer this question, we need to zoom further in to the level of the private and particular. Squatter settlements mirror a mode of development that may be unplanned, but is none the less the fruit of complex interactions and negotiations over space and time. Over space: contrary to their recurrent definition as 'spontaneous', squatter settlements rarely maintain any trace of spontaneity – and in fact, in Bengali, these areas are known as bosti (settlement) and are thereby distinguished from the decayed and cramped areas characterizing, for example, Dhaka's old town, which are commonly called 'slums'. Their inhabitants not only obey specific rules and power hierarchies controlling the land that can be respectively occupied or rented. They may also, from case to case, raise collective funds for the construction of common facilities, such as a water pump or a community mosque, or for the repair of roads and paths after the rainy season.[35] And over time: the utilization patterns of space throughout the day (but also throughout the year, as the monsoon in particular can strongly affect space in this sub-tropical country) must necessarily be extremely dynamic to accommodate the needs of multifarious inhabitants, differing in age and gender, professions, routines and so on. Apart from 'functional spaces', transit and gathering spaces obeying rules known to everybody, recognized protected areas may be called 'female spaces', such as the shared courtyards or the dwellings' respective interiors, where women are responsible for all kinds of household and private matters, from cooking, to washing, to taking care of small children.[36] Their good functioning – which I identify with rare trespass of a privacy border at the wrong moment – does not primarily rely on segregation, as could be the case in Old Dhaka's bazar. Contrary to the old town's three- or four-storey houses opening out only on one road, the compounds in most squatter settlements are only partially enclosed and, hence, accessible for husbands, neighbours, sellers, carpenters, children and their friends. It thus has to depend on a strict regulation of daily routines, allowing women and girls free rein during definite periods of time. Thus, for example, a group of girls can appropriate a kitchen courtyard in the absence of adults and, for a short time, gather for singing and dancing, oblivious to the outer world in their own 'space-time of desire'.

Finally we take a quick close-up of those faces, those wrinkles and well-tied sari.[37] They work as carpenters and street sellers, drive cycle-rickshaws or stitch T-shirts in sweatshops; they are employed as domestic helpers, guards and construction labourers. They have been arriving in Dhaka for more than 40 years, pushed by war, natural disasters and exploitation, and have ever since provided services that boosted its growth. In spite of that, they continue to be called the 'urban poor' and involved in humiliating aid programmes classing their self-made dwellings as 'shanties' and them as 'slum dwellers' who need 'accommodation'. It's high time for that image to be reversed.

IN THE MIDDLE OF URBANIZATION

> *Methods of thought which claim to give the lead to our world in the name of revolution have become, in reality, ideologies of consent and not of rebellion.*
> *(Albert Camus, The Rebel (1956 [1951]))*

The regressive–progressive procedure, as operationalized above, was expected to fulfil a twofold task: to enable conjunctures and to disclose differential time. Through its zooms, it displayed on one and the same level something that general methods of urban analysis often miss: the spatial and temporal interrelatedness and variability of urban phenomena. The application showed that the procedure enables not only an intellectual–historical, but also a perceptional–spatial recognition of coexisting space-times of Dhaka. Such is the case with the developments that have occurred in the neighbourhood of Dhanmondi, where the one- and two-storey residences built thanks to leases extended by a development trust clash with eight- and nine-storey apartment buildings, fruit of real-estate speculation, while the inhabitants are seen descending to the streets to protest against the consequences of unchecked construction. Here, differential time manifests itself: at one moment, urbanization seems to take a certain direction and specific actors seem to dominate others, but both direction and actors can change and be challenged in unexpected ways by a variety of factors and groups.

The planner or activist informed by such recognitions of space-time should be able to correlate social relations and recognize in them a variety of existing possible presents, thus discovering possible fields of action not merely for reformist, but also revolutionary urbanization.

With regard to the discussion on urbanization in non-European countries, Dhaka with its progress by fits and starts, high fragmentation and intermingling of 'urban' and 'rural' ways of life, emerged from the application as 'neither urban nor rural'. This definition derives from the realization that the main feature of such a diverse urbanization is of a temporal, and not spatial, character. It consists of the simultaneity of the 'rural', 'industrial' and 'urban' that was repeatedly evidenced by the different zooms, whereby all phases are evidently negated or neutralized, leaving room for a diverse kind of social relations. The otherness of these social relations (including the relations of production) in relations to Western precursors needs to be acknowledged and carefully analysed in future urbanization studies.[38] Towards this aim, the procedure, conjugating knowledge, perception and intuition, may constitute the basis for the 'dialectical anthropology' envisioned by Lefebvre – an anthropology that, developing from an urban problematic and adopting logical reason, does not content itself with the production of reports and taxonomies, but strives to grasp which elements of social life are conducive to a new, thoroughly human, 'rationality of fulfilment' beyond the capitalist one (Lefebvre 2003a: 71–2).

Keeping these insights in mind, I move on to discuss the assumption of 'complete urbanization' by highlighting one conceptual and one methodological problem implicit in some of the most popular interpretations of this hypothesis. First, the urbanization hypothesis is often substantiated by means of the statistic that more than half of the world's population live in urban areas (which *per se* merely indicates that urbanization, if it is progressing at all, is just about half way to completion). Yet the assumed relationship between the number of human beings living in 'urban' areas and urbanization is by no means given. We should not conflate the process of urbanization with one of its manifestations, that is, the increasing number of people living in urban areas. The 'half of the world's population' argument may lend itself to talk about 'urban growth', but the latter should be carefully distinguished from 'urbanization'.[39] Second, the description 'urban' is, both at an administrative and a conceptual level, a methodologically ambiguous one: politicians, development experts and demographers fight over it, as the declaration of a certain area as urban often has implications for its eligibility to receive special funds.[40] Vis-à-vis the high exposure to manipulation, measuring urbanization on the basis of mere demographic data seems questionable. The problem becomes particularly clear when we look at absolute numbers in South Asia: in Bangladesh and India, two countries renowned for their 'urban explosion', around 72 per cent of the total population, or 103 million and 864 million people respectively, still live in rural areas.[41] To add to this picture, consider that, for example in India, at least 53 per cent of the population is at present occupied in agriculture (UN 2013). This points to the still huge relevance of non-urban lifestyles and environments – and, considering the data on 'rural' poverty and on the increasing economic gap between megacities and hinterlands (Kundu and Saraswati 2012) – also to the urgent necessity to redirect research and funds beyond cities.[42]

Understanding urbanization, with Lefebvre, as the historical context within which phenomena occur, the question of how to count urbanization is rather irrelevant. In *Le droit à la ville* (1968), he writes: '[The expansion of the urban fabric] leads ... to the depopulation and the "loss of the peasantry" from the villages which remain rural while losing what was peasant life: crafts, small local shops'.[43] He thereby draws attention to an important phenomenon: the village can remain rural although peasant life changes, for example due to emigration as well as to the centralization of production and consumption, strangling local economic activities. In other words, urbanization does not manifest itself primarily in physical or demographic changes, but in the way we live, which means that to be deemed 'fully urbanized', society does not require an urban setting, but an urbanized everyday life. This take on urbanization as the process of routinization of everyday life has been poorly reflected in Lefebvre's reception in the last two decades, which, under the effect of the 'spatial turn', concentrated on spatial aspects of social and specifically urban life, on the political aspects of the production of space as well as on utopia. In my view, the very core of Lefebvre's thought is here: at the junction between his interest in space and his long-time engagement with the everyday. Precisely at this junction, Lefebvre localises the urban revolution, intending a profound change of the ways of life (in urban and rural settings) linked with the changed – but not yet transformed – relations of production. Thereby, he hinted at the fact that the urban *problematique* does not consist in the urban revolution as a historical process, but in the necessity of reshaping the relations of production that it causes. This transformation of the relations of production could happen with people realizing the extent to which urban routines have been homogenized and hence starting to search for different rhythms, lives and social forms. Such a concerted, collectively wanted and negotiated transformation would be in effect synonymous with a revolution, whereby a liberation from the homogenized–routinized life often typical of cities is meant. Whence Lefebvre defines the task of social analysis as 'retrieving' virtualities, that is, forgotten or hidden possibilities, at the conjunctures of everyday space-time.

As a result of these reflections, we should acknowledge that, rather than being in a phase of 'complete urbanization', we are in the very midst of the urban revolution. Understanding this entails significant benefits:

- It frees us from the representation of the industrial phase as 'absorbing' the agricultural and introducing the urban phase, thereby allowing the acknowledgement of other/different social forms, where practices that reflect mixed forms of life and production emerge or may already have emerged, as the example of 'ruralized' Dhaka indicated. This will boost new concepts and models grounded in these societies, their experiences and narratives, whereby neither the 'urban' nor the 'rural' should be considered as 'closed' systems: on the contrary, vibrant transformation processes are ongoing there.[44]
- It opens researchers' views on to forms of habitation, organization, livelihood, production and so on presently maturing in circumstances

of 'diverse urbanization'. This change of perspective will allow a better understanding of the lives of people who inhabit, and thereby produce, megacities such as Dhaka – as well as the fast-growing 1-million-plus cities coming up in their shadow, not only in the South Asian context.[45]

- It brings to the fore the relationship between production, urban life and consumption – or the question of access to resources. Acknowledging and further analysing this relationship could boost the search for tools that benefit not only the inhabitants of countries currently coping with the effects of fresh industrialization and liberalization, but also those of the 'old world', where social space has been attacked and progressively privatized in the last four decades.

If this is to turn into reality, social analysis must learn to examine the conjunctures. Only then may social and especially urbanization studies again be the sites of production not only of accumulative knowledge ('*savoir*'), but of socially useful cognition ('*connaissance*').

NOTES

1   Respective authors have worked out the triad of perceived, conceived and lived space; structured their studies according to the global, urban and private levels; dealt with rhythmanalysis; or, like Fraya Frehse in Chapter 12 of this book, trained a 'transductive' reading of specific urban spaces.

2   The *Eid-Al-Fitr* and *Eid-Kurban* festivals represent the two most important religious festivities for the mostly Muslim population of Bangladesh.

3   I dealt with the production of space in Dhaka in my PhD thesis, *Fragmented Dhaka* (Bertuzzo 2009).

4   In the project *Archives of movement*, carried on at TU-Berlin, I am currently seeking suitable approaches by focusing on people's actual modes of representation and narration of movement, conceptualized as the dimension at which space and time are thought of and experienced jointly.

5   Also the ambiguous meaning Lefebvre gave to the urban itself is often ignored, as I argue in the concluding section.

6   See UN-DESA-PD 2012. The controversial role of statistics backing the definitions 'urban' and 'rural' is treated in the concluding section.

7   Historian Malcolm McKinnon (2011) works out the urbanization/globalization/nation-building interaction in Asian cities and demonstrates the inadequacy of Western paradigms to explain them. Partha Chatterjee (2003) pointed to the discontinuity between Europe-generated terms and their meaning in the Indian context.

8   The term stems from the popular urban geographer Nazrul Islam (2005: 2).

9   Lefebvre explained his regressive–progressive procedure on various, but scattered, occasions. I refer to his essay *Perspectives on Rural Sociology* (1953; English translation 2003b). In her chapter 'For Difference "in and through" São Paulo', collected in this volume (Chapter 12), Fraya Frehse provides an excellent explanation of the procedure; her focus on historical times in space somewhat contrasts with my stress on the

conjunctures of historicities in space. I consider this divergence as a result of our different points of departure, as she concentrates her analysis on a specific place and its peculiar history.

10   See Hess (2004): '*Il s'agit de cette passion pour le moment où les structures n'arrivent plus à dominer leurs propres éléments, où ces éléments se rassemblent et forment une conjoncture novatrice*' (It's this passion for the moment, in which the structures can no longer dominate the elements, in which these elements take their own shape and form an innovating conjuncture).

11   Benjamin (1968) wrote about the *angel of history*, recognizing, among the ruins of history, hints of lost possibilities. He understood the *flâneur* – strolling in the city and thereby collecting, thus 'rescuing', traces from the past in the present – as such an 'angel', who for him was embodied by the poet Charles Baudelaire.

12   'There is a blind spot on the retina, the center – and negation – of vision. A paradox. The eye doesn't see; it needs a mirror. The center of vision doesn't see and doesn't know it is blind. Do these paradoxes extend to thought, to awareness, to knowledge?' See Lefebvre (2003a: 29).

13   I am referring here to Lefebvre's conception of three levels: the global or general (meaning the state and globalised networks); the urban or mixed; and the local or private (comprising the everyday and dwelling). The urban, as he put it, moderates between the two. See Lefebvre (1991: 12; 155).

14   See Lefebvre (2003b [1953]: 112–13) as well as Hess (2004).

15   One could elaborate on the possible parallels between Lefebvre's *conjuncture* and Benjamin's *illumination*, which would require a (long overdue) study of the role of Surrealism in both thinkers' work.

16   Dhaka dwellers understand by *bazar* single roads in the old city, where specific items are fabricated and sold; it does not describe an entire market area (as is the case in oriental cities).

17   An analysis of this fluctuation should start from as early as India's Partition (1947), during which migration of Hindus and Muslims in the Subcontinent was boosted and many a Hindu *bazar* in Old Dhaka was deserted. A second phase followed during Bangladesh's Liberation War, when many Hindu families were forced to migrate by persecution and expropriation. On this issue, see Kathun (2003), Bertuzzo (2009: 69–72).

18   Lungi are garments worn by men around the waist. On the *kutti*, see Bertuzzo (2009: 115–17).

19   Puja (forms of worship) are performed daily by Hindus in the private sphere; on specific occasions, however, the celebrations take place in public spaces, often accompanied by processions.

20   Old Dhaka was long ignored by the real-estate sector, which instead expanded from the city outwards. However, in recent years, the overall pressure on space makes even its tiny plots attractive. The construction boom soon awakened concerns about the destruction of architectural and cultural heritage in the old town; see https://openblogbd.wordpress.com/2012/08/25/none-to-look-after-old-dhakas-historic-sites/ (accessed 19 April 2013).

21   I refer to Doug Saunders's best-seller *Arrival City* (2011), which claims that the future of megacities depends not on their urban qualities nor on an urban revolution, but, in a more pragmatic way, on their ability to create good 'arrival conditions' for newcomers.

22   The ready reception of classic modern architecture in Bangladesh is mainly due to the seminal work of the Bangladeshi architect Muzharul Islam (1923–2012), a graduate from the AA School of Architecture, London and from Yale University at New Haven; see also Bertuzzo (2012).

23   On Bangladesh's Language Movement and Liberation War, see Alam and Delwar (2011).

24   See http://shahbagmovement.com/; Anam (2013).

25   Cf. Lefebvre (1968), translated into English in Lefebvre (1996 [1968]: 62–183).

26   In several interviews, residents from all income groups stated that they continued to live in the area in spite of the possibility of moving to newer, less congested neighbourhoods or to cheaper, less central areas of Dhaka. Their reasons ranged from logistical and infrastructural advantages to the presence of an accessible lake, but also mirrored their identification with the area's overall lifestyle, or what could be called its spirit. Cf. Bertuzzo (2009: 119–40); see also later in this section.

27   Rural areas are 'peripheral' to urban centres, but we can also conceive of a country such as Bangladesh as 'peripheral' to the global centres of production, as dependency theory maintained. See for example Amin (1976).

28   Infrastructural improvements implementing World Bank schemes for economic growth are however ongoing in various parts of the country: besides eight already existing EPZs (Export Processing Zones), the government is planning the instalment of SECs (Special Economic Zones) in the near future. While EPZs host solely manufacturing establishments, SEZs are equipped for manufacturing, trade and services activities, both export and domestic market oriented. They offer higher tax benefits for investors and also generally provide housing and further facilities for the workers.

29   Prepared by a consortium of foreign firms, Dhaka's first master plan recommended to zone the urban areas. In 1995, a Metropolitan Development Plan co-funded by the government of Bangladesh and UNDP/Habitat followed. Its principal authors were, again, foreign consultants backed by local firms.

30   The period concerned is 1971–2001, in which a growth rate of 6 per cent was registered (see UN/DESA/PD 2012). On this process, see also Islam (2005).

31   DIT, reorganized and renamed RAJUK in 1987.

32   On the overall consequences of leaving planned urban residential development in the hands of private firms, see Ghafur (2011).

33   Especially the fringes of Dhaka's east and north-east, which according to the master plan should serve as monsoon-water retention areas and thus kept free of construction, were occupied by real-estate projects. See for example Ali (2012).

34   Although both the richer and poorer sections of society were pursuing illegal activities, the government repeatedly tried to repress, often by forced eviction, encroachment only by the poor. An exception was the 2007–08 'caretaker government', installed to tackle a deep political crisis. The advisers acting as ministries during this period engaged in a straightforward fight against illegal encroachment by the rich as well, sometimes ordering the demolition of irregular buildings. The current government is not, however, pursuing this example. See Shafi (2011) and Bertuzzo (2009: 80–82; 170–80; 206-7) on the caretaker government's actions.

35   On negotiations for space in Dhaka's settlements, see Bertuzzo (2011) and Hackenbroch (2013).

36   See Bertuzzo (2011).

37   Sari are garments about 6 metres long, variously printed or embroidered, traditionally worn by women.

38   As Lefebvre suggested, we are not asked for 'urban studies' but for studies of/on urbanization.

39   See also the critique of the urban age thesis by Brenner and Schmid (2014).

40   UN-Habitat (2006: 5) for example admits that the definition of 'urban' varieshighly from country to country: some follow administrative criteria; others demographic ones, for example population and density; others economic characteristics and again others the availability of urban infrastructure.

41   My own calculations based on the respective rates of urban population, estimated at about 28 per cent for both nations, as well as on the Bangladesh 2011 Census (total population: 142,300,000) and on the India Census 2011 (total population: 1.2 billion). According to UN/DESA/PD 2012, Bangladesh's current annual urban growth rate is 3.5 per cent, opposed to 0.46 per cent rural growth; India's urban growth is 2.73 per cent and rural growth is 1.68 per cent.

42   Following the Indian sociologist Jai Sen's remark that 'the urban poor are the rural poor' (1976: 3), it becomes evident that an overall perspective on *regional*, and not urban, development is necessary.

43   He continues: 'If the same phenomena are analysed from the perspective of cities, one can observe not only the extension of highly populated peripheries but also of banking, commercial and industrial networks and of housing'. See Lefebvre (1996 [1968]: 72).

44   Concerning the transformation of villages in South Asia, see, for example, Mines and Yazgi (2010).

45   On the relevance of this hitherto neglected aspect of urbanization, see, for example, Bhagat (2011).

REFERENCES

Alam, M. and Delwar Hossain, A.M. 2011. *Dhaka in the Liberation War 1971*. Dhaka: ASB.

Ali, T. 2012. 'Govt Making Those Legal' (online), 31 July. Available at http://archive.thedailystar.net/newDesign/news-details.php?nid=244221 (accessed 19 April 2013).

Amin, S. 1976. *Unequal Development: An Essay on the Social Formations of Peripheral Capitalism*. New York: Monthly Review Press.

Anam, T. 2013. 'Shahbag Protesters Versus the Butcher of Mirpur'. *The Guardian* (online), 13 February. Available at http://www.guardian.co.uk/world/2013/feb/13/shahbag-protest-bangladesh-quader-mollah (accessed 19 April 2013).

Benjamin, W. 1968. 'Theses on the Philosophy of History', in *Illuminations*, edited by H. Arendt. New York: Schocken Books, 253–64.

Bertuzzo, E.T. 2009. *Fragmented Dhaka. Analysing Everyday Life with Henri Lefebvre's Theory of Production of Space*. Stuttgart: Franz Steiner Verlag.

Bertuzzo, E.T. 2011. 'Till Water Rises – Tactics Making for Infrastructure in Karail Bosti' (online). Available at http://www.bauwelt.de/cms/bauwerk.html?id=5514169&lang=en#.T4BjtpjwPzl (accessed 10 August 2013).

Bertuzzo, E.T. 2012. 'Muzharul Islam. Botschafter der Moderne' (online), 19 October. Available at http://derarchitektbda.de/botschafter-der-moderne/ (accessed 10 August 2013).

Bhagat, R.B. 2011. 'Emerging Pattern of Urbanisation in India'. *Economic and Political Weekly*, XLVI, 20 August, 10–12.

Boltanski, L. and Chiapello, E. 2005. *The New Spirit of Capitalism*. London: Verso.

Brenner, N. and Schmid, C. 2014. 'The "Urban Age" in Question'. *International Journal of Urban and Regional Research* 38(3): 731–55.

Camus, A. 1956 [1951]. *The Rebel*. New York: Alfred A. Knopf Inc.

Chatterjee, P. 2003. 'Are Indian Cities Becoming Bourgeois At Last?', in *Body.City: Siting Contemporary Culture in India*, edited by I. Chandrasekhar and P.C. Seel. New Delhi: Tulika, 171–92.

Ghafur, S. 2011. 'Imprints of the Changing Doctrines on Housing in Dhaka', in *400 Years of Capital Dhaka and Beyond*. Vol III: 'Urbanization and Urban Development', edited by R. Hafiz and G. Rabbani. Dhaka: ASB, 153–68.

Hackenbroch, K. 2013. *The Spatiality of Livelihoods: Negotiations of Access to Public Space in Dhaka, Bangladesh*. Stuttgart: Franz-Steiner-Verlag.

Hess, R. 2004. 'La méthode d'Henri Lefebvre'. *Multitudes* (online magazine), winter. Available at http://1libertaire.free.fr/AnalyseInstitutionnelle01.html (accessed 19 April 2013).

Islam, N. 2005. *Dhaka Now*. Dhaka: BGS.

Khatun, H. 2003. *Dhakaiyas on the Move*. Dhaka: Academic Press.

Kundu, A. and Saraswati, L.R. 2012. 'Migration and Exclusionary Urbanisation in India'. *Economic and Political Weekly* XLVII, 30 June: 219–27.

Lefebvre, H. 1991 [1974]. *The Production of Space*. Oxford: Blackwell.

Lefebvre, H. 1996 [1968]. 'The Right to the City', in *Writings on Cities* by H. Lefebvre, edited by E. Lebas and E. Kofman. Oxford: Blackwell, 63–182.

Lefebvre, H. 2003a [1970]. *The Urban Revolution*. Minneapolis, MN: University of Minnesota Press.

Lefebvre, H. 2003b [1953]. 'Perspectives on Rural Sociology', in *Henri Lefebvre: Key Writings*, edited by S. Elden, E. Lebas and E. Kofman. London and New York: Continuum, 111–20.

McKinnon, M. 2011. *Asian Cities: Globalization, Urbanization and Nation-Building*. Copenhagen: NIAS.

Mines, D.P. and Yazgi, N. 2010. *Village Matters*. New Delhi: Oxford University Press.

Murshed, M.M. 2011. 'Water Logging and Health Problems in Dhaka City', in *400 Years of Capital Dhaka and Beyond*, Vol III, 'Urbanization and Urban Development', edited by R. Hafiz and G. Rabbani. Dhaka: ASB, 387–98.

Saunders, D. 2011. *Arrival City*. New York: Pantheon.

Sen, J. 1976. 'The Unintended City' (online). Available at http://www.india-seminar.com/2001/500/500%20jai%20sen.htm (accessed 19 April 2013).

Shafi, S.A. 2011. 'Ecological Versus System' (online). Available at http://www.bauwelt.de/cms/bauwerk.html?id=5514169&lang=en#.T4BjtpjwPzl (accessed 12 April 2013).

UN-Habitat. 2006. 'The State of the World's Cities Report 2006/2007'. Nairobi: UN-HABITAT.

UN-Statistics Division. 2013. India (online). Available at http://data.un.org/CountryProfile.aspx?crName=INDIA#Economic (accessed 19 April 2013).

UN/DESA/PD. 2012. 'World Urbanization Prospects, the 2011 Revision' (online). Available at http://esa.un.org/unpd/wup/Analytical-Figures/Fig_2.htm (accessed 12 August 2013).

3

Where Lefebvre Meets the East: Urbanization in Hong Kong

Wing-Shing Tang

Henri Lefebvre has enjoyed wide currency over the past two decades. One of his path-breaking contributions to urban research is the thesis of complete urbanization, producing an urban society that is not only real but also virtual. This thesis has enlightened research on urbanization across the world. Nevertheless, like other great thinkers at any time, Lefebvre, being a Frenchman born at the turn of the twentieth century, as well as someone who experienced the rapid rise of industrial capitalism since the 1950s, the turbulent years of the 1960s and the significant change in the nature of state intervention since the 1970s, is very much spatiotemporally bounded (Gardiner 2000: 10–17; Merrifield 2006: 8). Smith (2003: xx–xxi) has objected that *The Urban Revolution* is incapable of addressing the rapidly expanding urbanizing world as well as the more complex web of capital and the state in the present day. In response, there are numerous attempts either to defend Lefebvre by commenting that he had already foreseen these 'anomalies' or to explore seriously the ways to extend Lefebvre over time and across space. As an example of the latter, Kipfer et al. (2008: 299) think that it is straightforward: just extend Lefebvre by taking into account colonialism and patriarchy. Globalizing Lefebvre entails 'linking considerations of everyday life to a broad critique of the imperial and patriarchal aspects of capitalist world order'. How feasible is this task?

It is the objective of this chapter to interrogate this Lefebvrean tradition. It argues that the literature is dominated by a bias that mostly considers the non-West as mere empirical objects for theories developed in the West. Lefebvre himself has neglected the non-West in constructing his widely acclaimed thesis; so do his many critics and followers. At the end of the day, while theories in the West continue to excel in abstraction, the non-West is poorly understood with inappropriate conceptual categories. To redress the balance, I argue that we need to trace the historical trajectory of the urban society in question and elaborate its development in relation to global urbanization. This chapter attempts to develop this contention by elaborating on the urbanization of Hong Kong.[1]

THE COMPLETE URBANIZATION THESIS AND ITS CRITICS

The Thesis

In *The Urban Revolution*, Lefebvre (2003: 7–16) deciphers urbanization by means of a schematic representation along an axis from 0 to 100 per cent, from the complete absence of urbanization to the completion of the process. At the zero point, there is pure nature. In history, then, humans started to form villages, which were accompanied by the city. The earliest town was the political city occupied by skilful conquerors. What Lefebvre has in mind was the Greek *polis* or the Roman city. This symbolized the beginning of organized social life and politics. The political city administered a vast territory, the peasants and communities within which paid tribute in exchange for the effective protection offered. In a sense, the city was parasitic on the countryside, which was, however, functionally integrated into the life of the city. Nevertheless, exchange and trade started to grow to such an extent, as in the case of Europe at the end of the Middle Ages, that even the political city failed to resist the successful penetration of the market and the merchants. The struggle, which, according to Lefebvre (2003: 10, my italics), 'create[d] not only *a* history but history *itself*', finally replaced the agora and the forum with the marketplace. This led to the birth of the merchant city. Commercial exchange became an urban function, in urban and architectural forms, producing a new urban structure. Besides the commercial function, the merchant city distinguished itself from the countryside by its special legal status. There was a moment in which the town emerged as a mediator between everyday life and nature. This development related to the growing importance of the state, and the development in rationalism that cumulated in Descartes. The primacy of the countryside was replaced by the priority of the urban. When industry 'gradually made its way into the city in search of capital and capitalists, markets, and an abundant supply of low-cost labor' (Lefebvre 2003: 13), the industrial city developed. Industrialization laid the foundation for urbanization, which in turn expedited the dissolution of the city itself (Schmid 2012: 46). The urban fabric was developed by the process of implosion–explosion, which denotes the tremendous concentration of people, capital, objects and thought, and, simultaneously, the immense explosion to the periphery, resulting in the disappearance of the peasantry, the complete subordination of agricultural production to industrialization and the extension of the urban fabric as suburbs, vacation homes and satellite towns. Finally, there will be a moment in which the effects of implosion–explosion are most fully felt due to globalization. Having supplanted its precedent industrial counterpart, the urban problematic becomes the motive force of historical change. This is emphasized with the urban question being increasingly integrated with the global economy. The urban problematic would give way to the production of differential space only by an urban revolution. Urban development arrives at a critical phase that can be understood as the point on the urban axis that approaches closest to complete urbanization.[2]

Central to the thesis is the town–country relationship. Although it signifies one of the most fundamental divisions of labour, Lefebvre sees the relationship as a historical one that is mediated by industrialization, the rise of the state and the advance of technology, and that is to be understood as a dialectical contradiction that develops with time. When nature dominated, the countryside was the norm. With the formation of the political city, the town was still parasitic on the countryside. When the market and the merchants concentrated in the merchant city, contradiction between town and country developed. It changed its character in the industrial city, as the town dominated the countryside, and agricultural production was subordinated to industrial production. Nevertheless, as the contradiction further developed, it reached a critical phase, where the town–country relationship gave way to the centre–periphery relationship (Lefebvre 2003: 118). This has, according to Schmid's (2008, 2012) eloquent philosophical interrogation, been an improvement of Lefebvre over Marx in the understanding of contradiction. Put differently, the thesis of complete urbanization documents the development of contradictions over time.

Lefebvre reminds us that the thesis should be examined not only in terms of time but also of space. It is spatial because the process of urbanization extends through space. When nature dominated, there was a spatial grid that basically attached the peasants to the soil. For the political city, there were walls and castles with an agora/forum at the centre of the town. In the merchant city, the market took place in the square at the centre of the city, alongside the church and the town hall. On the whole, the urban function, form and structure were no longer the same. The industrial city is not only packed with industrial plants and industrial activities, but is also different from its countryside in terms of landownership, the logic of spatial restructuring, the relationship with everyday life and the representation of space. In other words, Lefebvre draws our attention to space-time (Lefebvre 2003: 37).

Critiques of the Thesis

Many have criticized Lefebvre for being vague on details of his theorization. Focusing on Lefebvre's treatment of modalities of power in operation, Allen (2003: especially 159–88) challenges him for emphasizing domination/authority at the expense of other modalities such as coercion, persuasion, manipulation, seduction, induction and negotiation. According to Allen, the power of abstract space to erase traces of others is never complete; there are many spatial practices to negotiate the dominant coding. These modalities would have different spatial reaches, of which we should take note. In terms of the thesis of complete urbanization, the extent to which, for example, the critical phase can develop depends on the constitution of politicking, or the entanglement of a rich array of modalities of power, performed by various actors.[3] This is an important extension, but it has, argued Kipfer (2009), missed the crux of the matter. Having drawn on Eurocentric philosophy, Lefebvre has still stopped short of paying due attention to historical colonialism. In particular, he is more interested in employing colonization to decipher the crushing of everyday life in the West by capitalist commodification, state planning and the possible urban revolution. During the more recent crises of capitalism, Lefebvre remarks, various peripheries, including the former colonies, are reconnected to the metropolitan centres. The problem with Lefebvre is, for Kipfer (2009: 29), that he has failed to 'specify the distinction between *different varieties* of "colonization" and their *particular* forms of determination'. The specificity of colonization as a particular form of alienation must be explored. To make up for this, Kipfer invites us to look to Fanon for insights.

We must applaud Kipfer for broadening our understanding of Lefebvre and taking seriously his suggestion of linking the centre–periphery relation with colonization. Lefebvre is certainly Eurocentric. Deep in his mind in the formulation of the thesis of complete urbanization is Europe alone. In discussing the transition from the political city to the merchant city, he considers the European path as *the history*. Elden (2004: 130) also reminds us that Lefebvre once proclaimed that '[o]ne can, therefore, think, following Marx, that *Weltgeschichte*, worldwide history, was born with the city, of the city and in the city: the oriental, ancient, medieval city'. Having elaborated the reasons behind the formation of the urban as a 'blind field', Lefebvre (2003: 44) is confident that '[u]sing these concepts, we can study the current situation in the United States, South America, nonsocialist Asia, and so on'. On the issue of whether the peasants have been able to halt the crushing by the industrial bourgeoisie, he was authoritative regarding the Maoist experience (Lefebvre 2003: 113):

> The revolutionary capacity of the peasantry is not on the rise; it is being readsorbed [reabsorbed – WST] … On the contrary, a kind of overall colonization of space by 'decision-making centers' seems to be taking shape. Centers of wealth and information, of knowledge and power, are beginning to create feudal dependencies. In this case, the boundary line does not divide city and country but cuts across the urban phenomenon, between a dominated periphery and a dominating center.

Yet this authority was replaced by scepticism a few years later when he published *The Production of Space*. There, in discussing the possibility of extending his concepts of space of representation and representation of space to different socio-political contexts, Lefebvre (1991 [1974]: 42) remarks:

> Furthermore, it is not all clear a priori that it can legitimately be generalized. Whether the East, specifically China, has experienced a contrast between representations of space and representational spaces is doubtful in the extreme. It is indeed quite possible that the Chinese characters combine two functions in an inextricable way, that on the one hand they convey the order of the world (space-time), while on the other hand they lay hold of that concrete (practical and social) space-time wherein symbolisms hold sway, where works of art are created, and where buildings, palaces and temples are built. I shall return to this question later – although, lacking adequate knowledge of the Orient, I shall offer no definite answer to it.

Simply put, even Lefebvre is clear that due to different articulations of various socioeconomic forces, his theory of complete urbanization and the politics of the production of space may not be easily applicable to China. This reservation echoes more closely his earlier statement in *The Urban Revolution* that 'the general question of the relationship between the city and the countryside is far from being resolved' (Lefebvre 2003 [1970]: 8).

Can Kipfer's suggestion of bringing in colonization overcome the Eurocentric demerit? Although Kipfer is critical of metropolitanism in urban Marxism, his recommendation of focusing on different varieties of 'colonization' and their particular forms of determination is also very metropolitan, as his interest remains in those segregated areas in metropolitan countries (for example, immigrant workers and their sub-standard housing). What he has added is to relate these workers and their social conditions to neocolonialism in, say, North Africa. But he has devoted no time to unravelling how these countries have developed their neocolonialism from their past. Without such an understanding, it is difficult to evaluate whether the conditions underlying the transition from one type of city to another are really there – whether, as Lefebvre (2003: 32) himself has pointed out, these moments can coexist and generate problems of different kinds, and whether the possibility of change can exist or not. Then, if Kipfer's suggestion to take Lefebvre to a new height – or 'globalizing Lefebvre' – is to have any effect, one has to seriously subject Lefebvre to the real test imposed by the processes and conditions of historical colonialism.

COLONIZATION UNDER HISTORICAL COLONIALISM

Marx has acknowledged the role of colonies in the primitive accumulation of the classic English case, but he has analytically focused on modern capital accumulation. He has, therefore, deliberately confused primitive accumulation constructed as an event in the earlier stages of the English case with capital accumulation as an ongoing process detectable across the world nowadays (Hart 2002: 214–16). Concomitantly, the historical geographies of primitive accumulation in the colonies constitute invaluable knowledge in itself, as well as being a prerequisite for an informed understanding of modern capital accumulation.

Araghi and Karides (2012) have, from the perspective of the world-systems theory, highlighted the transformations of land rights in relation to the history of capitalism. They divide the global history of commodification of land rights into four historical periods: primitive accumulation; colonialism; developmentalism; and globalization. From the perspective of the colonies, each stage entails a form of land grab and the concomitant impacts on agriculture and development, in alignment with the developmental needs of the metropoles. This kind of thinking can easily be challenged by post-colonial positions such as that held by Tibebu (2011: xxi–xxii), in that it is still Eurocentric: the world-systems approach still has mostly concentrated on the core region, while treating the periphery peripherally. The insistence of these post-colonial positions on distinguishing 'History 2' from 'History 1' has, however, been criticized by Lazarus and Varma (2008) for ignoring their inter-relationships. Accordingly, Goswami's (2004) recommendation, as informed by Lefebvre's global framework, to resolve the post-colonialist's dilemma by the concept of co-determination is welcome. Nevertheless, and convincing though this may be, Goswami has emphasized co-determination at the expense of the colony's own history and geography. Thus the relational effect from the perspective of space has been emphasized at the expense of that of time. To redress this imbalance, it is necessary to underscore the nurturing of some kind of 'subjectivity' – a distinguishable rationality and its derivative strategies, tactics and practices – accumulated over time. This 'subjectivity' has its distinguishable logic of development, which, in turn, affects, and is affected by, the form and process of correlativity with others.[4] But it does not convey the notion of positionality, something essential to a post-colonialist account, as it does not exist socially through discourse and by discoursing: it is constantly situated in a material context and interaction. Nor does it resemble the notion of path dependency (Streeck and Thelen 2005: 6–9), since, far from being linear and repetitious, it has developed out of its own contradictions and in contradiction with other processes. In other words, the relational is intertwined not only spatially but also temporally. It is the intertwining of open geography with open history that matters. For a better understanding of the historical geographies of primitive accumulation of the colonies, therefore, one must situate the forms, processes and patterns of land grab within the historical development of each colony's 'subjectivity'.

This concept of 'subjectivity' can be elaborated by Coronil's (1997) call for a more political and global conception of capitalism. He criticizes Marx for, first, concentrating on the exploitation of labour while excluding that of nature from the analysis of capitalist production and, second, attributing the value of commodity to social relations at the expense of the role of nature. From the perspective of the periphery, land has to be taken into serious consideration as an active social force. Once land is returned to its significant position, according to Coronil, the state can be a landlord who can contribute to resources on which domestic capitalists depend for their revenue making. It is conceptually sufficient for Coronil (1997: 8), a post-colonial researcher himself, to argue that the periphery – Venezuela in his case – is the site of subaltern modernities, as the landlord state is an independent economic agent. It is, however, far from being insightful if we stop short of deciphering the exact ways that land has been contributing to creating wealth. Obviously, colonial landed property varied from the modern one. If each colony has its 'subjectivity' and if the land system within it also has its distinguishable logic of development, the ways the colonial government and the local regime, including the pre-colonial regime, fought against each other in configuring landownership and creating wealth from land must be clarified if our objective is to understand land grab in the colony. This complexity is elaborated below by the Hong Kong case.

THE URBANIZATION OF HONG KONG

Hong Kong, comprising geographically Hong Kong Island, Kowloon Peninsula and the New Territories, has urbanized tremendously since British colonial rule began in 1842. According to the mainstream account, everything started at 'Victoria City', one of the very first urban settlements in Hong Kong. Development grew as a result of the burgeoning *entrepôt* trade. It later spread northwards to the other side of Victoria Harbour, the Kowloon Peninsula. In comparison, the New Territories, a prosperous rice cultivation region, recorded in the 1911 Census that 70 per cent of its population were still agricultural by occupation (Chun 2000b: 91). Industrialization did not transform the colony systemically until 1952, when the UN imposed a trade embargo on China. Many capitalists and labourers across China migrated to Hong Kong after the civil war, energizing labour-intensive industrialization. On the one hand, while flatted factories mushroomed in urban Hong Kong, propelling the economy to take off, urban development started to encroach on the then urban fringe. On the other, declining rice cultivation forced many villagers to go abroad, to Europe in particular, for employment, to grow vegetables or take up diversified occupations almost identical with those in urban Hong Kong. This development was captured in the Labour Force Survey from 1980 (Government Information Services 1981: 50), as only 1.35 per cent of the total employed population was involved in agriculture and fishing, mining and quarrying, whereas manufacturing accounted for 41.7 per cent. The launching of the new town programme in the 1970s marked a new stage of urban development, as selected spots in the New Territories were transformed into high-density settlements. By 1981, the population exceeded 1.3 million – a big increase from 456,404 in 1961 – comprising 26 per cent of the total population of the colony (Chan 1999: 233). Urban development has accelerated ever since the 1980s, with redevelopment projects in the inner city, on the one hand, and, on the other, further urban encroachment on the fringe. For example, the Urban Renewal Authority announced in 2007 that it was going to redevelop 30 projects in the course of succeeding seven years (Ming Pao Daily 2007), while the latest proposal for 'North East New Territories New Development Areas' involves about 787 hectares of land, displacing 15 villages and affecting close to 10,000 persons (Cheng and Chan 2012: 96).

The above account appears to exemplify Lefebvre's thesis of complete urbanization. There was, first of all, commercial development in Victoria City, the centre, while agriculture dominated in the New Territories, its countryside. Later, industrialization expedited urbanization, encroaching first on the urban fringe and then on the countryside. Then an urban society emerged, as reflected in the changing occupational structure of the population as well as the disappearance of the rural. While redevelopment increased its pace both in the city centre and in the outlying area, the town–country relation increasingly gave way to a centre–periphery relation dominated by collusion between government and business (Tang 2008, Tang et al. 2012).

This description is, I regret to say, the appearance, but not the reality. Empirically, the built-up area as of the end of 2011 still comprised only 26.4 per cent of the total area of 1,108 km² (*Hong Kong Annual Report 2011*). This may be explained in part, as mainstream accounts have done, as due to the hilly topography. But there must be some other reasons behind the slow urban conversion since British rule started 170 years ago. In sum, the picture is more complicated than it looks.

To reveal the true picture, it is methodologically necessary to situate urbanization in Hong Kong within the history of British colonialism. Hong Kong was colonized with the construction of the British Empire in mind. Yet colonization, the construction of new social and legal property and labour relations by regulating time and space, inevitably confronted the history of Chinese society. Therefore we refer to the intertwining of two spatiotemporalities in a local setting – Hong Kong – that is far from being a spatial container (an empty space with a fixed boundary). These subtleties help explain the reality of urbanization in Hong Kong in a more informed manner.

HONG KONG UNDER THE AUSPICES OF THE CHINESE AGRARIAN EMPIRE

Before British colonial rule, Hong Kong was part of the Chinese agrarian empire. To facilitate control, each dynasty was keen to restrict the financial power of society, culminating in the policy of promoting agriculture at the expense of commerce. Accordingly, commerce could never have prospered, even so far as to achieve independent status, while rural activities dominated, inducing Mote (1977: 105) to remark that '[t]he rural defined the Chinese way of life' and that urban structures were indistinguishable from their rural counterparts. Besides, dialectically, the emperor was keen to develop his pastoral care. In an agrarian society with acute land and resource constraints, the quest was to fully absorb family labour and, concomitantly, encourage regional migration of agricultural surplus labour.

Xian-cum-Cheng

The territory of the empire was so big that the emperor was left with no alternative but to rely on his local agents for control. However, given the emphasis on hierarchy and collective responsibility, the local government system was still haunted by lack of autonomy (Huff 2003: 251–63). In areal terms, a county (*xian*) was an administrative local government with a walled city. Within the county, there was at the centre the walled city, the *cheng*, accommodating the local agents of the empire, and the rest – a few towns and numerous villages (Huff 2003: 260, Lewis 2006: 8). Accordingly, *cheng* and *xian*, figuratively speaking town and country respectively, were interchangeably employed, as they belonged to the identical administrative unit *xian* (Zhou 2005: 33–4). There were rural activities within the city wall, and urban activities outside it. This is confirmed by Feng's (2005) study of town–country relations during the Ming (1368–1644) and Qing (1644–1912) dynasties. In short, unlike in the West, cities and towns in China were never the locus of autonomous administrative units, the town was never separated from the countryside, and the merchant 'guilds' were never endowed with legal powers.

Hong Kong resembled other parts of China in that there was no clear-cut town–country distinction. By mid-Ming, the Pearl River Delta region, to which Hong Kong belongs, was further commercialized due to the internationalization of trade. Traditional markets and regional commercial centres started to prosper (Liu 1997:

23–6), but the urban and the rural were not functionally and legally separated. Guangzhou was a case in point: back in late Qing, it was part of two counties, Panyu and Nanhai. It was not until 1920 that Guangzhou was finally designated as an autonomous city (Tsin 1999: 21–2). Hong Kong, which was situated in the southern part of Xin'an County (with county seat at Nantou, now a district in Shenzhen), was administratively under the auspices of Guanfu Assistant Magistrate Division in 1819 (Liu 1999: 8) and another division in Kowloon Walled City in 1898 (Hase 2013: 6). The New Territories themselves were further divided into sub-districts, which, in most cases, were centred on a market town or a market village (Hayes 1984). In short, the town–country non-duality was vivid.

The Chinese Land System

This administratively defined empire-space was complicated by differences produced by the land system. Over time, the Chinese imperial land system had been adapted to nurture small-scale family farms in response to land constraint (Yang 2010: 28–34). Three developments are worth highlighting. First, collective landownership by lineage, clan and so on started to emerge during the Song (906–1279) dynasty. Second, there was separation of the right to use from the right to own since the Ming dynasty, rendering it possible for tenant farmers to transfer the right to use to others. Third, the more formal system of 'perpetual hereditary tenancy' (yongtian zhi) was popular in the richer regions of Su'nan, Fujian and Guangdong. Arable land was divided into two landholders: one refers to the topsoil (dipi); and the other to the subsoil (digu). Owners of topsoil, who maintained perpetual hereditary tenancies irrespective of any changes in the ownership of the subsoil, were free to inherit, mortgage, transfer and dispose of it (Yang 2010: 30–31). This system expedited the transition to a land-based taxation system: tax on landlords rather than tax on headship of peasants became the major source of revenue for the emperor as well as his economic means to intervene in land activities (Jin 2005: 65–78, Liu 1997: 8–13). Yet ownership of subsoil was important as it was still considered genuine proof of one's native place, the prerequisite for the right of entry to the imperial examination held at the prefecture level (Hase 2013: 42–9, Liu 1997: 9), the cornerstone of the meritocratic system of imperial China. Faure (1986: 36–44) reminds us that ownership meant rights of settlement too. In addition to inability to develop independent industrial and commercial activities, the 'perpetual heredity tenancy' system, which permitted peasants to survive by ploughing fields, had the societal effect of restricting the peasants to the rural area, instead of, like their counterparts during the enclosure movement in the West, dispossessing them and, in turn, forcing them to sell their labour power in the city (Jin 2005: 56).

By the time the British came to China, the pattern of land development in the Pearl River Delta had been set. The aforementioned commercial development in Guangdong since the Ming–Qing dynasty induced the localization of the gentry class. Besides exhibiting a more acceptable attitude towards commercial development, the latter was urged to reinforce lineage relations and networks by constructing ancestral halls, recording genealogy, purchasing arable land and converting it into collective ownership, and formalizing the customs and rituals of worshipping the ancestors and so on. As a result, more arable land was under the auspices of ancestral or communal 'trusts' (*tongs, zu*) (Liu 1997: 15–32). Besides, any matters related to land had to be handled by the county magistrate, who was located in Nantou, which entailed a long and difficult journey for the villagers (Hase 2013: 91). As a result, customary practices started to simplify, or rather complicate, the Chinese land system to such an extent that it has led many, including Hase (2013), to differentiate between the imperial land laws, applicable formally to most of the country, and the customary land laws practised in Guangdong. Moreover, although the first group of settlers (Punti, the Cantonese) in the New Territories dated back to the twelfth century, this simple social structure and the associated landownership pattern was complicated by, among other things, the Coastal Evacuation Policy (1661–69), which forced everyone living near the coast to retreat inland. After the abolition of the policy, only some of them returned. In response, the county magistrate encouraged newcomers, the Hakka (guest) people, to settle in the area and cultivate as much land as possible. Small grants of money and the promise of 'easy-terms' tenancies were offered to them, complicating the original landownership and owner–tenant relationships.

Concomitantly, the land system in Hong Kong comprised, according to Hase (2013: 50), 'layers of ownership within the village, and layers of landholders each with rights over the land'. The old land grants belonged to a customary land system in which the landholder of the subsoil was responsible for paying the land tax, while the cultivator of the topsoil had the perpetual and inheritable right of cultivation. The cultivator was free to sublease the topsoil to another tenant without the consent of the landlord, resulting in situations in which the topsoil landholder was not the actual cultivator of the land. It was commonplace that the tenant was not a real person either, but the clan or village community as a whole, or an ancestral 'trust'. Similarly, the right over the subsoil was usually owned by an ancestral or communal 'trust'. In other words, for any plot of land there were two lordships, one for the topsoil and another for the subsoil, but many more persons, an actual man or a *persona ficta*, with rights over the land. At the village level, while the topsoil right of the entire village was owned by an ancestral 'trust', individual village families cultivated the land as its sub-tenants. Some families made a small contribution payment to the 'trust', whereas others in other villages did not. All the relationships between the tenant and sub-tenants, articulated orally and bound by village customs, were supervised by the manager of the main 'trust'. To complicate matters, there were two types of deed, one red, and the other white. When the purchaser of a land transaction registered the deed with the official, the deed was called a 'red deed'. Deeds that were issued for the sale of topsoil rights, and others for the subsoil that did not register officially, were called 'white deeds' (Hase 2013: 71). The customary land system so described refuses to put tenants and landlords into straitjacket dualistic categories and, conversely, allows for the interaction of complementary oppositions.

HONG KONG IN TIME AND SPACE: BRITISH COLONIALISM

It was on the foundation of this locally articulated Chinese empire-space that the British constructed the colonial Hong Kong space. The British were interested in, as the great architect of British colonial rule Lord Frederick Lugard once remarked, both nature and natives in the tropics, bringing the colonial people 'forward into modernity' and incorporating them into a 'European-inflected spatiality' (Moore 2005: 13). In practice, before Hong Kong, the British had already colonized Australia, Ceylon, India and Malaya, and many of these provided experiences that were convenient models to emulate. Relevant to our discussion are, among others, the Torrens system from Australia, the Straits Settlements and Malacca (Sihombing 1984: 298–302) and the ruling against the Chinese *tong* in Penang (Chung 2010: 1416). These inputs from other countries, all connected by British colonialism, were the exemplar of correlativity of space in Hong Kong.

Correlativity was substantiated by the politico-legal manner in which Hong Kong was actually colonized over time and across space. Given the objective of expanding their empire on to Chinese soil, the British managed to take over Hong Kong Island on cession after the Treaty of Nanking in 1842. Colonization continued to extend northwards to the tract of Kowloon Peninsula south of Boundary Street after the Convention of Peking in 1860. To facilitate better administration, the British finally borrowed an even bigger tract north of the latter – later called the New Territories – for 99 years after the signing of the Convention for the Extension of Hong Kong Territory in 1898. This temporal account of colonization underscores the fact that the Hong Kong colony under British rule comprised two jurisdictional spaces, one eternally ceded, and another borrowed for 99 years only. The rest of this section elaborates on how this jurisdictional division complicated the development of the colonial space in Hong Kong in a way that contradicts Lefebvre's expectation.

The Emergence of an 'Urban' Centre within the Spatiality of the British Empire

Unlike other colonies, the construction of 'urban' Hong Kong did not involve the expansion of export-dependent monocultures for the reproduction of European labour and capital. Instead, given their strategic desire to colonize the Chinese mainland, the British were most eager to develop Hong Kong as an *entrepôt*. Hong Kong soon became a centre of modern trade, with economic activities located around the port. At the beginning, most of these modern traders were British, including those from the East India Company. They were 'brought in' from outside, not 'indigenously' bred. Although there were street market vendors before colonization, autonomy of the urban bourgeois did not exist. As time proceeded, Chinese traders came from Macao, and from the mainland due to civil war. As a result, the Hong Kong urban landscape exhibited a feature similar to other colonial cities – social and spatial segregation with one zone being restricted to the British and others opened to the Chinese ('Victoria City' vs 'China Town').

When the Treaty of Nanking was signed in 1842, the land relationships in 'urban' Hong Kong were drastically changed. As land on Hong Kong Island was declared Crown owned, villagers were, according to Hase (2013: 26), 'dispossessed' from land required by the new regime. The Hong Kong governor was empowered to make grants of land according to English common laws, not in perpetuity, only for a fixed lease period – 75 years in 1844. Grants of land were made available by auction, granting the right of development to the highest bidder (Nissim 2008: 9–15). Generating revenues from land became a major source of income for the colonial government (Nissim 2008: 11). This concern for revenues had made an impact on the land system in 'urban' Hong Kong. Unheard of elsewhere, property development had thus occupied a central position even in an early stage of development. At the same time, the system was also the product of local resistance. When 'urbanization' expanded to the Kowloon Peninsula, more villages were affected (Hayes 1984: 58), and as villagers learnt more about the notorious experience of previous land grabs, there were more records of resistance. The result was the explicit enactment of one clause in the Convention of Peking, prohibiting dispossession of land from villagers in Kowloon Peninsula. Owners were to be compensated, including buildings and agricultural produce, whereas those without official proof of ownership were allowed to continue farming the land as 'squatters' until resumption by the colonial government (Cheung 2013: 62–3).

The resulting urban–rural relationship was more complicated than one might have expected. First, the relationship took on a distinguishable form even at an embryonic stage. While 'urban' Hong Kong developed apace on the island between 1842 and 1860, the ceded part of Kowloon Peninsula did not enter this picture until the Convention of Peking was signed. Between these years, 'urbanization' also took place on land reclaimed from the harbour, besides the usual method of grabbing land from the indigenous villagers. During the years immediately after 1860, due to 'jurisdictional' expansion, 'urban' Hong Kong suddenly expanded into the 'countryside'. Put differently, there was urban explosion, in the Lefebvrean sense, even at the embryonic stage of 'urbanization'. Second, this explosion was achieved without land dispossession, as foreseen in many other colonies. In the case of land resumption in Tsim Sha Tsui, landowners were granted land of similar size in other parts of the peninsula, allowing them to continue farming. Many affected villagers relocated themselves to the district in the north, some as 'squatters' (Cheung 2013: 66–8). Third, the urban could not be isolated from the rural, due to the peculiar landownership. Many of the affected villagers in 'urban' Hong Kong actually paid rents to the subsoil owners belonging to the clans in the countryside of Kam Tin and Yeun Long (Hayes 2012: 10). The 'countryside' was always interwoven with the land grab in the 'urban'. Thus, when we talk about 'urban' development in 'urban' Hong Kong, it is difficult to exclude the rural in our discussion.

On the whole, the British developed an 'urban' centre specializing in trade and focusing on property development. They did this easily, because it took place in permanently ceded regions – legally under their ownership in perpetuity. This was a big contrast to the New Territories.

'Urban' Extension into the 'Alienated' Countryside

In advocating the gradual introduction of modern laws and ordinances into the New Territories, Lockhart, the colonial officer who surveyed the New Territories in 1898, nevertheless admitted the prevalence of 'great difference' between the ceded and the newly borrowed parts of the colony (Hayes 2012). The 'great difference' revealed, among other things, the hard fact that the New Territories was lent to the British for 99 years only. Against this politico-administrative backdrop, the British had encountered serious Chinese resistance in defence of their landownership in perpetuity (Sit and Kwong 2011: 39–46). There are debates in the literature about whether there was, as in other British colonies, indirect rule or whether Chinese customs had played a significant role in moulding the resultant landownership (Chan 1999, Chiu and Hung 1999, Chun 2000a, Liu 1999). In theoretical terms, there was the question of whether this development should be interpreted according to Eric Hobsbawm's 'invented tradition' (Chan 1999) and related to Benedict Anderson's 'imagined communities', Michel Foucault's 'colonial governmentality' (Chun 2000b), Theda Skocpol's 'social movement' (Chiu and Hung 1999), or Alfred Schütz's life-world (Cheung 2012). The relevant point for our immediate discussion is that a new territory was to be made, in correlativity with another territory that differed from it, yet informed its making. In particular, local resistance had forced the colonial government to proclaim the continuation of the Chinese way of life, and the safeguarding of its commercial and landed interests and, even for those without ownership titles, their rights in long occupation of land (Hayes 2012: 25–6).

The colonial government encountered difficulties in establishing a new, common law and a modern, scientific land registration system based on cadastral surveys for collecting taxes and revenues. In the end, according to the New Territories Land Ordinance of 1905, the government managed to formulate a land system of Block Crown Lease that favoured a clear-cut documentation of registered land rights (Hase 2013: 87–93, Hayes 2012: 29–41) in which many topsoil cultivators were privileged at the expense of their subsoil counterparts (Chiu and Hung 1999). The most significant point to note is that it had in fact incorporated many Chinese elements into the system. In accommodating urban expansion into the New Territories in the 1920s, the government encountered the land expropriation problem. Since they did not own the land, they could not expropriate it for development purposes. In the end, they needed to silence the opposition by stipulating new restrictions in 1923: any conversion of land for house-building purposes required applying for a licence and paying a premium. For renting house land to outsiders (that is, post-1898 settlers) in particular, the act of charging tax penalties above the low Crown Rent created a double standard in land administration. It constructed and concretized a category of self-proclaimed 'primordial inhabitants' whose rights to land and community were tied to Chinese traditional rights (Chun 2000b: 93–4). This colonial creation of a distinction between indigenous people and outsiders, which preserved rurality, has epitomized the continual coexistence of the urban and rural since the early 1900s. The two parts of the Hong Kong colony, the ceded and the borrowed, were, in 1898, disparate communities, each with its own dynamics but in interaction with each other. This led Hayes (2012: 2) to suggest borrowing the Chinese concept of *yin–yang* to characterize the dialectical relationship of town–country in Hong Kong.

The Coexistence of Convergence and Divergence

The duality urbanity–rurality became further fossilized over time. Immediately after the Second World War, world geopolitics rendered Hong Kong a strategic place in the fight against communism – the territorial containment of Chinese communism in particular. The massive influx of capital and labourers from Mainland China could destabilize society if there were too few investment opportunities and jobs. On the one hand, the government reluctantly modernized the economy by implementing an inactive industrial policy. Unlike many developing countries undertaking import-substitution policies after de-colonization, the government insisted on developing commerce, permitting the British *hongs* (traders) to bridge the gap between local manufacturers and foreign importers. Accompanied by governmental provision of infrastructure, public housing included, industrial development produced urbanization on the fringe in the 1950s (Tang et al. 2007). On the other, there was an urgent practical need to satisfy people's food supply and newly arrived immigrants' job requirements as well as the political urgency to prohibit the infiltration of the communists into the New Territories. The general tactic was to encourage these immigrants to cultivate unoccupied areas or plots rented from the landlords with the aid of a number of government-sponsored rural cooperatives, including the Vegetable Marketing Organization (Airriess 2005, Chun 2000b, Chiu and Hung 1999). In addition, there was a new concern with the condition of the colonies after the establishment of the United Nations. The newly elected British Labour government enacted The Colonial Development and Welfare Act, bringing basic improvements to countryside life in Hong Kong (Hayes 2012: 72–3). In sum, while industrialization-led urbanization took place on the urban fringe, rurality further developed in the outlying area by encouraging people to farm and settle there.

Developments since the 1960s had the effect of expediting urbanization in the New Territories and, concomitantly, attenuating the urban–rural difference. Rice cultivation declined due to the traditional small landholding operation; the construction of six reservoirs in the New Territories to meet increasing urban water consumption need; and the construction of country parks to protect water catchment areas. Other forces included the construction of new towns to accommodate people, and the introduction of voting by geographical constituency. While some forces were attributable to natural and international causes, others were due to the tactics of the government to resolve socio-spatial contradictions in the inner city. Civic pride, to be nurtured by modern designed living, was then desperately needed by the British in the negotiation with the Chinese on the future of Hong Kong (Tang et al. 2007). The effects of urbanization on the New Territories are conspicuous: newcomers have outnumbered the indigenous population; high-rise buildings compete with each other; youngsters wear clothing and live a lifestyle not dissimilar from that of their counterparts in the urban area; and it is even now administered by an urban-style local administration (Hayes 2012). An urban way of life has emerged in the countryside.

This is one side of the story only, as developments have, conversely, fossilized rurality. In light of customary land practice, the government needed to confront legal and pragmatic issues to expedite development in the New Territories. Hayes (2012: 83) remarks that this could not have been done without the restructuring of Heung Yee Kuk, a political organization of rural interests (Chiu and Hung 1999, Sit and Kwong 2011). After factional struggles in the 1950s, the Kuk had turned out to be supportive of urban development. Its flexibility has enabled the government to match the timing of land resumption with tight land formation and civil engineering schedules in development areas in the New Territories, converting the difficult and problematic land formation into the achievable.

Other 'costs' were involved, however. The government formulated a new compensation scheme for land resumption. The 'primordial inhabitants' were granted full cash compensation or could 'exchange' their agricultural land within the proposed development area for newly formed building land at a later date using 'Letters B' certificates. In doing this, the government legally solidified the 'primordial' status of the inhabitants, which it had tried desperately to dilute half a century before. Besides, as population grew in the New Territories, squatters increased by leaps and bounds. 'Primordial inhabitants' complained vehemently about the seemingly unjust government regulations on house building. As the government was keen to produce developable land amidst these complaints and resistance, it, after serious negotiation with the Kuk, finally entitled each of the male 'primordial inhabitants' to build for himself one small house in his village during his lifetime, the 'Small House Policy' of 1972. Application for a small house was permitted in established pre-1898 villages. To align with this new policy, amendments were made to the existing land policy too. In and around old villages, the administration is required to cordon off a plot of land called 'village expansion area' for this purpose. In doing this, the government has conceded to the 'primordial inhabitants' their inalienable customary right to live on the land, although it maintained its right to village land as property of the Crown (Chun 2000b: 149–56). Moreover, although the countryside is increasingly regulated by an urban-style administration, the power of rural interests has not been drastically curtailed until recently. For almost half a decade, the colonial government had relied on the village elders or representatives to rule the New Territories. Service provision as well as dispute resolution were provided by the Rural Committees. When the District Advisory Committee was formed, it still had to call upon the services of the members of those committees. The latter were active in putting on operas, festival activities and so on, thereby prolonging the rural culture in the community (Hayes 2012: 120). In other words, while the countryside is increasingly governed by an urban-style administration, rurality lingers on. This persistence can be deemed a product of the 'positive' non-intervention of the colonial government in the countryside in the first place.

Finally, rurality has been perpetuated legally due to the strenuous efforts of the Kuk. The power of the Kuk was strengthened after the support it offered to the government during the 1967 riots. Since then, the Kuk has stretched its influence to the Chinese communities and the British Parliament. In the negotiations on the future of Hong Kong, it stretched its influence to Beijing too (Hayes 2012: 163–7, Sit and Kwong 2011). To maintain the status quo, both the British and the Chinese governments were interested in preserving rural interests. Clause 2 in Annex III of the Sino-British Joint Declaration in 1984 is testimony to this perpetuation: the Old Schedule Lots could remain in the hands of the indigenous proprietors – largely in thousands of lineage trusts (Hayes 2012: 167). On the one hand, this rural emphasis has serious implications for urban redevelopment in the inner city by raising the already high-density development to ever new heights (Tang 2008; Tang et al. 2012). On the other, the urban outlook developed since the 1970s began to openly confront the rural outlook of the 'deep' countryside. This confrontation was aggravated by some of the malpractices of the indigenous inhabitants, who illegally sold their certificates to build a small house to developers. In contrast, to maintain their status as 'primordial inhabitants', villagers definitely would not sell the ancestral house, *zu wu* – literally the very first house where the whole clan lived – as it stands as a symbol of lineage (Chan 2012). No wonder one common scene in the New Territories is the encirclement of the *zu wu* by high-rise, high-density development. The town–country contradiction has clearly persisted and expanded.

Summary

The above has argued emphatically that if one examines the history of urban development in Hong Kong, one finds a distinguishable process and pattern. Undoubtedly, one sees urban encroachment on the two sides of Victoria Harbour and on the New Territories. Superficially, the latter's development has already exhibited all the characteristics of urban conversion, including the decline in the percentage of agricultural population, the shift from staple rice cultivation to vegetable growing and the increasing number of industries. Yet, in reality, the rural has not disappeared, due to the continual intervention of many political practices that have tried desperately to perpetuate the existing rural power structure. There have been two parallel developments since 1898, confirming the coexistence of the urban and the rural. On the one hand, while the New Territories has become increasingly urbanized over time, it is simultaneously perpetuating its rurality. On the other, since 1984, and especially once Hong Kong was returned to Chinese sovereignty in 1997, Hong Kong is becoming another city in the Chinese urban system. Increasing concerns are expressed not only about politico-economic but also about spatial integration with the mainland. Urban Hong Kong is increasingly non-urban in the sense that, being enclosed within a greater space, the power structure underlying the production of colonial Hong Kong in the first place has been declining in importance.

DISCUSSION: BEYOND LEFEBVRE

It is apparent from the Hong Kong case that Lefebvre has great difficulties in understanding urbanization under colonialism. The land relations and their politics have played a significant role in accounting for urbanization. The Chinese customary land practice entails non-dualities between ownership and tenancy, between transferability and perpetuity, between individual and collective (that is, ancestral), between urban and rural, and so on. It is difficult to accommodate these non-dualities in the duality-informed common laws.[5] When it comes to the politics of land, it is more complicated than the contradiction between collective production and individual appropriation of social benefits. It is always difficult to simplify the community 'trust' as either individual or collective. Its nature has been subject to successive rounds of politics, and then interpretation. Urbanization under colonialism is more dynamic than a Eurocentric Lefebvrean thesis of complete urbanization would have us believe. Even the trialectics proposed by Lefebvre is unable to account for a situation in which the duality of town–country does not occur in the first place. The Hong Kong case has demonstrated that while urbanization continues apace, the urban and the rural have coexisted, becoming each other, due to the persistence of the Chinese customary land practice. It stands at odds with the Eurocentric prediction of the disappearance of the town–country relationship and of the emergence of centre–periphery.

Urbanization in Hong Kong, for example, cannot be explained without knowledge of its past in correlativity with other countries and places. Hong Kong has been part of China, which has intimate relationships with, say, other countries in East and South-east Asia. China had its way of governing and its land system and practice. The British had their own experience of colonizing many parts of the world. These two practices interacted more seriously when the New Territories was lent to the British. They interacted again during the Cold War, demanding a more active encroachment on the countryside. More recently, they interacted again to decide on the future of Hong Kong, adding for the first time a larger rural component into the city. These temporal and spatial developments have nurtured some kinds of Hong Kong 'subjectivity'. This has affected the form and process of correlativity emphasized so much by those who try to apply Lefebvre to the developing world. Accordingly, to advance Lefebvre, especially for the non-West, requires us to construct a spatial story for the urban societies under investigation: their governing, including in particular their land system and practice. These societies play a more active role in either encouraging or deterring urbanization, necessitating a more nuanced open-geography and open-history analysis of the town–country relationship than a 'globalized' Lefebvre can afford. This leads us to have reservations about the recent surge in the urban literature to study global urbanization, which is still based mostly on a more or less Eurocentric view (for example, Merrifield 2013).

The Hong Kong case urges us also to sound a cautionary note regarding the recent calls for comparative urban studies. Recently, informed by post-colonialist theory, Robinson (2006) argued that there are ordinary cities in the non-West. As there is no single account that can capture the diversities, some of which are incommensurable, it is even difficult to derive formal comparative methodologies. The appropriate approach is to think of city space 'as a simultaneity of multiplicities or trajectories and thus historically and politically radically open to future possibilities' (Robinson 2011:

18). Robinson's call for diversity has been echoed by many others, including Bunnell and Maringanti's (2010) proposal of alternative practices in doing urban and regional research in Asia beyond metrocentricity. Instead of elaborating metrocentric theories with Asian cases, they call for theorizing from these cases. But these comparative studies have ignored the significance of a 'subjectivity'-cum-correlativity that the Hong Kong case has illustrated. On the other hand, in order to understand colonization better, Kipfer (2008: 1006), for example, demands that we carry out more case studies. The crux is, as our preliminary critique of the post-colonialist positions has shown, not so much diversity in the selection of case studies, because quantity itself cannot be a substitute for a more informed qualitative understanding with the recognition of the 'subjectivity' of the cities concerned. Lefebvre has his limitations, and it is difficult to resolve these by merely studying a few more cases. The only option open to us is to decipher a more open-geography- and open-history-informed spatial story of the cases concerned. As a final note of recommendation: one may consider Hayes's (2012) call to study Hong Kong's urbanization as *yin–yang* as an interaction between town and country; *yin–yang*, based on non-duality, may overcome Lefebvre's theoretical and methodological limitations.

NOTES

1   Thanks are due to the Research Grants Council of Hong Kong (GRF 250012) for their partial financial support of this research. The author would also like to thank Christian Schmid for his constructive comments.

2   This thesis of complete urbanization has been further developed into a history of space in *The Production of Space*.

3   For a similar attempt, see Harvey's (2006: especially 133–48) spatial matrix.

4   I have in mind the *tongbian* concept of 'dialectics' as informed by the Chinese philosophical principle of correlativity (see Tian 2005).

5   It is not so much another case of ambiguous property rights, as some Western-inclined arguments would have us believe, but one of a completely different nature – non-duality.

REFERENCES

Airriess, C. 2005. 'Governmentality and Power in Politically Contested Space: Refugee Farming in Hong Kong's New Territories, 1945–1970'. *Journal of Historical Geography* 31: 763–83.

Allen, J. 2003. *Lost Geographies of Power*. Oxford: Blackwell.

Araghi, F. and Karides, M. 2012. 'Land Dispossession and Global Crisis: Introduction to the Special Section on Land Rights in the World-System'. *Journal of World-Systems Research* 18: 1–5.

Bunnell, T. and Maringanti, A. 2010. 'Practising Urban and Regional Research Beyond Metrocentricity'. *International Journal of Urban and Regional Research* 34: 415–20.

Chan, K-s. 2012. 'Women's Property Rights in a Chinese Lineage Village'. *Modern China* 39: 101–28.

Chan, S.C. 1999. 'Colonial Policy in a Borrowed Place and Time: Invented Tradition in the New Territories of Hong Kong'. *European Planning Studies* 7: 231–42.

Cheng, C.S. and Chan, Y.M. 2012. 'Shenzhen-Hongkong Integration: Who Really Benefits From the New Territories Northeast Development Planning?' *Ming Pao Weekly* 2290, 29 September: 96–119.

Cheung, S.K. 2012. 'Portraying the Life-World of Village Settlements in the New Territories: Land, Development and Transformation', in *Locality Discourse 2011: Imagining the New Territories*, edited by Locality Discourse Editorial Committee and SynergyNet. Taipei: ABD Books, 117-41 (in Chinese).

Cheung, S-W. 2013. *Demolishing Village: The Disappearance of Villages in Kowloon*. Hong Kong: Joint Publishing (in Chinese).

Chiu, S.W.K. and Hung, H-f. 1999. 'State Building and Rural Stability', in *Hong Kong's History: State and Society under Colonial Rule*, edited by T.-W. Ngo. London: Routledge, 74–100.

Chun, A. 2000a. 'Colonial "Govern-Mentality" in Transition: Hong Kong as Imperial Object and Subject'. *Cultural Studies* 14: 430–61.

Chun, A. 2000b. *Unstructuring Chinese Society: The Fictions of Colonial Practice and the Changing Realities in 'Land' in the New Territories of Hong Kong*. Amsterdam: Harwood Academic Publishers.

Chung, S.P.-Y. 2010. 'Chinese *Tong* as British Trust: Institutional Collisions and Legal Disputes in Urban Hong Kong, 1860s–1980s'. *Modern Asian Studies* 44: 1409–32.

Coronil, F. 1997. *The Magical State: Nature, Money, and Modernity in Venezuela*. Chicago, IL: The University of Chicago Press.

Elden, S. 2004. *Understanding Henri Lefebvre: Theory and the Possible*. London: Continuum.

Faure, D. 1986. *The Structure of Chinese Society: Lineage and Village in the Eastern New Territories, Hong Kong*. Hong Kong: Hong Kong University Press.

Feng, Y. 2005. 'Town-Country Relations in China During the Ming-Qing period – An Investigation Along the Path of Scientific History'. *East China Normal University Journal (Philosophy and Social Sciences Edition)* 37: 113–21 (in Chinese).

Gardiner, M.E. 2000. *Critiques of Everyday Life*. London: Routledge.

Goswami, M. 2004. *Producing India: From Colonial Economy to National Space*. Chicago, IL: The University of Chicago Press.

Government Information Services. 1981. *Hong Kong 1981*. Hong Kong: Government Printer.

Hart, G. 2002. *Disabling Globalization: Places of Power in Post-Apartheid South Africa*. Berkeley, CA: University of California Press.

Harvey, D. 2006. *Spaces of Global Capitalism: Towards a Theory of Uneven Geographical Development*. London: Verso.

Hase, P.H. 2013. *Custom, Land and Livelihood in Rural South China: The Traditional Land Law of Hong Kong's New Territories, 1750–1950*. Hong Kong: Hong Kong University Press.

Hayes, J. 1984. 'The Nature of Village Life', in *From Village to City: Studies in the Traditional Roots of Hong Kong*, edited by D. Faure, J. Hayes and A. Birch. Hong Kong: Centre of Asian Studies, University of Hong Kong, 55–72.

Hayes, J. 2012. *The Great Difference: Hong Kong's New Territories and Its People 1898–2004.* Hong Kong: Hong Kong University Press.

Hong Kong Annual Report 2011, www.yearbook.gov.hk/2011/en/pdf/Appendices.pdf (accessed on 10 May 2013).

Huff, T.E. 2003. *The Rise of Early Modern Science: Islam, China, and the West*, 2nd edn. Cambridge: Cambridge University Press.

Jin, X. 2005. *A Research on Institutional Arrangements and Legislative Issues of Farmland Rights in China.* Beijing: Zhongguo Shehui Kexue Chubanshe (in Chinese).

Kipfer, S. 2008. 'Comparative Perspectives on "Colonization" and "Urbanization". Debates and Developments'. Contribution to 'Writing the Lines of Connection: Unveiling the Strange Language of Urbanization'. *International Journal of Urban and Regional Research* 32(4): 989–1027.

Kipfer, S. 2009. 'Urban Marxism and the Postcolonial Challenge: Henri Lefebvre and "Colonization"'. Paper to the conference on 'Urban Research and Architecture: Beyond Henri Lefebvre'. ETH Zurich, 24–26 November.

Kipfer, S., Schmid, C., Goonewardena, K. and R. Milgrom. 2008. 'Globalizing Lefebvre?', in *Space, Difference, Everyday Life: Reading Henri Lefebvre*, edited by K. Goonewardena, Stefan Kipfer, Richard Milgrom and Christian Schmid. London: Routledge, 285–305.

Lazarus, N. and Varma, R. 2008. 'Marxism and Postcolonial Studies', in *Critical Companion to Contemporary Marxism*, edited by J. Bidet and S. Kouvelakis. Leiden: Brill, 309–31.

Lefebvre, H. 1991 [1974]. *The Production of Space.* Trans. D. Nicholson-Smith. Oxford: Blackwell.

Lefebvre, H. 2003 [1970]. *The Urban Revolution.* Minneapolis, MN: University of Minnesota Press.

Lewis, M.E. 2006. *The Construction of Space in Early China.* Albany, NY: State University of New York Press.

Liu, R. 1999. *The Abridged History of the New Territories.* Hong Kong: Joint Publishing (in Chinese).

Liu, Z. 1997. *Between the State and the Society: A Study of Household Registration System in Guangdong during the Ming and Qing Period.* Guangzhou: Zhongshan Daxue Chubanshe (in Chinese).

Merrifield, A. 2006. *Henri Lefebvre: A Critical Introduction.* London: Routledge.

Merrifield, A. 2013. 'The Urban Question under Planetary Urbanization'. *International Journal of Urban and Regional Research* 37(3): 909–22.

Ming Pao Daily. 2007. 'URA Demolishes 400 Old Buildings and Relocates 10,000 Persons in 7 Years'. *Ming Pao Daily* 22 March 2007: A18.

Moore, D.S. 2005. *Suffering for Territory: Race, Place, and Power in Zimbabwe.* Durham, NC: Duke University Press.

Mote, F.W. 1977. 'The Transformation of Nanking, 1350–1400', in *The City in Late Imperial China*, edited by G.W. Skinner. Stanford, CA: Stanford University Press, 101–53.

Nissim, R. 2008. *Land Administration and Practice in Hong Kong*, 2nd edn. Hong Kong: Hong Kong University Press.

Robinson, J. 2006. *Ordinary Cities: Between Modernity and Development.* London: Routledge.

Robinson, J. 2011. 'Cities in a World of Cities: The Comparative Gesture'. *International Journal of Urban and Regional Research* 35(1): 1–23.

Sihombing, J. 1984. 'The Torrens System in the New Territories'. *Hong Kong Law Journal* 14: 291–305.

Schmid, C. 2008. 'Henri Lefebvre's Theory of the Production of Space: Towards a Three-Dimensional Dialectic', in *Space, Difference, Everyday Life: Reading Henri Lefebvre*, edited by K. Goonewardena, S. Kipfer, R. Milgrom and C. Schmid. London: Routledge, 27–45.

Schmid, C. 2012. 'Henri Lefebvre, the Right to the City, and the New Metropolitan Mainstream', in *Cities for People, Not for Profit: Critical Urban Theory and the Right to the City*, edited by N. Brenner, P. Marcuse and M. Mayer. London: Routledge, 42–59.

Sit, F-S. and Kwong, C-M. 2011. *The History of New Territories Heung Yee Kuk: From Borrowed Land to One Country Two Systems*. Hong Kong: Joint Publishing (in Chinese).

Smith, N. 2003. 'Foreword', in *The Urban Revolution* by H. Lefebvre. Minneapolis, MN: University of Minnesota Press, viii–xxiii.

Streeck, W. and Thelen, K. 2005. 'Introduction: Institutional Change in Advanced Political Economies', in *Beyond Continuity: Institutional Change in Advanced Economies*, edited by W. Streeck and K. Thelen. Oxford: Oxford University Press, 1–39.

Tang, W.-S. 2008. 'Hong Kong under Chinese Sovereignty: Social Development and a Land (Re)development Regime'. *Eurasian Geography and Economics* 49(3): 341–63.

Tang, W.-S., Chan, K.C., Wong, K.P., Kwok, C.Y. and Man, P.Y. 2007. 'Transcend the Central Value by its Historical Geography – Recall "Shatin Value"'. Occasional Paper 76, The Centre for China Urban and Regional Studies, Hong Kong Baptist University, Hong Kong (in Chinese).

Tang, W.-S., Lee, J.W.Y. and Ng, M.K. 2012. 'Public Engagement as a Tool of Hegemony: The Case of Designing the New Central Harbourfront in Hong Kong'. *Critical Sociology* 38: 83–100.

Tian, C. 2005. *Chinese Dialectics: From Yijing to Marxism*. Lanham, MD: Lexington Books.

Tibebu, T. 2011. *Hegel and the Third World: The Making of Eurocentrism in World History*. Syracuse: Syracuse University Press.

Tsin, M. 1999. 'Canton Remapped', in *Remaking the Chinese City*, edited by J.W. Esherick. Honolulu, HI: University of Hawaii Press, 19–29.

Yang, S. 2010. *The Research on the Evolution of Land Rights System during Late-Qing and the Republican Periods*. Beijing: Zhongguo Shehui Kexue Chubanse (in Chinese).

Zhou, Z. 2005. *The History of China Local Administrative System*. Shanghai: Shanghai Renmin Chubanshe (in Chinese).

4

Henri Lefebvre and 'Colonization': From Reinterpretation to Research

Stefan Kipfer and Kanishka Goonewardena

The metaphor of colonization is frequently used to characterize contested urban dynamics. It is less common for researchers to elaborate on how neocolonial forces actually shape urbanization today. A comparative volume on gentrification, for example, identifies gentrification as 'a new urban colonialism' (Atkinson and Bridge 2005). Yet most contributions to this book do not examine any substantive connection between colonialism and gentrification beyond casual analogy. The meaning of the colonial in relation to colonial history remains vague if present at all, as does the rhetorical suggestion here that gentrifiers be called colonizers (ibid.: 14). In the francophone context, Jean-Pierre Garnier (2010: 12) occasionally deploys the notion of colonization to illustrate how the French state, landed capital and petty-bourgeois class fractions reclaim the remaining working-class neighbourhoods in east-central Paris and some adjacent suburban municipalities. Here too, colonization is used to describe class-based, state-led and land-rent-induced displacement. The specifically neocolonial aspects of these processes remain opaque.

Loosely metaphorical uses of colonization to describe urban development are insufficient, indeed problematic. Our objections are not to metaphor per se, however. As we know from Antonio Gramsci, among others, metaphors are fundamental to the life of language and its role in mediating social relations. They help 'translate' meaning from context to context (Ives 2004: 84–9). Moreover, in active, self-reflexive use, metaphors can politicize by bringing familiar experiences (urban redevelopment) in contact with seemingly unrelated others (colonialism). For example, describing gentrification in North America as 'frontier' development alludes to the history of colonial settlement while capturing gentrification as a boundary-shifting process (Smith 1996, Blomley 2004: 79). But metaphors cease to play a de-familiarizing role if they obscure the critical work of translation that is involved in the juxtaposition of meanings derived from apparently distant contexts. In our case, using colonization indiscriminately and mechanically ('spontaneously', as Gramsci would say) risks undermining one's regard for the (neo)colonial realities to which the metaphor alludes. Such disregard makes it difficult to trace the links between the specifically racialized neocolonial and other, class-based and gendered aspects of urban strategies. This is particularly problematic where neocolonial spatial organization *coexists* with unbroken forms of colonialism, as in France's overseas territories or in Canada's white-settler relations with indigenous peoples.

In what follows, therefore, we develop a not purely metaphorical conception of 'colonization'.[1] First, we sketch Henri Lefebvre's own journey from an almost exclusively metaphorical understanding of colonization in the early 1960s to a conceptualization of 'colonization' as a historically and geographically varied modality of organizing hierarchical territorial relations in the late 1970s, a journey very much inspired by the intervening anti-colonial struggles. While noting the analytical promise of Lefebvre's move for purposes of urban research, here we follow Kristin Ross's (1995) path-breaking work to argue that Lefebvre's concept must be substantively transformed and enriched with those who shared much of his philosophical orientation but truly understood the fundamentally racialized nature of colonial relations – especially Frantz Fanon and his teacher Aimé Césaire. Second, we hope to demonstrate the difference such a transformed conception of 'colonization' makes in urban research today by focusing on a highly influential urban strategy that forcefully intervenes in race and class relations of metropolitan cities on both sides of the Atlantic. What commands our attention here on the basis of our ongoing research in Toronto and Paris are not the most direct and ongoing forms of colonization such as those exercised on indigenous peoples in Canada, but the more mediated, *neo*colonial strategies that we have identified in exemplary public-housing redevelopment projects in both cities. These are expressed most clearly in the aggressively promoted place-based urban policy called 'social mix', which we argue is a new modality of 'colonization' that has partly superseded the spatial separatism of postwar functionalism. This claim takes us beyond urban policy, housing and architecture; it urges us to reformulate the right to the city and returns us to a basic concern dear to Lefebvre and Fanon: the relationship between politics, social transformation and the appropriation of space.

LEFEBVRE ON 'COLONIZATION'[2]

In matters of colonialism, Lefebvre was typical both of the French left and urban Marxism. These questions play a secondary and often submerged role in his life and work. Lefebvre participated in two of the few historical conjunctures in which anti-colonial mobilization played a key role in French politics. In the mid-1920s, before joining the Communist Party (PCF), Lefebvre was briefly interned for getting involved in the PCF's campaign against France's role in suppressing the Rif uprising in Morocco (Burkhard 2000: 49–52, 60). But in contrast to close fellow travellers André Breton and Paul Nizan, Lefebvre's engagements here left no significant trace in his texts of the inter-war period. In the late 1950s, before and after his expulsion from the PCF, Lefebvre worked against the party line and supported

Algerian independence by linking dissident Communists to the network of people supporting the Algerian Liberation Front (FLN), the *porteurs de valises* (Hamon and Rotman 1979: 108–9, 167–9). Impressed by the Algerian war and the Cuban revolution, and liberated from the 'narrow, stifling nationalism' of the PCF (Lefebvre 1973: 9), he began making explicit use of the language of colonization in the late 1950s.

In 1961, Lefebvre and Guy Debord came to an agreement that the problematic of everyday life in France could be understood in analogy with the geopolitical situation of the colonies. Lefebvre wrote: 'everyday life has literally been "colonized".' It has been brought to an extreme point of alienation, in other words, dissatisfaction, in the name of the latest technology and of "consumer society"' (2002 [1961]: 110). A comparison is made here between, on the one hand, the relationship of colonizing and colonized countries and, on the other, the relationship between dominant and dominated sectors in the latest stage of imperial capitalism that intensified accumulation in new areas such as leisure and urbanism. This comparison expressed the thesis that 'daily life replaces the colonies' (2005 [1981]: 26) as capital accumulation shifted from the colonies to the metropolitan home market. Lefebvre recognized later that this thesis was 'excessive' and 'hypercritical' (ibid.) in stretching the meaning of colonization at the very moment when colonialism was deemed to recede into the background as far as capitalist development was concerned. His own claims notwithstanding (2002: 316), colonization remained a loose metaphor for metropolitan everydayness, which he treated as discontinuous with colonialism. While he described both colonialism proper and the bureaucratic administration of mass consumption as different forms of alienation (2009 [1939]: 4–5), he did not explain how these distinct forms relate concretely to each other – or why the latter should described in the terms of the former.[3]

Fifteen years later, Lefebvre proposed a more substantive conceptualization of 'colonization' as a state-bound practice of producing hierarchical territorial relations, and thus one crucial aspect of the role of the state in producing abstract (homogeneous, fragmented and hierarchical) space. As he said in the chapter on 'colonizers and colonized' in volume four of *De l'État*, 'wherever a dominated space is generated and mastered by a dominant space – where there is periphery and centre – there is colonization' (1978: 174). Lefebvre's formulation derived from detailed discussions of Lenin's, Luxemburg's, Amin's and Frank's theories of imperialism and colonialism in volumes two and three of *De l'État*. He insisted, unlike Lenin, that colonial plunder (and 'original accumulation' more generally) is not a mere phase in the transition of capitalism but an ongoing and persistent feature of capitalist development. He also argued that a proper analysis of 'colonization' must go 'beneath the economic facts' (ibid.: 170–71) of the relations of production driving imperialism (capital exports, external market penetration and unequal exchange) to focus on (1) relations of domination with all the humiliating and degrading aspects that macropolitical–economic analyses of imperialism sometimes occlude; and (2) the spatial, territorial forms in which state-bound domination is organized.

Lefebvre's intervention is intriguing for urban research because he insisted that 'colonization' can be compared across the divide between (neo)colonies and imperial centres. The opposition of centre and periphery thus 'extends to the heart of the metropoles' (1977: 18–19). Far from being a phenomenon restricted to world order and international relations, 'colonization' – the organization of political domination through hierarchical, territorial relations – becomes also pertinent to understanding relations between regions and within urban regions. Forms of 'colonization' can be compared, then, at various scales within and across different social formations. For example, in the age of Empire, colonial exploitation intensified under the pressure of inter-imperialist competition for territorial control. In this era, Lefebvre identified as the typical colonial form the Haussmannite 'suburban style' of *peripheralizing* workers in Paris and colonial subjects in colonial cities (1978: 178). In mid-twentieth-century capitalism, formal decolonization goes hand in hand with a 'world-wide extension of the colonial phenomenon' (ibid.), including the 'internal colonization' (ibid.: 180) of peripheral regions (the *Bretagne*, the *Pays Basque*, the *Pyrénées*), towns and urban centres according to the functionalist 'model of isolated units'. This latter model helped order space into a hierarchical and fragmented 'collection of ghettos', disperse workers and administer mass consumption, with men acting as 'foremen' for the big 'phallocrats' of state and capital (ibid.: 308–9, 174–5, 183).

What explains this shift of meaning of colonization from the early 1960s to the late 1970s? The main answer lies in Lefebvre's observation about the period of intense urban struggle before, during and after 1968.[4] In France, May 1968 and its aftermath revealed a peculiar contradiction between 'the democratic revolution, the great French revolution (with its consequences: the rights of man), on the one hand, and, on the other, imperialism, the clever and very tough bourgeois dominant class, the super-exploitation of foreign workers (which number three and a half million in France)' (1972: 257). Lefebvre recognized that, if claims to the right to the city and its double, the right to difference, included the 'refusal to allow oneself to be removed from urban reality by a discriminatory and segregative organization' (1996: 195), then de-segregation did not necessarily mean the same thing for French students, workers and immigrant workers (with their particular experiences of super-exploitation and precarious housing). Whereas in the early 1960s Lefebvre used colonization to describe a shift in accumulation from external colonialism to internal market penetration, the urban struggles in the late 1960 and early 1970s showed Lefebvre that 'internal' or 'semi-colonization' was tied to forms of territorial organization that entrenched segmentations among subaltern classes (1972: 258–9). No longer simply deploying a loose metaphor to capture the resemblance between colonialism and the colonization of everyday life, Lefebvre now indicated that these segmentations of the subaltern can be described in 'colonial' terms in part because of ongoing, not just historic, links between colonialism proper and French Fordism – at the heart of which lay the flows of migration of peoples from the former to the latter.

The recognition of these transnational links helped concretize Lefebvre's suggestion that '1968' (and the right to the city) be articulated in worldwide terms as a constellation of struggles in peripheries 'near' (in French suburbs) and 'far' (in Latin American barrios and African American ghettos). In his reflections on Che,

Mao, Castro, Lenin, Luxemburg and Amin (which can be found in his major urban works published between 1968 and 1973), Lefebvre concluded that this worldwide conjuncture of struggles of peripheralized social forces for sociopolitical and geographic centrality revealed territorial fault-lines *within* an urbanizing world, and no longer between the historic city and the countryside (2003 [1970]: 113). Derived from his observations of worldwide struggle, Lefebvre's conception of 'colonization' as a territorial relation of domination, while much less loosely metaphorical than in the early 1960s, is still not without limits. It does not adequately capture the distinction between *varieties* of 'colonization' and their *particular* forms of determination. With reference to Paris, he mentions that organizing hierarchical territorial relations means different things for students, women, male French workers and immigrants; yet he does so descriptively, without theorizing why this might be the case. Even the Lefebvre of the late 1970s does not fully live up to the promise of a comparative analysis of neocolonial spatial organization. Despite its potency for research on racism and colonialism,[5] his work still risks substituting homology for a theory of the relationship between colonial spatial strategy and 'colonization' in post-colonial times (Müller 2001).

Lefebvre's notion of 'colonization' must thus be developed further with theoretical influences that do more than allude to the specificities of colonial social relations: super-exploitation, pervasive humiliation and racist violence. The best candidate for this theoretical operation is Frantz Fanon, the intellectual among the counter-colonial generation of the immediate postwar years who was most adamant that colonialism and racism be understood as mediated by a contradictory set of spatial relations (Kipfer 2011). In this regard, Fanon dwelt on a variety of spatial forms: the geographically mobile visual and bodily regime of distancing established by gestures and the look in the public space of postwar France and the gendered forms of confinement established by patriarchy and racialized physical segregation in colonial Algeria. For Fanon, it was through these daily spatial practices and state-enforced geographical demarcations that racism managed to give colonial social relations their particularly ossified, caste-like character. The conceptual upshot of this insight is clear: the concept 'colonization' can only be deployed without losing sight of colonialism, past and present, if it helps us understand both the racialized dimension of spatial relations of domination and how these relate to (neo)colonial realities. In turn, this also means that today, genuine decolonization and the quest for a future without race so dear to Fanon must also be considered through their spatial mediation as a revolutionary project to appropriate time and space at various scales.

FROM THE 'MODEL OF ISOLATED UNITS' TO 'SOCIAL MIXITY'

Lefebvre and Fanon focused on the mid-twentieth century. What Lefebvre described as the paradigmatic form of abstract space in neocapitalism – the funtionalist model of isolated units – could be best observed in the suburban housing estates, bungalow districts, university campuses and factory zones as well as the central city renewal areas of the 1950s and 1960s. Characteristic of a crucial (Paris) and significant, if highly residual (Toronto) element of rented social housing, postwar functionalism was part of a worldwide effort of urban modernization with (neo)colonial dimensions. In the 1950s, the compartmentalized Algiers known to Fanon was infused with vulgar modernist and racially segmented social housing construction under the *Plan de Constantine*, the Gaullist effort to modernize colonialism that was also an important reference point for regional planning in Paris (Fredenucci, 2003). In Paris, functionalism had a number of facets. While the *grands ensembles* were meant to be diverse in class terms so as not to replicate the revolutionary working class *faubourgs* (Chamboredon and Lemaire 1970, Butler and Noisette 1977), they were off limits to most migrant workers until the 1970s. Colonial techniques of separating migrants helped identify *faubourgs* (now called *îlots insalubres*) for redevelopment and build transitional housing for immigrant workers, who were deemed in need of 'acculturation' before moving into regular social housing. In Toronto, mass suburbanization and urban renewal (including public housing construction) were to normalize pathologized and, sometimes, racialized working-class space: zones of self-built housing and central city 'slums' like Cabbagetown, the Ward and Chinatown. In some cases, but not all, the model of isolated units – Debord's 'technique of separation' – combined functional segregation with social separation.

Since the 1970s, state-led strategies of desegregation have selectively supplanted functionalism. While in the global South such strategies have taken forms such as forced dispersal through military urbicide and 'slum' clearance or managed informality through gradual 'slum' upgrading, official desegregation in Euro-America typically happens under the banner of 'diversity' or 'mixity'. Planning for diversity or social mixity typically mobilizes idealized conceptions of life in pre-modernist small towns or urban villages, assuming that physical proximity produces social harmony and resolves the 'dysfunctions' of postwar modernism. The distinction between planning for homogeneity (functionalism) and planning for diversity (postmodernism) was not clear-cut socially. However, under the influence of movements against postwar planning (including urban renewal and legally sanctioned forms of racial segregation), diversity planning has helped re-territorialize state intervention focused on place, neighbourhood or street. Today, mixity planning is typically explained as a medium of gentrification (Lees 2008, Bridge et al. 2012), neoliberalized state rescaling (Brenner 2004), or the exercise of symbolic violence in managing advanced marginality (Wacquant 2008). More broadly, practices of mixity reshape relations of domination along lines of class, 'race', gender and sexuality (Tissot 2011). In the realm of public housing redevelopment, we suggest, with Lefebvre and Fanon (as well as Gramsci), that 'social mix' is not *only* a result of state-managed gentrification and neoliberal state rescaling. It also represents a racialized technique of recasting relations of domination through contradictory combinations of territorial dispersal and proximity.

In Paris and Toronto, diversity and social mixity rose to the forefront in two phases: the first in the 1970s and 1980s, and the second in the 1990s and first decade of the 2000s. Large-scale public housing redevelopment became a central feature in the second, increasingly neoliberal and revanchist period. Since the 1970s, place-based mixing operations in Paris have taken various forms, including gradual, mixed-use strategies of rehabilitating central city neighbourhoods and, most notably, the arsenal of policies (labour-market training, social animation, special education programmes, physical renovation, neighbourhood policing) known now as *la politique de la ville* (Dikeç 2007, Tissot 2007). Territorially focused on a dizzying array of mostly, but not only, suburban social spaces diligently represented with government maps and statistics – and consistently preoccupied with limiting the concentration of 'problem' populations, notably residents of colour, French or immigrant – this arsenal has also included projects to redevelop housing estates along lines of mixity – of social composition, tenure and physical form. Since the late 1990s, these redevelopment efforts have taken centre stage in French urban policy, most notably under the auspices of *L'Agence Nationale de la Rénovation Urbaine* (*ANRU*) since 2004 (Epstein 2008, Lelévrier 2010). Nationally coordinated, dozens of projects are under way in the Paris region to break up housing estates and central neighbourhoods by means of varying combinations of demolition, rehabilitation, reconstruction and securitized redesign. Our focus has been on 16 projects in 13 municipalities where the role of housing estates (including public housing) varies significantly in terms of morphology, spatial position, proportional weight, social composition and ideological connotation.[6]

In Toronto, diversity planning emerged in the 1970s, with neighbourhood preservation and rehabilitation initiatives as well as efforts to build social housing with mixed-income populations (as in the case of housing cooperatives) and at a scale more amenable to physical integration (into existing mixed-use built environments) (Caulfield 1994, Slater 2004). With a fragmented federal state, whose historic role in urban policy was weak in comparison to its French equivalent, Toronto moved to a concerted place-based and public housing renovation strategy only in the new millennium, and this under the almost exclusively local auspices of the City of Toronto and its housing corporation (TCH: Toronto Community Housing). Both were the result of a forced amalgamation process legislated by the Province of Ontario that created the current City of Toronto out of six municipalities (including the smaller 'old' Toronto) in 1998. This second stage began in 2002 with strategies to demolish and redevelop public and social housing in the central city (Don Mount, Regent Park, Alexandra Park) and the Fordist suburbs (Lawrence Heights) (Kipfer and Petrunia 2009, August and Walks 2012, Hatcher 2012). While quite similar to the Paris cases with respect to the overall goal of mixing up the social and tenure composition and physical design of housing estates, redevelopment in Toronto follows mostly complete, not partial, physical demolition and is much more aggressive in focusing reconstruction on developer-built ownership housing. Starting in 2005, public housing redevelopment became embedded in broader inter-institutional networks and labour-market, recreation, policing/security, and housing rehabilitation policies targeted on 13 'Priority Neighbourhoods' (now renamed 'Community Improvement Areas') (Siciliano 2010, Allahwala 2006).

The Toronto and Paris cases do not represent isolated objects. They are best understood not only in their national contexts but also relationally, as cases co-defined by transnational dynamics. They both arose out of a common if highly uneven and multi-pronged crisis of postwar capitalism: the restructuring and rescaling of welfare states. In hindsight, one can also see how early experiments in diversity planning contributed to gentrification processes, albeit not always, and not always in unambiguous ways. Today, of course, gentrification, while highly path-dependent, is transnationally articulated with the help of a globalizing development industry and forms of policy transfer – including those facilitated by the European Commission and those reaching Toronto from Britain and the USA. Likewise, our main point – that an analysis of mixity as a new modality of 'colonization' must pay particular attention to how strategies of breaking up public housing districts respond to perceived threats from racialized 'problem areas' – also has transnational dimensions. Symbols of sociopolitical threat that help sustain mixing strategies do travel, and not only from the USA outwards (Wacquant 2008). While the African-American 'ghetto' is still mobilized as the symbolic counterpoint to Toronto and Paris, the image of the French 'banlieue' has also been exported, including to Toronto, to illustrate the evils of 'concentrated poverty'.

Postwar functionalism hit a double impasse in the 1970s. On the one hand, it faced the fall-out from '1968'. In Paris, this included sometimes radical resistance to central city urban renovation projects, the urban trade unionism (Manuel Castells) of existing housing estate tenants, and the struggles of immigrant workers against the methods that confined them to marginal housing forms (shantytowns, workers' hostels, transitional housing) outside regular social housing (Hervo 2012, Pitti 2008, Hmed 2008). First imported from Algeria in the 1950s, these methods were modified and generalized to limit the proportion of migrants from the colonies in regular housing estates once they started arriving there in large numbers in the 1970s (Blanc-Chaléard 2012, Blanchard 2012, De Barros 2005, Cohen and David 2012). In Toronto, a combination of urban reform movements against urban renewal and usually women-led public housing tenant movements (for democratic management and proper building maintenance in housing estates like Regent Park) de-legitimated key planks of postwar planning. In the 1970s, this constellation of forces (led by midde-class reformers) ushered in a reform-oriented City Council that began deploying Jacobsian notions of diversity to pursue neighbourhood preservation and develop non-functionalist public housing. In the same period, public housing estates underwent qualitative social change, becoming increasingly non-European in composition and thus subject to explicitly racialized stigmatization (Purdy 2003).

Contemporaneously, the crisis of postwar Keynesianism and the first signs of neoliberalism squeezed postwar functionalism from the top, as it were, putting an end to the construction of social housing superblocks in the early 1970s in favour of resurging market and ownership housing in Paris and of cooperative, non-governmental and non-profit housing in Toronto, where, in contrast to Paris, housing policy never ceased to be overwhelmingly market- and property-oriented. In both cases, place-based social mixing went hand in hand with a qualitative rescaling of the state. In France, place-based urban policy was instituted through the decentralization reforms begun under Mitterrand. In the 1980s and 1990s, public housing redevelopment was typically a product of complex multi-scalar negotiations until the creation of *ANRU* in 2004 (under Chirac and Sarkozy) gave the central state a greater coordinating role in local renovation projects (Epstein 2008). In Canada, the neoliberal deconstruction of the federal state in the 1980s and 1990s helped squeeze social housing provision by reducing it to an essentially provincial affair. In Ontario, forced devolution culminated in the late 1990s, when the provincial government stopped social housing construction, devolved the responsibility for managing social housing to municipalities, and made it easy for housing officials in Toronto to argue that public housing redevelopment could only be achieved by leveraging private real estate.

If Lefebvre-inspired work on state rescaling (Brenner 2004) is pertinent for our case, so is research on public housing redevelopment as one form of 'municipally-managed gentrification' (Hackworth and Smith 2001). In Toronto, gentrification is built into the financing model of redevelopment, which structurally depends on private real-estate investment and the construction of private ownership housing, which, given the extremely low average household incomes of public housing tenants, caters almost exclusively to incoming residents and reduces the proportion of public housing tenants on site to a small minority of total residents. Land-rent considerations help explain both the timing and the location of such public housing redevelopment efforts, which began with two central city projects (Regent Park, Don Mount) that are within walking distance of the financial district and were quickly engulfed by the rapidly expanding gentrification frontier after the end of the deep real-estate slump in the 1990s. Even in Toronto, where the highly residual character of public housing leaves little room for internal upgrading, gentrification does not have the same intensity everywhere. Except for Lawrence Heights, which is a 30-minute subway ride from the central business district, public housing redevelopment has hardly begun in the inner suburbs where most public housing is located.

In the Paris region, gentrification is of uneven importance in renovation. In general, land-rent valorization and private real estate are significant in the design and the implementation of redevelopment (Lelévrier and Noyé 2012), even though the social diversity and political weight of social housing are much higher than in Toronto. Next to projects adjacent to subway and regional transit stations (in new town Cergy, for example), land-rent pressures are most evident in the Goutte d'Or area in Paris proper and projects close to central Paris (in Montreuil and Saint-Denis). There, gentrification *qua* renovation is part of a process that prolongs, in some respects, an older, state-led history of peripheralizing the subaltern from central Paris. Now managed by modernizing – Green, reform Communist or Socialist – factions in Paris and in the old Red Belt, land-rent valorization is often ambiguous or limited to particular zones, however (Clerval 2013: 173-206, Bacqué and Fijalkow 2012, Tissot 2007). Elsewhere, redevelopment is at some distance from the gentrification frontier. In Aulnay-sous-Bois, outer Saint Denis and Sarcelles, the Socialist municipality dominated by its famous *grand ensemble*, valorization is so far limited to building beachheads of market housing or 'upgrading' social housing: shrinking the most subsidized segments and imitating private property lines with physical design. In cities dominated by bungalow owners and the right (Sartrouville, Mantes-la-Jolie), police access rivals land rent as the prime mover of housing demolition, limiting social housing reconstruction and de-densifying housing estates in Cité des Indes and Val Fourré.

The emphasis on supply-side gentrification and state rescaling is thus insufficient to capture the sociopolitical dynamics of public housing redevelopment *qua* mixity. Not only in US cities, as Wacquant implies in his comparison of territorial stigmatization in Chicago and La Courneuve (2008), but also in Toronto and Paris social mixing functions as an ethno-racially coded technique of state intervention to reorganize spatial relations between and within social classes. This is hardly surprising given the degree to which state territorial strategies have mediated the transnational colonial and imperial histories of France and Canada. In Canada, white-settler colonialism (Stasiulis and Jhappan 1995) has been an essential feature of state formation. Linked to the active role Canada played in the British Empire, 'settler urbanization' has instituted private property regimes in two ways: dispossessing indigenous peoples (Blomley 2004) and segmenting immigrant populations along ethno-racial lines between British and Euro-Canadian inhabitants and other non-indigenous minorities. In France, the peculiar contradictions of French Republicanism to which Lefebvre alluded are, in part, explicable with reference to the role colonial–imperial networks played in forming the modern French state in the late nineteenth century (Cooper 2005). Since the late 1950s, these colonial links have been re-articulated not the least with state strategies of territorializing social relations: urban policies, housing provision and administrative practices of managing the mobility, settlement and daily life of post-colonial populations (Sayad 1999, Gallissot et al. 1994).

How can we detect the racialized and neocolonial aspects of social mixing? First, social housing estates have become to a very significant (Paris) or overwhelming (Toronto) degree highly diverse social spaces inhabited by people of colour since the 1970s. Whether or not targeted at inhabitants of colour, policies and projects to 'normalize' housing estates with a combination of physical redesign, social mixing/dispersal and privatization have had disproportionate effects on social groups variably racialized – homogenized – immigrant, black or Muslim. Second, social mixity is a mostly unspoken code to limit threats said to emanate from 'problem' populations such as working-class residents of colour. In Toronto, this threat is mostly diffuse but pervasively rooted in long-standing, racialized forms of stigmatizing housing projects as havens of crime, 'social disorder' and 'dysfunctional' families led by single mothers (Purdy 2003, James 2012). Following the 2005 revolts in France, place-based social policy and paramilitary police raids targeted at 'guns and gangs' were sometimes justified as ways to pre-empt a supposed 'French problem' in Toronto's postwar suburbs (Siciliano 2010: 8–10). In Paris, mixity has been promoted *also* to contain the movements and riots against police violence that emerged from large housing estates themselves in the late 1970s (Kirszbaum 2008, Belmessous 2006). The political character of demolition is most evident where estates are directly identified with riots: Mantes-la-Jolie, Sartrouville, Clichy-Montfermeil and Saint Denis (Francs-Moisins). Also, the allocation and distribution of social housing units in the relocation process is a key technique to change the 'image' of a municipality by limiting the concentration of precarious inhabitants and 'large [read: African] families', a technique that refracts the late colonial 'quotas' imposed on migrants in social housing (Tanter and Toubon 1999, Simon 2003, Tissot 2005). This example, and the way in which housing estates are redesigned physically to facilitate policing and counter-insurgency (Belmessous 2010, Garnier 2012), shows how the 'reconquest' of housing estates is part of a 'colonial counter-revolution' (Khiari 2008).

Territorialized social policy and housing redevelopment are thus more than state-led gentrification and neoliberal state rescaling. They help reorganize spatial forms of political domination along racialized and neocolonial lines. Breaking up housing estates and dispersing resident populations (accompanied by territorially targeted flanking measures) is intended to tame 'problem populations' by making them more subject to state authority and exposing them to the 'responsible' forms of behaviour exhibited by more stable, preferably propertied working- and middle-class fractions. Herein lies a third crucial racialized dimension of place-based social mixing: paternalism. Precarious and racialized segments of the working class are assumed to be incapable of governing themselves and require the aid of the more 'respectable' social groups with whom they are brought into contact and who are to spread the work ethic and other such proper, 'civil' attitudes. This paternalism rearticulates not only nineteenth-century views of the dangerous classes that helped justify early social housing construction. It also resonates with colonial civilizing missions and their habit of denying agency to the colonized – peoples without history. If stigmatized inhabitants play a role in social mixing, it is on the culturalist terms of the dominant. In Toronto's Regent Park, some consultation processes were organized along ethnic lines and public housing tenants (children and teenagers of colour) were recruited to aestheticize the housing estate during cultural festivals designed for outsiders (McLean 2013). In the Goutte d'Or, the left-liberal City Hall expresses selective support for cultural diversity (a new mosque) even as it promotes 'commercial mixing' to dilute and manage the presence of African shops and markets in the streetscape of the neighbourhood.

Place-based social mixing cannot avoid the contradictions produced by social polarization, segregating real estate, mixo-phobic racism. In Paris, public housing demolition re-segregates as much as de-segregates the most precarious public housing tenants (Lelévrier and Noyé 2012) due to low reconstruction rates for the most subsidized housing categories and mixo-phobic resistance by 'respectable' jurisdictions to accept displaced residents. In some municipalities, the emphasis is thus less on dispersing than on containing old and new residents on site. In conservative Mantes-la-Jolie, for example, mosque construction is seen as a way to deepen clientelist relations between City Hall and community leaders to pacify the Val Fourré estate. In both Paris and Toronto, physical design (fences, sharp demarcations between building envelopes) can underscore the micro-segmentations between different housing forms (ownership and subsidized housing in Toronto; market housing, upgraded and highly subsidized social housing in Paris). Even where mixing operations are deemed successful in the eyes of the authorities, relative physical proximity between different social groups does not stop the kind of bodily confinement Fanon analysed in his phenomenology of racism. New residents often distance themselves in their routines from existing tenants while the police engage in racial profiling. What was true two generations ago still holds now, in a post-colonial context: mixing social groups territorially can go hand in hand with social separation and political domination (Chamboredon and Lemaire 1970).

Despite these contradictions – and the structural violence in imposing social mix from above – public housing redevelopment includes hegemonic elements that undermine opposition. In Toronto, expressions of discontent by inhabitants have not translated into lasting organized opposition, making it easy for politicians and NGOs to present public housing demolition as a progressive policy. In Paris, housing demolition has been much more politicized. It arguably contributed to the 2005 riots in some areas (Epstein 2008) and pushed local tenant movements against 'social cleansing' in others (Poissy, Gennevilliers and Sarcelles) to form a broader network of resistance ('*La coordination anti-démolition des quartiers*'). Politicization has modified some projects and made it difficult to justify full-scale demolition. Yet even there, opposition has failed to break a cross-party consensus about the merits of social mixity. Why? As in Toronto, redevelopment through mixity *promises* to 'normalize' the targeted projects. The symbolic and material destruction of people's lived space is offered as the only way to improve housing conditions or escape stigmatization. In Toronto and Paris, the promises of redevelopment are advanced through relocation processes that force households to negotiate with housing authorities individually, thus countering collective definitions of resident interest (Deboulet 2006). Finally, consultation processes and ways of managing resident relations (*gestion de proximité* in Paris, social development in Toronto) tend to shift political power from existing to new inhabitants (August and Walks 2012, Bacqué and Fijalkow 2012).

THE RIGHT TO THE CITY?

Borrowing from Lefebvre and Fanon, we suggest that the recent shift to place-based mixing strategies represents a new and reinvented modality of hierarchical territorial organization intent on supplanting functionalist spatial separation and concentration by projects of spatial proximity and dispersal. While strategies of dispersal exist in different forms around the world, including slum clearance and military urbicide, our research sketched here focused on mixity by public housing redevelopment in Toronto and Paris. We term these cases forms of 'colonization' to emphasize that they are not reducible to supply-side land-rent dynamics (Hackworth and Smith), state rescaling processes (Brenner) and generic forms of state-bound symbolic violence (Wacquant). To call place-based mixing 'colonial' is to highlight their specifically political and racialized character as responses to the perceived threat of populations of people of colour, who represent the predominant target of mixing operations and are deemed in need of pacification and civilization from above, in terms reminiscent also of colonial paternalism. Although more mediated than the directly colonial strategies imposed on indigenous peoples, with which it sometimes overlaps in Canada (Blomley 2004: 87–93), 'colonization' as state-imposed desegregation rearticulates colonial history. It is more than a loose metaphor.

What are the implications of this conclusion for Lefebvre's notion of the right to the city (which also included a de-segregating dimension and a demand for difference)? For some, mixing strategies such as the US HOPE VI programme (which has influenced Toronto planners) may, under certain conditions, facilitate a right to the city for inhabitants (Duke 2009). This pragmatist interpretation treats the right to the city as a set of liberal rights to stay in or move to existing physical spaces (gentrifying neighbourhoods, previously white suburbs). They prolong the institutional appropriation of Lefebvrean insights (Stanek 2011, Garnier 2010) by ignoring the *fundamental* contradiction between the right to the city and the privatizing, disciplinary and reifying character of spatial dispersal under HOPE VI (Jones and Popke 2010). For Lefebvre, the right to the city was a revolutionary claim and thought. With it, he outlined how various revolutionary demands for political power and the social surplus emanating from multiple peripheralized and segregated social spaces (inhabited by workers, immigrants, students, inhabitants of informal settlements) may converge in part by *producing* typically momentary forms of spatial centrality. In this light, de-segregation is emancipatory only if (1) it takes place on the democratically defined terms of the segregated, not the state; and (2) makes it possible for subaltern groups to encounter each other in an open-ended dynamic of collective struggle. This view resonates with Fanon's own view about the relationship between spatial form, political struggle and social transformation. For Fanon, proper *decolonization* involved an appropriation and production of space (street, nation, world order) and a concomitant transformation of colonized peoples in an open-ended, democratic, socialist and feminist liberation struggle.

The implications of state-bound 'colonization' thus go much beyond housing policy, planning and architecture. First, social mixing operations, which undermine networks of solidarity, not only make it difficult to sustain opposition to public housing demolition. They also threaten to pre-empt a dialectic of the right to the city – a convergence of distinct struggles – by further segmenting distinct points of mobilization (against racism, precariousness, austerity) from each other. Second, our two cases remind us that *de*-segregation, not just segregation, can be a territorial technique of domination (Kipfer, 2013). We thus need more than a rigorous debate about the particular (and today largely illusory) conditions under which social mix *as policy* may be considered emancipatory (De Filippis and Fraser 2010). It obliges us to revisit 'mixity' not as forcible de-segregation but as a *form of struggle* linking multiple subaltern social groups (and their self-organized capacity to articulate the specificity of their respective situations) to each other and against dominant forces (Delphy 2008). Movements like the *Forum Social des Quartiers Populaires* and the *Parti des Indigènes de la République* in Paris and No One Is Illegal in Toronto are searching for ways of articulating neighbourhood activism (against police violence, housing demolition, precarity, deportation, Islamaphobia) to broader struggles (against austerity, racism, imperialism) without dissolving the former into the latter. In such spatially nuanced strategies that link autonomy with alliance formation, a defense of segregated, stigmatized social spaces is both necessary and insufficient.

NOTES

1   To underline that colonization may exceed colonialism proper – including the ongoing colonial subjection of indigenous peoples in white-settler colonies – and include racialized forms of territorial hierarchy in post- and neocolonial contexts, we use the term in quotation marks ('colonization').

2   This section borrows from an in-depth exposition (Kipfer and Goonewardena 2013).

3   Lefebvre was not alone. Activists with the *Mouvement de libération des femmes* (*MLF*) described women as a 'colonized people' or 'the black continent', analogies that were politically explosive but tended to sidestep the specificities of colonialism (Boggio Ewanjé-Epée and Magliani-Belkacem 2012: 40–42).

4   Lefebvre's use of colonization as a concept benefited from his work on the transformations of the French countryside, where his interest in urbanization originated. Also, Lefebvre followed Mario Gaviria (1974) when he called Mediterranean tourist areas products of 'neocolonization' (1991 [1974]: 58), thus linking the rise of leisure to bourgeois hegemony and uneven development. Thanks to Łukasz Stanek for the reference.

5   This potency has been demonstrated not only by Kristin Ross but also, in different ways, by Ferndando Coronil, Gillian Hart, Manu Goswami, James Tyner and Eugene McCann.

6   Aulnay-sous-Bois, Cergy, Clichy, Montfermeil, La Courneuve, Gennevilliers, Mantes-la-Jolie, Montreuil, Paris (Goutte d'Or), Poissy, Saint Denis, Sarcelles, Sartrouville.

REFERENCES

Allahwala, A. 2006. 'Weak Policies for Strong Neighbhourhoods?' *Relay* 13: 1719.

Atkinson, R, and Bridge, G. (eds.) 2005. *Gentrification in Global Context: The New Urban Colonialism*. London: Routledge.

August, M. and Walks, A. 2012. 'From Social Mix to Political Marginalization', in *Mixed Communities: Gentrification by Stealth*, edited by G. Bridge, T. Butler and L. Lees. Bristol: Policy Press 27397.

Bacqué, M.-H., and Fijalkow, Y. 2012. 'Social Mix as the Aim of a Controlled Gentrification Process: The Example of the Goutte d'Or District in Paris', in *Mixed Communities: Gentrification by Stealth*, edited by G. Bridge, T. Butler and L. Lees. Bristol: Policy Press 115–31.

Belmessous, H. 2006. *Mixité sociale: une imposture*. Nantes: Atalante.

Belmessous, H. 2010. *Opérations banlieues*. Paris: La Découverte.

Blanc-Chaléard, M.-C. 2012. 'Les quotas d'étranger en HLM: un héritage de laguerre d'Algérie? Les Canibouts à Nanterre (1959–1968)'. *Métropolitiques* 16 mars, http://www.metropolitiques.eu/spip.php?page=print%id_article=301.

Blanchard, E. 2012. 'La police et les médinas algériennes en métropole'. *Métropolitiques* 8 février, http://www.metropolitiques.eu/spip.php?page=print&id_article=279.

Blomley, N. 2004. *Unsettling the City: Urban Land and the Politics of Property.* New York: Routledge.

Boggio Ewanjé-Epé, F. and Magliani-Belkacem, S. 2012. *Les feministes blanches et l'empire* Paris: La Fabrique.

Brenner, N. 2004. *New State Spaces.* Oxford: Oxford University Press.

Bridge, G., Butler T. and Lees L. (eds) 2012. *Mixed Communities: Gentrification by Stealth.* Bristol: Policy Press.

Burkhard, B. 2000. *French Marxism Between the Wars: Henri Lefebvre and the Philosophies.* New York: Humanity.

Butler, R. and Noisette, P. 1977. *De la cité ouvrière au grand ensemble: la politique capitaliste du logement sociale 1875–1975.* Paris: François Maspéro.

Caulfield, J. 1994. *City Form and Everyday Life.* Toronto: University of Toronto Press.

Chamboredon, J.-C. and Lemaire, M. 1970. 'Proximité spatiale et distance sociale. Les grands ensembles et leur peuplement'. *Revue française de sociologie* 111: 333.

Clerval, A. 2013. *Paris sans le peuple: la gentrification de la capitale* Paris: La Découverte.

Cohen, M. and David, C. 2012. 'Les cités de transit: le traitement urbain de la pauvrété à l'heure de la decolonisation'. *Métropolitiques* 2 February.

Cooper, F. 2005. *Colonialism in Question.* Berkeley, CA: University of California Press.

De Barros, F. 2005. 'Des franco-musulmans aux 'immigrés': l'importation declassification coloniale dans les politiques du logement en France'. *Actes de la recherche en sciences sociales* 159(4): 26–53.

Deboulet, A. 2006. 'Le résident vulnérable. Questions autour de la démolition'. *Mouvements* 47–48: 4–5.

De Filippis, J. and Fraser, J. 2010. 'Why do we want mixed-income housing and neighbourhoods?' in *Critical Urban Studies*, edited by J. Davies and D. Imbroscio. Albany, NY: SUNY Press, 135–48.

Delphy, C. 2008. 'La non-mixité, une necessité politique: domination, ségrégation et auto-détermination': http://www.indigenes-republique.org/spip.php?article1220 (accessed 31 March 2008).

Dikeç, M. 2007. *Badlands of the Republic* London: Blackwell.

Duke, J. 2009. Mixed Income Housing Policy and Public Housing Residents''right to the City'. *Critical Social Policy* 29(1): 100–120.

Epstein, T. 2008. 'Gouverner à distance : la rénovation urbaine, démolition-reconstruction de l'appareil d'Etat'. Thèse de Doctorat. Ecole Normale Supérieure Cachan.

Fredenucci, J.-C. 2003. 'L'urbanisme d'Etat': nouvelles pratiques, nouvelles acteurs'. *Ethnologie française* 37: 13–20.

Gallissot, R., Boumaza, N. and Ghislaine, C. 1994. *Les migrants qui font le prolétariat.* Paris: Méridiens Klincksieck.

Garnier, J.-P. 2010. *Une violence éminemment contemporaine.* Marseille: Agone.

Garnier, J.-P. 2012. *Un espace indéfendable.* Grenoble: Le Monde à l'envers.

Gaviria, M. 1974. *España a go-go: turismo charter y neocolinialisme del espacio*. Madrid: Ediciones Turner.

Hackworth, J. and Smith, N. 2001. 'The Changing State of Gentrification'. *Tijdschrift voor Economische en Sociale Geografie* 92(4): 468–70.

Hamon, H, and Rotman, P. 1979. *Les porteurs de valises. La résistance française à la guerre d'Algérie*. Paris: Albin Michel.

Hatcher, K. 2012. 'Alexandra Park: Dynamics of Redevelopment'. Major Paper, Masters Programme in Environmental Studies, York University.

Hervo, M. 2012. *Nanterre en guerre d'Algérie. Chroniques du Bidonville: 1959–62*. Paris: Actes du Sud.

Hmed, C. 2008. 'Des mouvements sociaux 'sur une tête d'épingle': le rôle del'espace physique dans le processus contestataire à partir de l'exemple des mobilizations dans les foyers de travailleurs migrants'. *Politix* 145–65.

Ives, P. 2004. *Language and Hegemony in Gramsci*. Winnipeg: Fernwood.

James, C. 2012. *Life at the Intersection*. Black Point, NS: Fernwood.

Jones, K. and Popke, J. 2010. 'Re-envisioning the City: Lefebvre, Hope VI, and the Neoliberalization of the Urban Space'. *Urban Geography* 31(1): 114–33.

Khiari, S. 2008. *La contre-révolution coloniale en France: de de Gaulle à Sarkozy* Paris: La Fabrique.

Kipfer, S. 2011. 'The Times and Spaces of (De-)Colonization', in *Living Fanon: Global Perspectives*, edited by N. Gibson. London: Pluto, 93–104.

Kipfer, S. 2013. 'Urbanisation et racialisation: déségrégation, émancipation,hégémonie', in *Penser l'émancipation*, edited by H. Buclin, J. Daher, C. Georgiou and P. Raboud. Paris: La Dispute, 68–83.

Kipfer, S., and Goonewardena, K. 2013. 'Urban Marxism and the Postcolonial Challenge: Henri Lefebvre and "Colonization"'. *Historical Materialism* 21(2): 76–117.

Kipfer, S. and Petrunia, J. 2009. '"Colonization" and Public Housing in the Competitive City: A Toronto Case Study'. *Studies in Political Economy* 83: 111–39.

Kirszbaum, T. 2008. *Mixité sociale dans l'habitat*. Paris: La documentation française.

Lees, L. 2008. 'Gentrification and Social Mixing: Towards an Inclusive Urban Renaissance?' *Urban Studies* 45(12): 2449–70.

Lefebvre, H. 1972. 'La bourgeoisie et l'espace', in *Le droit à la ville suivi de Espace et politique* by H. Lefebvre. Paris: Anthropos, 45–61.

Lefebvre, H. 1973. *La somme et le reste*. Paris: Bélibaste.

Lefebvre, H. 1977. *De L'État Volume 3*. Paris: Union Générale des Editions.

Lefebvre, H. 1978. *De L'État Volume 4*. Paris: Union Générale des Editions.

Lefebvre, H. 1991 [1974]. *The Production of Space*. Trans. Donald Nicholson-Smith. Oxford: Basil Blackwell.

Lefebvre, H. 1996. *Writings on Cities*. Trans. Eleanore Kofman and Elizabeth Lebas. Oxford: Blackwell.

Lefebvre, H. 2002 [1961] *Critique of Everyday Life: Volume II. Foundations for a Sociology of the Everyday*. Trans. J. Moore. London: Verso.

Lefebvre, H. 2003 [1970]. *The Urban Revolution*. Trans. R. Bononno. Minneapolis, MN: University of Minnesota Press.

Lefebvre, H. 2005 [1981]. *Critique of Everyday Life: Volume III*. Trans. J. Moore. London: Verso.

Lefebvre, H. 2009 [1939]. *Dialectical Materialism*. Trans. J. Sturrock. Minneapolis, MN: University of Minnesota Press.

Lelévrier, C. 2010. 'Action publique et trajectoires résidentielles: un autre regard sur la politique de la ville'. Habilitation. Université de Paris-Est.

Lelévrier, C, and Noyé, C. 2012. 'La fin des grands ensembles?' in *A quoi sert la rénovation urbaine?*, edited by J. Donzelot. Paris: PUF, 185–221.

McLean, H. 2013. 'Cracks in the Creative City: The Contradictions of Community Arts Practice'. Unpublished manuscript.

Müller, J. 2001. 'Alltagsleben – Rassistische Diskriminierung und Kritisches Denken'. *Jungle World – Subtropen* 5(6): 9–11.

Pitti, L. 2008. 'Travailleurs de France: voilà notre nom: les mobilizations des ouvriers étrangers dans les usines et le foyers durant les années 1970' in *Histoire politiquedes immigrations (post)coloniales*, edited by A. Boubeker and A. Hajjat. Paris: Amsterdam, 95–111.

Purdy, S. 2003. '"Ripped Off" By the System: Housing Policy, Poverty and Territorial Stigmatization in Regent Park Housing Project, 1951–1991'. *Labour/Le Travail* 52: 45–108.

Ross, K. 1995. *Fast Cars, Clean Bodies* Cambridge, MA: The MIT Press.

Sayad, A. 1999. *La double absence* Paris: Seuil.

Siciliano, A. 2010. 'Policing Poverty: Race, Space, and Fear of Crime after the Year of the Gun (2005) in Suburban Toronto'. PhD thesis. University of Toronto, Department of Geography.

Simon, P. 2003. 'Le logement social en France et la gestion des 'populations à risques'. *Homme et Migration* 1246: 76–91.

Slater, T. 2004. 'Municipally Managed Gentrification in South Parkdale, Toronto'. *Canadian Geographer* 48(3): 303–25.

Smith, N. 1996. *The New Urban Frontier: Gentrification and the Revanchist City*. New York: Routledge.

Stanek, Ł. 2011. *Henri Lefebvre on Space: Architecture, Urban Research and the Production of Theory*. Minneapolis, MN: Minnesota University Press.

Stasiulis, D. and Jhappan, R. 1995. 'The Fractious Politics of a Settler Society' in *Unsettling Settler Societies*, edited by D. Stasiulis and N. Yuval-Davis. London: Sage, 95–131.

Tanter, A. and Toubon J.-C. 1999. 'Mixité sociale et politique de peuplement'. *Sociétés contemporaines* 33–34: 59–87.

Tissot, S. 2005. 'Une discussion informelle? Usages du concept de mixité sociale dans la gestion des attributions du logement HLM'. *Actes de la recherche en sciences sociales* 159: 54–69.

Tissot, S. 2007. *L'Etat et les quartiers*. Paris: Seuil.

Tissot, S. 2011. *De bons voisins: enquête dans un quartier de la bourgeoisie progressiste*. Paris: Raisons d'agir.

Wacquant, L. 2008. *Urban Outcasts: A Comparative Sociology of Adanced Marginality*. Cambridge, UK: Polity.

PART II
Contradictions of Abstract Space

Plan Puebla Panama: The Violence of Abstract Space

Japhy Wilson

Abstract space is the central concept of Henri Lefebvre's magnum opus, *The Production of Space* (Lefebvre 1991 [1974]).[1] Subsequent appropriations of Lefebvre have tended to treat the concept as a signifier denoting 'the space produced by capitalism' (Brenner 2004: 43). In this chapter, however, I argue that the critical value of abstract space lies less in its conceptualization of space than in its theorization of abstraction. The concept of abstract space should be understood as an attempt to grasp the ways in which the space of capital embodies, facilitates and conceals the complex intertwining of structural, symbolic and direct forms of violence that Lefebvre refers to as 'the violence of abstraction', and it is in this sense that the concept offers a unique contribution to our understanding of the capitalist production of space. Furthermore, the concept of abstract space can serve as a nucleus around which to orient Lefebvre's seemingly diffuse ideas on abstraction, violence, history, the state, *autogestion* and the politics of difference. I develop this reading of abstract space through a critical analysis of the Plan Puebla Panama (PPP), a regional development programme for southern Mexico and Central America, which was launched in 2001 and abandoned in 2008. The formulation and implementation of the PPP is interpreted as an 'actually-existing' abstract space that embodies the structural, symbolic and direct forms of violence inherent to the process of abstraction.

The chapter begins by sketching an initial interpretation of abstract space, understood as both an emergent historical–geographical reality and a specific technology of power, which embodies both multiple forms of violence and the possibility of a post-capitalist 'differential space'. The second section introduces the PPP as an actually-existing abstract space, revealing the structural and symbolic violence of its political-economic logic and discursive construction. The third section focuses on three place-based resistances to the implementation of the PPP, demonstrating the contradictions that emerge through the concretization of abstract space. The final section then traces the evolution of Plan La Realidad-Tijuana, a counter-project initiated by the Zapatistas, which I interpret as a strategy for the production of a differential space, and which was ultimately repressed by direct state violence. I conclude that the case of the PPP reveals the multidimensional violence of abstract space, the transformative political possibilities generated by its contradictions, and the instrumentality of abstract space itself in preventing the realization of these possibilities.

THE VIOLENCE OF ABSTRACT SPACE

Lefebvre is best known in Anglophone academia for his writings on space, despite the fact that this was only his primary concern during the late 1960s and early 1970s (Lefebvre 1991, 1996 [1968], 2003a [1970]). In contrast to this relatively transient focus on space, 'the critique of the practical power and force of abstraction is a leitmotif that runs throughout the whole of Lefebvre's work' (Schmid 2008: 32). For Lefebvre, abstraction is a complex and inherently violent process through which a richly differentiated socio-spatial reality is progressively emptied of its substantive content and reduced to the 'economic' abstractions of money and the commodity, the 'cultural' abstractions of quantification and calculability, and the 'political' abstraction of state power (Lefebvre 2009a: 109). Following Marx, Lefebvre roots this process in the dynamics of capital accumulation, in which value is measured in terms of abstract labour – labour in general stripped of all qualitative differences and reduced to a quantitative measure of socially necessary labour time, expressed in the form of money (Lefebvre 1991: 307). Through the coercive laws of competition at the level of the world market, the drive to maximize surplus value becomes all-encompassing, constituting what Postone (1993) has called an 'abstract form of domination', which appears to operate objectively beyond our individual or collective control, despite the fact that it is the aggregate outcome of our (alienated) productive activity (Lefebvre 1996 [1968]: 187, 2006: 243). Lefebvre argues that this has profound consequences, not only in terms of the material subsumption of diverse use values within the abstract equivalence of exchange value, but also in terms of the representational erosion of differentiated symbolic systems by an instrumental rationality, which reproduces the logic of homogeneity and calculability characteristic of the commodity form (Lefebvre 2006: 258, 2008: 56).

It is in the context of this wider concern with abstraction that Lefebvre develops his concept of abstract space. In *The Production of Space*, Lefebvre traces the historical development of abstract space in relation to the formation and consolidation of accumulative societies – societies oriented towards growth and the production of surplus value. Through this process, 'the economic sphere becomes predominant and determining' (2002 [1961]: 324), abstract representational systems homogenize pre-capitalist symbolic orders, and the abstract space of capitalist modernity emerges, founded on a fragmentary grid of private property and national boundaries, and a homogeneous 'urban fabric' of cities, infrastructure networks and globalized production systems (2003a: 3–4, 1991: 53). In the twentieth century, space becomes increasingly instrumentalized as a means to both the expanded reproduction of capital and the territorial consolidation of the national state (1991: 307). Abstract space is therefore both the result of a vast and largely uncoordinated set of historical–geographical processes, and a technology of power through which space as a whole is increasingly organized 'according to a rationality of the identical and the repetitive that allows the state to introduce its presence, control, and surveillance in the most isolated corners (which thus cease to be corners)' (2003b: 86).

Throughout *The Production of Space*, Lefebvre repeatedly emphasizes the extent to which abstract space is permeated and underpinned by violence, insisting that 'there is a violence to abstraction, and to abstraction's practical (social) use' (1991: 289). Lefebvre neglects to provide a precise definition of violence, but from his use of the term it is clear that the violence of abstraction is not limited to 'direct' physical violence, but also possesses what Slavoj Žižek has conceptualized as 'structural' and 'symbolic' dimensions. Žižek argues that our commonsense understanding of violence limits it to direct acts performed physically by one agent upon another, normalizing the structural violence embodied in the socially exploitative and ecologically destructive dynamics of capital as an abstract form of domination (Žižek 2008: 11), while drawing attention away from the subtle symbolic violence of economic and technological abstractions that 'simplify the designated thing, reducing it to a single feature ... destroying its organic unity' (ibid.: 52). For Lefebvre, abstract space embodies violence in each of these respects. In structural terms, abstract space constitutes the grids, nodes, and networks of property, production and exchange through which the law of value exerts its abstract domination (Lefebvre 1991: 341, 404). This structural violence is enabled by a symbolic 'violence enthroned in a specific rationality, that of accumulation, that of bureaucracy ... a unitary, logistical, operational and quantifying rationality' through which social space is discursively homogenized and stripped of qualitative content in order to function as a 'passive receptacle for the planners' (ibid.: 280, 420). This intertwining of structural and symbolic violence is in turn profoundly dependent on the direct violence of state power through which abstract space is produced and reproduced – 'A founding violence, and continuous creation by violent means' (ibid.: 280). The seemingly apolitical form of abstract space – as the space of economic infrastructure and technocratic planning – functions to conceal its violence, appearing as the neutral backdrop and container of society through which 'contradictions ... are smothered and replaced by an appearance of consistency' (ibid.: 363). Yet Lefebvre insists that 'within this space violence does not always remain latent or hidden', as its constitutive antagonisms imply 'the constant threat, and occasional eruption, of [direct] violence' (ibid.: 57).

These antagonisms include the contradictions between exchange value and use value, between the conceived space of the planners and the lived space of the inhabitants, and between the abstract space of the state and the traces of pre-existing spatial practices and representations. Together, they hold open the concrete possibility of a post-capitalist 'differential space' dwelling within 'the cracks and fissures of planned and programmed order' (Lefebvre 1991: 52, 1996: 129). Lefebvre sees this possibility expressed in a proliferation of place-based struggles in and against abstract space, characterized by assertions of diversity against homogenization, territorial *autogestion* against state domination, and commonality against privatization and fragmentation (1991: 368, 2008: 168, 2009b: 148–50). To the extent that such struggles remain as isolated particularisms, however, Lefebvre is adamant that they will merely contribute to the reproduction of abstract space, the very homogeneity of which is sustained through such processes of fragmentation (1991: 64). A differential space would therefore not only accentuate diversity and complexity against reduction and homogenization, but would also 'restore unity to what abstract space breaks up – to the functions, elements, and moments of social practice' (ibid.: 52). For Lefebvre, it is only 'class struggle' in this non-homogenizing, differential sense of the term that 'prevents abstract space from taking over the whole planet and papering over all differences' (ibid.: 55).

    In summary, then, abstract space can be understood both as the spatial outcome of the complex and contested historical–geographical dynamics of capitalist development, and as a specific technology of power that attempts to rationalize the contradictions inherent in this process, through the production of a space that simultaneously advances capital accumulation and extends state power while reducing constitutive differences and presenting itself as a pragmatic response to economic necessity in the interest of the common good. This project, however, remains necessarily incomplete – an incompleteness that is both a cause and a consequence of the direct, structural and symbolic violence of abstract space. This incompleteness is constituted by gaps and ruptures within which differential space exists as an immanent possibility, the realization or negation of which is determined through the contingencies of political struggle. It is this incompleteness and contingency that Lefebvre wishes to emphasize, insisting that we must not 'bestow a cohesiveness it lacks upon a totality which is in fact decidedly open – so open, indeed, that it must rely upon violence to endure' (1991: 11). It is in this spirit that I develop my interpretation of abstract space in the remainder of this chapter, through an analysis of the PPP as an actually-existing and fiercely contested abstract space. The following section reveals the structural and symbolic violence contained within the apparently apolitical technocratic language of the Plan itself, while subsequent sections draw attention to the direct violence involved in its implementation.

PLAN PUEBLA PANAMA (PPP) AS AN ABSTRACT SPACE

PPP was first announced in November 2000 by the newly elected president of Mexico, Vicente Fox Quesada, and was officially launched in June 2001. It was originally conceived as a 20-year, US$25 billion regional development programme, backed by the Inter-American Development Bank (IDB),[2] and incorporating the nine states of southern Mexico, and the Central American national states of Belize, Costa Rica, El Salvador, Guatemala, Honduras, Nicaragua and Panama.[3] The Plan sought to integrate this 'Mesoamerican' region more fully into the global economy, through the construction or modernization of transport and energy infrastructures, combined with the harmonization of border regulations, the liberalization of trade, and the promotion of foreign direct investment in tourism, light manufacturing and agribusiness (Inter-American Development Bank 2001). The vast geographical scale and international complexity of the PPP are beyond the scope of this chapter, and my focus here is limited to Mexico, which is of particular significance as the political centre of the PPP, and as the state in which the PPP was most concertedly implemented and most forcefully resisted. While it had the full support of the other states in the region, the PPP was planned by the Mexican government in conjunction with the IDB, and was to be the flagship development project of the Fox administration, which remained committed to the neoliberal agenda that previous regimes had been implementing since the 1980s (Rodríguez 2010).[4] Within the Mexican context, the PPP was intended both as a populist public works programme and as a central component of the ongoing process of neoliberalization, constituting the physical space through which the 'successes' of the North American Free Trade Agreement (NAFTA) could be extended to the 'backward' south (Wilson 2011), and countering the widespread resistance to NAFTA from peasant and indigenous social movements in the region.

From the perspective of these movements, NAFTA threatened to deprive the peasantry of the economic security and cultural significance of commonly held land, while exposing them to 'free competition' with the heavily subsidized and highly industrialized forces of US agribusiness (Van der Haar 2007). When NAFTA came into force on 1 January 1994, the predominantly indigenous Ejercito Zapatista de Liberación Nacional (EZLN) launched an armed uprising in Mexico's southernmost state of Chiapas, seizing control of several municipal capitals, and calling for a national revolution. Despite being swiftly driven back into the Lacandon Jungle by the Mexican military, the EZLN succeeded in securing a truce agreement, through which large tracts of land seized during the uprising were ceded to the movement. This land provided the material basis for a network of Zapatista Autonomous Municipalities operating independently of the state (Burguete Cal and Mayor 2003, Stahler-Sholk 2007). In 1996, the Mexican government signed the San Andres Peace Accords, which committed the state to constitutional reforms granting all indigenous peoples the right to the autonomous control of the natural resources and political administration of their territories.[5] However, the Accords were not implemented, and negotiations between the state and the EZLN collapsed. Following the election of Fox in 2000, the EZLN once again called on the government to implement the Accords, leading a month-long march across southern Mexico, generating widespread popular support for indigenous autonomy, and culminating in a 200,000-strong demonstration in Mexico City in March 2001.

In terms of the nature of its demands and its level of support, the march can be interpreted as a moment in which a differential space based on territorial *autogestion* and unity-in-difference was revealed as a concrete possibility. It is no coincidence, therefore, that Fox chose the day following the demonstration to unveil the Mexican 'chapter' of the PPP, confronting the Zapatistas' demand for a differential space of multiple indigenous autonomies with an economistic vision of 'great road and rail corridors, gas pipelines and electricity systems, ports and airports that rapidly and efficiently connect the development zones being created from Panama to Mexico' (Fox, quoted in Romero 2001: 18). The document that Fox presented contained a strategy for the radical socio-spatial restructuring of southern Mexico, which would transform this 'backward' region, with its legacy of semi-subsistence agriculture, strong indigenous cultures and social unrest, into a modernized node of the global economy. The Plan was centred upon the production of an integrated multimodal transport network, which would reorient the economic space of the region away from Mexico City and towards export markets in Europe and the USA. This would be complemented by an upgraded energy grid, connected to a series of hydroelectric projects designed to capitalize upon the vast water resources of the region. On the scale of Mesoamerica as a whole, these infrastructure projects would contribute to the two central infrastructure systems of the PPP – the International Network of Mesoamerican Highways (RICAM), and the Central American System of Electricity Integration (SIEPAC). Combined with continued land privatizations in the context of the broader process of neoliberalization, these infrastructure networks would allow the region to maximize its 'comparative advantages' in natural resources and cheap labour and improve its 'productivity and competitiveness', attracting foreign investment and catalysing the economic transformation of southern Mexico into a space of large-scale export-oriented agriculture, export processing zones, natural resource extraction, bioprospecting and luxury ecotourism.[6]

The PPP thus constituted an abstract space in the sense of a strategy that aimed 'to structure space in the perspective of unlimited growth' (Lefebvre 1976 [1973]: 113), while simultaneously negating the substantive cultural and political–economic differences that existed within the region. As such, it embodied the structural and symbolic violence characteristic of abstract space. In structural terms, the PPP would function to open southern Mexico more fully to the forces of global competition. As the World Bank noted in its strategy for southern Mexico, which reproduced the logic of the PPP:

> Firms that are located in areas with better infrastructure will be more integrated into the ... global market system ... Firms that are located in highly accessible areas are also more exposed to competition, and are thus forced to improve productivity. (World Bank 2003: 19)

In southern Mexico, of course, the majority of 'firms' are *campesinos* (peasant farmers), and being 'forced to improve productivity' implies the abandonment of the land and the transition to wage labour – in other words the primitive accumulation that Marx identified as the foundational violence of capitalist social relations (Marx 1977: 873–940). The World Bank's logic thus illustrates the structural dimension of the violence of abstraction, in which capitalist social relations are imposed through apparently objective processes without resort to direct violence, and the law of value is exerted as an abstract form of domination.

In the case of the PPP, the violence intrinsic to this process was further concealed by the discursive reduction of southern Mexico to a purely formal and quantitative space, defined only by high poverty statistics, low productivity, long transport times and underexploited resources, and stripped of any trace of the Zapatista uprising or the subsequent movement for indigenous autonomy (Presidencia de la República 2001: 127–65). This representation of the region as a depoliticized space of inadequacy, deprivation and wasted potential embodied the symbolic violence of abstraction, erasing the representational spaces of southern Mexico's diverse population and the history of struggle through which these spaces had been produced, developed and defended. This symbolic violence had very real effects, to the extent that it facilitated and legitimated the material erasure of the socio-spatialities that it discursively denied. In the weeks following Fox's presentation of the Mexican section of the PPP, the Mexican Congress passed the 'Indigenous Law of Rights and Culture', which claimed to fulfil the San Andres Accords, but which in fact limited indigenous autonomy to a multiculturalist assertion of cultural diversity, while rejecting claims to political autonomy and the control of natural resources (Harvey 2004: 124–5). The EZLN responded by breaking off all communications with the Mexican state and retreating to their Autonomous Territories. Questioned at the official launch of the PPP in June 2001 over the possibility of the Plan provoking further conflict with the EZLN, Fox replied:

> There is no longer any conflict … We should not grant any more space or power to zapatismo … The PPP is a thousand times greater than zapatismo or some community in Chiapas. (Quoted in La Jornada 15 June 2001)

This assertion of coherence and denial of substantive contradictions is central to the logic and practice of abstract space (Lefebvre 1991: 363). By negating the political antagonisms of southern Mexico, and presenting itself as a pragmatic response to economic necessity and social deprivation, the PPP functioned to obscure the material contradiction between abstract space and the differential space that was gestating within it. As Lefebvre argues, abstract space not only operates *positively* through the planned production of space, but also 'relates *negatively* to something that it carries within itself and that seeks to emerge from it: a differential space-time' (ibid.: 50, emphasis added). The irony of this strategy in the case of the PPP, however, was that it sought to eliminate the constitutive antagonisms of southern Mexico through an intensification of the very processes of neoliberalization that had caused these deep-rooted contradictions to explode in the form of the Zapatista uprising. The following sections trace the reassertion of these contradictions through the process of the PPP's concrete implementation, and mark the moments of direct violence through which these contradictions were both expressed and ultimately contained.

THE CONTESTED IMPLEMENTATION OF PLAN PUEBLA PANAMA (PPP)

From its launch in 2001 to its abandonment in 2008, the PPP was opposed by numerous place-based social movements that challenged its reduction of social space to an abstract factor in the logic of accumulation, and that emphasized the profound connection between space, identity and social practice in the history of Mexico's indigenous and peasant populations. In contrast to the abstract official representations of the PPP, these place-based movements demonstrated that social space 'is not merely economic, in which all parts are interchangeable and have exchange value ... [and] is not merely a political instrument for homogenizing all parts of society' (Lefebvre 2009c: 191). In this section I briefly detail three examples of localized resistance to the PPP, in order first to indicate something of their breadth and diversity, and second to demonstrate the tendency for these forms of resistance to articulate a common politics of *autogestion* and difference that resonated with Lefebvre's vision of a differential space.

On 22 October 2001, four months after the official launch of the PPP, the Mexican Ministry of Communications and Transport (SCT) announced the construction of an international airport 20 miles outside Mexico City. The airport was to be constructed on agricultural land in the Texcoco Valley, requiring the expropriation of 4,550 hectares of communal land belonging to the *ejido* (collective agricultural community) of San Salvador Atenco. Without consulting the *ejiditarios* (collective proprietors), the federal government announced the expropriation of the land on grounds of 'national interest', at a price of 7 pesos (US 70 cents) per square metre. Although it was located slightly outside the official geographical perimeter of the PPP, the proposed airport followed the same economic logic, was being implemented by the same administration and would be integrated into the same infrastructure networks. It was therefore interpreted by the local population and other social movements as constituting the PPP's symbolic and material initiation. The *ejiditarios* of San Salvador Atenco rejected the airport, forming the FPDT (People's Front in Defence of the Land), and framing their struggle as the first resistance to the PPP.[7] In December 2001, faced with state strategies of bribery and repression, and drawing inspiration from the Zapatista Autonomous Territories, the FPDT declared Atenco a 'municipality in rebellion', expelling government officials, occupying state buildings, and constructing barricades against the threat of military and police incursions. Tensions with the state escalated over the following months, culminating in July 2002 in a violent confrontation with the federal police, in which a member of the FPDT was killed (Pascual 2002, Stolle-McAllister 2005). Faced with growing public support for the FPDT following this event, the Fox administration was forced to cancel the airport project. The cancellation shook the confidence of potential investors in the PPP, leading *The Economist* to comment that 'problems now cloud the Plan Puebla Panama', due to the fact that it 'runs through many communal lands occupied by indigenous people' (*The Economist* 10 August 2002). Equally, the victory of the FPDT strengthened the resolve of other social movements opposed to the Plan, demonstrating the continued material significance of the lived spaces of southern Mexico, despite their discursive erasure in the planning documents and political discourses of the PPP. In the words of one of the leaders of the FPDT, 'We will continue to insist that the *campesinos*, their world, and their *cosmovisión* have to be understood.

If they are not taken into account, then it is logical that such development programmes will fail' (quoted in *La Jornada* 18 July 2002).

The centrepiece of the PPP in southern Mexico was to be the Isthmus of Tehuantepec Megaproject, including the construction of a 'dry canal' between the Pacific and Atlantic coasts – a high-speed road and rail link connecting deep-water ports across the narrowest point of the Mexican landmass, which was to compete for international trade against the increasingly congested Panama Canal. The Megaproject combined the dry canal with forestry plantations, fish farms, oil refineries, road networks, energy projects and tourist resorts (Presidencia de la República 2001: 135). The Project awakened historical memories of similar regional development programmes implemented in the 1960s and 1970s in southern Mexico, which had been characterized by corruption, forced resettlements and economic failure (Scott 1982), and was forcefully opposed by social movements in the Isthmus. As in the case of the airport project in Atenco, the planners found themselves confronted by the persistence of communal land ownership and the strength of community organization. Road construction for the section of the PPP's highway network (RICAM) between Oaxaca and Tehuantepec was blocked by impoverished communities who lacked both the vehicles and the toll fees necessary to make use of the roads crossing their lands, and who argued that the projects would only benefit haulage companies, agribusinesses and the high-end tourist industry (Red Oaxaceña de Derechos Humanos 2004). Similar arguments were articulated by UCIZONI (Union of Indigenous Peasants of the Northern Isthmus) in their opposition to the expropriation of 100,000 hectares of land for the construction of wind farms for the generation of electricity for the PPP's transnational energy grid (SIEPAC). UCIZONI argued that the grid would bypass the local *ejidos*, and that the energy generated on their land would instead by utilized by the multinational corporations that the PPP was designed to attract to the region (UCIZONI 2006). When interviewed, a leader of the movement explained that, like the FPDT, UCIZONI had drawn inspiration from the Zapatistas in developing autonomous forms of organization, including education projects and production cooperatives, and based on a shared recognition that 'Land ownership (*la tenencia de la tierra*) is the foundation of the power to resist'.[8]

Southern Mexico has extensive hydroelectric potential, and a number of dam projects were undertaken in the mid-twentieth century, resulting in the dispossession and displacement of *campesino* communities (Barkin and King 1970). As with the Isthmus of Tehuantepec Megaproject, the PPP's planned 'extension of hydroelectric projects in the region' (Presidencia de la República 2001: 42) was consequently one of the most controversial of its proposals (Pickard 2004). In January 2003, the government of the southern Mexican state of Guerrero announced the construction of La Parota, a 765 MW dam at an estimated cost of $US1 billion (*Business News Americas* 30 January 2003). La Parota was named as one of the 'strategic projects' of the PPP (Presidencia de la República 2001: 171), and was immediately rejected by many of the local *ejidos* facing displacement. Following the examples of the FPDT in Atenco and UCIZONI in the Isthmus of Tehuantepec, these communities established CECOP (Council of *Ejidos* in Opposition to La

Parota) to organize their opposition to the dam, which they claimed would destroy 36 communities, flood 17,000 hectares of land and displace 25,000 people. In the context of the recent victory of the FPDT in Atenco, and the growing resistance to the PPP in the region as a whole, CECOP posed a significant challenge not only to the future of the PPP, but also to the symbolic authority of the state and its power to control and transform the national territory. The state responded to this threat with a range of tactics similar to those deployed in Atenco. In the *ejidal* assemblies that it organized to gain approval for the project, the Mexican Federal Electricity Corporation (CFE) was accused of buying votes, changing assembly locations without informing CECOP, and physically barring the entry of CECOP members. CECOP leaders were arrested and received death threats, and intra-community divisions were generated between those supporting and opposing the project, resulting in violent confrontations in which two community members were killed.[9]

The cases of Atenco, the Isthmus of Tehuantepec and La Parota illustrate the processes through which the violence concealed within technocratic representations is manifested in the concretization of abstract space. Taken together, these examples also serve to demonstrate the tendency for the internal contradictions of abstract space to inspire practices of *autogestion* and assertions of difference, which for Lefebvre constitute the incipient praxis of a differential space.[10] As a prominent anti-dam activist explained when interviewed, 'Capital is after territory (*va por el territorio*), and what we have to promote is territorial autonomy, the defence of food security and natural resources'.[11] Yet in the absence of articulation within a broader movement, as Lefebvre himself recognized, such struggles are condemned to remain as fragmented particularisms that may achieve local victories, but that are incapable of fundamentally challenging the forces of abstraction. Furthermore, without a clearly articulated political vision and strategy, forms of resistance of this kind can easily become conservative protections of the local status quo – which is invariably characterized by its own entrenched hierarchies and exclusions – instead of serving as catalysts for social transformation. Lefebvre therefore repeatedly emphasized the need for 'counter-plans' and 'counter-projects' with which to draw such movements together, while asserting the continued significance of class identity and anti-capitalist politics in achieving the required unity and the necessary transformative vision (Lefebvre 1991: 373, 383, 419, 2003b: 88). The following section interprets the Zapatistas' 'Other Campaign' as a counter-project of this kind, which wove the fragmented struggles in Atenco, the Isthmus of Tehuantepec and La Parota into a broader revolutionary movement that combined assertions of *autogestion* and the right to difference with an increasingly class-based and explicitly anti-capitalist project.

THE OTHER CAMPAIGN AS A STRUGGLE FOR A DIFFERENTIAL SPACE

In August 2003 the EZLN returned to the public sphere after over two years of silence following the implementation of the *Ley Indigena*. In a series of statements marking their return, they emphasized their rejection of the PPP, and announced the launch of a counter-plan, which they called 'Plan Realidad-Tijuana' in reference to the southernmost Zapatista Autonomous Territory on the Guatemalan border, and the northernmost Mexican city on the border with the USA.[12] The name indicated their desire to construct a national movement of resistance against the logic of the PPP, which they interpreted as not only homogenizing in terms of its extension of the space of state and capital, but also fragmentary, to the extent that it sought to manage southern Mexico as a reserve of natural resources for global capital distinct from the rest of the nation (EZLN 2006a). The statements referred to their counter-project by the shortened name of 'Plan Reali-Ti', in order to mock the abstraction of the PPP, its distance from the lived reality of southern Mexico, and its failure to be fully concretized in the image of its representations. In the words of the EZLN spokesperson, Subcomandante Marcos:

> Plans on paper are one thing, and reality is another … The growing resistance of groups, collectives, and communities has impeded the full application of the Plan, and where it has managed to install itself, it presents all the solidity of a cardboard stage-set. (EZLN 2006a: 18)

The objective of Plan Reali-Ti was to 'connect all the resistances in our country, and with them, reconstruct the Mexican nation from below' (ibid.: 21), drawing the multiple resistances to the PPP into precisely the integrated-yet-differentiated movement that Lefebvre insists is necessary to challenge abstract space, but doing so on a national basis instead of allowing the movement to be defined by the geographical scale of the PPP itself. While declining to impose a fixed plan or model of their own, the EZLN set out seven Accords that were to serve as the basis for Plan Reali-Ti. Of these Accords, the first two expressed the very principles of *autogestion* and difference so central to Lefebvre's vision of a differential space, calling first for 'Reciprocal respect for the autonomy and independence of the social organizations' of all the marginalized and excluded sectors of Mexican society, and second for the 'Promotion of forms of self-government and *autogestion* throughout the national territory' (EZLN 2006b: 51).[13]

Plan Reali-Ti thus constituted a counter-project to the PPP that echoed Lefebvre's vision for a differential space, aiming to build a movement of unity-in-difference, based on collective self-management, and opposed to fixed models and hierarchical structures. However, it was not until 2005, with the issuing of the 'Sixth Declaration of the Lacandon Jungle', that the vision set out in Plan Reali-Ti was developed into an explicit programme for action on a national scale. The Sixth Declaration definitively abandoned all negotiations with the state, and proposed the construction of a national project independent of electoral politics and political parties. Whereas previous Declarations had maintained a political focus on the issue of indigenous rights, the Sixth Declaration acknowledged the necessity for the Zapatistas to evolve beyond identity politics and to contribute to a class-based anti-capitalist movement that would overcome Mexico's entrenched social divisions between the *indígena* and the *mestizo*, the *campesino* and the worker, and the rural and the urban (EZLN 2005: 11). The Sixth Declaration thus aimed to incorporate the scattered resistances against the PPP into a broader transformative movement with the potential to overcome the fragmentary and conservative tendencies of individual place-based struggles, while at the same time rejecting the homogenization, hierarchy and dogmatism that had come to be associated with traditional class politics in Mexico.

The Sixth Declaration became the political strategy of the EZLN's 'Other Campaign' (*La Otra Campaña*), the name of which emphasized both the rejection of the party politics of the 2006 Mexican presidential election campaign, and the significance of difference and 'otherness' within the movement (Mora 2005). In January 2006 the Other Campaign *caravana* left the Zapatista Autonomous Territories and began to work its way across Mexico, aiming to visit every state in the country in order to incorporate Mexico's multiple, diverse and fragmented social struggles into a national anti-capitalist movement (EZLN 2005: 11–13). Although it longer defined itself by its opposition to the PPP as Plan La Realidad-Tijuana had originally done, the Other Campaign encountered and came to incorporate many of the resistances to the Plan, including those against the Atenco airport, the Isthmus of Tehuantepec Megaproject, and the La Parota dam. In February 2006, for example, the *caravana* passed through the Isthmus of Tehuantepec, where it was joined by UCIZONI and other groups opposing the Megaproject. Speaking in the Isthmus, Marcos described the Megaproject in terms that captured the contradiction between abstract space and the space of lived experience, locating it within the long history of struggle over the right to the production of space in southern Mexico:

> There is a plan, a project to convert to colour, dignity and rebellion ... of the Isthmus into ... the grey of concrete and money ... If this nightmare arrives, the Isthmus will be filled with highways, railroads, factories ... huge hotels and offices. They won't respect ejidal property, they will sell it ... They won't respect the labour of the campesinos, they will dispossess them of their land. They won't respect indigenous culture, they will crush it as they have done for five hundred years, but this time for ever. (Quoted in La Jornada 8 February 2006)

In April 2006, the *caravana* visited the proposed site of the La Parota dam, where it was received by CECOP. Declaring that 'the lands of La Parota are also Zapatista lands', Marcos warned Fox that the construction of the dam 'could only be achieved through a war in southern Mexico' (quoted in *La Jornada* 17 April 2006). Two days later, the state announced the cancellation of the dam project (*La Jornada* 19 April 2006). Within a week of this symbolic victory, the Other Campaign arrived at the site of the cancelled airport project in Atenco, where it was joined by the FPDT, who then provided security for the EZLN as the *caravana* participated in the Labour Day celebrations in Mexico City on 1 May (Gibler 2006). By this stage, the Other Campaign had grown to include over 1,000 social movements, and was attracting significant national attention. By drawing high-profile struggles such as those in Atenco and La Parota into an increasingly broad-based and explicitly anti-capitalist movement premised on *autogestion* and the right to difference, and leading that movement into the heart of Mexico City on Labour Day in the year of a presidential election, the EZLN had succeeded in demonstrating the concrete possibility of a differential space in terms that posed a significant challenge to the territorial power of the state. Two days after Labour Day, a confrontation occurred between state police and the FPDT on the outskirts of Atenco, during which police shot and killed a 14-year-old boy and arrested the leader of the FPDT. From Mexico City, the EZLN issued a statement in support of the FPDT, and large numbers of the *caravana* began arriving in Atenco. At dawn the following day, 3,500 state and federal police entered Atenco. Houses were raided, inhabitants and *caravana* members were beaten, and a 20-year-old student was fatally injured with a tear-gas canister. Altogether 217 people were arrested, of whom 30 women and one man were raped while in custody. Fearing further violence, the EZLN suspended the *caravana*, closed off all access to the Zapatista Autonomous Territories, and shifted the focus of the Other Campaign from the construction of a national anti-capitalist movement to a more limited campaign for political prisoners and victims of repression (Giordano 2006, Cuninghame 2007, Amnesty International 2008).

The police incursion in Atenco was represented by the state and the mainstream media as an unfortunate but necessary response to the belligerence of the local population.[14] From the Lefebvrean perspective developed here, however, the event appears not as an isolated incident, but as an explosion of direct violence that gave expression to the profound socio-spatial tensions of southern Mexico. The PPP had simultaneously denied and attempted to resolve these contradictions, through a strategy that paradoxically served only to intensify them by further deepening the structural and symbolic violence of abstract space. The implementation of the Plan had provoked numerous resistances, through which the alternative spatial practices pioneered in the Zapatista Autonomous Territories began to be generalized. The Other Campaign sought to weave these resistances into a national anti-capitalist movement, grounded in the praxis of *autogestion* and the politics of difference that Lefebvre identified with his vision for 'a differential space, which represents for capitalism an antagonistic and ruinous tendency' (Lefebvre 2003b: 98). At the point at which this alternative became a concrete possibility, however, the state resorted to its unparalleled capacity for direct violence. For those involved in the Other Campaign, the message was clear. As a member of the *caravana* present in Atenco during the police raid explained when interviewed, 'The state had to strike Atenco symbolically, in order to say 'Your autonomy goes no further than this'.[15] The violent occupation of the autonomous municipality of Atenco should thus be understood as a material and symbolic assertion of the territorial dominance of the state, through which the possibility of a differential space was ultimately obstructed, demonstrating the extent to which, in Lefebvre's phrase, 'State power only endures by virtue of violence directed towards a space' (Lefebvre 1991: 169).

CONCLUSION

Having begun his six-year presidential term with the prediction that the PPP would 'end the backwardness of southern Mexico in order to incorporate the region into the corridors of world commerce' (quoted in *Financial Times* 18 June 2001), Fox thus ended it by sanctioning the violent repression of movements rejecting the Plan.[16]

Despite being re-launched in 2007 by the newly elected president, Felipe Calderón Hinjosa, it quickly became apparent that the PPP had become unworkable. The continued level of organized resistance to the Plan, the consequent suspicion with which it was regarded by potential investors, and the absence of state funds due to persistent low growth in the Mexican economy all contributed to making its further continuity both politically and economically unviable. In June 2008, the PPP was officially abandoned and replaced by the Mesoamerica Project for Integration and Development – a regional development programme of far less scope and ambition.[17] As Lefebvre concludes:

> The bourgeoisie and the capitalist system thus experience great difficulty in mastering what is at once their product and the tool of their mastery, namely space. They find themselves unable to reduce ... socio-spatial practice to their abstract space, and hence, new contradictions arise and make themselves felt. (1991: 63)

Lefebvre goes on to suggest that this 'spatial chaos ... despite the power and rationality of the state, [might] turn out to be the system's Achilles heel' (1991: 63). However, while it is vital to defetishize the monolithic appearance of abstract space and to reveal the contradictions and possibilities that dwell within it, it is equally necessary to acknowledge the limitations of these possibilities, and the ruthless effectiveness of the state in closing them down. Despite its continued existence, the Other Campaign never recovered the momentum that it had gathered before its repression in Atenco. The Zapatistas have become increasingly politically isolated in recent years within the confines of their Autonomous Territories, and other struggles have generally dissolved back to the level of fragmented particularisms. While the PPP has not succeeded in producing southern Mexico in the image of its abstractions, thus far the resistances and transformative struggles in the region have also failed to achieve significant progressive change, and southern Mexico remains economically impoverished, politically marginalized, and increasingly embroiled in the 'drug war' that is engulfing the country. This, then, is the reality of abstract space in the case of the PPP – neither the space of smooth flows and geometric order imagined by the planners, nor a space yet ripe with the possibility of another world that the EZLN have sought to realize. Instead, in the wake of the PPP and its counter-plans, southern Mexico remains a space of failed technocratic projects and shattered revolutionary dreams, which continues to be marked by the more prosaic realities that have long defined the ragged peripheries of global capitalism – poverty, inequality, violence and struggle.

NOTES

1   This chapter is a shortened version of a paper that first appeared in the *International Journal of Urban and Regional Research*, entitled 'The Violence of Abstract Space: Contested Regional Developments in Southern Mexico'. I would like to thank the journal's editors for agreeing to its publication in this volume. Thanks to Greig Charnock, Paul Chatterton, Stuart Shields, Christian Schmid, Guido Starosta, Julie-Anne

Boudreau at IJURR, and five anonymous referees for helpful comments on earlier versions of this chapter. Any mistakes are of course my own. A version of this paper was presented at the 2010 annual conference of the Society of Latin American Studies, Bristol, UK. I acknowledge the financial support of the Economic and Social Research Council in funding much of the research presented here.

2   The Inter-American Development Bank (IDB) is a regional development bank for Central and South America and the Caribbean, and is the biggest source of development financing for the region. It is headquartered in Washington DC and the USA holds 30.01 per cent of its shares and voting power, compared to a total of 50.02 per cent of shares and votes held by the 26 Latin American and Caribbean member states together. As in the cases of the Word Bank and the International Monetary Fund, the USA is therefore the dominant state actor in the IDB, and the IDB is consequently regarded as an agent of imperialism by many on the Latin American Left.

3   Colombia was incorporated into the PPP in 2006. The Mexican states included in the PPP were Campeche, Chiapas, Guerrero, Oaxaca, Puebla, Quintana Roo, Tabasco, Veracruz and Yucatan.

4   The unusual scale of the PPP – encompassing a sub-region of one national state and the entirety of seven others – is due to a compromise between the respective agendas of Mexico and the IDB. The PPP was publicly presented as a Mexican initiative, and was promoted in Mexico as the realization of Fox's electoral campaign promise of a regional development programme for the impoverished south of the country. However, according to a member of the IDB closely involved with the early stages of the PPP, representatives of the IDB had met with Fox following his election, and had privately requested that he promote a regional development programme encompassing Mexico and Central America. The scale of the PPP can therefore be understood as representing an accommodation between these two agendas (interview with a senior member of staff at the IDB, Mexico City, 15 January 2008).

5   Official government statistics for 2000 classified 9,854,301 of the Mexican population – or 9.5 per cent – as indigenous. Of this population, 74.4 per cent were located in the nine southern Mexican states participating in the PPP, although the region contains only 28 per cent of the national population as a whole (Coordinación General del Plan Puebla Panamá 2003).

6   As such, the PPP was representative of a broader trend within neoliberal restructuring, which 'seeks to reorient state intervention away from monopoly market regulation and towards … the social, physical, and geographical infrastructures that support, finance, subsidize, or otherwise promote new forms of capital accumulation by providing the relatively fixed territorial structures that permit the accelerated circulation of capital and the relatively unhindered operation of market forces' (Swyngedouw et al. 2002: 200).

7   The representation of the airport as part of the PPP enabled the FPDT to attract added media attention, and to gain support from other social movements in the region. In the words of one activist closely involved in the resistance to the PPP, 'It's not important what is formally inside or outside the PPP – it's all part of the same strategy. But the PPP made this strategy visible' (Armando Bartra, Interview: Mexico City 28 November 2007).

8   Carlos Beas Torres, a leading member of UCIZONI (interview, Mexico City, 1 February 2008).

9   Much of the information for this section is drawn from interviews with José Martín Velásquez, an activist involved in organizing resistance to the PPP (Mexico City, 23 January 2008), and Citlali Jiménez Rodríguez, a Mexican activist and academic who

had conducted extensive research into the La Parota conflict, including interviews with CECOP members (Mexico City, 13 December 2007). See also *La Jornada* 30 July 2004, 15 December 2004.

10   Other examples of the place-based conflicts generated by or attributed to the PPP's implementation in southern Mexico include: opposition to the forced displacement of communities inhabiting the Montes Azules Biosphere Reserve in Chiapas; Unión Hidalgo's struggles against the construction of industrial shrimp farms on the Pacific coast of the Isthmus of Tehuantepec; local resistance to the 'La Celula' urbanization project in Puebla; and struggles against dispossession resulting from the construction of tourist resorts and transportation infrastructure in Quintana Roo (see Wilson 2009: 137–77).

11   Gustavo Castro Soto, founding member of the Mexican Movement against Dams and in Defence of Rivers (MAPDER) (interview, San Cristobal de las Casas, 20 March 2008).

12   The Mesoamerican Forum constituted another significant attempt to construct a counter-project to the PPP, bringing together communities and intellectuals from across the region in a series of meetings in opposition to the Plan between 2001 and 2005. Unlike Plan Realidad-Tijuana, however, the Mesoamerican Forum remained a space for the exchange of information and ideas, instead of becoming the base for a concrete political movement (see Wilson 2009: 130–77 for a detailed discussion).

13   The other five Accords were: the promotion of resistance and rebellion against the state and the established political parties; solidarity with the victim against the aggressor; the formation of a trading network among small-scale producers; resistance to the privatization of nationalized industries; and the formation of an alternative cultural and media network (EZLN 2006b: 51).

14   On the afternoon of the incursion, Fox made a televised statement emphasizing 'The commitment of my government to the Mexican people is to guarantee the rule of law.' That evening, Enrique Peña Nieto, then Governor of the State of Mexico, announced: 'I am the first to regret what occurred in San Salvador Atenco. We acted to restore order and tranquillity. My government is firmly committed to protecting you and your family' (footage in Defosse 2010). At the time of writing, Peña Nieto has recently been inaugurated as president of Mexico. His inauguration was marked by clashes outside the National Palace between police and protesters opposing both the alleged fraudulence of his election and his role in the violence in Atenco.

15   An activist closely involved in the Other Campaign (interview, San Cristobal de las Casas 12 January 2009).

16   The state violence in Atenco was repeated in Oaxaca in November 2006, immediately before Fox's departure from office, when federal police entered the centre of Oaxaca City to end its occupation by the Popular Assembly of the Peoples of Oaxaca (APPO). The APPO had taken control of the city five months earlier, in opposition to government corruption and policies including the PPP, and had run it according to principles of direct democracy and *autogestion*. Over the course of this period 29 APPO members and sympathizers died as a consequence of state and paramilitary violence (Esteva 2006, 2010, Roman and Edur 2008).

17   The Executive Commission of the PPP calculates that between 2001 and 2008 US$7.9 billion was invested in the PPP in Mesoamerica as a whole, of which 96.6 per cent was dedicated to RICAM and SIEPAC – the transport and energy infrastructures (Comisión Ejecutiva del Plan Puebla Panamá 2008). Whereas the PPP included over 100 separate projects, the Mesoamerica Project includes only 20. Many of the PPP projects excluded from the Mesoamerica Project, however, have reappeared within the context

of development programmes operating at different scales (see Wilson 2013 for a discussion of this process in the case of Chiapas).

REFERENCES

Amnesty International 2008. 'Mexico: Torture and sexual violence against women detained in San Salvador Atenco – Two years of injustice and impunity'. *Report* 29 April 2008 http://www.amnestyusa.org/research/reports/mexico-torture-and-sexual-violence-against-women-detained-in-san-salvador-atenco-two-years-of-injust?page=show (accessed: 27 June 2013).

Barkin, D. and King, T. 1970. *Regional Economic Development: The River Basin Approach in Mexico.* Cambridge: Cambridge University Press.

Brenner, N. 2004. *New State Spaces.* Oxford: Oxford University Press.

Burguete C. and Mayor, A. 2003. 'The de Facto Autonomous Process: New Jurisdictions and Parallel Governments in Rebellion' in *Mayan Lives, Mayan Utopias,* edited by R. H. Rus, J. Hernández Castillo and S. L. Mattiace. Lanham, MD: Rowman and Littlefield, 191–217.

Comisión Ejecutiva del Plan Puebla Panamá. 2008. *El PPP: Avances, Retos y Perspectivas.* Villahermosa: Comisión Ejecutiva del Plan Puebla Panamá.

Coordinación General del Plan Puebla Panamá. 2003. *Plan Puebla Panamá: Por un Desarrollo Equilibrado y Socialmente Incluyente.* Mexico City: Secretaria de Relaciones Exteriores.

Cuninghame, P. 2007. 'Reinventing An/Other Anti-Capitalism in Mexico: The Sixth Declaration of the EZLN and the "Other Campaign"'. *The Commoner* 12: 79–109.

Defosse, N. 2010. *Viva México.* Mexico: Terra Nostra Films.

Esteva, G. 2006. 'The Asemblea Popular de los Pueblos de Oaxaca: A Chronicle of Radical Democracy'. *Latin American Perspectives* 34: 129–44.

Esteva, G. 2010 'The Oaxaca Commune and Mexico's Coming Insurrection'. *Antipode* 42(4): 978–93.

EZLN. 2005. Sixth Declaration of the Selva Lacandona, http://www.ezln.org/documentos/2005/sexta3.en.htm (accessed: 8 January 2007).

EZLN. 2006a. 'La Treceava Estela (Cuarta Parte): Un Plan' in *Caracoles* by EZLN. San Cristóbal de las Casas: Edición Pirata, 17–22.

EZLN. 2006b. '"La Fiesta de los Caracoles". Palabras de los Comandantes, Comunicados y Planes' in *Caracoles* by EZLN. San Cristóbal de las Casas: Edición Pirata, 37–58.

Gibler, John. 2006. 'Crackdown in Mexico: Death, Injuries, and Jail'. *Global Exchange* 6 May, http://chiapas.mediosindependientes.org (accessed: 11 May 2006).

Giordano, A. 2006. 'Mexico's Presidential Swindle'. *New Left Review* 41: 5–28.

Harvey, N. 2004. 'Disputando el Desarrollo: el Plan Puebla Panamá y los Derechos Indígenas' in *El Estado y Los Indígenas en Tiempos del PAN,* edited by R. A. Hernández, S. Paz and M. T. Sierra. Mexico City: Miguel Ángel Porrua, 115–36.

Inter-American Development Bank. 2001. *Plan Puebla Panamá: Iniciativas Mesoamericanas y Proyectos.* Washington, DC: Inter-American Development Bank.

Lefebvre, H. 1976 [1973]. *The Survival of Capitalism.* London: Allison and Busby.

Lefebvre, H. 1991 [1974]. *The Production of Space.* Oxford: Blackwell.

Lefebvre, H. 1996 [1968]. 'The Right to the City' in *Writings on Cities* by H. Lefebvre, .eds E. Kofman and E. Lebas. Oxford: Blackwell, 63–182.

Lefebvre, H. 2002 [1961]. *Critique of Everyday Life Volume 2.* London: Verso.

Lefebvre, H. 2003a [1970]. *The Urban Revolution.* Minneapolis, MN: University of Minnesota Press.

Lefebvre, H. 2003b. 'Space and the State' in *State/Space: A Reader*, edited by N. Brenner, B. Jessop, M. Jones and G. Macleod. Oxford: Blackwell, 84–100.

Lefebvre, H. 2006. *La Presencia y La Ausencia: Contribución a la Teoria de las Representaciónes.* Mexico City: Fondo de la Cultura Económica.

Lefebvre, H. 2008 [1981]. *Critique of Everyday Life Volume 3.* London: Verso.

Lefebvre, H. 2009a. 'The State in the Modern World' in *State, Space, World: Selected Essays* by H. Lefebvre, edited by N. Brenner and S. Elden. Minneapolis, MN: University of Minnesota Press, 95–123.

Lefebvre, H. 2009b. 'Theoretical Problems of *Autogestion*' in *State, Space, World: Selected Essays* by H. Lefebvre, edited by N. Brenner and S. Elden. Minneapolis, MN: University of Minnesota Press, 138–52.

Lefebvre, H. 2009c. 'Space: Social Product and Use Value' in *State, Space, World: Selected Essays* by H. Lefebvre, edited by N. Brenner and S. Elden. Minneapolis, MN: University of Minnesota Press, 185–95.

Marx, K. 1977. *Capital Volume 1.* New York: Random House.

Mora, M. 2005. 'Zapatista Anti-capitalist Politics and the "Other Campaign": Learning from the Struggle for Indigenous Rights and Autonomy'. *Latin American Perspectives* 34: 64–77.

Pascual, M. 2002. 'Atenco: From Local Battle to National and Global Cause', http://www.narconews.com/print.php3?ArticleID=1396&lang=en (accessed: 27 June 2013).

Pickard, M. 2004. 'The Plan Puebla Panama Revived: Looking Back to See What's Ahead'. *La Cronique des Ameriques* 12: 1–7.

Postone, M. 1993. *Time, Labour and Social Domination.* Cambridge: Cambridge University Press.

Presidencia de la República. 2001. *Plan Puebla Panamá: Capitulo México – Documento Base.* México DF: Presidencia de la República.

Red Oaxaceña de Derechos Humanos. 2004. *El Plan Puebla Panama: Un Proceso en Marcha.* Oaxaca: Red Oaxaceña de Derechos Humanos.

Rodríguez, A. O. 2010, 'The Emergence and Entrenchment of a New Political Regime in Mexico'. *Latin American Perspectives* 37(1): 35–61.

Roman, R. and Edur, V. A. 2008. 'The Oaxaca Commune: The Other Indigenous Rebellion in Mexico'. *Socialist Interventions Pamphlet Series*, no. 99.

Romero, M. 2001. 'El Plan Puebla Panamá: Apuesta Contra el Atraso'. *Vertigo* 15 April: 17–23.

Schmid, C. 2008. 'Henri Lefebvre's Theory of the Production of Space: Towards a Three-dimensional Dialectic' in *Space, Difference, Everyday Life: Reading Henri Lefebvre*, edited by K. Goonewardena, S. Kipfer, R. Milgrom and C. Schmid. London: Routledge, 27–45.

Scott, I. 1982. *Urban and Spatial Development in Mexico.* Baltimore, MD: Johns Hopkins University Press/World Bank.

Stahler-Sholk, R. 2007. 'Resisting Neoliberal Homogenization: The Zapatista Autonomy Movement'. *Latin American Perspectives* 34: 48–63.

Stolle-McAllister. 2005. 'What Does Democracy Look Like? Local Movements Challenge the Mexican Transition'. *Latin American Perspectives* 32(15): 15–35.

Swyngedouw, E., Moulert, F., and Rodriguez, A. 2002. 'Neoliberal Urbanization in Europe: Large-Scale Urban Development Projects and the New Urban Policy' in *Spaces of Neoliberalism: Urban Restructuring in North America and Western Europe*, edited by N. Brenner and N. Theodore. Oxford: Wiley-Blackwell, 195–229.

UCIZONI. 2006. *El Plan Puebla Panamá Existe y Mesoamérica Resiste*. Oaxaca: UCIZONI.

Van der Haar, G. 2007. 'Land Reform, the State, and the Zapatista Uprising in Chiapas' in *Rural Chiapas Ten Years after the Zapatista Uprising*, edited by S. Washbrook. London: Routledge, 68–91.

Wilson, J. 2009. 'Abstract Space and the Plan Puebla Panama: A Lefebvrean Critique of Regional Development in Southern Mexico'. Unpublished PhD thesis, University of Manchester.

Wilson, J. 2011. 'Colonising Space: The New Economic Geography in Theory and Practice'. *New Political Economy* 16(3): 373–97.

Wilson, J. 2013. 'The Urbanization of the Countryside: Depoliticization and the Production of Space in Chiapas, Mexico'. *Latin American Perspectives* 40(5): 218–36.

World Bank 2003. *Mexico: Southern States Development Strategy*. Washington, DC: World Bank.

Žižek, S. 2008. *Violence*. London: Profile.

6

'Greater Paris': Urbanization But No Urbanity – How Lefebvre Predicted Our Metropolitan Future

Jean-Pierre Garnier

Translated by Kim Sanderson

> **It is worth remembering that the urban has no worse enemy than urban planning and 'urbanism', which is capitalism's and the state's strategic instrument for the manipulation of fragmented urban reality and the production of controlled space.**
>
> **(Lefebvre 1976 [1973]: 15)**

It is always difficult to cast a critical eye over a project that has yet to be built. Thus we are unable to assess the material reality of a specific project even when many measures under way or planned before the launch of this project (or group of sub-projects: more than 650) have subsequently been subsumed into the same 'brand'.[1] We can certainly examine the course the project will take, and formulate hypotheses on its *raison d'être* and probable impact on residents' lives (see Figure 6.1). This is, however, a risky venture, made riskier still by the complete lack of any analysis calling into question the project's positive impact.

The 'Greater Paris' project is precisely such a project, designed to encompass 15,000,000 people by 2050, and to affect a still-undefined 'metropolitan' region with fluid boundaries and a current population of just over 11,700,000.[2] One would be hard pressed to find, among the many media reports and copious comments on this project, any argument running counter to its advocates' claims.

Yet some doubts have been expressed here and there about the project's feasibility at a time when the crisis of financialized capitalism has imposed a new norm: economic austerity and the resultant drastic reduction in public spending. The fact that architects were the first port of call, asked in an international consultation to outline the future Greater Paris – also known as the 'capital region' – without any knowledge of the socio-economic context, invited questions and even recriminations. Equally, the priority given to the creation of an automatic orbital super-métro transport service as the first stage of concrete implementation has met with a somewhat mixed response among certain stakeholders in the planning process – not to mention the squabbles over seniority arising from the division of responsibilities between the various government bodies responsible for implementation. So disparate and contradictory are the interests and therefore the

Fig. 6.1   Greater Paris, 650 sub-projects

opinions of the various political and administrative bodies (including the regional council, Paris municipality and communes) that the question of 'metropolitan governance' has often been raised without an institutional answer having been found.

On the other hand, nobody has thought to contest the basic justification for this project by linking the promotion of a Greater Paris with the imperatives resulting from the new modes of capitalist urban development. Yet we are aware that these have negative effects on the majority of city dwellers.

The official *raison d'être* for Greater Paris, unanimously approved both among right- and left-wing political leaders and among planning professionals (including planners, architects, teachers and researchers), not to mention in the world of business, is common knowledge in France because it has been drummed into the populace by the media. It is encapsulated in the text of the prospectus from the Société du Grand Paris, the body responsible for overseeing and coordinating the project's implementation while the issue of 'governance' is resolved.[3] The title sums up the matter at hand: 'Fierce global competition' (SGP 2010). The text explains:

> Greater Paris was born in response to a vital question for our country: how can we establish France sustainably amidst the international economic competition? For several decades, the world has been evolving at truly dizzying speed and countries which yesterday seemed to lag behind are today developing apace. In the face of such change, the United States and the United Kingdom are arming

themselves with a new weapon: global cities. Thus New York and London have changed tack and are attracting a steady stream of new development potential … In this age of constant competition between world-ranking cities in the aim not only of driving their economies but also of becoming strategic centres for commerce, technology and logistics, our targeted response is the Greater Paris project …

In view of this, we believe it is appropriate to turn to the late Henri Lefebvre for help with the counter-arguments. Lefebvre is certainly someone who, had he come into the world a little later and therefore been able to witness the gestation of such a project during his lifetime, would have brought a note of discord to disrupt the chorus of approval that has greeted Greater Paris. Naturally we do not claim here to speak for him, to take the liberty of guessing what he would have thought of the future now promised to Paris and the Parisians (who were turned into 'Franciliens' with a wave of the magic wand of bureaucracy).[4] We will simply borrow some conceptual tools from the late urban thinker in an attempt to see beyond the façade of the universally lauded Greater Paris project, and thus enter into a discussion extending beyond mere apology.

FROM MASTER PLAN TO GREATER PARIS: CHANGE IN CONTINUITY

The praise that was heaped on President Nicolas Sarkozy's April 2009 launch of Greater Paris into media orbit, when he presented to the public the proposals from the project's ten winning teams of architects, might indicate that this was a novel initiative. He emphasized that this was the world's first study on this scale of the phenomenon that is the modern metropolis, and the work that had been done was unprecedented (Sarkozy 2009), enthused the president. However, all this statement demonstrates is his lack of long-term memory. Besides the exaggeration inherent in his claim that the architect teams had accomplished a world first, a precedent actually existed on the president's home turf. Indeed, a few months after the elections that brought him into power, Nicolas Sarkozy had himself acknowledged this fact, confirming the need to consider a 'new, all-encompassing development project for Greater Paris', and thus admitting not only that others had already introduced the idea, but also that they had garnered the means to implement it. As he stated, now, 40 years after the first steps taken by General de Gaulle and Prefect Paul Delouvrier, the errors of the past must be made good, and he drew attention to the scale of what happened 50 or 60 years ago, when there was no fear about conjuring up a vision of the future (Sarkozy 2007).

In 1965, almost half a century earlier, another 'grand design' for the future role of the French capital and its environs had in fact been proclaimed with great fanfare, also accompanied by drawings on the same grand scale: a planning and development master plan entitled 'Schéma Directeur d'Aménagement et d'Urbanisme de la Région Parisienne (SDAURP)'. The plan was poured straight from the minds of the state's technocrats, and was fed by the ambitions of major industrial firms, banking consortiums and property groups; this provided Henri

Lefebvre with yet another occasion to criticize what in *The Right to the City* he would call 'de-urbanized urbanization', that is, an urbanization without urbanity in the sense that it precludes the existence of an 'urban man for whom and by whom the city and his own daily life in it become oeuvre, appropriation, use value (and not exchange value)' (Lefebvre 1996 [1968]: 78).

This criticism might also be applied to the Greater Paris project. In fact, although according to President Sarkozy the intention behind this project was to 'make good the errors of the past', the project actually reprises the planning principles set out in the 1965 Master Plan rather than breaking with them. This will undoubtedly involve reproducing mistakes. Lefebvre's verdict on urban development projects copied from the Master Plan blueprint must therefore also apply to the Greater Paris project.

The report presenting the 1965 Master Plan contains most of the arguments that would, just over 40 years later, justify the Greater Paris project. The organization of this forthcoming project also meets the objectives proposed all those years earlier, which even then were presented as imperatives.

Then as now, the aim was not to slow the spatial expansion of the Parisian agglomeration, but rather to promote it by channelling this expansion into two priority axes.[5] The main reason given for this remains the same. Admittedly, in the 1960s there was no talk of 'free and fair competition', an unwritten rule that implicitly governs today's urban environment as it does all other spheres of human activity in Europe, from one global city to the next. However, the Gaullist political elite and the urban planners they employed did consider that competition with metropolises in neighbouring countries, in particular with London, meaning there was a pressing need to let Paris emerge from the 'intra muros' constraints of its city walls,[6] as Paul Delouvrier repeatedly explained. Delouvrier was a senior civil servant whom Général de Gaulle appointed to 'bring some order to this bloody shambles' – by which he was referring to the Parisian agglomeration[7]– and to shape it into a major urban centre to rival those elsewhere in Europe. The concept of a 'world city' had not yet been devised, but only because capitalism had not reached the globalization stage.

The Greater Paris project slots into a framework of transnational capitalism in which competition plays out on a global scale between 'world cities', and not merely at the European level, which was the reference point for the SDAURP. Nevertheless, the issue of competition facing the officials responsible for developing and planning the Paris region remains basically the same as in the early 1960s.

In the 1965 Master Plan, three objectives were set that would allow the Paris urban region to step up to the mark as a European metropolis: 'To promote an organised urban expansion'; 'To restructure the suburbs by providing them with urban centrality'; and 'To unify the regional labour market' using 'an appropriately planned transport network' (IAURP 1965). These arguments are also advanced by advocates of the Greater Paris project; in presenting a metropolitan vision of a Greater Paris, they are simply building on their predecessors' vision.

This may initially appear astonishing given that the economic, institutional and political backdrops to these two projects contrast starkly. The first project was launched at the height of France's 'thirty glorious years' of economic prosperity following the Second World War, the product of a Fordist model of capital accumulation. The state was centralizing and interventionist, the government resolutely right-wing. The second project was launched in times of financial crisis and ongoing recession that followed the dawning of an era of neoliberal capitalism based on flexible, financialized accumulation. Today, power in terms of urban planning has been decentralized towards local authorities and there is a left-wing majority of 'socialists' and greens in the Île de France Regional Council and in the office of the Mayor of Paris. Finally, the 1965 Master Plan was drawn up under the direction of a technocracy of engineers, whereas teams of architects were charged with setting the main direction for planning Greater Paris.

One constant remains, above and beyond the different contexts, and it is something that requires explanation: the same class logic and the same ideology are at work within the urban planning choices being made. These are the same logic and ideology that Henri Lefebvre continually denounced in his critical reflections on changes in towns and cities and the effect of capitalism on urban areas.

The first of Lefebvre's targets is conceptual, the ideological 'naturalization' of the production of space. Some 40 years have passed since Henri Lefebvre's major works on urban matters were first published. Yet the public bodies responsible for town and country planning, both national and local, carry on regardless. They consider, or pretend, that urban concentration, polarized growth and the accompanying socio-spatial inequalities – euphemistically known as disparities – emerge naturally or (ultimately the same thing) spontaneously. In his books and articles, Lefebvre repeatedly underlined the structural relationship between urban concentration and the concentration of capital. Urban concentration has only been growing since his day, with the same cause producing the same effect as the concentration of capital has become increasingly transnational, technological, flexible and financial. People persist in labelling the resulting urban transformation 'mutation', a concept borrowed from biology. Lefebvre (1969) queried the use of this term due to its naturalizing and thus depoliticizing connotations, which invite us to believe that we know where this urban evolution is headed, whereas in fact we do not know where we are going.

Lefebvre's second target is the techno-bureaucracy, and the technocratic rationalism that colours its concept of urban policy. The SDAURP was drawn up in the highest echelons of the state by a team composed mainly of architects/planners, geographers and graduates from the Ecole nationale polytechnique, under the direction of a senior civil servant reporting directly to the president and prime minister. Besides the undemocratic nature of the conditions in which the Master Plan was produced, the accompanying maps, plans and report perfectly illustrate Lefebvre's definition of urban planning: 'Planning as ideology formulates all the problems of society into questions of space and transposes all that comes from history and consciousness into spatial terms' (Lefebvre 1996 [1968]: 48). Judging from the planning choices made and the justifications proffered by the architects who made them, the Greater Paris project is certainly broadly in line with this ideology. The project represents yet another claim to have found spatial responses to uncomfortable questions that we are reluctant to ask, questions about social contradictions that we seek to camouflage in order to avoid uncovering the class issues underlying all urban policy in a capitalist regime.

The decentralization of responsibility for urban development that Lefebvre had been fervently hoping for in the 1960s and 1970s failed to produce the outcome he expected. He had expressed some reservations about any decentralization driven from on high, asking how the centralized state could take charge of centralization. It would be a façade, a caricature (Lefebvre 1970). Just as Lefebvre had hoped, bodies at local, regional and département level have eventually acquired 'real autonomy, a real authority to manage' (ibid.). And still decisions on the future of towns and cities are being decided by a politico-technocratic oligarchy, rather than by their residents. Change has occurred, but it is merely a change in the level at which this oligarchy sits within the overall hierarchy.

The oligarchy no longer exercises its power at national level, but at regional level. Although it was a right-wing French president who officially approved the project and although several ministries and prefectures have a presence within the 'Société du Grand Paris', the supervisory body for project implementation, representatives from the relevant local authorities (communes, regions and départements) are in the majority on the Société's Supervisory Board. This is also the case for the Atelier International du Grand Paris (AIGP), a public–private joint venture (GIP). Its technical board comprises some 15 international teams of architects and sets out the research, design, value-adding, awareness-raising and promotional campaigns associated with planning a Greater Paris. This association also works closely with local elected representatives and their colleagues.

Thus local power may have been freed from government control, but it is not necessarily any more democratic. Now more than ever, citizens are distanced from the process of making decisions that will affect part of their lives as city dwellers. From this point of view, the consultation procedures, public debates and other mechanisms for public participation established by local elected representatives act as alibis for democracy, with no real influence on planning choices except on matters of detail. In short, the 'popular consultation' touted in municipal, regional or département propaganda remains a fiction. Having witnessed only a few years of this, Lefebvre drew his own conclusions that the municipalities were clearly organized on a state model, reproducing in a smaller format the management habits and dominance of the high-level state bureaucracy. In this scenario city dwellers were seeing their theoretical rights as citizens dwindle, alongside the possibility of exercising them fully (Lefebvre 1991b).[8] Indeed, why should things have played out differently? The municipalities form part of the state apparatus: they are its local, elected arm. Decentralization has given technocrats in planning departments the option of completing their political or administrative careers at commune or city level as well as at national level. They still have access to the usual urban development tools, redolent of an overly quantitative and technological approach.

Henri Lefebvre had a third target: town planning, and in particular the Paris Master Plan, the outline of which he saw emerging on the ground. Despite the simultaneous promotion of the major provincial cities as 'balancing metropolises', he claimed that 'The centrality of Paris is continually reinforced … a mechanical means of compensating Paris, on paper, within French space' (Lefebvre 1970: 11). Indeed, as Lefebvre had predicted, metropolization policies pursued since that time and intended to benefit both the regional capitals and the 'capital region', inspired by 'neoliberal critiques of Paris' centrality', have actually given rise to a 'semi-colonialism involving underdeveloped regions and zones in a relationship with decision-making centres, especially Paris'. The consequence of this, which was already identifiable in Lefebvre's day, is perfectly encapsulated here: 'Imperialist France has lost its colonies, but an internal neo-colonialism has grown up. France is now home to over-developed, over-industrialised, over-urbanised zones, as well as a number of zones in which under-development is increasing …' (Lefebvre 1991a [1974]: 258). In this respect, the Greater Paris project will only accentuate a trend already manifest in the 1960s: 'The capital attracts everything towards it: people, brains, riches. It is a centre for decisions and opinions. Around Paris subordinate, hierarchical spaces extend; these spaces are simultaneously dominated and exploited by Paris' (ibid.).

As in the 'good old days' of Gaullist era 'indicative planning', the key today is to manage, channel and direct, but above all not slow down the urban development of Paris. The old notions popular with the Délégation à l'Aménagement du Territoire et à l'Action Régionale (Delegation for planning, development and regional action, DATAR) and the Institut d'Aménagement d'Urbanisme de la Région Parisienne (Planning and development office for the Paris Region, IAURP) are being trotted out once again, without so much as an initial pause to dust them off. These notions are supposed to help bring order to urban chaos, if not in practical then at least in intellectual terms. At the inauguration of the Société du Grand Paris headquarters in November 2011, the Minister for Urban Areas celebrated the excellence of a project that he believed deserved 'quadruple-A status': it represented ambitious architecture and forward-looking planning;[9] apparently he did not notice that these were the very values, and indeed the very words, that constantly cropped up in 1965 speeches praising the Master Plan. As for the 'vision of tomorrow's metropolis, with its new links and new centres' (Leroy 2011b), which the minister was so keen to promote, its manifestation is strongly reminiscent of that previous metropolitan implementation: after the Réseau Express Régional (RER) and the new towns spawned by the 1965 Master Plan come the Grand Paris Express and the new competitiveness clusters.

RESTRUCTURING SOCIO-SPATIAL POLARIZATION AND SEGREGATION

The inequality of urban development will not be ended by the latest local competitiveness clusters in the city's inner or outer peripheries, any more than it was by the new towns that have been erected over the decades since the Master Plan was published: it is inherent in the capitalist dynamic. The current clusters will merely push urban development into new socio-spatial moulds (see Figure 6.2). Lefebvre

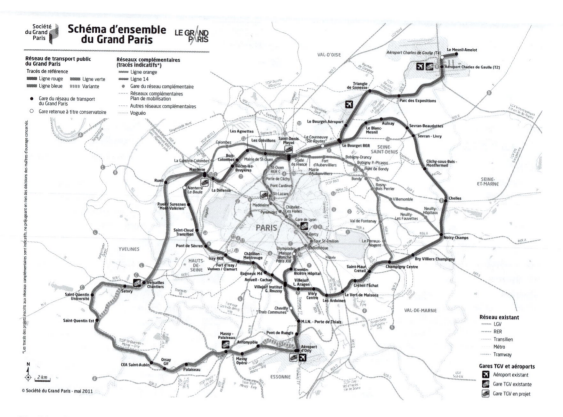

Fig. 6.2   Greater
Paris Express

had noted that the earlier new towns, expected to inject an urban 'centrality' into outlying urban development, would nevertheless remain both subordinate to and dependent on the capital. Without an autonomy or identity of their own, these towns acted as satellites, unable to break free from the capital's orbit. 'New towns bear only too visibly the marks of technocracy, indelible marks which show the futility of any attempt to animate them, whether through architectural innovation, information, cultural events or community life' (Lefebvre 1991b). Residents still feel as if they live in the suburbs, as if they are 'second-class citizens' compared to the privileged residents remaining in Paris itself.

However, in contrast to the new towns, the predominant focus for the seven 'world-class track competitiveness clusters' planned by and for the Greater Paris project is not urban but economic. To be precise, the focus lies on the ideology of economism, which has risen to a position of even greater dominance under the (as yet feebly contested) reign of neoliberalism. The clusters will be situated in 'project areas' where in some cases some of their individual components already exist. In the 1980s, they would have been dubbed 'technopoles'. These days, they are known even in French as 'clusters' – a term imported from the USA. They are made up of high-tech industrial manufacturers, research and higher education establishments that are interlinked, complementary and share an area of specialist expertise. Each cluster, which will be planned and developed in accordance with a 'territorial development contract' between central government and the relevant communes, will centre on a single specialism: finance to the west of Paris (La Défense–Seine Arche), cultural creation based on visual arts and social sciences to the north (Plaine Saint-Denis), a business airport plus aeronautical activity such as training and trade fairs further north (Le Bourget), an airport, conference and international trade fair platform even further north (Roissy–Villepinte–Tremblay), a focus on environment and sustainable development to the east (Cité universitaire Descartes), a 'biotech valley' to the south-east (from Ivry-sur-Seine to the new town of Evry), scientific and high-tech research to the south-east (Saclay), and logistics and sustainable transport ('confluence') downstream on the Seine towards the port of Le Havre.

No doubt the urban dimension will not be altogether absent from these 'world-class excellence clusters', but will be mainly commercial in nature. Housing is planned to accommodate some of the 'matière grise (grey matter)' – current concretizing parlance in France for highly qualified employees and the students destined to join them. Apart from that, commercial zones will be developed within and around the 70-odd new or renovated stations for the 'Grand Paris Express' that will serve the clusters (see Figure 6.2). The architect tasked with outlining these 'next-generation stations' and expected to grant them and the surrounding districts their own identity, with all the high-tech audiovisual models at his disposal, has proposed what Batiactu (2012) called a sensual station design, both a laboratory for contemporary urban life and a space in which to experiment with new ways of living and being together. Thus ways of life and existences are treated as mere commodities.

The creation of this automatic metro network, which will mainly run underground in a large-capacity double loop (175 km of extra track is planned by 2025), is presented as a priority, if not *the* priority. It is intended to connect with the existing metro, RER and suburban railway lines on the outskirts of Paris, linking the competitiveness clusters with one another and with the capital, which will thus retain its monopoly on the role of high-class centre. Once again, the 'polycentric design of urban space' that Lefebvre often advocated, both to avoid a dispersal of the main centre due to saturation and to reduce the peripheral areas' dependency, will take a hierarchical form, thus slightly reducing the inequality between areas without making it disappear. The public transport network will be strengthened and modernized as a cornerstone of the Greater Paris project. This will in turn reinforce a phenomenon that Lefebvre had highlighted as deeply worrying: the 'dissociation of the city dweller and the citizen'. He stated in one of his last articles that being a citizen meant staying in an area for a long time, and that, despite this, in modern urban areas city dwellers were in perpetual motion: they moved around; if they did settle down, they soon detached themselves from the place or attempted to do so (Lefebvre 1991b). We might add that future city dwellers will have no choice but to move around. Indeed, to the supporters of a Greater Paris, be they politicians, administrators, experts or researchers, the metropolitan space represents above all a 'space for flows and networks'. Hence the pride of place granted to 'mobility', which is equated with 'freedom'.

Homo metropolitanus is destined to be in perpetual motion, a passer-by in a vehicle: a passenger whose everyday life will no longer play out within a limited area, but on a regional scale. Yet any vision or project in which residents aim to reclaim the city on the basis of shared experience, arising from a stable sense of belonging to an identifiable place that they all frequent, must be based on localism. The 'Franciliens' of the future will always be prepared to leave their residential environment for work, study or entertainment and will no longer seek out a favourite or regular place to frequent within the urban area. Residents with no attachment to any particular area will always be prepared to move elsewhere.

A public exhibition was held at the Cité de l'Architecture et du Patrimone in spring 2012, deploying major illustrative resources in the organizers' aim to 'close the cycle of reflection on the Greater Paris project'. They consider an efficient transport system to be a unique opportunity to change people's lives (Duthilleul 2012). The exhibition's title sums up the urban philosophy that was its inspiration: 'Transport – when our movements shape cities'.

In the minds of the planning technocrats and their attendant local elected representatives, the urban space of tomorrow will not be consigned to the same fate as the space of yesterday. Lefebvre unstintingly illustrated and demonstrated this fate: 'Capitalism and neocapitalism have produced abstract space, which includes the "world of commodities", its "logic" and its worldwide strategies, [as well] as the power of money and that of the political state' (Lefebvre 1991a [1974]: 53). To the technocrats, tomorrow's space is our just reward as transient city dwellers, and not the product of a logic and of social forces over which we have absolutely no influence!

In reality, it is imperative that the Greater Paris project connects to the networks and flows of the transnational economy, as do other metropolises, and that it proves with metropolitan marketing campaigns that it is equally if not better capable of harnessing these flows than its foreign competitors. As its elected officials and their advisers repeat incessantly, Greater Paris must demonstrate that it is competitive and therefore attractive. The ground rules are clear: either it gathers the resources to grow bigger and wider, developing its own area by concentrating a maximum of resources there for its own benefit (or, more precisely, for the good of those people who benefit from this concentration) and joining the 'highly selective metropolis club' to cite a catchphrase in decision-making circles, or it will be destined to marginalization and potentially terminal decline. The French president declared that,

> in order to remain first-class, city dwellers needed to think a long way ahead, and to think big. Thus the Greater Paris project meant more than merely expanding beyond the boundaries of Paris – Greater Paris meant a willingness to envisage the Paris of the future in a much wider perspective than the constraints of the périphérique, much wider than the Petite Couronne ring of suburbs, and much wider even than the l'Ile de France. (Sarkozy 2010)

Of course this step change will do nothing to lessen the socio-spatial inequality and segregation inherent in capitalist urbanization, contrary to the claims of certain experts who state that situating the Paris metropolis as a major hub within the global marketplace would facilitate its future economic success and therefore generate the potential to redistribute some of the wealth thus produced to benefit disadvantaged groups. Quite the reverse: this endless expansion of cities over an ever-greater area will only reinforce the physical separation and attendant socio-ideological separatism between the increasingly security-conscious 'beaux quartiers' – or residential suburbs reserved for the rich – and the zones with increasing surveillance to which the poor are relegated. Equally, the contrast between the centre and the outskirts will not diminish, but will continue to grow.

In a process analysed and criticized by Lefebvre, some of the urban area will disperse and be diluted by the wider agglomeration, while the rest will become concentrated and consolidated according to a hierarchy. At the heart of the city centre, and at the heart of the entire future capital region, will be the high-ranking activities and population. On the outskirts a few technical and scientific 'excellence clusters' will be granted a partial, secondary urban centrality in which property speculation will widen the divide between the salaried white-collar workers who live in situ and can enjoy this excellence and people who are less well qualified and paid, and obliged to live elsewhere. Indeed, zones of popular housing will be scattered across the remaining metropolitan area; they will lack facilities and decent public transport links. In conclusion, the centralization of capital, which is accentuated by its transnationalisation, will be accompanied by a spatial concentration of its strategic urban components – at the expense of the areas allocated to non-profit-making activities and/or less solvent residents.

As a result, the 'noble' functions will continue to gather in the central part of Greater Paris, as Lefebvre observed: those functions that give direction or make decisions. For both professional and cultural reasons, the urban centre will be associated with the 'upper tertiary' sector, now also known as the 'quaternary' (leadership, information, innovation), alongside services (finance, consultancy, advertising, hotels, restaurants and high-class leisure pursuits) and the attendant facilities, as well as the bourgeois and new petty bourgeois, spearheaded by the fashionable bohemian bourgeois – the 'creative class'.

In order to make room for the above groups, campaigns will take place to recapture territory in those pockets of popular housing that remain at the heart of the agglomeration, be they districts in the northern and eastern arrondissements or in what were the working-class inner suburbs – known as 'red' when their local authorities were under French Communist Party control and the Party still called itself revolutionary. Such 'renovation' or 'regeneration' schemes claim to reinvigorate specific neglected zones, to redevelop certain disadvantaged areas, to contribute to urban renewal. Yet their aim remains the same: to replace the existing population and improve the spaces this 'frees up', thus benefiting contractors, property developers and speculators; to improve the quality of the areas then reserve them for 'people of quality'.

In short, the working classes will be cleared from the centre of the metropolis, since their very presence as residents is deemed to be at best useless and at worst an encumbrance – although they will be welcome as workers, since the service sector in a 'global city' is constantly expanding, as we will see below (Sassen 1996). Thus they will be despatched to ever more distant suburbs, as will any facilities playing secondary or subordinate roles, (polluting industries, power plants, waste incineration, warehouses), which may be indispensable to the operation of the metropolis but are deemed burdensome due to the pollution they cause.

As we can see, Paris will retain its wealth and its wealthy people, but spread over a wider area, and export all obstacles to the distant outskirts, deemed to be a dumping ground. From the late 1960s, Henri Lefebvre had described the capitalist metropolis to come:

> The ideal city, the New Athens, is already there to be seen in the image which Paris and New York and some other cities project. The centre of decision-making and the centre of consumption meet. Their alliance on the ground based on a strategic convergence creates an inordinate centrality ... Strongly occupied and inhabited by these new Masters, this centre is held by them. (Lefebvre 1996 [1968]: 161)

The promotion of a Parisian centrality that is ever more exclusive, in both senses of the word, might be described as a 'restriction to an elite of the right to the city', to borrow from the 'radical' geographer David Harvey (Harvey 2008).

Nevertheless, dispossessed of this right, the residents ousted to the outskirts will still have access to the heart of the metropolis in order to provide the aptly named 'services' – for is their role not first and foremost that of servants to the metropolitan elite? They might also visit from time to time as consumers and users of any urban amenities within their credit limits. How, then, to reconcile the greater social and spatial divide characteristic of the current organization and operation of metropolitan areas with the 'imperative of solidarity' that the managers of the 'global city' repeatedly pronounce to their populace? The two are reconciled by a public transport system that is constantly being upgraded and improved. Mobility is supposedly synonymous with the ability of all people to access all parts of the metropolis. Yet this is just a means of making a positive out of the negative that is the obligation for marginalized citizens to commute constantly, either for work or just to spend occasional leisure time in the lofty urban heights that have been usurped from them.

Thus in *The Right to the City* Lefebvre described the coming capitalist metropolis as 'the ideal city, the New Athens'. Yet all the indications are that the Greater Paris project will merely reproduce the existing socio-spatial organization. The centre, although expanded beyond the boundaries of Paris itself, would still be occupied and held by the 'new Masters', who would possess this privileged place 'without necessarily owning it all'. Surrounding the centre, distributed in the outlying areas according to a hierarchy, would live a multitude who 'provide a multiplicity of services for the Masters of this State'. Lefebvre asked, 'Could this not be the true New Athens, with its minority of free citizens, possessing and enjoying social spaces, dominating an enormous mass of subjugated people, in principle free, genuinely and perhaps voluntarily servants, treated and manipulated according to rational methods?' Yet he made a distinction within these servile masses between the workers and employees directly subject to wage-slavery and the 'new notables': executives, engineers, artists, writers, entertainers and media people.

It would of course also be possible to include planners and architects here, always ready to accommodate those in power – not forgetting 'the scholars, sociologists leading,' whom Lefebvre did not hesitate to rank as 'the servants of State and Order, under the pretence of empiricism and rigour, of scientificity' (Lefebvre 1996 [1968]: 161). The spaces planned and reserved for this staff of graduates prefigured the excellence clusters in the Greater Paris: 'these secondary elites are assigned to residence in science parks, university campuses – ghettos for intellectuals'. As for the rest of the populace, 'The mass, under pressure from many constraints,' will still be relegated to 'more or less residential ghettos' (ibid.: 162).

In all likelihood, the Greater Paris project will merely constitute a new step along the road towards an urban extension that will be accompanied by the death of urbanity in terms of an 'art of living in cities and of experiencing the city' (Lefebvre 1968: 154). On an ever greater scale, the project will facilitate the pursuit of the threefold process of capitalist urbanization, as highlighted by Lefebvre: the homogenization, fragmentation and hierarchization of urban space.

GOVERNANCE OF THE PARIS METROPOLIS: STRUCTURAL INTER-CLASS COLLABORATION

The question remains: why does the Greater Paris project or more broadly the 'metropolis model' win unanimous approval among local elites, elected or otherwise, in major agglomerations? Why have they agreed to be governed by an unwritten imperative (as described above) that applies to all life in this European capitalist society, the principle of 'free and fair competition' that pits individuals, businesses, social strata and nations against one another, and involves cities in reciprocal rivalry?

An initial response to this question might lie in the superficial attractiveness of this project, launched as it was with major media fanfare. The models, plans and audio-visual simulations presented for the public to peruse at the Cité de l'Architecture et du Patrimoine showed the Greater Paris of the future in its very best light. This attractiveness was boosted by a stirring speech made by the French president at the official opening of this spectacular exhibition, and echoed for several weeks by journalists with their own particular blend of enthusiasm and complacency. The exhibition presented proposals from ten teams of architects, 'among the greatest in the world', selected to work on the future Greater Paris (Sarkozy 2009).

Although Nicolas Sarkozy had, not unexpectedly, posited in his speech the need for a global city to stand out from its rivals in the global economy, this was not his primary point of reference in establishing the direction the project should take. Instead, he claimed this direction was inspired by aesthetic and even humanist considerations; hence the calculated choice of the heritage-laden Cité de l'Architecture et du Patrimoine as the venue for this presentation. The president began by declaring that 'Studies by planners and architects have formed the starting point in drawing up this highly symbolic Greater Paris project', arousing some astonishment and even anger in urban planning circles. The president went on to explain why such specialists had been tasked with determining the spatial impact of the Greater Paris project.

Without wishing to linger excessively over a speech probably written by one or more special advisers – in contrast to Général de Gaulle or François Mitterrand, Nicolas Sarkozy never claimed any literary prowess – we should note that the argument, developed in a lyrical, almost poetic or even grandiloquent style, makes a change from the arid, off-putting language usually used by urban development technocrats. It constitutes no more and no less than 'putting architecture back at the heart of our policy decisions' (Sarkozy 2009). The president elaborated further: 'Civilisation begins at the point where policy and aesthetics meet.' His oratory even reveals some borrowings from Lefebvre's critical thinking:

> It is a question of not allowing the financier alone to make the decisions, restricted to a purely quantitative approach ... of breaking with the dreadful habit of holding that art is superfluous whereas it actually meets a very deep human need. It is a question of breaking with a rationalism which is so excessive, so cold that it ends up being opposed to life itself. It is a question of breaking with the functionalism that caused such damage in our cities by increasing specialisation and separation where it should have mixed and combined. It is a question of breaking with everything which in past decades has contributed to the dehumanisation of our cities. (Sarkozy 2009)

President Sarkozy was not the first statesman to dip into Lefebvre's theory in order to justify a particular urban development policy. From the mid-1970s onwards Lefebvre had been complaining that his urban theories, deemed 'subversive' when he first expounded them, were now being adopted by officialdom as 'trivial and self-evident' (Lefebvre 1991a [1974]: 352). He was subsequently obliged to take a stand, since the more he was plagiarized, the fewer citations from his work would be properly attributed to him. Fragments of Lefebvre's conceptualizations were taken up, often as slogans, by right-wing proponents of 'urban planning à la française' during the presidency of Valéry Giscard d'Estaing (Garnier and Goldschmidt 1977a), and then by elected representatives of the institutional left who had reached the upper echelons of municipal authority in 1977 (Garnier and Goldschmidt 1977b), before becoming common currency among the leaders of the Parti Socialiste. This was after the party had gained power in May 1981, when its leaders were busy swapping the 'socialist project' that had helped them to victory for an idea of 'urban civilisation' expected to calm the troubled waters of France's popular suburbs (Garnier 1997).

Yet the Greater Paris project is emerging against a political and ideological backdrop clearly controlled by 'the markets', in which there is little reason – besides the discussions of architecture – to conceal the urbanization of the capital beneath a cultural carapace. The following can be found on the website of the Société du Grand Paris, under the heading 'An exceptional set of opportunities':

> For companies, the Grand Paris project represents major development potential. This is of course the case for companies participating directly in

project implementation. But it also applies to companies benefiting from its indirect effects, such as improved transportation. For real-estate investors, the emergence of new urban centres and the growth in employment mean new opportunities. (Leroy 2011a)

If further proof were needed that Grand Paris is in harmony with capitalist interests, this could be found in a speech given by Urban Areas Minister Maurice Leroy, who was responsible for the project, at a July 2011 seminar held in London. The title speaks for itself: 'The Greater Paris project: financial and real estate opportunities' (Leroy 2011a). The minister addressed investors whose 'time is precious and accounted for', going straight 'to the heart of the matter' as he put it:

As investors, you have choices to make and as such need information so you can make comparisons and take the most appropriate decisions in terms of development potential and profitability. Above all, you need a vision, the ability to see yourself in the future as clearly as possible and make the most accurate possible projections for your investments. (Ibid.)

Before handing things over to his French financier companions, who wanted to speak to their UK counterparts, the minister reassured the investors of 'the economic ambition of the project: I would like to explain how Greater Paris will be constructed and why you would be right to invest and believe in this project's success'. He did not speak at length about art, culture or urban civilization, but spoke briefly with more figures than words in the aim of proving to UK businessmen that the Greater Paris project could be a good deal (ibid.).

Once again, the same refrain about 'the increasing competition facing major cities' was in evidence; the cultural, humanist angle was completely absent. The minister elaborated: 'We will face this competition with an enterprising spirit and with our enterprises themselves: with the relevant objectives, methods and capacities. We are counting on the future just as you are counting on the future of your companies.' The message did come across loud and clear; as the minister emphasized in his concluding remarks: 'France has chosen excellence, Paris is transforming, capitalising and looking to the future. We certainly have the assets, and we're inviting you to share in and make the most of them!' (Ibid.)

In response to this and the president's speech at the Cité de l'Architecture, we might be justified in quoting from Lefebvre: 'When there is talk of art and culture, the real subject is money, the market, exchange, power. Talk of communication actually refers only to solitudes. Talk of beauty refers to brand images. Talk of city-planning refers to nothing at all' (Lefebvre 1991a [1974]: 389). This last judgement, inspired by an excessively polemical approach, actually contradicts a proposition that Lefebvre endeavoured to prove elsewhere: far from playing a negligible role, city planning helps make urban space 'a space which is determined economically by capital, dominated socially by the bourgeoisie, and ruled politically by the state' (ibid.: 227). This critique might itself need some fine-tuning, and brings us back to the initial question: why does the Greater Paris project meet with unanimous approval, at least among all those who pay it any sustained attention?

This question can be answered by posing a second question: who benefits from the process of metropolization? To answer that it is primarily the global, or globalizing, bourgeoisie would hardly constitute an original insight, although this is no doubt the case. This answer overlooks the fact that this bourgeoisie does not implement the underlying urban policy, although it is directly represented among the leadership and in national and local government, and although these same bourgeois representatives do help shape policy and play a key role in decision-making. A third, and threefold, question might bring us closer to a definitive response: who manages the city, who promotes and organizes the process of metropolization, and how?

'It's a matter of governance!' sings the chorus of local elected representatives and bosses alike, with their words echoed by aligned researchers. Yet 'governance' is a pseudo-concept that, as with so many in technical planning newspeak, cannot be precisely defined – which of course is why it's so handy. The smokescreen of such code and the machinations of technocracy actually conceal a 'metropolitan governance' that is first and foremost concerned with the spatial accumulation of capital while also ensuring – to a greater or lesser extent depending on the interplay between the forces currently at work – that the collective needs of the population are met. This applies regardless of the geographical and administrative boundaries imposed and the institutional formula finally adopted.[10] It is called 'governance', a term imported from the English-speaking business world, because it involves close cooperation between state bodies and businesses; its three-letter acronym, like the entity itself, is also imported from English and borrowed from business: the 'PPP' or 'public–private partnership'.

The private partners are easily identified. We can refer to them collectively as 'capitalists': financiers, bankers, contractors, construction companies, property developers and the like. Most are represented by chambers of commerce and industry that bring together the most influential business people in the Paris region. They are also represented by the many networks and pressure groups that spring up around local power bases, not to mention those capitalists who sit directly on various councils and committees.

Lefebvre and many later progressive and/or 'radical' researchers have endeavoured to demonstrate how and why urban development is primarily used to slot the production of space into the framework of commerce, to prepare the way for capital in search of the most profitable investments. Lefebvre (1970) noted some 40 years ago that capital seeks out a second circuit, in addition to the normal or habitual production and consumption circuit, in case the first should falter. This is precisely what has been happening for the past few years, when a surplus of capital has threatened to cause devaluation. The strategy defined by Lefebvre is increasingly coming into play, namely to normalize this secondary circuit, property, while perhaps keeping it as a compensatory sector (ibid.). The Greater Paris project certainly fits the description of this strategy. To confirm this, rather than reading the supposedly learned words of researchers who fail to distinguish explaining from promoting, one need only read the financial press.

The main players in metropolization are the public partners. In the Paris region, as in other major French agglomerations, these partners originate from a class or class fraction that has been given various labels in successive periods and by successive researchers, mostly sociologists: 'salaried middle class', 'new petty bourgeoisie', 'classe de l'encadrement capitaliste' (including managers, senior officials and so on), 'intellectual petty bourgeoisie'. We have opted for the last, since it is the intellectual capital of this class that it employs to act as intermediary and mediator in capitalist relations of domination, as we will see below. This raises the question: by what means can part of this class exercise political power at local level? Lefebvre sets us on the right track in his four-volume work on the state. His 'central theory' reads: 'The middle classes, despite their diversity, across political differences, literally support the State: they provide material and ideological support, by any means and at all costs' (Lefebvre 1974: 462–3). Without undertaking any analysis in this respect, he also glimpsed the place occupied and role played by a fraction of these middle classes in reproducing capitalist production relations. It is a fraction that, at whatever level of the state apparatus and however closely embroiled in the cogs of state, determines its own actions and ensures these are implemented 'on the ground', especially in terms of urban development.

In a 1981 work, again spanning several volumes, Lefebvre made a comment that brings us closer to finding an answer. He said that we were indeed faced with a society in which the ideology of the middle classes predominates, under the hegemony of major investors. The middle classes in question are none other than the intellectual petty bourgeoisie, which possesses primarily educational and cultural capital. It falls to this intellectual petty bourgeoisie to link the dominant class, which has the monopoly on leadership (private or state bourgeoisie) with the classes it dominates, which are expected to undertake any implementation (working class and salaried proletariat). The social division of labour assigns it the task of mediation (design, organization, monitoring, ideological inculcation). The intellectual petty bourgeoisie further subdivides into hierarchical strata: its middle and upper levels are a product of universities, subject to a greater or lesser amount of subsequent finishing. Its most highly qualified members emerge from the 'grandes écoles', extremely selective higher education establishments that train France's intellectual elite: senior civil servants, managers of laboratories and high-tech businesses, senior university academics. Thus the hegemony of the bourgeoisie today relies on a bloc being in power, as Gramsci would have described it, with the ruling class treating the new petty bourgeois elite as a new ally in perfecting its dominance.

In its role of intermediary, middleman and mediator, this university-educated oligarchy is far from all-powerful. As a subordinate agent in the reproduction of capitalist production relations, it bends to or even anticipates the will of the bourgeoisie. For example, it rolls out the red carpet – or rather the green carpet, given the mantra of sustainable urban development – in the form of urban development plans and programmes to attract investors, entrepreneurs and property developers to the capital, along with their servants, engineers, executives, technicians, and all sorts of 'creators' and 'creatives' (including architects and landscape architects, designers, advertising professionals).

The intellectual petty bourgeois supplies the vast majority of the political and administrative staff who 'manage' urban space, in the Paris region as elsewhere. At commune, département and regional levels of the state apparatus, it is responsible both for making planning and development decisions and for following up their practical implementation. Thus support from the technocracy – which is also inclined to decentralize – and backing from experts enables local elected officials to organize 'tomorrow's metropolis': the urbanization of new zones, installation of new 'competitiveness clusters' within 'project areas', establishment of a high-capacity automated public transport system, 'redevelopment' of popular areas and industrial wasteland, and so on. Everything claims to contribute to 'sustainable development'. 'Social purpose' is often added for good measure, but in fact amounts to precious little in terms of commitment.

Given the above, the political hue of the local authority and region, or rather of its politicians, is of little significance since the sociological pedigree and business/management ideology of the key post-holders and people with their hands on the levers of power in the metropolis vary very little. The urban policies that they implement are also remarkably consistent, with very few variations. What is peculiar to Paris is that the upper echelons of the state are involved in the metropolis project, although their involvement neither alters nor adds to the nature of the project. The Mayor of Paris and the president of the Ile de France region, both leftist politicians, nevertheless echoed the calls made by right-wing President Sarkozy in their determination to strengthen Paris' world city status.

Incidentally, we should not overestimate the role played by Nicolas Sarkozy. The Greater Paris project had been emerging since at least the beginning of the century, and nobody queried the need for it at any of the numerous debates held before its official launch, or indeed during the debates that followed.

Pierre Mansat, 'communist' deputy to the 'socialist' Mayor of Paris Bertrand Delanoë, confirmed in 2012 that the Mayor had been 'convinced since 2001 that developing Paris, maintaining its status of global metropolis, of world city, is only conceivable if we go beyond the boundary of the péripherique' (Mansat 2012). He noted at this juncture that he too was a keen supporter of the Greater Paris project: 'I believe that this project has a future. It should be placed in the context of the efforts made over ten years. There can be no going back on the awareness that has been raised, neither among citizens nor among elected officials.'

Until recently, the same message was being sent by the green politicians: 'It may not please everybody, but the metropolis has already arrived. And the implementation of coordinated, sustainable and democratic development is the next step' (Contassot and Monod 2012). We note the obligatory reference to 'sustainable development', which is now a feature of all French urban development plans, and had already been highlighted by the former president as he launched the consultation on the future of Greater Paris in 2007: the teams of architects were required to reflect on the future potential for a '21st-century post-Kyoto metropolis'. This was an opportunity to reinforce the project's green credentials and a further argument intended to curry favour with the public, as witnessed by the prevalence of greenery on the models, maps and plans displayed. The chorus of elected officials, planners and architects gathered under the auspices of the Atelier International Paris Métropole also all foretold of a 'post-Kyoto city' – a risible claim, when everyone knew that even the modest 1997 Kyoto protocol targets would be nowhere near achieved by the 2012 deadline. The fiasco of the December 2009 Copenhagen Climate Change Conference merely confirmed how pointless these predictions were. Once again, it was clear to see that the official narrative on Greater Paris was somewhat fictitious.

Regardless of its veracity, belief in this narrative was to be upheld. Party leaders aided and abetted this process when the Parti Socialiste was returned to government in 2012, appointing the 'green' Cécile Duflot as Minister for Territorial Equality and Housing, under a 'left-wing' banner. The minister was tasked with guiding the Greater Paris project in the stead of the previous government's Minister for Urban Areas, Maurice Leroy. Yet instead of taking a 'green' angle, Cécile Duflot adopted a 'social' approach, referring to the needs and aspirations of the populace, to the campaign-promised future 'change' of direction for Greater Paris. Without questioning the need for the project, she proposed a reorientation towards a 'vision centred on the expectations of the Franciliens themselves rather than on the competition between metropolises' (Duflot 2012). Thus breaking with the dominant discourse, she confirmed that 'Greater Paris will mean nothing if it is built for its competitors and not for its residents. Greater Paris cannot become Dubai-sur-Seine'. As regards linked-up public transport, she also distanced herself from the 'vision presented by her predecessors, who deemed it sufficient to link the excellence clusters to one another … for a marketing brochure'. For Minister Duflot, the question was one of 'renewing everyday public transport', starting with the overcrowded, ageing and breakdown-prone RER. However, the only person the minister's statements committed was her, in so far as she was a green isolated in a majority socialist government and coming up against the main players in Grand Paris policy, the local, regional, département and municipal elected officials, who were all convinced that priority should be given to economic criteria, who obeyed the dictates of globalization, who were governed by the 'laws of the market'.

In fact, the return of the institutional left to power in spring 2012 did not change the genral direction of the Greater Paris project, despite the stated aim of new Prime Minister Jean-Marc Ayrault to distinguish himself from Nicolas Sarkozy by naming his project 'New Greater Paris' (Ayrault 2013b). In fact, this 'novelty' was purely a matter of terminology. In a well-publicised interview, he had announced in March 2013 his decision to 'grasp the Grand Paris dossier firmly', while also confirming that the priority the previous right-wing government had accorded to developing the rail transport network, with the creation of 72 stations, would remain (Ayrault 2013a). Nor were the arguments employed any more innovative. As Sarkozy had before him, Jean-Marc Ayrault emphasized 'economic performance and competitiveness' in order for 'the Ile de France to reach the summit of global metropolises from an economic and attractiveness point of view', but placed more importance on the 'solidarity' which the project was expected to generate – socialism oblige. Overall, neither the new socialist French president nor the new prime minister has opened up new prospects, except perhaps in terms of housing. Even these have precious little chance of becoming reality due to budgetary restrictions decided in the context of an 'austerity' policy implemented in the months following François Hollande's election to the Élysée Palace. Generally speaking, the realization of the prime minister's promise, made in the interview quoted above, that Greater Paris, this 'considerable project', 'will indeed be completed in 2030', looks set to meet the same fate.

Doubts have been and are being cast on only a few planning choices and the institutional methods for realizing the Greater Paris project, at least by those who have a voice at such assemblies in one capacity or another. Yet these doubters represent a minority of the population that will be affected, in the Ile de France and even further afield. Marginalized by the mechanisms of 'representative democracy', the majority has so far remained silent. This problem may be due to a failure to transcend the economic, technical, planning, scientific and cultural/aesthetic domains to which this debate is usually confined, and within which it is addressed from a political angle.

Whereas the Greater Paris project is political because it is supported by the political (le politique) in the Lefebvrean sense of the word, that is, the state, it seems that it has so far escaped from politics in the materialist sense (la politique) that Lefebvre and Marx would also have employed: class struggle. Indeed, with the exception of rare, isolated and fleeting instances of minority popular resistance to a particular scheme or other, no social force has opposed either the end or the means of the overall Greater Paris project with any consistency. Having for a long time counted on the working class to 'change the city' as well as changing society, in the mid-1970s Lefebvre noted that this was a vain hope: 'There is no getting around the fact that the bourgeoisie still has the initiative in its struggle for (and in) space' (Lefebvre 1991a [1974]: 56). The consensus of approval currently enjoyed by the Greater Paris project, ranging from the 'parties of government' (Parti Socialiste, Parti Communiste Français, Parti de Gauche, Écologie-Les Verts, Union pour un Mouvement Populaire) to the employers and planning professionals, certainly confirms the current accuracy of Lefebvre's dismayed recognition.

From the late 1960s, Henri Lefebvre had envisaged what could occur in the absence of conscious, organized 'political forces which are in fact social forces' which might check the speed of capitalist urbanisation (Lefebvre 1996 [1968]: 163). They are penned into:

> planned suburbs, and other more or less residential ghettos ... These masses who do not deserve the name of people or popular classes, or working class live relatively well. Apart from the fact that their daily life is remote controlled and the permanent threat of unemployment weighs heavily on them, contributing to a latent and generalized terror. (Ibid.: 162)

Lefebvre emphasized that their passivity and silence could only prolong and worsen segregation, and vice versa: 'segregation will continue resulting in a vicious circle. Segregation is inclined to prohibit protest, contest, action by dispersing those who [could] protest, contest and act' (ibid.: 163).

Half a century later, all over France, standards of living for the dominated classes are much worse, and for many people unemployment is no longer a threat but a reality. The spatial dispersion of these classes has grown continually, and the Greater Paris project will merely put the finishing touches to their atomization throughout the agglomeration. Should we therefore subscribe to the pessimistic, disillusioned conclusion that Henri Lefebvre drew? 'If the inhabitants of various categories and strata allow themselves to be manoeuvred and manipulated, displaced anywhere under the pretext of social mobility, if they accept the conditions of an exploitation more refined and extensive than before, too bad for them' (Lefebvre 1996 [1968]: 163).

This conclusion certainly seems a desperate one. However, in contrast to the consensus among left-of-centre intellectuals, it is not always realistic to end a publication or conference on the obligatory optimistic note. Whereas proponents of campus radicalism always end their exposés with a flourish of 'social movements' and 'urban struggle' – without actually participating in practice – we prefer to take stock of the state of play between the relevant forces. The current dearth of mobilization among residents must be noted; active opposition to the Greater Paris project amounts at present to a periodic, loosely structured conjunction of small, scattered collectives. Yet most stakeholders are aware that if there must be an anticapitalist revolution, as unlikely as this might appear in the current political climate, then despite the past claims of Henri Lefebvre and present claims of David Harvey (Harvey 2008) it would not be primarily 'urban'. Nevertheless, perhaps it might be partly urban.

NOTES

1   Bertrand Lemoine, Director General of the Atelier International du Grand Paris: 'Le Grand Paris n'est pas un projet mais une multitude de projets'. Conference at the Institut de France, 24 May 2012.

2   In fact, the area directly affected by the Greater Paris project, the limits of which remain uncertain, extends across only two-thirds of the region, with a population of some 8 million.

3   In the meantime, before the somewhat problematic creation of a new metropolitan state body, a Société du Grand Paris was established by law on 3 June 2010 ('Loi no. 2010-597 du 3 juin 2010 relative au Grand Paris'). As a public institution, it brings together the relevant state (ministries and préfectures) and local authorities (communes, regions and départements).

4   In 1976, the 'District de la Région parisienne', under the administrative authority of a delegate-general appointed by the government, became the 'Région Île-de-France'. The implementation of a law on decentralization turned this region into a 'collectivité locale' (local authority) with representatives elected through universal suffrage. The region's residents were thus renamed 'Franciliens'.

5   The 1965 Master Plan predicted that the population would be 14 million in 1985.

6   'Paris intra-muros' originally denoted the capital's last fortified city walls, and now refers to the central area enclosed by the périphérique ring road.

7   General de Gaulle expressed this intention, in the barrack-room language he liked to use in private, to the newly appointed delegate-general for the Paris Region after a helicopter flight over the capital.

8   Several territorial reform bills have been debated that would restructure the institutional framework for the Paris metropolis, but the question of who governs Greater Paris has been subject to several challenges, to which there has as yet been no response. In contrast to other metropolitan areas in France such as Greater Lyons, or abroad such as Greater London, France's main metropolis still has no joint government structure.

9   The French terms he used all begin with 'A': *ambition, architecture, avenir, aménagement*.

10   Since the end of 2012, the official level of unemployment among people of working age in France has risen to over 10 per cent.

REFERENCES

Ayrault, J.-M. 2013a. Interview. *Le Parisien* 6 March: 1–2.

Ayrault, J.-M. 2013b. Speech at the Université de Marne-la-Vallée, *Le Monde* 7 March: 1 and 4.

Batiactu 2012. 'Les "gares sensuelles" de Jacques Ferrier sont sur les rails'. Available at http://www.batiactu.com/edito/les-gares-sensuelles-du-grand-paris-signees-ja-32482.php (accessed 26 June 2012).

Contassot, Y. and Monod, C. 2012. 'Pour une démocratie efficace et écologique: la Métropole du Grand Paris'. *Métropolitiques*. Available at: http://www.metropolitiques.eu (accessed 17 February 2012).

Duflot, C 2012. Speech at the Maison de l'Architecture de l'Île-de-France, 26 June. Available at: http://www.territoires.gouv.fr (accessed 26 June 2012).

Duthilleul, J.-M. 2012. Interview with François de Mazières, Head of the Cité de l'Architecture and Jean-Marie Duthilleul, exhibition organizer. *Le Journal du Dimanche*, 1 April, 3.

Garnier, J.-P. 1997. *Des barbares dans la Cité: De la tyrannie du marché à la violence urbaine.* Paris: Flammarion.

Garnier, J.-P. and Golschmidt, D. 1977a. *La comédie urbaine: Ou, La Cité sans classes.* Paris: Maspero.

Garnier, J.-P. and Golschmidt, D. 1977b. *Le socialisme à visage urbain: Essai sur la local-démocratie.* Paris: Editions Rupture.

Harvey, D. 2008. 'The Right to the City', *New Left Review* 53, September–October.

IAURP 1965. *Schéma directeur de la région parisienne, Rapport de présentation.* Paris: La Documentation française.

Lefebvre, H. 1969. 'La crise de l'urbanisme contemporain', in *L'homme et la ville dans le monde actuel*. Paris: Desclées de Brower, 23–37.

Lefebvre, H. 1970. 'Réflexion sur la politique de l'espace'. *Espaces et Sociétés* 1, November.

Lefebvre, H. 1974. *De l'État*. Tome IV, Paris: 10/18 UBE.

Lefebvre, H. 1976 [1973]. *The Survival of Capitalism. Reproduction of the Relations of Production*. London: Allison and Busby.

Lefebvre, H. 1981. *Critique de la vie quotidienne, III. De la modernité au modernisme (Pour une métaphilosophie du quotidien)*. Paris: L'Arche.

Lefebvre, H. 1991a [1974]. *The Production of Space*. London: Blackwell.

Lefebvre, H. 1991b. 'Les illusions de la modernité', *Le Monde diplomatique – Manière de voir* 13: 14–16.

Lefebvre, H. 1996 [1968]. 'The Right to the City', in *Writings on Cities* by H. Lefebvre, edited by E. Kofman and E. Lebas. Oxford: Blackwell, 63–182.

Leroy, M. 2011a. Speech at the seminar 'The Greater Paris project: financial and real estate opportunities', London, 12 July. Ministère de la ville.

Leroy, M. 2011b. Speech by Maurice Leroy, Minister for Urban Areas, 29 November, www.ville.gouv.fr.

Mansat, P. 2012. *Paris métropole fédérée*. Blog by Pierre Mansat. Available at www.pierremansat.com (accessed 12 May 2012).

Sarkozy, N. 2007. Speech on 17 September 2007 at the inauguration of the Cité de l'architecture et du patrimoine. *Le Monde* 18 November: 1–5.

Sarkozy, N. 2009. Speech on 29 April 2009 at the Cité de l'architecture et du patrimoine, at the exhibition 'Le Grand Paris de l'agglomération parisienne à la Cité'. *Le Monde* 30 April: 1–4.

Sarkozy, N. 2010. Speech on 29 November 2010 at the Cité de l'architecture et du patrimoine. *Le Monde* 30 November: 4.

SDAURP 1965. *Présentation du Schéma directeur de la Région Parisienne de 1965*. Available at http://www.driea.ile-de-France.developpement-durable.gouv.fr/presentation (accessed 3 July 2006).

SGP 2010. *Le Grand Paris : une compétition impitoyable*. Available at: http://www.mon-grandparis.fr/presentation-de-la-sgp-la-societe-du-grand-paris (accessed 7 December 2010).

Sassen, S. 1996. *La ville globale*. Paris: Descartes & Compagnie.

7

The Production of Urban Competitiveness: Modelling 22@Barcelona

Greig Charnock and Ramon Ribera-Fumaz

Over 20 years have passed since Richard Florida and Martin Kenney announced that 'capitalism is undergoing an epochal transformation from a mass production system where the principal source of value was human labour to a new era of "innovation-mediated production" where the principal component of value creation, productivity and economic growth is knowledge' (1991: 637).[1] For many, this argument retains its validity today, evidenced by the proliferation of 'knowledge economies' throughout the world. Such economies are said to be 'characterised by the de-materialisation of production, a shift away from dealing with raw materials and machines towards dealing with other minds … The term knowledge economies is also intended to capture a sense of accelerating technological change and, related to this, the need for continuous innovation' (Bryson et al. 2000: 2–3). In this 'new epoch', cities and city-regions are deemed crucial (Simmie 2001; Rodríguez-Pose 2008). Eminent economists, such as Paul Krugman and Michael Porter, have today popularized an 'urban hypothesis' (Drejer and Vinding 2005) that highlights the importance of industrial location and agglomeration for trade, and clustering of industries to foster innovation and competiveness, with obvious corollaries for urbanism. Others see cities as ideal centres of the kinds of 'creative industries' that constitute the new economy (Aage and Belussi 2008), as well as poles of attraction for the 'creative class' (Florida 2005). This is significant since 'the driving force behind the development of a city turns out to be its ability to attract and retain creative individuals' (Lazzeretti et al. 2008: 551), widely referred to in the knowledge economy literatures as 'talent' (see Karlsson et al. 2009). Generally, such literatures support the OECD's (2007) conclusion that 'competitive cities' have become 'a new entrepreneurial paradigm in spatial development'.

In this chapter, we examine '22@Barcelona', a project of urban transformation that appears to epitomize this 'new entrepreneurial paradigm' and which has been internationally branded in terms of creating 'a new space for knowledge and people'. Drawing on Lefebvre's theory and in particular on his critique of representations of space, we present a critical analysis of contemporary strategies to engineer urban competitiveness. We argue that the functionalist and reductive representations of 22@Barcelona betray an ideological concern with the globally competitive abstract space, the reduction of difference and the closing of the circuit of everyday life.

FROM (RE-)PRODUCTION TO REPRESENTATION: ABSTRACT SPACE AND THE CRITIQUE OF EVERYDAY LIFE

The idea that the sphere of everyday life can explain the survival of capitalism into the late twentieth century – as well as illuminate the role of formal logic, modelling and social planning as ideology – leads Lefebvre (1976 [1973]: 21, original emphasis) to the now well-known thesis that 'capitalism has found itself able to attenuate (if not resolve) its internal contradictions for a century … *by occupying space, by producing a space'.* Lefebvre reveals that capitalism produces its own (urban) space and, in so doing, creates the permissive conditions for the reproduction of the totality of bourgeois society (an argument that knowingly implicated the former communist bloc as much as the West — see Brenner 2008). Time, understood in the abstract as concerning work, the production of commodities and of surplus value, has been 'reduced to constraints of space' (Lefebvre 2009: 187) – circumscribed and suppressed within the *urban form.* The process of mediation that re-produces the social relations of production in a contradictory form, according to Lefebvre, is therefore that of urbanization – the production of (urban) space (Lefebvre 1976, 2003 [1970]).

Lefebvre's critique of everyday life places emphasis upon the extent to which, by the 1970s, time had become dominated by space, the growth of the forces of production by the development of the social relations of production, and in the urban form. The relativization and simultaneity of everything particular in space had, after the Second World War, become the means by which capital reproduces itself. In short, capital does indeed strive to create a world in its own image, as Marx and Engels observed in *The Communist Manifesto* (2004 [1848]). But, Lefebvre suggests, this entails more than the simple 'annihilation of space by time' or the melting of 'all that is solid into air'; rather, the reproduction of capitalism occurs by means of the totalizing drive to concretize an *abstract space* (Lefebvre 1991 [1974]: ch. 4; Stanek 2008: 76), which is 'abstract inasmuch as it has no existence save by virtue of the exchangeability of all its component parts, and concrete inasmuch as it is socially real and as such localised' (Lefebvre 1991 [1974]: 341–2). In other words, Lefebvre explains how the production of this space is at the same time a process of the reproduction of alienated social relations. The human subjects that go about their individual everyday lives locked into a seemingly self-regulating circuit of production–consumption–production socially constitute such a space.

Lefebvre is adamant that this process also provides clues as to the possibility of a dis-alienated totality that already exists in the mode of being denied. Analytically, this poses the question of form *and* content. The key here is to recognize that 'urban space-time, as soon as we stop defining it in terms of industrial rationality – its project of homogenisation – appears as *differential'* (Lefebvre 2003: 37). That is, 'abstract space *is not* homogenous; it simply *has* homogeneity as its goal, its orientation, its "lens"' (Lefebvre 1991: 287). For Lefebvre, the identification of the potentially revolutionary content of the analysis of the production of space and critique of everyday life follows from the insight that the production of space can only proceed via a relational process of homogenization/differentiation (Lefebvre 1991: 308 and 342; Stanek 2008: 71–2). Urbanization brings human subjects together in space in such a way that is necessary for the reproduction of the social relations of production, but which also exacerbates the contradictions of this abstract space – for example, it creates centres in which 'once groups and classes succeed in meeting face to face, once they come to grips, a free dialogue explodes under the dialectical impetus' (Lefebvre 2000 [1971]: 185). Homogenizing abstract space is therefore constituted by social relations that simultaneously constitute a 'differential space', which 'is different because it celebrates particularity – both bodily and experiential' (Merrifield 2000: 176). So, while Lefebvre explains the necessity of urbanization from the point of view of capital, he also identifies 'the existence of *irreducibles*, contradictions and objections that intervene and hinder the closing of the circuit [of everyday life], that split the structure' (Lefebvre 2000: 75, original emphasis). And it is this insight that holds the key to understanding the limits to the production of abstract space in an urban form. Everyday life is, according to Lefebvre, the sphere in which such irreducibles are to be found. It is 'the sociological point of feedback' (Lefebvre 2000: 32); 'the ill-defined, cutting edge where the accumulative and the non-accumulative intersect' (Lefebvre 2008a [1961]: 335); and 'the point of delicate balance and that where imbalance threatens' (Lefebvre 2000: 32). And, critically, it is the sphere that holds the key to revolutionary action: 'a revolution takes place when and only when, in such a society, people can no longer lead their everyday lives' (ibid.).

For Lefebvre, a defining characteristic of the developed capitalist mode of production is that knowledge itself becomes a productive force (Lefebvre 1991: 44). Indeed, those who wield it are able to mould society and space instrumentally – it becomes 'a serviceable (operational) tool for the analysis of spaces, and of those societies which have given rise to them and recognised themselves in them' (ibid.: 45). Lefebvre defines such knowledge under the category '*representation*'. Such knowledge, after all, is ideological for as long as it is rooted in formal logic and the will to abstract from concrete, lived experience (*le vécu*). 'Knowledge falls into a trap when it makes representations of space the basis for the study of "life", for in doing so it reduces lived experience' (ibid.: 230). Formal logic is characterized by the principles of identity, equivalence, recurrence and repetition. Lefebvre's dialectical logic, on the other hand, reveals the limits to formal logic at the level of abstraction, but also at the level of serviceable representations that have a 'real' effect. For Lefebvre (1991: 289), '*there is a violence intrinsic to abstraction*, and to abstraction's practical (social) use'. '*A pure (formal) space defines the world of terror* ... this aspiration to a pure abstraction imposing its laws and its structures is part of the power of forms, it endows them with the power to terrorise' (Lefebvre 2000: 179, original emphasis).

Lefebvre is highly critical of the intellectual division of labour characteristic of the modern university system, as well as of the social role of 'techniques, technicians, technocrats, epistemology, and the research of a purely technical or epistemological order' (Lefebvre 2009: 175) that serve to dissect the total movement of human social praxis, compartmentalize various spheres or activities of everyday life (paradigmatically, in the circuit production–consumption–production), and mould concrete space according to the logic of pure form, recurrence and coherence. To deny difference is to be dogmatic, and to aim to reduce differences and close the circuit of everyday life is to be implicated in the generalized terrorism of the bourgeoisie (Lefebvre 2000: ch. 4). Lefebvre therefore rails against 'models' – abstract but serviceable representations of a projected, planned space in which some kinds of spatial practice are condoned and others dismissed as pathological. He writes 'the physician of modern society sees himself as the physician of a sick social space ... The cure? It is *coherence* ... he will systematise the *logic of the habitat* underlying the disorder and apparent incoherence' (Lefebvre 1996 [1968]: 82–3). There is violence intrinsic to such abstraction: 'the "plan" ... does not remain innocently on paper. On the ground, the bulldozer realizes "plans"' (Lefebvre, cited in Wilson 2010: 136). In terms of political action, then, Lefebvre is certain that 'to clear a path, we have to destroy the models' (Lefebvre 2003: 163).

Lefebvre (2009: 246) considers the logicians and modellers of space to be 'agents of the state' precisely because they persist despite the fact that the production of space is a contradictory process in which difference cannot be wholly reduced. 'Abstract space (or those for whom it is a tool) makes the relationship between repetition and difference a more antagonistic one ... It reduces differences to induced differences: that is, to differences internally acceptable to a set of "systems" which are planned as such, prefabricated as such' (Lefebvre 1991: 396). Chief responsibility for suppressing the realization of a dis-alienated urban society through the concretization of abstract space lies in the modern state ('the quintessential limiter' – Lefebvre 2003: 163). The state has, for Lefebvre, assumed ever-increasing responsibility for circumscribing and cohering the process of urbanization and sustaining the alienation inherent in everyday life (Lefebvre 2008b [1981]: 124–5). The social role of instrumental representations of space is therefore political at the same time. Its practitioners:

> conceive and construct dominant spaces ruling over dominated spaces ...
> They subject space to a logistics, believing thereby that they can ether suppress
> conflicts and contradictions, or at least understand them in order to combat
> them. Against this, however, the intrinsic connection between logic and violence
> suggests that these agents in fact revive conflicts and aggravate contradictions.
> (Lefebvre 2009: 46)

For Lefebvre (2009: 174), then, 'there is a politics of space because space is political'. So, to conclude this theoretical discussion, we see that Lefebvre's general critique of the process of urbanization carries along with it a politically focused critique of reductive forms of knowledge, and of instrumental representations of space. And it is not unreasonable to suggest that little has changed since Lefebvre wrote that:

> today the state and its bureaucratic and political apparatuses intervene
> continually in space, and make use of space in its instrumental aspect in order
> to intervene at all levels and through every agency of the economic realm.

> *Consequently, social practice and political practice tend to join forces in spatial practice, so achieving a certain cohesiveness if not a logical coherence. (Lefebvre 1991: 378)*

With this in mind, our discussion now turns to consider the 22@ project in the Poblenou district of Barcelona.

MODELLING 22@BARCELONA

> *Nowhere in Barcelona symbolises the way in which the city has evolved towards becoming an information society as the 22@ District in Poblenou. (Ajuntament de Barcelona 2007: 11)*

In Barcelona, the primary laboratory for the production of a planned, globally competitive space is the district of Poblenou ('new town' in Catalan), the former industrial manufacturing heartland of the city, located on the coast to the south of the river Besós delta. From the mid-nineteenth century, a vibrant and successful textile sector developed there, earning it the moniker 'the Catalan Manchester'. Since then, a historical process of largely unplanned industrialization has produced a relatively haphazard layout that has long distinguished it from the main city, and in particular the gridiron-like Eixample district it borders. Since 2000, the city has designated Poblenou a new 'knowledge district' and rebranded it '22@Barcelona'. Oriol Clos, former Director of Urbanism at 22@bcn, SA, and also the former city council's chief architect, explains that:

> *the 22@ Plan establishes the criteria and terms for the conversion of the old industrial areas into a sector suited to the new forms of productive activity, based on information and knowledge technology, and on a new balance of urban, residential, productive and service functions, in which all are integrated into a hybrid fabric, constructed around the historical morphology of the sector. (Clos 2004: 193–4)*

In other words, and notwithstanding the constraints set by the pattern of urbanization in Poblenou, the district will be transformed in accordance with the conceived goals of engineering urban competitiveness and 'quality of life' for its inhabitants – into 'a new space for knowledge and people'. Furthermore, it is clear that the logic servicing the transformation of this specific space is at once local *and* global.

This championing of the 22@ Plan by the city council reflects the concerted effort made since 2000 to transform Poblenou into 'a new model for a *compact city*, where companies on the cutting-edge of innovation co-exist with universities, research, training and technology-transfer centres, as well as homes, infrastructures and green areas' (Ajuntament de Barcelona 2008: 2, original emphasis). The project is on a considerable scale, covering 198.26 hectares, and leading to the estimated transformation of 1,159,626 m^2 of existing industrial land and the potential creation of around 3,200,000 m^2 of new construction. It will involve the legal recognition of 4,614 existing homes and the construction of around 4,000 new subsidized units; 114,000 m^2 of green area land; and a total investment in infrastructure of around €180 million – making it the largest project of its kind in Europe (see Charnock and Ribera-Fumaz 2011). The project is being marketed in terms of large-scale urban redevelopment, with a strong emphasis on fostering both economic growth and social cohesion. On the one hand, the area is being remodelled to facilitate innovation and enhanced competitiveness in the global economy, and primarily through the promotion of 'clusters' (in the specific areas of media, information and communication technologies, medical technologies, and energy and design), the establishment of technology and R&D centres in collaboration with the main Catalan universities, and the implementation of a 'new special infrastructure plan' oriented to meet sustainable development goals but also to enhance digital telecommunications provision throughout the district. On the other hand, the district is said to be designed to promote the quality of work and life in the district, this being defined in terms of aiding entrepreneurs and supporting vocational training and labour market entry,[2] promoting knowledge-based learning in schools, making information and communication technologies (ICT) more accessible to the elderly, and making the most of the district's proximity to the city's famed beaches and entertainment centres so as to attract and retain that all-important 'talent'.

Our purpose here is to ask whether those terms are themselves representative of 22@ as abstract, produced space, and constitutive of the very process Lefebvre saw as being the means by which capitalism secures its 'survival'. For expositional reasons, we divide the analysis of the representations of 22@Barcelona into their two principal 'logics': the first is broadly urbanist, the second sociological.

The Compact City: Competitiveness and Formalism

Lefebvre was damning of planners who saw the city as a 'sick social space' (Lefebvre 1996 [1968]: 82–3). In 22@Barcelona presentations, Poblenou is 'diagnosed' in terms of post-industrial 'obsolescence and decay' and represented in photographs of derelict industrial premises (Ajuntament de Barcelona 2009). Elsewhere, the former Director of Urbanism on the project describes the morphology of Poblenou as being characterized by 'the coexistence of industrial, residential and service sector buildings, of greatly varying size, importance and styles, in very close proximity with what are, at times, brutal discontinuities and breaks. *A highly irregular fabric is formed, with little homogeneity*' (Clos 2004: 192, emphasis added). Yet, fortuitously, the existing morphology of Barcelona is deemed to hold the key to its own rescue. The key to this is its 'compactness' (*compacitat*), which, as Joan Busquets – former head of urban planning for the city and now Harvard professor – explains (2005: 15), makes Barcelona the 'prototype of a Mediterranean European city with a long urban tradition', characterized by 'the density and compactness of [its] urban form'. The 'compact city' – an aspirational form for urbanists involved in the transformation of cities the world over – is already in existence in Barcelona, as a product of evolution or an almost 'natural' or 'ecological' outcome common to many Mediterranean cities. And, it would appear that compactness provides a solid spatial basis for global competiveness. According to *La Ciutat Digital* (Pacte Industrial de la Regió Metropolitano de Barcelona 2001: 189), 'its formal continuity, multifunctionality, heterogeneity and diversity are the basis for a social life with cohesion and quality of life, while it is also the platform for a competitive economy'. This is congruent with the received wisdom on compact cities, which holds that:

> talent is attracted to sociable communities – places with destinations, public
> and civic spaces, environmental amenities – where they can come together
> with colleagues and friends, either through planned or chance encounters
> ... [T]he new economy demands physical infrastructure that reduces the
> cost of business. This means buildings that can be quickly reconfigured and
> constructed, housing of varying types and costs, development patterns that
> are predictable, and transportation systems which increase mobility. (Smart
> Growth online)[3]

Through a process of intensification of compactness, Poblenou is to be transformed into the competitiveness-oriented palimpsest 22@. The city council envisaged an increase of build ability from 2 m^2 of ceiling/m^2 of land under code 22a regulations to a possible 2.7 m^2 under code 22@ (Ajuntament de Barcelona 2009). In this high-density planning, mixed uses are promoted both vertically (with individual buildings housing city institutions, universities and business, such as the MEDIA-TIC building, or the expansion of loft construction) and horizontally (newly planned plots, again for mixed use). But, more importantly, this physical intensification will also supposedly intensify the competitiveness of the district: first, as a place of economic innovation and transformation; and, second, as a place of a vibrant popular culture based on the civic cultural tradition of Poblenou, and further strengthened by the 'bohemian' milieu of various artists' studios, small creative companies and communities that have been resident in the district since the 1980s.

From a Lefebvrean conceptual point of departure, the compact city is but another exercise in 'modelling' – conceiving a serviceable, reductive representation of the urban in accordance with the logic of pure form. As Neumann writes, with particular focus upon the 'sustainability' aspect of the model but with a more general critical point in mind:

> Like those a century ago, today's new urbanist and compact city architects
> prepare a design for a place to be built according to a plan. It is not evolutionary
> ... Form, as biologists and geologists understand it, is an outcome of evolution.
> Form is a snapshot of process ... Form, in and of itself, is not measurable in terms
> of sustainability. (Neumann 2005: 22–3)

Yet the 22@ project is being driven by an overriding concern with *compacitat*, and the allure of an urban form that, as one city council publication puts it, is synonymous with 'cohesion, consistency, solidity, unanimity, union and agreement' (Guidoni 2007: 134) – characteristics Lefebvre held to be representative of formal logic itself. In this context, 22@Barcelona, as Gdaniec (2000: 381, original emphases) notes, is hardly an outcome of evolutionary social praxis, as city planners claim: 'in terms of the city's aims and projects, the district Poblenou *is* relevant in its local, physical form, but only insofar as it provides *space*, potential, and some historic/ cultural features (such as factory chimneys – some of which are left as quasi "public art" or décor)'. It is perhaps telling that the 22@ clusters are often depicted in 22@ Barcelona presentations as jigsaw-piece-shaped 'spaces of transformation' – at first discrete pieces digitally superimposed on to an aerial photograph of Poblenou to show the actual clusters' locations, and which are then pieced together through animation to make a seamless whole. That such envisioned compactness lends itself to the intensified production of a space conducive to global competiveness in the 'new economy' is a boost to the planners' formal-logical appeal to representations of coherent, homogeneous space.

A New Space for Knowledge and People': Closing the Circuit of Everyday Life

Our second criticism concerns the 'sociological' representation of 22@. As was explained in the first section of this chapter, Lefebvre argued that reproduction was both a spatial and a temporally determined process; however, the survival of capitalism depended upon the modern state's insidious capacities, through planning and architectural practice for example, to organize space in such a way as to assert the dominance of a particular experience of time – accumulative – over another – non-accumulative (Lefebvre 2008a: 334–7). Knowledge about abstract space, and the power to control that it engenders, makes the necessary closing of the circuit of production–consumption–production plausible, at least from the point of view of capital.

Lefebvre writes that, while in 'the street … consumption gleams in all its hallowed splendour', 'far away, in the factories … [and] on the working class estates, everything is functional, everything is a signal – the repetitive gestures by which the labour force keeps on going in its everyday life' (Lefebvre 2008a: 312). Of course, for Lefebvre it was this spatio-temporal disarticulation that made everyday life in this 'bureaucratic society of controlled consumption' (2000: ch. 2) a domain of alienation but also a depository for the sources of possible dis-alienated human praxis. But in 22@ – the 'new space for knowledge and people' – such disarticulation could, it appears, be overcome. The envisaged morphology of this form is one in which workers no longer have to be segregated in an immediate manner. There is no significant commute to speak of; rather the space is compact and characterized by mixed use (coincidentally, making it 'environmentally sustainable' to boot). It is a spatial form in which consumption itself is elevated and reintegrated into the process of production, albeit in an ideologically obfuscated form. Workers' own consumption patterns are those that enhance their attributes as a particular form of human capital – 'knowledge workers' – or as entrepreneurs. They work flexible hours, socialize and meet frequently with others in this innovative milieu, but not necessarily in 'the office', and invest in their own training and familiarity with the latest instruments of production. Their spatial practice is conducive to the overall competitiveness of that space, as opposed to others. They no longer see themselves as 'workers'. Here, the social relations pertaining to the commodity form are 'obsolete'. They are 'talent', whether 'home-grown' or attracted from all over the world, and deserve to inhabit this space by virtue of being so.

In return for taking their talent to Barcelona, these people get to live and work in a city the European Cities Monitor has consistently ranked first for providing the 'best quality of life' for employees in Europe (Cushman & Wakefield Inc. 2009). Whether working at home or in the office, the talented are a stone's throw away from one of Europe's most iconic beaches and sea-front developments. If they wish to go further afield to 'network' and consume, huge resources are being invested in European and international transport connectivity. They live in a city revered internationally for its culture, its architecture, its food, its football team and so on. This new space takes advantage of such attributes; as the 22@Barcelona Chief Executive, Josep Miquel Piqué, has said, 'knowledge infrastructure is not just fibre and telecoms. You also need things like good food, wine, and aesthetics, so cities can become neuro-centres of the knowledge economy' (in Engardio 2009). In going about their everyday lives, in which the traditional division between production and consumption is blurred, the talent of 22@Barcelona will make this space a fully functional 'neuro-centre'. In this 'space for knowledge and people', the circuit of everyday life will be closed.

THE CONTRADICTIONS OF SPACE

Judged on its own terms, the 22@ project has enjoyed some success. According to the City Council, by 2011, 70 per cent of the area had been transformed, 4,500 companies and institutions had been established and the number of new jobs in 22@ since 2000 was estimated at 56,000 (Ajuntament de Barcelona 2012). However, a city-council-commissioned study by London's Imperial College Business School found that the project faced significant challenges: inadequately educated human capital within the district; a very low incipient level of local entrepreneurship; scarce venture-capital resources; a lack of large firm presence (with most preferring to locate in Madrid); and an inferior level of 'global connectivity' with business communities in cities in Europe and, surprisingly, Latin America (Leon 2008: 239). It concluded that, while 'Barcelona's attraction for the creative classes is evident from many different market research studies', the:

> jobs that have been created under the attraction policy tend to be in the
> construction sectors and retail and leisure services, not the knowledge economy.
> The driver for this is paradoxically the desire of a well-educated, mobile
> international community for high quality housing and services to support the
> lifestyles that attracted them to the city in the first place. (Leon 2008: 245)

The 22@ district became the new hub for office space in the city at the height of the last Spanish real-estate boom (*El Periódico* 2005; Charnock et al. 2014a: ch. 4). However, it is clear that the district has not become the space for knowledge-based entrepreneurial enterprise that the City Council envisaged. Occupancy rates of newly constructed real estate have increased, but the new tenants have tended to be local, medium to large service firms relocating in search of cheaper rents and well-equipped buildings.[4] And nor has the district lived up to the planners' notion of a space characterized by mixed-use activities. Clear zoning between businesses, commercial premises, housing and public services has achieved the greater density associated with the notion of compactness, but has created isolated islands of business parks surrounded by disintegrated residential and commercial areas.

The economic crisis that has dramatically affected Spain since 2008 also revealed significant problems in the 22@ district. In 2005, the district represented around 70 per cent of all office real-estate investment in the city. By 2011, however, a precipitous fall in demand meant that vacancy rates doubled to 14.2 per cent from 2009 (Charnock et al. 2014b). In this scenario, and with a change of leadership in the City Council in May 2011, the city's development strategy for 22@ shifted from attracting entrepreneurial talent and knowledge workers towards courting investors with projects such as the Smart City Campus at 22@, in partnership with such firms as Telefónica, Abertis, Cisco, Schneider Electric and Agbar (Suez).

Meanwhile, in a district with a history of active neighbourhood associations and a strong industrial working-class heritage, residents have been challenging the City Council over the implementation of the 22@ plan.[5] Clua and Albet (2008) have documented the early emergence of the 'Associació d'afectats del 22@', an affected residents' organization, and the 'Coordinadora contra el 22@' youth organization, whose anti-capitalist graffiti daubed Poblenou's walls. They also explain how a nineteenth-century textile factory, Can Ricart, has proved to be a focal point in resistance to the 22@ project. The civic platform 'Salvem Can Ricart' succeeded in halting plans to redevelop the complex, which has for some time been home to many artisanal workshops and artists' studios. Many of these have since been evicted in any case. In late 2006, Can Ricart became the focus of further controversy when La Makabra, a group of squatters, occupied the complex in protest at evictions here and elsewhere in Poblenou and openly challenged the City Council's new Strategic Plan for Culture (Swartz 2008). Under pressure from Poblenou's residents, the City Council declared Can Ricart a 'Cultural Asset of National Interest' in 2008, and agreed to a regeneration plan taking into account the demands of the local community. Five years later, however, the project had stalled, and some of the flagship projects, such as the installation of Linguamon (a UNESCO-sponsored institution to preserve and diffuse languages across the world) in Can Ricart have been terminated due to a lack of funding (*El Periódico* 2013).

But perhaps the clearest sign of the failure to create a new space for knowledge and people concerns the district's newest residents. Ironically, the district has succeeded in attracting a new class of creative and talented young people – albeit not quite the people the planners had in mind. They are mostly *sans papiers* from Sub-Saharan Africa and recent immigrants from Romania. In the immediate vicinity of the new office towers and flagship developments, such as Jean Nouvel's Poblenou Central Park, the *sans papiers* inhabit abandoned warehouses and new developments left half-constructed in the fallout from the crisis. They were attracted to the district before the crisis, making a living dealing with the abandoned waste generated in the tearing down of old factories and warehouses and the construction of new office buildings. Today, they have become an everyday, familiar sight in the 22@ district, scouring building sites and refuse containers with supermarket shopping trolleys, looking for scrap to sell.

According to the City Council, by 2013 there were over 700 people living in 63 squatted settlements in the city, many of them in Poblenou. In 2012 and 2013, several warehouse owners attempted to evict squatter settlements with the help of the City Council – with mixed success. Together, squatters, local residents and social movements have physically prevented police from executing evictions, and have also carried out public demonstrations so as to make visible the 'terrorism' imposed by the crisis and the 22@ project on the district's most vulnerable inhabitants. Probably the most emblematic recent example of such struggle concerned a squatted factory – Puigcerdà 127 – just a few blocks away from the Jean-Nouvel-designed park and Can Ricart. At one point just a few years ago, the factory was home to some 300 *sans papiers*, living without running water or electricity. During the summer of 2013, around 120 of them remained in the building, with hundreds more passing through every day (*ElDiario.es* 2013a). They had resisted evictions on many occasions, with the support of the neighbourhood association of Poblenou and other urban social movements. But on 23 July 2013, the police forcefully evicted all remaining squatters from the warehouse. Although the City Council has committed to 'normalizing' the immigrants and to providing shelter, at the time of writing most of them were still awaiting a resolution to their predicament (*ElDiario.es* 2013b).

The irony of this situation is twofold. First, this warehouse is set in one of the two spots in Barcelona where the City Council envisions constructing a super-block based upon the principles of incentivizing local production, energy self-sufficiency and the efficient management of resources. And second, the very developer that owns the warehouse and went to court to evict the *sans papiers* also has a charity that helps women deemed to be at risk of social exclusion – a risk faced every day by the recently evicted residents of Puigcerdà 127.

CONCLUSIONS

This chapter has examined 22@Barcelona, a concrete project conceived with the aim of engineering urban competiveness in the so-called 'new economy'. In this, Henri Lefebvre's writings on abstract space and the critique of everyday life have been a useful resource for critically analysing the project's underlying logic and the manner of its execution – but also its limits and contradictions. We have argued that the functionalist and reductive representations of 22@Barcelona betray an ideological concern with the concretization of globally competitive abstract space, the reduction of differences, and the closing of the circuit of everyday life in Poblenou. For us, being able to use Lefebvre's work as a point of departure in subjecting to critique such a cutting-edge and large-scale project illustrates the enduring critical potency of Lefebvre's work beyond the specificities of 'the bureaucratic society of controlled consumption' which he critically analysed in the 1960s and 1970s (Lefebvre 2000).

NOTES

1   This is an abridged and updated version of Charnock and Ribera-Fumaz (2011). The authors acknowledge the support received by the Spanish Ministry of Innovation and Science in carrying out the research informing this chapter (grant reference CSO2010-16966).

2   Barcelona Activa, the city's local development agency, is now located in Poblenou and is the key component of the city's competitiveness strategy, promoting entrepreneurialism and business creation, incubation facilities, job-seeking facilities tailored to knowledge economy human capital needs, and knowledge-based vocational training (see OECD 2009). A recent initiative was 'Do it in Barcelona', a strategy to attract global entrepreneurs and foreign 'talent' to the city (see http://www.doitinbcn.com/portal/web/do-it-in-barcelona).

3   Source: 'Smart Growth Issues: Economics', http://www.smartgrowth.org/about/issues/issues.asp?iss=3), accessed 1 October 2009. It is, of course, also advantageous for Barcelona's urbanists to appeal to a compact city model which, according to Scheurer (2007: 13), 'resonates with the sustainability agenda, promotes a culturally appealing, innovative and dynamic urban milieu, takes active measures against socio-spatial segregation and reinvigorates local self-governance'.

4   The most recently available data, from 2006, reveal that office relocations from other parts of the city represented 75 per cent of total newcomers to the district (*El País* 2006a). By 2006, new 'knowledge-intensive' and ICT companies represented only one-third of new businesses relocated in 22@ (*El País* 2006b). In 2008, the City Council received 40 requests from small companies for office space of less than 250 m². All were unable to locate there as developers argued that the cost of transforming large floors for start-ups was too expensive (*Cinco Días* 2008).

5   For an account of how heritage and alternative arts and social centers were driven from Poblenou see Martí-Costa and Pradel i Miquel (2012).

REFERENCES

Aage, T. and Belussi, F. 2008. 'From Fashion to Design: Creative Networks in Industrial Districts'. *Industry and Innovation* 15(5): 475–91.

Ajuntament de Barcelona 2007. *The Innovation Route in Barcelona*. Barcelona: Ajuntament de Barcelona.

Ajuntament de Barcelona 2008. *22@Barcelona: The Innovation District*. Barcelona: Ajuntament de Barcelona

Ajuntament de Barcelona 2009. *Presentation: 22@Barcelona*, http://www.22barcelona.com/documentacio/22barcelona_2009_eng.pdf (accessed: 31 August 2014).

Ajuntament de Barcelona 2012. *Current State of 22@*. http://www.22barcelona.com/content/blogcategory/38/157/lang.en/ (accessed: 27 February 2013).

Brenner, N. 2008 'Henri Lefebvre's Critique of State Productivism', in *Space, Difference, Everyday Life: Reading Henri Lefebvre*, edited by K. Goonewardena, S. Kipfer, R. Milgrom, C. Schmid. London: Routledge, 231–49.

Bryson, J.R., Daniels, P.W., Henry, N. and Pollard, J. 2000. 'Introduction', in *Knowledge–Space–Economy*, edited by J. R. Bryson et al. London: Routledge, London, 1–12.

Busquets, J. 2005. *Barcelona, the Urban Evolution of a Compact City*. Boston: Nicolodi, Roverento and Harvard University Graduate School of Design.

Charnock, G., Purcell, T. and Ribera-Fumaz, R. 2014a. *The Limits to Capital in Spain: Crisis and Revolt in the European South*. Basingstoke: Palgrave Macmillan.

Charnock, G., Purcell, T. and Ribera-Fumaz, R. 2014b. 'City of Rents: The Limits to the "Barcelona Model" of Urban Competitiveness'. *International Journal of Urban and Regional Research* 38(1): 198-217.

Charnock, G. and Ribera-Fumaz, R. 2011. '"A New Space for Knowledge and People?" Henri Lefebvre, Representations of Space, and the Production of 22@barcelona'. *Environment and Planning D* 29(4): 613–32.

Cinco Días 2008. 'Edificios grandes, oficinas pequeñas' (Large buildings, small offices). 20 November.

Clos, O. 2004. 'The Transformation of Poblenou: the New 22@ District', in *Transforming Barcelona*, edited by T. Marshall. London: Routledge, 191–202.

Clua, A. and Albet, A. 2008. '22@bcn Plan: Bringing Barcelona Forward in the Information Era', in *Knowledge-Based Urban Development: Planning and Applications in the Information Era*, edited by T. Yigitcanlar, K. Velibeyoglu and S. Baum. Hershey: Information Science Reference, 132–47.

Cushman & Wakefield Inc. 2009. *European Cities Monitor 2009*. Available at: http://www.europeancitiesmonitor.eu/wp-content/uploads/2009/10/ECM_2009_Final.pdf (accessed: 30 January 2010).

Delgado, M. 2007. *La Ciudad Mentirosa: Fraude y Miseria del 'Modelo Barcelona'*. Madrid: Libros de la Catarata.

Drejer, I. and Vinding, A. L. 2005. 'Location and Collaboration: Manufacturing Firms' Use of Knowledge Intensive Services in Product Innovation'. *European Planning Studies* 13(6): 879–98.

Elden, S. 2008. '*Mondialisation* Before Globalisation: Lefebvre and Axelos', in *Space, Difference, Everyday Life: Reading Henri Lefebvre*, edited by K. Goonewardena, S. Kipfer, R. Milgrom and C. Schmid. London: Routledge, 80–93.

ElDiario.es 2013a. 'Puigcerdà 127: a la espera de agua corriente y una vida digna' (Puigcerdà 127: waiting for running water and a dignified life). 4 March.

ElDiario.es 2013b. 'L'incompliment d'acords complica la situació dels desallotjats dels assentaments del Poblenou' (The noncompliance of agreements complicates the situation of Poblenou settlements' evicted people). 7 August.

El País 2006a. 'La inversión en oficinas bate récords y rebasa los 1.600 millones en Barcelona' (Office investment breaks records and rebases 1,600 million in Barcelona). 16 January.

El País 2006b. 'Sólo el 30% de las 226 empresas instaladas en el 22@ se dedica a la comunicación' (Only 30% of the 226 businesses installed in 22@ are dedicated to communications). 23 March.

El Periódico 2005. 'Las nuevas áreas de negocio de Barcelona se consolidan' (The new business areas of Barcelona are consolidated). 5 July.

El Periódico 2013. 'Can Ricart agoniza a los 5 años de ser declarado bien cultural' (Can Ricart in agony 5 years after being declared a cultural asset). 6 May.

Engardio, P. 2009. 'Barcelona's Big Bet on Innovation'. *Business Week* 8 June, available at http://www.businessweek.com/print/innovate/content/jun2009/id2 (accessed: 30 January 2010).

Engels, F., Marx, K. 2004 [1848]. *Manifesto of the Communist Party*. Available at: https://www.marxists.org/archive/marx/works/1848/communist-manifesto/ (accessed 1 September 2014).

Florida, R. 2005. *Cities and the Creative Class*. Abingdon: Routledge.

Florida, R. and Kenney, M. 1991. 'The New Age of Capitalism: Innovation-mediated Production'. *Futures: The Journal of Forecasting and Planning* 25(6): 637–52.

Gdaniec, C. 2000. 'Cultural Industries, Information Technology and the Regeneration of Post-industrial Landscapes. Poblenou in Barcelona – A Virtual City?' *GeoJournal* 50(4): 379–87.

Guidoni, G.D. 2007. *Proyecto BCN*. Barcelona: Ajuntament de Barcelona.

Karlsson, C., Johansson, B. and Stough, R. 2009. 'Human Capital, Talent, Agglomeration and Regional Growth. Centre of Excellence for Science and Innovation Studies' working paper, 191. Available at: http://cesis.abe.kth.se/documents/191.pdf (accessed: 12 May 2012).

Lazzeretti, L., Boix, R. and Capone, F. 2008. 'Do Creative Industries Cluster? Mapping Creative Local Production Systems in Italy and Spain'. *Industry and Innovation* 15(5): 549–67.

Lefebvre, H. 1976 [1973]. *The Survival of Capitalism: Reproduction of the Relations of Production*. London: Allison and Busby.

Lefebvre, H. 1991 [1974]. *The Production of Space*. Trans. D. Nicholson-Smith. Oxford: Blackwell.

Lefebvre, H. 1996 [1968]. 'The Right to the City', in *Writings on Cities* by H. Lefebvre, edited by E. Kofman and E. Lebas. Oxford: Blackwell, 63–182.

Lefebvre, H. 2000 [1971]. *Everyday Life in the Modern World*. Trans. S. Rabinovitch. London: The Athlone Press.

Lefebvre, H. 2003 [1970]. *The Urban Revolution*. Trans. R. Bononno. Minneapolis, MN: University of Minnesota Press.

Lefebvre, H. 2008a [1961]. *Critique of Everyday Life, Volume 2: Foundations for a Sociology of the Everyday*. Trans. J. Moore. London: Verso.

Lefebvre, H. 2008b [1981]. *Critique of Everyday Life, Volume 3: From Modernity to Modernism*. Trans. G. Elliott. London: Verso.

Lefebvre, H. 2009. *State, Space, World: Selected Essays*, edited by N. Brenner and S. Elden. Minneapolis, MN: University of Minnesota Press.

Leon, N. 2008. 'Attract and Connect: the 22@Barceolona Innovation District and the Internationalisation of Barcelona Business'. *Innovation: Management, Policy & Practice*, 10(2–3): 235–46.

March, H., Saurí, D., Ribera-Fumaz, R. and Parés, M. forthcoming. 'Poblenou Barcelona, New Town, New Ecologies: A Trip Through Sustainability Extremes', in *Adventures in Urban Sustainable Development: Theoretical Interventions and Notes from the Field*, edited by S. Mössner, T. Freytag and R. Krueger. Cambridge, MA: MIT Press.

Martí-Costa, M. and Pradel i Miquel, M. 2012. 'The Knowledge City Against Urban Creativity? Artists' Workshops and Urban Regeneration in Barcelona'. *European Urban and Regional Studies* 19(1): 92–108.

Merrifield, A. 2000. 'Henri Lefebvre: A Socialist in Space', in *Thinking Space*, edited by M. Crang and N. Thrift. London: Routledge, 167–82.

Neumann, M. 2005. 'The Compact City Fallacy'. *Journal of Planning Education and Research* 25(1): 11–26.

Organisation for Economic Cooperation and Development 2007. *Competitive Cities: A New Entrepreneurial Paradigm in Spatial Development*. Paris: OECD.

Organisation for Economic Cooperation and Development 2009. 'Promoting Entrepreneurship, Employment and Business Competitiveness: The Experience of Barcelona'. LEED Programme Local Development Agency Review Series. Paris: OECD.

Pacte Industrial de la Regió Metropolitana de Barcelona 2001. *La Ciutat Digital*. Barcelona: Beta Editorial.

Rodríguez-Pose, A. 2008. 'The Rise of the "City-region" Concept and its Development Policy Implications'. *European Planning Studies* 16(8): 1025–46.

Scheurer, J. 2007. 'Compact City Policy: How Europe Discovered its History and Met Resistance'. The Urban Reinventors Paper Series, 2. Available at: http://www.eukn.org/binaries/eukn/eukn/research/2008/06/compact-city-policy.pdf (accessed: 25 November 2008).

Simmie, J. (ed.) 2001. *Innovative Cities*. London: Spon Press.

Stanek, Ł. 2008. 'Space as Concrete Abstraction: Hegel, Marx, and Modern Urbanism in Henri Lefebvre', in *Space, Difference, Everyday Life: Reading Henri Lefebvre.*, edited by K. Goonewardena, S. Kipfer, R. Milgrom and C. Schmid. London: Routledge, 62–79.

Swartz, J. 2008. 'Space-Run Artists: Art, Activism and Urban Conflict in Contemporary Barcelona'. *The Fillip Review*, 7. Available at: http://fillip.ca/content/art-activism-and-urban-conflict-in-contemporary-barcelona (accessed: 30 January 2010).

Wilson, J. 2010. *Abstract Space and The Plan Puebla Panama: A Lefebvrean Critique of Regional Development in Southern Mexico*. PhD diss., School of Social Science, The University of Manchester.

8

Reconstructing New Orleans and the Right to the City

M. Christine Boyer

Henri Lefebvre's famous invocation of the right to the city claimed that those segregated in ghetto enclaves, condemned to live in substandard housing, excluded from having an active role in the formation of the city, had the right to return to the centre, by which he meant the right to a decent urban life, the right to freedom, to education, to participate in and change decisions that affect them, including all that produces urban space (Lefebvre 1996 [1968]).[1] Every inhabitant had a right to appropriate space in order to guarantee security from harmful disruption in the pattern of their daily lives in homes, jobs or communities. This required a radical restructuring of the power relations that underlie both the production of urban space and the practice of urban democracy.

In New Orleans, the aftermath of Hurricane Katrina shattered all concepts entailed in the right to the city. In post-Katrina New Orleans all inhabitants should have been granted access to participate in meaningful discussions about the future of the city, protected against evictions, guaranteed a right to work and affordable housing, sheltered and protected in a place called home. But the damage created on 31 August 2005 left 80 per cent of New Orleans flooded with an estimated 107,000 occupied housing units inundated and an additional 27,000 sustaining wind damage, making this the largest residential disaster in US history (Brookings Institution 2009). It presented an emblematic portrait of today's risk society: uncertain, sudden disruption of daily life, arriving any time and any place, releasing a sustained cry for the right to the city and to life.

Disaster recovery enhances the spatial politics of planning, as land itself becomes the turbulent ground of perpetual crisis. In a state of emergency, the authority that controls the land retains the power to define what areas matter and which do not, who is disposable and who is not, what matters most and what does not. Consequently New Orleans is a shrinking city, and the neediest – African Americans, the elderly and children – were basically ignored in recovery efforts. The 2010 census revealed that the city's population stood at 343,829 or 71 per cent of its level in 2000 (Greater New Orleans Community Data Center 2011). There are 118,526 fewer African Americans compared to 2000, 24,101 fewer whites and 3,225 more Hispanics. Although African Americans still represent the majority of the city's population at 60 per cent, down from 67 per cent in 2000, they have been the ones to bear most of the pain of displacement, abandonment and re-segregation.[2] The loss of housing has occurred in tandem with the loss in population: in September 2009 there were still 65,888 unoccupied addresses, the next year 50,100 residential properties remained blighted, 47,738 stood vacant, and so the statistics of pain continue year after year (Greater New Orleans Community Data Center 2011).

The world is familiar with the images of fetid water inundating New Orleans in the days after the levees broke. The spectacle of the storm's violence and the spectacle of massive class inequalities were beamed around the world by satellite television. The cameras were there and then gone, displaying the inevitable hit-and-run media frenzy. But once the spectacle was normalized, someone of authority, under the cover of eroding municipal control, gave bulldozers the right to demolish wrecked homes, to clear away uprooted trees, to remove rotting refrigerators, trashed vehicles – whatever the debris. Once the cameras were no longer trained on the site, many fields – especially in the mostly African-American Lower Ninth Ward – were levelled and cleared.

Having taken the brunt of the worst flooding, by 2012 the Lower Ninth Ward appeared 'strangely eerily beautiful'. In this semi-tropical environment, fields of tall grass have sprung up everywhere, erasing the last vestiges of damage, so that no trace remains of where a cement platform for a house or a driveway once was. An entire Afro-American community has been erased, pocked-marked here and there with a few defensive houses built on stilts, a block or two of pale faux-Creole cottages erected by Habitat for Humanity or financed by the federal government, an array of architectural offerings commissioned by the film actor Brad Pitt's 'Make It Right' organization.

No relics of pain are left; no marks of the spectacular dismemberment appear in these fields of green. The New Orleans Diaspora has been ejected from the security of their homes, scattered to cities across the US. How did all this clearance and severed redevelopment come about as if we were blind? Who exactly controls these beautiful fields of grass, who has annexed this territory, who commands some lands to lie fallow and other parcels to be traded to outside developers? Who has the authority to select those inhabitants who have a right of return and those who are 'better off' banished from the playing fields of the Lower Ninth Ward? Is this void of belonging, are these ejected and scattered inhabitants, these fallow lands and enclave economies, the work of architects/planners and city shrinkers?

Bill Quigley, a public-interest lawyer in New Orleans, has claimed that in the wake of the hurricane, New Orleans is 'a developer's dream, and a resident's nightmare'. And even Nicolai Ouroussof, the *New York Times* architecture critic, has called the reconstruction of New Orleans 'one of the most aggressive works of social engineering in America since the postwar boom of the 1950s. And architecture and urban planning have become critical tools in shaping that new order' (Bill Quigley quoted in Nguyen 2007; Ouroussoff 2006). As one critique reported on New Orleans recovery:

> [t]he problem with urban planners is two fold. First, they work for the wrong
> people, the government, rather than for the citizens. As local governments have

become more corrupt and more beholden to the interests of a small number of developers and other businesses, urban planning has inevitably come to reflect these perverse priorities.

Second, urban planners believe in sweeping physical solutions to social problems … [this is] what G. K. Chesterton called the huge modern heresy of 'altering the human soul to fit its conditions, instead of altering human conditions to fit the human soul.' (Smith 2009)

Since 2005, there have been six different municipal plans and one federal non-plan for the reconstruction of New Orleans. Planning, Lefebvre noted in *The Urban Revolution*, involves a reduction in social and mental conceptualization, the result of both trivialization and specialization. Blind fields evolve from not-seeing and not-knowing. 'The blinding (assumptions we accept dogmatically) and the blinded (the misunderstood) are complementary aspects of our blindness' (Lefebvre 2003 [1970]: 30, 48). The architects/planners busily reconstructing New Orleans have been blind to biases against the poor and the displaced embedded in their plans. Even if their intentions were to foster integration and interaction, they refuse to see that they follow financial dictates not of social justice: passing laws that restrict, limit or ban the building – even renting – of homes that traditionally benefit poor and working-class people of colour. Couched in the specializing language of zoning, tax credits or permissive-use permits, such blindness has created re-segregation (Ratner 2008, Nguyen 2010). What lessons might be gleaned from studying the reconstruction plans in post-Katrina New Orleans? As one plan has metamorphosed into another, as segmented proposals split up or merged, has there been a principle of urban re-segregation, spatial fragmentation and neighbourhood triage at work?

ACTION PLAN TO REBUILD NEW ORLEANS

On 11 January 2006, the first reconstruction plan, 'The Action Plan to Rebuild New Orleans', from the Bring New Orleans Back Commission (BNOBC), was delivered to Mayor Nagin. The plan called for neighbourhood planning teams to begin work by 20 February and to complete their plans by 20 May, with a city-wide consolidated plan finished by 20 June. BNOBC called this plan an attempt to create 'a smaller, more manageable footprint', with rebuilding targeted at higher, drier ground rather than lower, more flood-prone parts of the city. In Lefebvre's words, it would 'condense' the city. This so-called plan for a 'new American city' recommended some flooded neighbourhoods be replaced with parks, and a four-month moratorium be imposed on building permits in neighbourhoods with the worst flooding.[3] In order to propel quick action in 'immediate opportunity areas', the plan recommended extending power to a new city agency, the 'Crescent City Redevelopment Corporation', to 'buy and sell property, for redevelopment, including use of eminent domain as a last resort', forcing buy-outs from those unwilling to sell their heavily damaged and flooded homes (BNOBC 2006: 50).

Thousands of New Orleans residents and evacuees were furious about this first recovery plan, which assumed that population and revenue would be severely and permanently reduced. They were especially outraged by the reconstruction map that spread large green patches over most of the low-lying districts. They were eager to return and begin the long process of recovery, but the plan held too many financial and security risks if their neighbourhood failed BNOBC's 'viability' test proving that half of a given district's population intended to return and rebuild. Unviable neighbourhoods with insufficient population to support 'equitable and efficient service delivery' would be ignored. While the plan recognized publicly subsidized housing as an asset, it claimed that this was an issue the federal government would address, thus washing its hands of responsibility for housing low-income inhabitants who had been given by Katrina essentially a one-way ticket out of town and no help to come home.

Sensing this plan was unpopular, Mayor Nagin, running for re-election in May 2006, took some distance: he lifted the moratorium allowing residents to rebuild anywhere, but warned that they did so in flood-prone neighbourhoods at their own risk. He recommended revamping schools, building a light-rail system, promoting new riverfront development and better flood protection. Some 20 or so neighbourhoods of New Orleans were to establish planning teams to investigate whether their areas were sustainable or not. And again these plans were to be completed by May 2006. When BNOBC's smaller footprint condenser plan failed to achieve federal support, the City Council inaugurated another plan.

NEIGHBORHOODS REBUILDING PLAN

Funded by the City Council and presented to the mayor's office in October 2006, the Neighborhoods Rebuilding Plan (Lambert Plans[4]) reported that all flooded neighbourhoods wanted to rebuild their housing stock, restore streets and other infrastructure, reopen schools, and bring back supermarkets and pharmacies (City of New Orleans 2006). Forty-seven neighbourhoods developed plans: 13 of these were communities where more than 50 per cent of children under the age of five lived below the poverty line; 11 of these had a level of 66 per cent. Thus the measuring stick for neighbourhood rebuilding was the extent to which these neighbourhoods would be allowed to improve the quality of life and stability beyond what they had achieved in 2005.

Via this plan the City Council granted residents a process to allow their voices to be heard and to define what their communities would become. Participants believed naively that funds at the heart of the rebuilding process provided by the Community Development Block Grant (CDBG) were to be used in areas of 'concentrated distress'. Non-flooded areas suffering minor problems such as poor refuse service or job loss were expected to recover on their own.

What this planning process unleashed, however, was an illusory practice: the number of meetings began to spiral out of control. It had been assumed that three meetings per neighbourhood would be sufficient to complete the required plans.

The 'executive' summary of the Neighborhoods Rebuilding Plan explained the contrary effect.

> Because the stakes were so high and emotions so deep, and because many neighborhoods had begun planning with little to modest direction on their own in order to 'prove their viability', it quickly became apparent that three very structured meeting [sic] was insufficient to build a rapport and trust with the neighborhood groups. (City of New Orleans 2006: 12)

Architects/planners remained blind to the reality, believing instead that their plans were transparent and in the interest of communities. In order to make their schemes clear to inhabitants who were judged to be 'frightened' by the planning process, consultants began to meet neighbourhood groups 'in homes, under tents, on the street, in playgrounds, and most importantly in houses of worship' (City of New Orleans 2006: 12).

It was obvious to community participants, however, that the city was developing a patchwork of proposals riddled with uncertainties. Urban proposals, Lefebvre had warned, don't go very far; they are a strategy papering over the fact that space harbours an ideology and so they perpetuate the illusion that space can be designed without bias or controversy (Lefebvre 2003: 157). Architects/planners make a compromise between state management in which free enterprise is ascendant, and a neoliberal position that calls for consensual planning activities (citizen participation). They slip into the crack between them, between public and private interests, accepting fragmentation of the city, even contributing to it with their representational plans and visualizations. Worthy inhabitants who remained behind in the stricken city were committed to participate in empty decision-making processes, aware that they were being trapped in meaningless debate, that their raised voices fell on deaf ears. Their daily struggles with survival, their tangible experiences of trauma, were excluded from the planning process – they were left to proceed on their own. Meanwhile a developer's game of triage took shape as a mask and a tool of reconstruction (Lefebvre 2003: 180).

A POLICY OF TRIAGE

Employed by BNOBC, the non-profit Urban Land Institute (ULI) drew outright fury after it suggested a few months after Katrina that a concept of triage should be put into practice. Their report, released in mid-November 2005, recommended that vast, mostly poor areas of the city should be left without services and aid. It gave the stamp of approval to the fact that the city's footprint would shrink and raised the vision of New Orleans rebuilt for developers, corporations and the well-to-do class. Without utilizing the word 'triage', their advice nevertheless implicitly divided the city into three parts: those areas that would recover with aid; those that would recover without aid; and those that would never recover. It suggested concentrating the delivery of services and money in 'viable' areas that would recover with aid and forget about the areas that would never recover (Urban Land Institute 2005).

By 2007 a triage system had been put into effect: the city focused on struggling areas such as Gentilly Boulevard and Elysian Fields Avenue, and viable areas that could benefit from investment such as Canal Street, but neglected to rebuild destroyed and flooded low-income areas – with the exception noted above of a few homes built by philanthropic organizations. No longer waiting for federal aid to arrive, by late March 2007, $1.1 billion from state and local funds was allocated for infrastructure repair and other projects with the hope of leveraging private investment to spur on new businesses and recovery projects.

THE UNIFIED NEW ORLEANS PLAN (UNOP) CITYWIDE STRATEGIC RECOVERY AND REBUILDING PLAN

Meanwhile, as a condition for releasing federal recovery funds, the Louisiana Recovery Authority (LRA) mandated that a plan for New Orleans must address city-wide recovery and rebuilding – not only areas that had flooded but also those that had not. With funds from the Rockefeller Foundation and with the approval of the LRA and the City Council, the UNOP effort was initiated, culminating in yet another plan delivered in June 2007 calling for an additional $14.3 billion for New Orleans' recovery (City of New Orleans 2007).

The planning process began in September 2006, when architects, city planners and neighbourhood residents created 13 Planning District Recovery Plans (containing 73 officially recognized neighbourhoods). It provided a two-tiered process: the integration of 50 previous Neighborhood Plans (from the Lambert Plans) into District Plans and these to be merged with the work of another set of planners detailing a comprehensive, city-wide plan. Planning districts, for example, might have a list of repair projects such as neighbourhood schools, parks, libraries and local streets, but these only achieved city-wide significance when grouped together into a larger project labelled 'Repair Renovate or Construct New District/ Neighborhood Parks'.

The plan highlighted the word 'recovery', pointing out that this was not a master land-use plan nor a comprehensive plan because it focused merely on capital projects and programmes to correct or repair the effects of disaster. 'Time is of the essence when lives have been disrupted, when businesses have been destroyed and communities torn apart' (ibid.:10). It set the limit for such 'recovery' within a span of ten years. While the city-wide plan recognized that people were living in every one of the neighbourhoods of the city, that every inhabitant had the right to return to New Orleans and that all neighbourhoods of the city must eventually be rebuilt, in the same breath, the report argued, the city was given a grand opportunity to reinvent itself in a smarter, stronger and safer manner with a higher quality of life (ibid.: 52–3, 56). But how to get there remained a challenging goal.

UNOP, as the other plans before it had, divided the city into three: a policy area A with 'less flood risk and/or higher repopulation rates'; a policy area B with 'moderate flood risk and/or moderate repopulation rates'; and a policy area C with 'highest flood risk and slowest repopulation risks' (Johnson 2007: 6). It proposed a 'Neighborhood Stabilization Program' to help people in the hardest hit areas, with the fewest people returning, to relocate to planned 'cluster developments' where there would be upgraded infrastructure, social and commercial services, and neighbours. Property owners remaining in abandoned areas would be assisted by two programmes: 'Elevate New Orleans' loans to raise their homes on stilts or the 'Slab-on-Grade Remediation' programmes to erase the last traces of their former homes.

Thus, after an 18-month planning process, New Orleans was about to receive the most comprehensive and detailed plan with wish-lists of projects district by district but with no priorities set, no timeline established and no budget allocated. Some of the city's inhabitants were getting worried. While they still believed in inserting their opinions into the planning and budgeting process, it was becoming apparent that citizen participation might be a colossal waste of time and energy, and that the various plans contained nothing but paper dreams and unfulfilled hopes.

THE 2007 REDEVELOPMENT PLAN (BLAKELY PLAN)

In late March 2007, while UNOP was undergoing review and revision, another plan was unveiled, this one promoted by Edward J. Blakely, the city's newly appointed Executive Director for Recovery Management (McKee 2007). His plan focused on 17 'hub sites' – zones approximately half a mile in diameter and dotted about the city – to act as magnets for commercial development. Blakely proclaimed: '[i]f I could pump life back in these places, you might pump life back into the entire city' (Blakely quoted in Nossiter 2007). Adopting a triage mentality, Blakely selected high-visibility sites, with sufficient land and other assets to attract investors and with adequate resources to catalyse developments such as schools and libraries. All hubs centred on old markets, on which the city was built in the first place. Even though 15 of those sites had not been hit by flood-waters or had begun to rebuild on their own, Blakely seized the opportunity to reinvest in these vital areas. Only two devastated areas received funds: one in the Lower Ninth Ward and a section surrounding Lake Forest Plaza shopping centre.

Jane S. Brooks, professor and chair of the Planning and Urban Studies Department at the University of New Orleans, proclaimed: '[p]eople can start to see where this targeted reinvestment is going to occur'. She attributed the wide acceptance of the Blakely plan to the broad public participation that led up to it. 'People are ready to understand that this is the first wave of investment … If this works, maybe there will be another wave of investment. There's no miracle here. What he's trying to do is use public money to attract private money' for neighborhood reinvestment (quoted in McKee 2007). As Lefebvre noted, planning based on class criteria results in segregation, even when the intention is to bring about integration and interaction (Lefebvre 2003: 90).

Yet one year after the plan's announcement, '[w]eary and bewildered residents [from the on-again off-again recovery plans], forced to bring back the hard-hit city on their own, have searched the plan's 17 "target recovery zones" for any sign that the city's promises should not be consigned to the municipal filing cabinet, along with their predecessors. On their one-year anniversary, the designated "zones" have hardly budged' (Nossiter 2008).

THE FEDERAL GOVERNMENT'S NON-PLAN TO DEMOLISH PUBLISH HOUSING

Soon after Katrina's impact became clear, Housing and Urban Development (HUD) Secretary Alphonso Jackson predicted that New Orleans would not be as black as it had been for a long time, if ever. He then worked to make that prophecy come true. While human rights lawyers admit that there are no precise figures on the racial breakdown of poor and working-class people from New Orleans who have been displaced, no one challenges the strong indications that they are overwhelmingly African Americans. Immediately following Katrina, the black population of New Orleans plummeted by 69 per cent, while the white population fell only 39 per cent, according to the Center for Constitutional Rights (July 2009). Areas that have recovered substantially are affluent and predominantly white.

Henri Lefebvre warned of blind spots in the process of planning. 'The blinding is the luminous source (knowledge or ideology) that projects a beam of light that illuminates *elsewhere*' (Lefebvre 2003: 31). The dazed and blinded stare at the ruins and what is left in the shadows; they cannot see crucial facts of displacement and re-segregation and so manipulate in the dark a limited set of indicators and indexes found in the viable areas. Their language is biased as well: the words 'derelict structure' substitute for somebody's 'home', while 'property' replaces the word for 'house'. Erroneous, if not illegal, demolitions and buyouts based on historic racial bias show scant respect for Lefebvre's right to the city or provide equitable access to homes, jobs and education.

Thus another blind spot loomed large on the horizon. In early 2006, James Glassman, writing in the *Wall Street Journal*, openly declared: 'It was planning – specifically, the horrifying housing projects, largely destroyed in Katrina; the stultifying school systems, the Superdome and other wasteful public-works projects – that held the city back.' He applauded the Katrina 'tragedy' for providing the nation with 'the most exciting urban opportunity since San Francisco [earthquake] in 1906' (Glassman, 2006: A13).

Despite a critical shortage of housing, the Housing Authority of New Orleans (HANO) proposed to demolish New Orleans' 'Big Four' public housing projects. In December 2007 demolition was approved without a plan for relocating the 20,000 residents already displaced from the projects by the storm but waiting to return, and in spite of the fact that public housing in New Orleans ranked among the nation's best. Scattered across the city, there were 4,500 units chartered for demolition by the summer of 2008. The city of New Orleans had boundless energy for reconstruction plans, but showed no interest in enacting a right of return for former residents of New Orleans public housing stock.[5]

Before Katrina, New Orleans had been a city of renters and low-income residents, but the storm destroyed more than half of these rental units and recovery planners could not see the problem. Davida Finger, a staff attorney at the Loyola Law Clinic working on housing issues, commented:

> What we saw after the storm was an emphasis on property owners all around, treating renters as second-class citizens ... To be forward-thinking, we have to take into account all that's happened to renters. There's no quick-fix policy, but there has been ... a recognition that so much of what determines a family's outcomes turns on housing. (Quoted in Nguyen 2009)

Sheila Crowley, president of the National Low Income Housing Coalition, at the DC hearing on the after-effects of Katrina in 2007, put it this way:

> Katrina is about wrenching hundreds of thousands of people from homes to which most will never return. Katrina is about the sudden and complete loss of all that home means – safety, respite, privacy, comfort and security.

The situation in New Orleans was so dire that it prompted United Nations officials to call for an immediate halt to the demolition of public housing, saying that demolition is a violation of human rights and will force predominantly black residents into homelessness. 'The spiraling costs of private housing and rental units, and in particular the demolition of public housing, puts these communities in further distress, increasing poverty and homelessness', said a joint statement by UN experts on housing and minority issues (Moreno Gonzales 2008). Despite these calls, demolitions and human security issues continued to deny citizens of New Orleans the right to the city.

REINVENTING THE CRESCENT RIVERFRONT PLAN

Carrying out the policy to bow before developers and ignoring the plight of African Americans, Mayor Nagin promoted a 'Reinventing the Crescent Riverfront' plan allocating $300 million for its implementation. Most of this money was intended to build parks, remove docks and wharves that were roadblocks to the creation of a riverside promenade down river from the famed French Quarter, but the plan also called for building residential towers that could attract wealthier, more creative people to shore up the city's tax base. The Crescent Riverfront site offered extraordinary views of the city and was a stone's throw away from the lucrative tourist quarter. It was far too valuable to remain an industrial zone. But the Port Authority believed otherwise: there was something 'authentic' and visually exciting about watching passing ships and barges: 'New Orleans is about this rich legacy of a port city. We want this mix' (DeGregorio 2008). And some residents in adjacent communities agreed, joining together to form the 'Riverfront Alliance'. 'We would rather see real maritime activity continue on ... It's really great to look at the end of the street and see ships there. It reminds you that you are in a river town' (DeGregorio 2008).

As Lefebvre noted, architects/planners slip into the cracks between the demands of developers and those of the authorities, and even when they think they are uniting the city they tend to increase its fragmentation (Lefebvre 2003: 158). The riverfront plan was proposed first in 2004, then delayed by Katrina, but given the green light in January 2008. The first phase of redevelopment, a 4.5-mile plan, was unveiled in 2009. It encompassed $163 million of improvements aimed to transform a gritty industrial zone marred by burnt-out cargo docks into verdant green space replete with bike paths, pavilions, two recreational piers and even electricity-generating windmills (DeGregorio 2009; Kennedy 2008). Like all the other plans, this one was not without controversy: in a city slow to rebuild affordable housing and make basic infrastructure improvements, some asked why there should be high-rises for the wealthy on the waterfront, and why those who owned waterfront property were leading the planning process.

MASTER PLAN FOR THE TWENTY-FIRST CENTURY: NEW ORLEANS 2030

In June 2008, the City Planning Commission called for yet another plan, this time a master plan prepared by the firm of Goody Clancy & Associates from Boston. A draft was released on 15 September 2009 with the expectation that after a few weeks of discussion and a few amendments offered, the plan would be voted into law, as occurred on 27 January 2010. Henceforth all land-use decisions and zoning codes, capital improvement programmes and capital budgeting are required to be in conformity with its proposals.[6]

Unfortunately the Master Plan is actually a vision plan, or set of goals to be achieved under ideal circumstances (Goody Clancy & Associates 2009: 17–22). Like most of the plans before it, this one fails to provide implementation policies, or set priorities among different proposals, and neglects to offer detailed plans, maps or criteria for the future physical development of the city such as land-use classifications and urban design projects. Nor does it discuss how to change the perception that New Orleans is not a safe place for investment as long as it remains at risk of another catastrophic flood.[7] 'The future land use plan and map' reveals only 'the desired distribution of land uses … that reflect the long-term vision, goals and policies' of the plan. It offers as well an urban design framework with the 'desired characteristics of new development' (ibid.: 116–19).

The vision plan appears to be a grab-bag of everyone's needs and desires. It offers lists of suggestions such as improving the city's website; recruiting multilingual fire-fighters; better training for the 311 system to report back to citizens on enforcement actions; and a ban on plastic bags in stores (ibid.: 84-86). It envisions over the coming years that key decisions will be made by nearly 20 new groups and expects 20 new plans or studies from newly formed commissions on housing, historic preservation, heritage tourism, cultural activities, pedestrian and bicycle provisions, climate change and so on. It calls for a 'rehabilitation-friendly building code' using tax credits and other incentives to achieve 'higher-value reuse' of old buildings. It advocates moving away from a 'curatorial' approach to preservation to one that merely gleans 'historic character' as a valuable contribution to contemporary life (ibid.: 3). And it calls for urban agriculture zones and describes an accelerating resettlement of neighbourhoods, with innovative land-assembly plans and density levels that can provide 'the critical mass needed to support vibrant commercial districts, walkable streets, convenient transit, lively parks and similar amenities' (ibid.: 20, 120). It has, in other words, accumulated many visions and desires presented in preceding plans to which it has added a list of its own.

David Dixon, the chief planner of the Master Plan, boasts that when the Army Corps of Engineers finishes levee improvements by 2011, the city will be protected from disaster coming from a once in a once-in-a-century storm. Thus New Orleans will no longer be a city of 'wet' and 'dry' neighbourhoods, but one in which all sections can plan confidently for the future. One might add: those sections remaining, which have not been bulldozed or had their fields stripped clear, and those inhabitants, mostly white, who will reap the harvest of a shrinking city. It is the new energizing entrepreneurial creative class that the plan expects to flow into this new New Orleans of rising opportunities. As the plan describes: '[t]he share of Americans who want to live in walkable urban neighborhoods will grow for the next 15 to 20 years', and those people 'are increasingly choosing amenity-rich mixed-use communities' such as those envisioned for New Orleans. In short, the dreamers of triage have won the battle for New Orleans recovery, envisioning a walkable, sustainable green city, a resource-efficient and smarter city, an economically healthy and resilient city. The plan predicts that gated and exclusive enclaves with landscaped canals, parks with water features, and shady, tree-lined streets will be the new norm (ibid.: 76–82).

As the *New York Times* observed in the aftermath of Katrina, there was an urge to rebuild 'that is as primal as the force that pushes grass up through the cracks in the sidewalk'. The *Times* did not specify, in offering such a homily, what force and where the grasses would grow.[8] 'How do you build a city with equity? There is no manual', a community organizer asked way back in 2005 (*New York Times* 2006: 3).

THE RIGHT TO THE CITY REVISITED

In post-Katrina New Orleans, race and income have inhibited the ability of the most vulnerable inhabitants to return to their homes, to participate in redevelopment plans and to rebuild their neighbourhoods. They have been excluded: they have no right to the city, no right of return to their homes, no right to be protected from discrimination. Yet the right to housing, which includes residential stability and security of tenure, is contained in the UN Guiding Principles on Internal Displacement, and while the US has accepted this policy in situations of international displacement it has failed to apply it domestically. Discriminatory post-Katrina plans have all prioritized economic viability over residents' needs, and economic incentives over crime prevention. Homelessness rates, which are nearly four times higher in New Orleans than in other American cities, continue to rise as reconstruction creates shortages of affordable housing and fewer rental units in its wake. No redevelopment plan has ever mentioned creating 'affordable rental units' and only meagre assistance has been offered through a rental repair programme (Flaherty 2010).

Reconstruction plans for New Orleans are a retrogression from Lefebvre's 'right to the city'. The plans for reconstructing New Orleans need to be radically rethought and refocused on the recipients' end of things, otherwise the power invested in planning authorities remains far from legitimate and their proposed actions deploy yet more violence against the most vulnerable. New Orleans will continue to be a blind spot of racism in the eyes of the nation, and the 'urban' as a problematic will remain unsolved. [9]

The notoriously flooded Lower Ninth Ward endures as a world of hurt and of economic sanctions casting a long shadow over New Orleans' reconstruction.

> 'Until the Lower Ninth Ward is back on its feet, the New Orleans recovery
> has failed,' says Patricia Jones, a resident and director of the Neighborhood
> Empowerment Network Association (NENA), a nonprofit working to restore
> the area … 'You get the feeling they're just waiting for all us so-called poor
> people to leave so they can turn the place into a resort area or something,'
> says resident Henry Holmes, 76, who owns a popular local restaurant,
> Holmes One Stop. 'But you can't have New Orleans without the Lower Ninth
> Ward …' (Padgett 2010)

Edward Blakely, the so-called 'recovery czar', claims that New Orleans was a dysfunctional city before Katrina hit: no longer the major port on the Gulf, nor a pre-eminent medical centre, its medium income was half of the national figure, its crime rate beyond understanding, its government incompetent, its school system failing, its economy reliant on an unstable tourism base. That is why he planned for total regional reconstruction, not merely disaster recovery (Blakely 2012: 90). No wonder neighbourhoods were left to recover every aspect of life for themselves, as planning reached only the conceptual, abstract, universal level. Blakely's neoliberal entrepreneurial growth poles – or any of the other unrealistic reconstruction plans – failed because New Orleans could not attract private investment to 'kick-start' recovery. The planners blame citizens of New Orleans as well! After low-lying neighbourhoods were covered with 'green dots' in the first recovery plan, citizens would never again trust professional planners, nor could they wait to be chaperoned by teams of urban planners who threw out their community's plans in order to substitute their own more professional ones (Wooten 2010). Community organizers had to lead the way through the mire of institutional red tape, government impediments, stymied recovery plans and paltry payouts.

In the wake of Katrina, Lefebvre's 'conceived' space of the planners and the 'lived' space of neighbourhood experience collided. Nothing seemed to hold the two in creative tension. No matter how one defines the 'right to the city' – socioeconomic rights to affordable housing, quality education, adequate transportation, fair wages, community services; the democratic right to have one's voice listened to; the legal right of return to one's community not someone else's idea of clustered development; the right to plan community facilities; the right of environmental, criminal, ethnic justice; the right of security against disruption of life – these rights are all incommensurable with the right to secure the economic viability of urban reinvestment.[10] Planners continue to see the urban space of New Orleans as capital property and 'most investments so far have been in the most populated and prosperous parts of town … Several areas are not part of any new plans.'[11] In times of crisis and recovery, keeping the 'right to the city' a fuzzy concept may have been strategically expedient for the planners, but it postponed for ever debate about the tradeoff costs between different rights and what type of city was being created. The form these rights take matters deeply; the level at which decisions are made is strategic; the belief that planners manage things and people in innovative and positive ways is an illusion. Loosely defined and emotionally held rights left little ground for their contradictions to be negotiated and their tradeoffs with 'creative destruction' mollified. Justice was not given a chance in the city of New Orleans.

NOTES

1   For an extended discussion of Lefebvre's claim for 'the right to the city' see Attoh 2011; Dikeç and Gilbert 2002; Dikeç 2005; Dikeç 2002; Harvey 2003; Harvey 2008; Lopes de Souza 2010; Marcuse 2012; Marcuse 2009; Mayer 2012; Mitchell 2012; Purcell 2002; Schmid 2012.

2   The population of New Orleans topped 300,000 for the first time since Hurricane Katrina, according to US Census estimates in March 2009, but four of the seven parishes in metropolitan New Orleans shrank since 2007, according to estimates of population on 1 July 2008. Maggie Merrill, Mayor Ray Nagin's director of policy, called the estimate a milestone because it was the first time since Katrina that an official estimate put the city's population at more than 300,000. Sociologist Troy Blanchard proclaimed 'The pace of the rebuilding process can vary … The fact that it has continued at this rate almost three years after the storm shows it's not tapering off. People are continuing to come back' (Scallan, 2009).

3   Each Neighborhood Planning District would consist of the following: Neighborhood residents; Planner/urban designer; Historic preservation expert; City Planning Commission representative; Environmental/public health consultant; Mitigation planner; Finance expert; Administrative/technology support; Community outreach; and would reach out to displaced residents by internet and other means.

4   Called the 'Lambert Plans' because Lambert Advisory of Miami provided the project management team.

5   Shortly after Katrina, Congress allocated $10.4 billion in Community Development Block Grants to Louisiana for housing recovery. The state got another $1.7 billion in low-income housing tax credits, called the Gulf Opportunity Zone Act or GO Zone, aimed at offering incentives for developers and non-profits to build affordable rental housing. The Housing Authority of New Orleans (HANO), and by extension its receiver HUD, is applying for these funds to redevelop the four public housing complexes that have been demolished (Nguyen 2007).

6   Once a year the Plan can be amended to allow capital improvements not mentioned in the Plan but consistent with it, and every five years it can be updated as well (Goody Clancy & Associates 2009: 2, 8, 115).

7   For detailed criticism of the draft Master Plan for New Orleans, see Bureau of Governmental Research 2009.

8   The *New York Times* quoted without reference (*New York Times* 2006: 4).

9   Bill Quigley's 'Katrina Pain Index 2012' tells the story: New Orleans continues to rank second on the list of American cities with the highest income inequality and with the highest homeless rate, 21 per cent of all residential addresses remain abandoned or blighted; 27 per cent of its people continue to live in poverty; overall population is declining; its school systems privatized, its public transportation reduced (Quigley and Finger 2012).

10   Kafui Attoh argues the rallying cry of 'the right to the city' taken from Henri Lefebvre, remains a 'black box'. The form each right takes is important, for they are not all commensurable, nor achievable (Attoh 2011).

11   Howard Hughes Corporation plans a $70 million renovation of Riverwalk in the tourist section of town, an upscale Fresh Market plans a complex near the upper income Garden district, and Costco plans a store, its location yet to be announced (Kennedy 2012).

REFERENCES

Attoh, K. A. 2011. 'What Kind of Right Is the Right to the City?' *Progress in Human Geography* 35(5): 669–85.

Blakely, E. J. 2012. *My Storm: Managing the Recovery of New Orleans in the Wake of Katrina*. Philadelphia, PA: University of Pennsylvania Press.

BNOBC 2006. *Action Plan for New Orleans: The New American City* (11 January).

Brookings Institution 2009. *The New Orleans Index: Tracking the Recovery of New Orleans and the Metropolitan Area*. Washington, DC: Brookings Institution Press.

Bureau of Governmental Research (BGR) 2009. *In Search of the Master Plan: Making the New Orleans 2030 Draft Plan Work* (14 October).

Center for Constitutional Rights 2009. 'International Human Rights Obligations and Post-Katrina Housing Policies Briefing' (Paper to the Technical Experts for the Advisory Group on Forced Evictions United States Mission, 26 July–1 August).

City of New Orleans 2006. *Neighborhoods Rebuilding Plan. Summary October 2006*. Available at: http://nolanrp.com/data/neighborhood/nola_nrp_summary.pdf (accessed 6 September 2014).

City of New Orleans 2007. *The Unified New Orleans Plan (UNOP) – Citywide Strategic Recovery and Rebuilding Plan*. Available at: http://www.nolaplans.com/plans/UNOP/UNOP_Citywide.pdf (accessed 6 September 2014).

DeGregorio, J. 2008. 'Reclaiming the River: An Ambitious Plan Calls for Opening the Riverfront, but the Port and Some Neighbors Have Other Ideas'. *Times Picayune* (5 April).

DeGregorio, J. 2009. 'Architects Present Concept for Redeveloping New Orleans Riverfront'. *Times \ Picayune* (14 January), http://www.nola.com/news/index.ssf/2008/04/on_the_waterfront_katrina_dama.html (accessed: 28 February 2009).

Dikeç, M. 2002. 'Police, Politics, and the Right to the City'. *GeoJournal* 58(2): 91–8.

Dikeç, M. 2005. '(In)Justice and the "Right to the City": The Case of French National Urban Policy', in *Right to the City*. Roma: Societa Geografica Italiana, 45–53.

Dikeç, M. and Gilbert, L. 2002. 'Right to the City: Home or a New Societal Ethics?' *Capitalism, Nature, Socialism (CNS)* 13(2): 58–74.

Dikeç, M. and Gilbert, L. 2008. 'Right to the City: Politics of Citizenships', in *Space, Difference, Everyday Life: Reading Henri Lefebvre*, edited by K. Goonewardena, S. Kipfer, R. Milgrom and C. Schmid. New York: Routledge, 250–63.

Flaherty, J. 2010. 'On the Fifth Anniversary of Katrina, Displacement Continues'. *Huffington Post* (27 August).

Glassman, J. K. 2006. 'Cross Country: Back to the Future'. *The Wall Street Journal* (12 January).

Goody Clancy & Associates 2009. *Draft Plan 21st Century New Orleans Master Plan.*

Greater New Orleans Community Data Center (GNOCDC) 2010. 'Benchmarks for Blight' (7 May), http://www.gnocdc.org/BenchmarksforBlight/index.html (accessed: 7 May 2012).

Greater New Orleans Community Data Center (GNOCDC) 2011. 'News Release: Facts for Features Hurricane Katrina Recovery' (August), http://www.gnocdc.org/Factsforfeatures/HurricaneKatrinaRecovery/index.html, (accessed 5 July 2012).

Harvey, D. 2003. 'The Right to the City'. *International Journal of Urban and Regional Research* 27(4): 939–41.

Harvey, D. 2008. 'The Right to the City'. *New Left Review* 53 (September–October): 23–40.

Johnson, L. A. 2007. 'Recovery and Reconstruction Following Large-Scale Disasters: Lessons Learned in New Orleans' (paper presented at the 2nd International Conference on Urban Disaster Reduction, 27–29 November).

Keleher, T. 2009. 'By the Numbers: Katrina Families Still Wait for Justice'. Colorlines Blog (1 September).

Kennedy, S. 2008. 'New Orleans Riverfront Plan Get Green Light'. *Business Week* (16 January).

Kennedy, S. 2012. 'Vitality Reborn, New Orleans Draws Developers'. *New York Times* (25 September).

Lefebvre, H. 1996 [1968]. 'The Right to the City', in *Writings on Cities* by H. Lefebvre, edited by E. Kofman and E. Lebas. Oxford: Blackwell, 63–182.

Lefebvre, H. 2003 [1970]. *The Urban Revolution*. Minneapolis, MN: University of Minnesota Press.

Lopes de Souza, M. 2010. 'Which Right to Which City?' *Interface* 2(1): 315–33.

Marcuse, P. 2009. 'From Critical Urban Theory to the Right to the City'. *City* 13(3): 185–97.

Marcuse, P. 2012. 'Whose Right(s) to What City?', in *Cities for People, not for Profit: Critical Urban Theory and the Right to the City*, edited by N. Brenner, P. Marcuse and M. Mayer. New York: Routledge, 24–41.

Mayer, M. 2012. '"The 'Right to the City" in Urban Social Movements', in *Cities for People, not for Profit: Critical Urban Theory and the Right to the City*, edited by N. Brenner, P. Marcuse and M. Mayer. New York: Routledge, 63–85.

McKee, B. 2007. 'New Orleans Recovery Plan Unleashed'. *ARCHITECT Magazine* (1 May). http://www.architectmagazine.com/design/new-orleans-recovery-plan-released.aspx (accessed: 20 February 2009).

Mitchell, D. 2012. *The Right to the City: Social Justice and the Fight for Public Space*. New York: The Guilford Press.

Moreno Gonzales, J. 2008. 'U.N. Weighs in Against Demolishing Public Housing'. *Housing Advocacy* (28 July). Accessible at: http://housingadvocacy.blogspot.com/2008/07/un-weighs-in-againstdemolishing-public.html (accessed 20 October 2009).

New York Times 2006. 'New Orleans Planning for a Better Future'. New York: The Rockefeller Foundation.

Nguyen, T. 2007. 'A Game of Monopoly'. *Colorlines* 38 (May/June).

Nguyen, T. 2009, 'They Can't Go Home Again'. *Colorlines* 51 (July/August).

Nguyen, T. 2010. 'Pushed Out and Pushing Back in New Orleans'. *Colorlines* (7 April 2010), http://colorlines.com/archives/2010/04/pushed_out_and_pushing_back_in_new_orleans.html (accessed: 7 May 2012).

Nossiter, A. 2007. 'Steering New Orleans' Recovery with a Clinical Eye'. *The New York Times* (10 April).

Nossiter, A. 2008. 'Big Plans are Slow to Bear Fruit in New Orleans'. *New York Times* (1 April).

Ouroussoff, N. 2006. 'Ideas & Trends: Unbuilding – Architecture, All Fall Down.' *New York Times* (19 November).

Padgett, T. 2010. 'New Orleans' Lower Ninth: Katrina's Forgotten Victim?' *TIMESPECIALS* (27 August), http://www.time.com/time/specials/packages/article/0,28804,2012217_2012252_2012673,00.html (accessed: 24 October 2012).

Purcell, M. 2002. 'Excavating Lefebvre: The Right to the City and its Urban Politics of the Inhabitant'. *GeoJournal* 58: 63–108.

Quigley, B. and Finger D. 2011. 'Katrina Pain Index 2011: Race, Gender, Poverty', http://www.informationclearinghouse.info/article28914.htm (accessed: 12 May 2012).

Randall, K. 2006. 'City Residents Denounce "Bring New Orleans Back" Rebuilding Plan' World Socialists Web Site (14 January). https://www.wsws.org/en/articles/2006/01/newo-j14.html. (accessed: 20 February 2010).

Ratner, L. 2008. 'New Orleans Redraws its Color Line', *The Nation* (27 August), http://www.thenation.com (accessed: 7 May 2012).

Scallan, M. 2009. 'New Orleans Population Tops 300,000 for the First Time since Katrina', *New Orleans Metro Real-Time News* (19 March), http://www.nola.com/news/index.ssf/2009/03/no_tops_300000_in_census_estim.html (accessed: 20 February 2009).

Schmid, C. 2012. 'Henri Lefebvre, the Right to the City, and the New Metropolitan Mainstream', in *Cities for People, not for Profit: Critical Urban Theory and the Right to the City*, edited by N. Brenner, P. Marcuse and M. Mayer. New York: Routledge, 42–62.

Smith, S. 2009. 'A New Bottom of the Ninth Urban Planning and New Orleans', *Progressive Review*, http://prorev.com/ningth.htm, (accessed October 2009).

Stickells, L. 2011. 'Editorial, The Right to the City: Rethinking Architecture's Social Significance', Special Issue *Architectural Theory Review* 16(3).

Urban Land Institute 2005. 'Moving Beyond Recovery to Restoration and Rebirth: Urban Land Institute Makes Recommendations on Rebuilding New Orleans' (18 November), http://www.uli.org/ResearchAndPublications/Reports/Advisory%20Service%20Panel%20Reports/NOLARelease.aspx (accessed: 12 May 2012).

Wooten, T. 2011. *We Shall Not Be Moved: Rebuilding Home in the Wake of Katrina*. Boston, MA: Beacon Press.

PART III
Everyday Architectures

Ground Exploration: Producing Everyday Life at the South Bank, 1948–1951

Nick Beech

> **On this vast field of human fragments, the state has built its watchtower.**
> **(Lefebvre 1995 [1961]: 121)**

The following is one sample of a larger research project that has mobilized the work of Henri Lefebvre in order to contest the 'canon' of mid-twentieth-century British modern architectural history.[1] The empirical base for the research lies in one of the more banal activities of the building process – soil mechanics, a technical practice that hardly impinges on the formal properties of architecture. As such, the research departs from Anglo-American architectural projects that engaged with Lefebvre's work at the turn of the century in that it provides openings for a reassessment of architecture's historical relationship to social democracy and the emergent welfare state of mid-twentieth-century Britain.

ANGLO-AMERICAN 'POSSIBILITIES' AT THE TURN OF THE CENTURY

At the turn of the century, Iain Borden published his 'theorised history' of skateboarding, a work that stands out as one of very few full operationalizations of Lefebvre's work in the discipline of architectural history (Borden 2001). In that work Borden made a claim for the usefulness of Lefebvre in countering the degeneration of post-structuralist critiques, exemplified in the architectural histories of North American theorists such as Beatriz Colomina, Anthony Vidler and Mark Wigley. These histories, Borden argued, whilst theoretically innovative and transformative of the interpretation of modern and contemporary architecture, had resulted in an endlessly folding narrative on a settled 'canon' (Borden 2001: 8). Lefebvre offered an alternative, by which the central figure of the 'architect' and the closed space of architectural production could be radically opened to other, 'everyday' practices of spatial production.

Borden's project to utilize Lefebvre was shared, in Britain and the USA, by a wide range of historians, critics and practitioners of architecture (Harris 1997,

McLeod 1996, Upton 2002). That wider movement of the late 1990s went further in identifying Lefebvre's work as potentially useful for the renewal of architectural practice. Not only was there a vocalization of growing discontent with the limitations of post-structuralism in history and criticism, but also a response to the emergence of 'neo-avant-garde' architects – Peter Eisenman, Zaha Hadid, Rem Koolhaas, Daniel Libeskind, for example – whose work, while stretching the formal possibilities of architecture, simultaneously abandoned any progressive or social role for the architect. It seems that Lefebvre's work offered, particularly in *The Production of Space* (1991 [1974]), a way out of an impasse generated by the split between a refined hyper-criticism in the academy and the continued production of the built environment with all its attendant problems of patronage, politics and economy.

'Neo-avant-gardism' – canonized, male/masculine, big-'A' and abstract – was to be displaced through the exploration and integration of the marginalized, female/feminine, domestic and 'concrete'. Thus the messiness of the kitchen table, the street and the alleyway was presented as a 'concrete' challenge to the formal abstractions of the neo-avant-garde and, most important of all, a 'subject/body' of inhabitation, or 'use' of architecture, was pulled into relation with architectural questions (on the urban, on order, on space, on ethical practice, on matter), both political and aesthetic (see for examples Confurius 2000, Harris and Berke 1997, Hill 1998, Wigglesworth and Till 1998).

As a consequence, and returning to Borden as an example, a marginal subject/body – for Borden the skateboarder, just as in other works of the period the housewife, the homeless, the child, the street walker, the cigarette smoker and so on – was understood as *the* location at which the production of the urban occurs (Borden 1998: 66). This figuration was in part due to a compression of Lefebvre's distinct 'triads' of the social production of space and the spatial reproduction of the body, in which the dialectical relation *spatial practice/representations of space/representational spaces* became synonymous with the *perceived/conceived/lived* body (ibid.: 39–40). At the same time, and despite persistent pleas to the contrary, Lefebvre's always conjunctural critique of everyday life, space and the state was conflated with both a prior architectural discourse on the 'ordinary', 'pop' and 'vernacular', and with the theoretical legacies of Michel de Certeau's anthropology of everyday practices, which invested so much hope in the creative and resistant capacities of 'the common hero' (de Certeau 1988 [1980]: n.p.).

Finally, though not true of Borden's work, Lefebvre's proposition that the urban should be understood as a transformative mediation of the abstract (architecture/planning) and the concrete (occupation of space) generally appeared as though he had understood the urban as a barely resistant 'medium' by which the citizen/subject and the state might be sucked into relation.[2] Relying on just such an interpretation drove Lawrence Barth to distraction, declaring Lefebvre redundant, anachronistic and satisfying 'only the most romantic among us' (Barth 2000: 24).

Despite attempts to the contrary, then, architecture was reduced to a 'representational' medium, mobilized by higher, abstract authorities – principally the state and the market – and resisted or transformed in various ways by creative, embodied subjects. Thus the 'canon' has been splendidly preserved and transcended in the crudest dialectical fashion.

The domestication of Lefebvre's revolutionary project into architectural discourse was not politically innocent, despite, and therefore because of, intentions. Discernible behind much of this work in architectural theory and practice is a broadly social democratic enterprise that, crucially, accepted the politico-economic constraints advanced by neoliberal political fractions – the very same political fractions who were the ashamed inheritors of constituencies historically enthusiastic toward a compromised, 'mixed-economy' programme for the capitalist state: the 'triangulating' administrations of Clinton in the USA, 1993–2001, and New Labour in Britain, 1997–2010.

In that context, the confusion over Lefebvre's project can be seen as a result of it being 'turned back on its head'. Whilst Lefebvre identified the urban as *the* location for the formation of revolutionary subjectivities in and through some kind of *autogestion*, this has to be understood within the original dialectical conditions that Lefebvre presupposed. The urban is such a revolutionary site precisely because it is the spatial realization of ever-increasing fragmentation and subjectification by advanced capitalist relations (Goonewardena et al. 2008). It is, we might say, the spatial equivalent of the 'real subsumption of labour' by machine production as opposed to the merely 'formal subsumption of labour' in pre-industrial manufacture. The result of this process of 'spatial subsumption' is the proliferation of 'identities', and even political 'groupuscules', towards which capital is not only apparently indifferent, but is largely *invested* (Lefebvre 1969 [1968]: 43–53): history leading bad (or back) side first.

The contemporary urban, as a specific level of the 'state mode of production', is, for Lefebvre, a 'space of catastrophe' (as the reading of Jameson 1991: xi suggests and Stanek 2011, confirms), a space that is at once both a summit of capitalist relations and precisely, therefore, the point at which revolutionary agency *might* occur. Not for nothing was the title of Lefebvre's account of Nanterre in 1968 volcanic. So understood, Lefebvre's work is useful for analyses of contemporary urban conditions, but obfuscating if mobilized in the celebration of the 'creative powers' of the partial, fragmentary subject produced in such spaces of catastrophe. This tends beyond obfuscation towards the dangerous if those fragmentary subjects are considered as prior to, and outside of, an equally prior form (let us say the state, institutions or the market), whose relation of externality is apparently 'mediated' (as in transmitted) through the urban.

The consequences for architectural theory and practice, and the arts and humanities in general, of the extension of normative neoliberal conceptions of the urban – as a domain in which the state 'captures' flows of capital for the production of sites of social goods and pleasure, coincidentally making those who are forced to reproduce such spaces in their daily lives 'more competitive' (see Charnock and Ribera-Fumaz 2011, for a critique of the contemporary urban development schemes that precisely targets this condition) – are of course far less serious than the reproduction, expansion and intensification of capital in daily life, state terrorism and environmental destruction. But they are no less tragic and they have a significance of sorts, a significance that extends through the muddle of the architectural canon understood for much of the twentieth century within a fundamentally idealist conception of architecture as a visual or representational art.

To summarize, architectural theory that mobilized Lefebvre in the late 1990s ended up retaining a conception of architecture as always signifying something outside of itself. This operated in two directions: first a prior, given, phenomenal subject/body; secondly a prior, given abstract state form. It is the contention of this chapter that Lefebvre offers a means to conceptualize *all three* – architectural space, the subject/body, and the 'state mode of production' – as *produced* in the metabolic relation between 'nature/human/matter', which are really holding terms or place terms that are themselves in constant transformation. The task then is to demonstrate that architecture, as a particular process of production, is also necessarily a particular process of production of subjects/bodies and a state mode of production. Or, to put that more accurately: the production of space, the production of subjects/bodies, and the production of state and market forms are all dialectically conditioned by each other.

THE SOUTH BANK AS A 'REPRESENTATION OF THE SOCIAL DEMOCRATIC STATE'

Since its opening (in May 1951), the Royal Festival Hall (RFH) and the South Bank Exhibition of the Festival of Britain (1951) have attracted considerable attention in architectural literature, much of it revolving around the articulation of social democracy with architectural modernism – that the RFH and the Exhibition constitute an exemplary kind of modern architecture that was able to represent the welfare state to largely passive political subjects (Conekin 2003, Curtis 1985/6, Forty 1976 and 1995, Pevsner 2010, and Richards 1951). We can observe at least three major reconfigurations of a distinct matrix – of state (as social democracy), technology (as modern architecture) and subject (as passive citizenry) – through the literature on the RFH and Exhibition over the past 60 years. Within these accounts, 'technology' – variously understood either as the technical conception of architectural space in modernism (formal), and/or its realization through advanced technological practices of construction (constructional) – has provided a problematic field for assessing the relative success or failure of the architecture of the South Bank.

Architectural commentators of the 1950s tended to understand the role of modern architecture in the formation of social democracy as more or less coincidental – that is, fundamental to the technical character of welfare-state projects, but equally outside the politics of the same. Whilst Nikolaus Pevsner had consistently argued that modern architecture was an appropriate formal and constructional mode for the mass production of building, the unfolding historical progress of that mode was depicted by him as occurring alongside and, even if lamentably, outside of developments of the state.

Indeed, what was exemplary about the Exhibition and the RFH for Pevsner, writing in 1951, was not the display of technological progress (the extent of which, as Reyner Banham (1976) later pointed out, was deeply ambiguous), but the dragging up of a historical planning principle – the 'picturesque' (Pevsner 2010: 198). It was this older device for conceiving the formal arrangement of space that, for Pevsner, was so representative of the modern English, liberal, social democratic state. Those 'viewers' of the RFH and the South Bank (the architectural subject always being optic for Pevsner) would *naturally* respond to the form of its spaces, given the deep cultural resonance of free, liberal, appropriative subjectivity now commanding the landscape. Modern architecture was to be harnessed by the social democratic state, now representative of welfare-state provision – full employment, health care, comprehensive education, housing for all. The state itself was fundamentally understood as a system of technocratic planning institutions, operating for the interests of all, 'all' here meaning a diverse citizenry of individual interests.

This initial position on the architecture of the South Bank – that it constituted a formal representation of technology, which was further utilized by the state – tended to harden through the 1960s. Commentators and historians (see, for example, Frayn 1963, and Jackson 1965) argued that modern architects were practically drafted in to the organization of production by the state during the 1940s due to the proclivity of the 'new empiricists' (as certain modernists in Britain were then dubbed) for organization, analysis and fast production. It was further argued that what was so attractive about British modern architecture and planning for the new 'compromised' social democratic state was that it was precisely *not* loaded with particular class or political interests or connotations, because it was manifestly 'pragmatic' and technocratic. This, despite the historic association of modern architecture in Britain with the socialism of William Morris and the work of various European social democratic and communist émigrés of the 1930s.

Such ideas were later 'theorized' in the 1980s through a Foucauldian analysis conducted by Barry Curtis (1985/6), who pushed the proposition further in suggesting that 'picturesque planning' was, itself, a disciplinary technology that constituted a new 'citizen/consumer', fortuitously resolving the antagonism of previous classical class antinomies. Despite the use of Michel Foucault's conceptualization of governmentality, however, Curtis still seems to have trodden on the secure grounds of 'the state' – state-planning institutions and state technocrats used architecture to weave a narrative into which the 'citizen/ consumer' was induced.

However, it is with the work of the architectural historian Adrian Forty (1976, 1995) that these different, though commensurate, settings of the state/technology/ citizen matrix have been most successfully thought through. For Forty, the Exhibition of 1951 was a fundamentally ideological project. Supposed to provide an expectant polity with a 'more real experience' of the welfare state than the 'waiting room of a doctor's surgery', the Exhibition in fact provided, Forty argued in 1976, a technocratic cover for the inadequacies of British social democracy to resolve the antagonism of labour and capital.

Looking back on modern architecture's mid-twentieth-century running to ground from the perspective of the mid-1990s, Forty presented a further refinement to this ideological critique. Modern architecture had not only represented social democracy; it had become identified with it – attacks on one were necessarily an assault on the other. This had come about principally due to modernism's technological language. Technology – whether formal or constructional – constituted a ready-made Fabian promise, an ideology of the always future resolution of the present inadequacies of redistributive liberalism.

Apparently so different in interpretation and consequence, what all these perspectives assume is that the state, however that is defined, operates outside of and prior to polity and architecture. Architecture is a 'medium' that the state can mobilize, either to construct its own polity or to communicate with a given, equally prior, polity. How to challenge such an entrenched, and powerful, account? Following Lefebvre's own critical procedure, let us start by acknowledging the truth of the 'appearance' in ideological projects, but assert that something is going on 'behind its back' that needs to be examined.

The assumptions made in the state/architecture/citizen matrix are both critically astute, in that they describe very well the ideology of mid-twentieth-century social democracy, and at the same time materially false. That is, the critiques of the South Bank architecture, and of other major projects of the period, commonly presented in architectural literature reproduce the ideological proposition that the 'state' can successfully redistribute the surplus of capitalist production without becoming, as Lefebvre argued it necessarily must, guarantor of capitalist production and social reproduction. It is time for Lefebvre's life-long project to be turned towards, and engage with, the conditions of production.

The following sets out to consider the material production of the RFH, in its most prosaic forms, in the instance given below – through soil mechanics. This follows Lefebvre's suggestions that the process by which a new state space is produced demonstrates its origins in certain compromises between capital and labour and how the necessarily contradictory nature of this compromise results in both new state institutional forms and new subjects/bodies.

This strand of Lefebvre's work has been substantially developed in critical geography, at at least two levels. On the one hand the mobilization of concepts such as 'metabolism' and 'circulation' in understanding the material reproduction of the urban has brought out the critical tension between apparently 'neutral' technical planning and production regimes, which are proven in the analysis to be no such thing, and evidently 'partisan' ideological projects, which are shown to contribute to the formation of technical and scientific knowledge (see Smith 1984, Swyngedouw 1999, 2006). In such work, the uneven development of material resources, urban security and urban governance are understood not as the result of 'misunderstandings' of how the urban 'works', but are the product of, and co-extensive with, race, gender and particularly class struggles.

On the other hand, a growing body of work has taken up Lefebvre's challenge to reconceive the state–space relation beyond moribund models of discrete, legitimate, juridico-national powers operating within strictly bounded flat, or 'hollow', territorial spaces (Brenner 2004, Brenner et al. 2003). In this work, 'space' and the 'state' are no longer considered as a priori *objects* that exist in abstract relation to one another, but as historical *processes*, conditioned by class struggle.

Similarly, bringing Lefebvre into architectural research could offer a chance to look at the 'nitty-gritty' of the nature/human/matter triad (Lefebvre 1988: 88) and the production of new forms of 'state–space' as this occurs at the scale of singular buildings and specific urban developments. Such an approach requires a thinking through of the dialectical relations of the material, social and ideological 'degrees' of production (Lefebvre 1968 [1939]: 152), in which material products and techniques are understood as but one degree, affected by and effective on social processes and products (the market and the state form) and symbolic expressions (rhythmic, social and spatial), though ultimately incommensurate with either.

GROUND EXPLORATION AT THE MATERIAL DEGREE

Ground exploration is a practice within the field of soil mechanics, carried out by engineers to ascertain the structural qualities of the ground on which a particular building will stand. To achieve this, samples of soil are taken from various locations on the site, analysed, and then described in terms of the internal structural qualities of each sample. In the past, such a practice involved extraction of soils that were then 'measured' in the engineer's hand on site – the soil would be crushed by the fingers, smelled, shaken in the hand to observe water dilation, and its textures and colours noted. Accurate assessment of ground conditions relied on the experience and 'know-how' of the engineer employed on the job. This necessarily precluded proper assessment in certain conditions. A tidal river (such as the Thames in London) poses considerable difficulties, given the complex stratification of soils and relationship to a rising and falling water level. To continue the example of the Thames – the soil found beneath the 'made-up ground' (of refuse, rubble, humus and so on) at the South Bank was commonly described as 'grey-blue silty clay', relatively soft to the touch, with some plasticity, some minor dilation, and a particular colour and smell found throughout the Thames valley – 'London blue clay' (see Figure 9.1).

A number of engineering, architectural and construction industry journals reported on the ground exploration conducted at the South Bank in 1948 (for example, Measor and New 1951, and Hole and Eales 1951). That these processes were discussed at all in the period is a result of the then relatively recent technical revolution in soil mechanics and ground exploration. Soil mechanics and analysis had radically advanced in large part due to US 'New Deal' projects of mass road building in the 1930s (Seely 1984). As part of the wider economic plan of federal government demand creation, the USA had entered into a road-building programme that soon resulted in widespread failures, as a large number of standardized road products collapsed.

As Bruce Seely demonstrates (1984: 820–25), the new soil mechanics was able to solve a problem that had proved intractable for either the historical 'know-how' practices or contemporaneous forms of laboratory research in structural

Fig. 9.1   Royal Festival Hall Progress

statics. Rather than simply develop ever more sophisticated forms of quantitative measurement of roadstrip products, soil mechanics – particularly as elaborated by the field's leading engineer/researcher, the Austrian émigré Karl Terzaghi – focused on analysing the structural qualities of soils on which any road product would have to stand. This resulted in the development of a progressively standardized set of interlocking practices for the sampling, recording and classification of soils according to their structural properties (Knight 1948, Nash 1951, Taylor 1948, Terzaghi and Peck 1948). Whilst in outline similar to earlier forms of ground exploration, the new methods developed by Terzaghi and others involved increasingly sophisticated mechanical apparatuses – on site and in the laboratory – so that a number of operatives were employed, at discrete moments in time and space, none of whom worked directly with 'soil', but assessed, measured and analysed various effects evident in the behaviour of those apparatuses. The results of the analysis could then be projected across the construction site, producing a stratigraphy whose structural interactions, with the projected loads of the proposed building structure, could be predicted.

Further progress in soil mechanics and ground exploration was made in Britain during the Second World War. This began, as in the USA, with road building, but soon developed with wartime airstrip production (Marwick and Webb 1946). Whilst this can be understood as simply one relatively minor development in the general transfer of construction materials, technologies, infrastructure and dollars from the USA to Britain during the Second World War (Kohan 1952), the development of soil mechanics displays some peculiarities.

The Building Research Station (BRS) – the national research and development institution for the building industry in Britain, established during the 1920s to provide technological solutions to mass social housing (Swenarton 2005/6, 2008) – was directed towards problems of immediate reconstruction during the Blitz. The Soil Physics Section of the BRS used soil mechanics in assessing insurance claims made against bomb-damage repairs by London property owners. The BRS was able to demonstrate that many of these claims were made against damage not caused by bombing, but by the shrinkage behaviour of 'London Clay', which resulted from the proximity of tree roots and exceptionally dry summers throughout 1941–45 (Charles et al. 1996: 138).

As a result, by 1948 'London Clay' had become one of the first soils in the world to have been systematically redefined through laboratory testing. Professional engineers and contractors were no longer satisfied by the description of 'London Clay' as a 'grey-blue silty clay', a description entirely lacking in the technical specificity required for any analysis of that soil's structural qualities. Rather, it was understood and described as a matrix of soil properties, expressed in the formalized 'trilinear soil classification scheme' (see Figure 9.2). 'London Clay' so described is no longer a 'natural' product, but is a 'product' of the warfare state-institutional apparatus. 'London Clay' is a systematized object in the sense that it is no longer a 'thing' (clay) found 'here' or 'there' (in parts of London) but is a 'structure' (of quantified silt, sand, clay and moisture content) with internal qualities (compressive and shear strength) and environmental properties (shrinkage, expansion, movement) that occur in relation to other 'structures' (gravels, sands, rocks) in a stratigraphy (London itself).

GROUND EXPLORATION AT THE SOCIAL DEGREE

The first mention of ground exploration at the South Bank is provided by *The Builder*, in February 1949:

> [A] number of samples were taken at various depths, enclosed in air-tight tins and taken for testing to the laboratories of the [London County Council's – LCC's] Chief Engineer's Department at the County Hall. Granular materials, such as sand and gravel, were tested for moisture content and particle size. Cohesive soils, such as silt and clay, were tested for moisture content, liquid limit, plastic limit and by triazial test for shear strength and angle of internal friction. (Anon. 1949a)

The report begins to indicate a network or 'circuit' of state institutions and the production of knowledge through laboratory testing of samples. Such a picture is further developed in a brief footnote to an account of this phase of construction at the South Bank provided by two architects in an early part of a series of reports provided for the *Architects' Journal* throughout 1949 and 1951. John Eastwick-Field and John Stillman produced these reports in collaboration with the lead architects

Fig. 9.2   Particle
Size Distribution

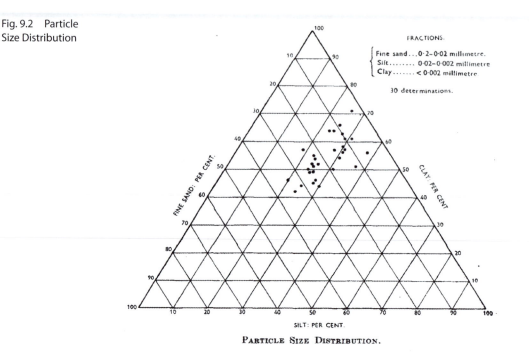

PARTICLE SIZE DISTRIBUTION.

for the concert hall – Robert Matthew, Leslie Martin, Edwin Williams and the engineer Guthlac Wilson of Scott & Wilson (Eastwick-Field and Stillman, 1950: 189). Eastwick-Field and Stillman note that the trial borings for the South Bank were subcontracted to Ground Exploration Ltd (Eastwick-Field and Stillman, 1950: 248).

The knowledge of the ground at the South Bank is then produced in two distinct 'loops' in this circuit. In the first 'loop', the private contractor Ground Exploration Ltd provides extracted samples in sealed tins that are distributed to a system of institutional laboratories at the LCC and the BRS, who conduct technical tests to gain information on the structural qualities of the soils; in the second 'loop', the same contractors (Ground Exploration Ltd) provide boring apparatus and labour for a private engineering firm (Scott & Wilson), which abstracts information from the borings on site. These data are then drawn up as sectional projections in the offices of Scott & Wilson, and distributed to the Architect and Chief Engineer at the LCC offices.

What does this add to our picture of a transformed technical practice? Here, it is worth emphasizing the effect that the development of ground exploration has on the conception of the technical subject. In already acting on a 'mediated' (or 'intermediary'), socialized process (the technical apparatus), rather than an 'unmediated', or 'natural', thing (soil), the technical subject is also transformed. The expert engineer, who gains understanding of a given soil through subjective experience and intuition, is replaced by a 'network' of institutions and practices, competences and knowledges that produces (or reproduces) a system of 'soils'. This implies an already fragmentary 'body/subject' – the individual labourer or engineer cannot possibly understand the soil mechanics of the South Bank *in toto*, but can only contribute to an already socialized process of knowledge production. The very forms of the apparatuses – the auger boring equipment, the wax-sealed cylinders containing the soil, the mechanical trial apparatus in the laboratories – preclude individual 'judgement' on the quality of the soil, requiring a social process of production to get any meaningful result.

At the same time, with the utilization of private engineering firms (here, Scott & Wilson) by state-sponsored institutions (here, the BRS), the operations of local government (here, the LCC) are engaged in more than 'provision' for a given, regional polity. Commentary on the architecture of social democracy and the welfare state has always relied on the language of redistributive politics – markets and capitalist production produce surpluses that are then redirected by the welfare state for the provision of social goods. But the evidence of ground exploration at the South Bank suggests something quite different – here we have a complex inter-relation of a public and a private institution, in which the former is deliberately engaged in the progressive support and development of the latter: the state mode of production. The fragmentary subject/body of ground exploration is socialized through contracts between private and state (local and national) authorities.

GROUND EXPLORATION IN THE IDEOLOGICAL DEGREE

This account of ground exploration, as an operation conducted by private technical institutions integrated with national and local state authorities, was further reported by *The Builder* only a month later, though in a different context. *The Builder* reported on a debate in the House of Commons arising from a question posed by the Tory MP Sir Ralph Glyn, who attempted to oppose the construction of the concert hall at the South Bank on the basis that the site was unsuitable for such a building. Herbert Morrison, Lord President of the Council, the political figurehead for the Festival of Britain, presented his defence of the concert-hall project based on the results of the trial borings:

> Mr H. Morrison said that he was assured by the Department of Scientific and
> Industrial Research ... experiments were in progress to reduce sound vibration
> at its source. Trial borings showing the nature of the sub-soil were also available.
> The question of made-up ground was not a factor at all as the building would
> have its foundations on ballast over blue clay, which was well known to be one of
> the best foundations available. (Anon. 1949b)

Whilst much of Morrison's response is based on other technical activities – acoustic testing – and the references to soil mechanics are technically incoherent, the point of interest lies in the extent to which ground exploration was presented as a product of scientific research conducted within state institutions – the BRS in particular.[3] That such a defence was necessary was due to political resistance (clearly represented by the Tory party, but evident on the Labour party benches too) to Morrison's long-term project of transforming the heart of London, starting with the reconstruction of Waterloo Bridge in the 1920s, continuing on with the new County Hall building (opposite the Palace of Westminster) and into the architecture of the RFH and the Festival of Britain Exhibition. The 'science' of the Department of Scientific and Industrial Research is here mobilized for the purposes of social democratic planning of the urban.

This disguises, however, a more fundamental relationship between urban governance, state institutional practices, engineering, construction, the market and the material conditions with which any urban development necessarily has to contend – the ground. In ideological terms, whilst it is quite clear that Morrison intended to mobilize state and market resources in the redistribution of social wealth (scientific, material and spatial), the material processes engaged can be described quite differently. As I hope the preceding has shown, ground exploration can be understood in terms of Lefebvre's theorization of the 'state mode of production' (Lefebvre 1977: 59–68) – in particular, his suggestion that social (re)production reaches a stage at which productive activity is directed toward the 'intermediary':

> The intermediary seizes the reality of those actors put in connection. Commodities and money connect individual labour and social labour; abstracted, they are concretised; it is advisable to study them in-and-for-themselves, so much so that one reduces (excises) that from which they proceed. (Ibid.: 65)[4]

I have understood this passage – and the work of which it is a part (De l'État) – in relation to the Grundrisse (Marx 1973), particularly as Marx relates the process by which the production of relative surplus value results in the creation of 'new needs', subsuming 'nature' within social reproduction (Marx 1973: 408–10). Taking the above comment by Lefebvre as a guiding statement for the analysis, the emerging technical practice of ground exploration can be understood as acting on the 'intermediary', even when this is commonly understood as some kind of an 'external' thing. Whilst ground exploration is ideologically mobilized in the period to overcome certain instrumental and pragmatic conditions – how to 'know' the structure of a given piece of ground for the purposes of constructing a large building – it is also both the product of and productive of new market conditions and new 'state forms' that are in turn expressive of transformative conditions for subject/bodies held in new social relations. In other words, I hope I have shown that 'soil' mechanics, while manifestly dealing with the same 'stuff', rarely has anything to do with the 'soil' that you and I would recognize were we to go down to the Thames riverbank and get our hands dirty.

NOTES

1   This chapter has been significantly revised and owes a great deal to critical commentaries provided by Łukasz Stanek and Christian Schmid. Its inadequacies are my own.

2   Cf. Stanek (2008), who provides a very different account of 'mediation' and its role in Lefebvre's critique of the social production of space in modernity.

3   *The Builder* presented a series of reports on ground exploration as developed by the Building Research Station (BRS). See Anon. (1948); Anon. (1949c); and Hammond (1949).

4   Translation of *De l'État* author's own.

REFERENCES

Anon. 1948. 'Tests for Soil Compaction: A Recent British Standard'. *The Builder* 175(5507): 289.

Anon. 1949a. 'The South Bank River Wall: Work Now Well under Way'. *The Builder* 176(5532): 252.

Anon. 1949b. 'In Parliament'. *The Builder* 176(5537): 404.

Anon. 1949c. 'Building on Made-Up Ground: A Research Station Digest'. *The Builder* 177(5560): 330–31.

Banham, R. 1976. 'The Style: "Flimsy … Effeminate?"', in *A Tonic to the Nation: The Festival of Britain 1951*, edited by M. Banham and B. Hillier. London: Thames and Hudson, 190–96.

Barth, L. 2000. 'Revisited: Henri Lefebvre and the Urban Condition'. *Daidalos* 75: 23–5.

Borden, I. 1998. *'A Theorised History of Skateboarding with Particular Reference to the Ideas of Henri Lefebvre'.* Unpublished doctoral thesis. London: University College London.

Borden, I. 2001. *Skateboarding, Space and the City.* Oxford and New York: Berg.

Brenner, N. 2004. *New State Spaces: Urban Governance and the Rescaling of Statehood.* Oxford: Oxford University Press.

Brenner, N., Jessop, B., Jones, M. and Macleod, G. (eds). 2003. *State/Space: A Reader.* Oxford: Blackwell.

de Certeau, M. 1988 [1980]. *The Practice of Everyday Life.* Trans. Steven Rendall. Berkeley, CA: University of California Press.

Charles, J.A., Driscoll, R.M.C., Powell, J.J.M. and Tedd, P. 1996. 'Seventy-Five Years of Building Research: Geotechnical Aspects'. *Proceedings of the Institution of Civil Engineers Geotechnical Engineering*, 119, 129–45.

Charnock, G. and Ribera-Fumaz, R. 2011. 'A New Space for Knowledge and People? Henri Lefebvre, Representations of Space, and the Production of "22@Barcelona"'. *Environment and Planning D: Society and Space* 29(4): 613–32.

Conekin, B.E. 2003. *'The Autobiography of a Nation': The 1951 Festival of Britain.* Manchester and New York: Manchester University Press.

Confurius, G. (ed.) 2000. *The Everyday.* Special issue of *Daidalos* 75.

Curtis, B. 1985/6. 'One Continuous Interwoven Story: The Festival of Britain'. *Block* 11: 48–52.

Eastwick-Field, J. and Stillman, J. 1950. 'Concert Hall Progress'. *Architects' Journal* 111(2869): 189–92.

Forty, A. 1976. 'Festival Politics', in *A Tonic to the Nation*, edited by M. Banham and B. Hillier. London: Thames & Hudson, 26–39.

Forty, A. 1995. 'Being or Nothingness: Private Experience and Public Architecture in Post-war Britain'. *Architectural History* 38: 25–35.

Frayn, M. 1963. 'Festival', in *Age of Austerity, 1945– 1951*, edited by M. Sissons and P. French. London: Hodder and Stoughton, 307–26.

Goonewardena, K., Kipfer, S., Milgrom, R. and Schmid, C. (eds). 2008. *Space, Difference, Everyday Life: Reading Henri Lefebvre*. London and New York: Routledge.

Hammond, R. 1949. 'Notes on Site Exploration and Foundations of Buildings'. *The Builder* 177(5574): 830–31.

Harris, S. 1997. 'Everyday Architecture', in *Architecture of the Everyday*, edited by S. Harris and D. Berke. New York: Princeton Architectural Press, 1–8.

Harris, S. and Berke, D. (eds) 1997. *Architecture of the Everyday*. New York: Princeton Architectural Press.

Hill, J. (ed.) 1998. *Occupying Architecture: Between the Architect and the User*. London and New York: Routledge.

Hole, E. and Eales, F. 1951. 'The Construction of the Royal Festival Hall'. *The Structural Engineer* 29(3): 78–91.

Jackson, A. 1965. 'The Politics of Architecture: English Architecture 1929–1951'. *Journal of the Society of Architectural Historians* 24(1): 97–107.

Jameson, F. 1991. *Postmodernism or, The Cultural Logic of Late Capitalism*. London: Verso.

Knight, B. 1948. *Soil Mechanics for Civil Engineers*. London: Edward Arnold.

Kohan, C.M. 1952. *History of the Second World War, United Kingdom Civil Series: Works and Buildings*. London: HMSO.

Lefebvre, H. 1968 [1939]. *Dialectical Materialism*. Trans. John Sturrock. London: Jonathan Cape.

Lefebvre, H. 1969 [1968]. *The Explosion: Marxism and the French Upheaval*. Trans. Alfred Ehrenfeld. London and New York: Monthly Review Press.

Lefebvre, H. 1977. *De l'État: Le mode de production étatique, tome III*. Paris: Union Générale d'Éditions.

Lefebvre, H. 1988. 'Toward a Leftist Cultural Politics: Remarks Occasioned by the Centenary of Marx's Death'. Trans. D. Reifman, in *Marxism and the Interpretation of Culture*, edited by C. Nelson and L. Grossman. London: Macmillan, 75–88.

Lefebvre, H. 1991 [1974]. *The Production of Space*. Trans. Donald Nicholson-Smith. Oxford: Blackwell.

Lefebvre, H. 1995 [1961]. *Introduction to Modernity: Twelve Preludes, September 1959–May 1961*. Trans. John Moore. London: Verso.

McLeod, M. 1996. 'Everyday and "Other" Spaces', in *Architecture and Feminism*, edited by D. Coleman, E. Danze and C. Henderson. New York: Princeton Architectural Press, 1–37.

Markwick, A.H.D. and Webb, S.B. 1946. *Road Research Bulletin, IV: Soil Survey Procedure and its Application in Road Construction*. London: HMSO.

Marx, K. 1973. *Grundrisse: Foundations of the Critique of Political Economy (Rough Draft)*. Translated by Martin Nicolaus. Harmondsworth: Penguin/New Left Books.

Measor, E. O. and New, D.H. 1951. 'The Design and Construction of the Royal Festival Hall, South Bank'. *The Institution of Civil Engineers Journal* 36(7): 241–305.

Nash, K. 1951. *The Elements of Soil Mechanics in Theory and Practice: Four Lectures Delivered at King's College, London*. London: Constable & Company.

Pevsner, N. 2010. 'Festival of Britain'. Trans. S. Eiche, in *Visual Planning and the Picturesque*, edited by Matthew Aithison. Los Angeles, CA: Getty, 195–8.

Richards, J.M. (ed.) 1951. 'Foreword', *South Bank Exhibition*. Special issue of *Architectural Review* 110(656).

Seely, B.E. 1984. 'The Scientific Mystique in Engineering: Highway Research at the Bureau of Public Roads, 1918–1940'. *Technology and Culture* 25(4): 798–831.

Smith, N. 1984. *Uneven Development: Nature, Capital and the Production of Space*. Oxford: Blackwell.

Stanek, Ł. 2008. 'Space as Concrete Abstraction: Hegel, Marx, and Modern Urbanism in Henri Lefebvre', in *Space, Difference, Everyday Life: Reading Henri Lefebvre*, edited by K. Goonewardena, S. Kipfer, R. Milgrom and C. Schmid. London and New York: Routledge, 62–79.

Stanek, Ł. 2011. *Henri Lefebvre on Space: Architecture, Urban Research, and the Production of Theory*. Minneapolis, MN: University of Minnesota Press.

Swenarton, M. 2005/6. 'Breeze Blocks and Bolshevism: Housing Policy and the Origins of the Building Research Station 1917–21'. *Construction History* 21: 69–80.

Swenarton, M. 2008. *Building the New Jerusalem: Architecture, Housing and Politics, 1900–1930*. Bracknell: IHS BRE Press.

Swyngedouw, E. 1999. 'Modernity and Hybridity: Nature, Regeneracionismo, and the Production of the Spanish Waterscape, 1890–1930'. *Annals of the Association of American Geographers* 89(3): 443–65.

Swyngedouw, E. 2006. 'Circulations and Metabolisms: (Hybrid) Natures and (Cyborg) Cities'. *Science as Culture* 15(2): 105–21.

Taylor, D. 1948. *Fundamentals of Soil Mechanics*. London: Chapman & Hall.

Terzaghi, K. and Peck, R. 1948. *Soil Mechanics in Engineering Practice*. London: Chapman & Hall.

Upton, D. 2002. 'Architecture in Everyday Life'. *New Literary History* 33(4): 707–23.

Wigglesworth, S. and Till, J. (eds) 1998. *The Everyday and Architecture*. Special issue of *Architectural Design* 134.

10

The Space of the Square: A Lefebvrean Archaeology of Budapest

Ákos Moravánszky

Budapest emerged as the capital of Hungary with the unification of the two cities Buda and Pest and the market town Óbuda in November 1873.[1] Enabled by the political compromise (*Ausgleich*) with the Austrian half of the Habsburg Empire (1867) and the ensuing economic upswing with an influx of foreign capital after post-revolutionary decades of so-called 'passive resistance' to Austrian imperial administration, Budapest became a European capital with an unprecedented population growth. Since its central area has a built substance originating in the decades between 1873 and 1914, the city is uniquely shaped by the economy and culture of liberal capitalism.

The basic tenets of Henri Lefebvre's theory were gained from the observation of the capitalist city. Since Budapest is a paradigmatic case of capitalist urbanization in the late nineteenth century, this theory offers adequate tools to analyse its complex spatiality. Budapest served as the mould for other models of society and production, of socialism and post-socialism as well, inspiring or even necessitating interpretations that address the relationship of a society to its conceived, perceived and lived spaces. Similar interpretations abound in the literature – Péter Nádas' *Évkönyv* (*Yearbook*, 1989), with observations about individuals and societies shaped by the form of houses and cities, is just one case in point. The launch of the journal of the Centre for Regional Research of the Hungarian Academy of Science, *Tér és társadalom* (*Space and Society*) in 1987, with references to neo-Marxist interpretations of social space – including Lefebvre's (Kiss 1987) – indicate that empirical research on territorial development, mobility and urbanization started well before the collapse of socialism. The intention behind many of the debates was to show the competing political interests and their social programmes behind the technical or professional arguments of urban planning. Since in a socialist economy competing positions were not based on opposed economic interests, they concluded that urban practice as disguised, economy-based social struggle would eventually give way to real social practice in the city – at least this was the hope of many theorists in search of an alternative model of socialism.

After the collapse of socialism and the return to a market economy, however, urban space became once again a battlefield – the privatization process and its profiteers, the interests of financially independent local (district) governments and of foreign and Hungarian investors and developers shattered the monolithic unity of state planning. Still, references to the historic urban structure of Budapest, the roots of the city in the *genius loci* and continuous refinements in a series of urban beautifications supported by *városatyák* (city-fathers) and visionary mayors and realized by architects and planners are abundant. We have to ask whether the notion of urban space itself has an ideological function, directing the attention to the topophilic, positive aspects of space, the unity of the perceived, conceived and lived, and away from the hard and more surface-bound rather than space-bound realities of real estate, where the basic facts of control over the city are established.

In this chapter, I will focus on four urban squares in Budapest to discuss their perceived, conceived and lived aspects, and to assess the performance of Henri Lefebvre's theory of social space – and to detect its possible blind spots. This approach was stimulated by a peculiarity of the Hungarian language. The word for space, *tér*, also means an urban square. *Tér* has Finno-Ugric roots, meaning breadth, width (for example, of a fishing net) or a wide area (Zaicz 2006: 840).

In most languages, the term 'urban space' (for example, *Stadtraum* in German) appeared as late as the second half of the nineteenth century, influenced by research and theoretical work in the physiology and psychology of visual perception (Moravánszky and Gyöngy 2003: 121–255, Moravánszky 2012). Before that, speaking about 'urban space' rather than of squares and streets must have appeared strange and abstract, more a metaphor than an empirically accessible entity – like speaking of 'musical space' today. Therefore German urban theorists of the nineteenth century spoke of 'Platz' (square) when they discussed the aesthetics of urban space – for instance Albert Erich Brinckmann in his important book *Platz und Monument* (Brinckmann 1908). Camillo Sitte referred in his early handbook of urban design, *Der Städtebau nach seinen künstlerischen Grundsätzen* (*City Planning According to Aesthetic Principles*), to the new urban illness that he diagnosed in the modern city with its wide and open streets and squares as 'Platzscheu' (the fear of the square) rather than as agoraphobia (Sitte in Collins 1965). We can conclude that the first 'spatial turn' of the nineteenth century was triggered by the recognition that visual perception in three dimensions provides a better explanation of the urban phenomenon than cadastral plans, plot structures and street axes. But in Hungarian, the homonymy of space and urban square was very likely a stimulus to raise the question whether the two dimensions of the square were sufficient to explain the problems created by urban modernization.

I selected the four urban squares along an imaginary straight line which I had drawn on the map of Budapest: the *Oktogon*, *Károly Kós tér*, *II. János Pál pápa tér* and *Nyugati tér*. In doing this, I wanted to emphasize that they are 'dissected' from the organism and the city to analyse their temporal layers rather than to observe their spatial connections when walking along the streets.

THE OKTOGON

Fig. 10.1 Satellite image of the Oktogon

The Oktogon is the most representative urban square of nineteenth-century Budapest. It marks the intersection of the two most important components of the new capital after unification: the Nagykörút (Grand Boulevard) that encircles the inner city on the Pest side, and the representative radial avenue Andrássy út, leading from the centre to the large city park, Városliget (see Figure 10.1).

The planning of the square was in the hands of a new institution, independent of the municipality: the Fővárosi Közmunkák Tanácsa (Council of Metropolitan Public Works), modelled after the Metropolitan Board of Works in London, cooperating first with a French–German–Hungarian building consortium that started to sell the plots and to build the first houses, including the four large buildings on the Oktogon. The director of the consortium was Lajos Lechner, winner of the competition in 1871 for the regulation plan (master plan) of Budapest. Lechner also developed the concept for the 2,200-metre avenue Andrássy út, with the two urban squares, the Oktogon and the round Körönd (Circus). These squares subdivided the street into three sections: the first, between the city centre and the Oktogon, is 32 metres wide, lined with four-to-five-storey buildings; the second, between the Oktogon and the Körönd, is 43 metres wide and three to four storeys high; and finally the third, between the Körönd and the large city park, Városliget, is 61 metres wide, with a row of terrace housing as its first subsection, and with free-standing urban villas in the section close to the park. The intention was to achieve a continuous decrease in scale and modulation of urban character when moving from the city towards the green space, the site of the big millennial exhibition at the time of the street's inauguration.

The Oktogon is the result of an urban 'clearing', to use Heidegger's reference to the etymological connection of space and clearing in the German language: 'a space is something that has been made room for, something that is cleared and free, namely, within a boundary …' (Heidegger 1977: 332). The Oktogon had to be carved out of the mass of small houses in Pest. The construction of a representative avenue that connects the inner city with the only large urban green on the Pest side was announced in 1868, immediately after the 'Compromise' of Hungary with Austria. The occasion for the inauguration of this large-scale urban monument was the Millennium in 1896, the celebration of the legendary foundation of the Hungarian state 1,000 years earlier when the chiefs of the land-conquering Magyar tribes elected Árpád as their first ruler.

The architect of the four large neo-Renaissance buildings of palatial dimensions that define the Oktogon was Antal Szkalnitzky; the building permit was issued in 1873. Lajos Hevesi, the journalist–critic later associated with the Vienna Secession, criticized what he thought was a discrepancy between the conceived and the perceived aspects the square:

> It is clear by now that the Oktogon, as it still existed on paper and as a plastercast [model], made a much bigger impression than in brick on the ground. It achieves something that appears almost impossible: narrowing by making wider. A very wide street became here a very narrow square. There is no development in the side direction. We see the four street junctions divided by four blocks of houses, which have neither sufficient façade widths nor sufficient depths, to counterbalance big gaps of the streets flowing into the square. This octagon is in reality a tetragon, since four of its eight sides are made of air. The masses that could seam the square, just like the square seamed by masses, are missing. The folding-screen character of the four blocks, which is very striking today, will probably disappear when the four big streets flowing into the square will be finished, but it will never become a decent public square; we also have to give up any dreams of a monumental fountain, a decorated memorial column or a marble sculpture, since they would block the center of Oktogon, which is needed for something else: traffic.[2]

The Oktogon was an unusually new, spacious dimension for the citizens of Budapest, even if the passers-by do not seem to suffer from agoraphobia in the photographs taken soon after the millenary festivities. The pictures show very clearly that the Oktogon was used simultaneously by trams, coaches and pedestrians as a 'shared space' (see Figure 10.2). But the Oktogon's task was not only functional. It had a representational role, for which the millennial exhibition was the historical occasion. It became an important link in the chain of political monuments, including the Körönd and culminating in the vast Hősök tere (Heroes' Square).

The different 'official' names the square was given at certain moments of history, like Mussolini tér (Mussolini Square), or November 7 tér,[3] never took root in everyday talk; the inhabitants of Budapest always used 'Oktogon' as a reference to the geometric form, to the conceived aspects of the space. The regular octagon as urban square is a distinctly artificial form, created on the drafting table to become a characteristic configuration for Renaissance fortifications and ideal, 'planned' cities. It aggravates the distance from the small streets and one-storey houses and

BUDAPESTER STADTBAHN
SIEMENS & HALSKE.

Ringstrassenlinie. — Kreuzung der Andrássystrasse.

gardens that were destroyed to erect it. The houses lined up on both sides of the street contrasted strikingly with the scale of the still-existing texture.

Fig. 10.2   The Oktogon around 1900

The critic Hevesi criticized the striking similarity of architectural form of the four buildings on the square, and jokingly proposed that kindergarten classes should be taken here to develop the child's mind by finding the slight differences between the corner blocks. Yet the symmetry of the Oktogon exists only on the map, and we can hardly trace this conceived quality in the perceived space of citizens. This imbalance is partly due to the described 'scenography' of Andrássy út, the change of scale of the buildings on the connecting streets; the square is a joint between two sections of the street, and the characters of these two sections were different by design. More importantly, the south-western side of the square, closer to downtown, is much more frequented by the public, due to the subway stations, restaurants and the upscale stores, while the eastern side lacks such functions. The famous restaurant Savoy and the Café Abbázia were on the downtown side of the square, regularly visited by well-known artists of that day.

Even with regard to its built spaces, the Oktogon is much more than an octagonal square surrounded by façades. There are hidden public and semi-public spaces concealed behind its façades, mediating the surrounding chessboard system and the geometry of the square. These concealed spaces are also part of the city, being especially important in Budapest, where the gateways and courtyards form a kind of intermediary space layer between the public spaces outside and private spaces inside. Hidden spaces of a different kind are the stations of the underground tramway, which was built beneath street level in an open ditch at the same time as the buildings lining the avenue. Budapest wanted to showcase the most modern transport infrastructure in continental Europe at the time of the 1896 millenary exhibition and festivities. The electric subway was a symbol of the modern city, a work of the engineer. While it is 'invisible', unlike the Eiffel Tower or the Lisbon elevator, it meant nevertheless the inclusion of a new level into the usage and imagination of the city. The mystery and magic of the modern metropolis were connected to the exploration of this subconscious world.

Night illumination played an important role in the atmospheric effect of the Oktogon. In 1929, a soap manufacturer installed a large electric billboard. With the power of 300,000 candles, it was one of the popular spectacles of urban illumination in Europe, with stars, the moon and, finally, a comet lighting up in a timed sequence. The crossing of Andrássy út and Nagymező utca, just two blocks to the south of the Oktogon, was the centre of nightlife with its variety shows, bars and operetta theatres, and – together with the illumination of the bridges on the Danube – this is the area where Budapest's image as national capital had to be reinvented as a cosmopolitan metropolis of commerce and entertainment. Then, after long decades of relative darkness on the square after the Second World War, in 1970, to commemorate the 25th anniversary of Hungary's 'liberation' by the Soviet army, the results of the 'new economic mechanism' – a cautious liberalization that allowed a de-centralization of economy with more chances for 'private initiatives' – were presented. New housing estates and a new subway line were built and new commodities were produced, with the 'neonization' of Budapest as an expression of the will to catch up with the consumer worlds of capitalist societies. This programme was adopted by the 10th Congress of the Hungarian Communist Party that same year, and a conference on advertising was organized as well. The function of advertising in an economy without a market was not clear at all – yet posters and billboards had to offer a semblance to Western cities (Kovács 2009: 222–45). In the neon trend of the 1960s, November 7 tér, as the Oktogon was then called, was the place to make the dream of glamorous Budapest come true. One popular song of the time celebrated the 'wonderful splendour' of 'neon-lit Budapest', while another, comparing streets and squares of the Hungarian capital with those in Paris, the *cité-lumière*, found that 'the Oktogon is the Place Pigalle'. Budapest's media image was formed by identifying the Oktogon with its spectacular counterparts in Paris or London. The 'perceived' as immersive environment include, so it seems, the 'conceived' aspects of the square, which are the result of the production of programmes and designs by urban authorities, developers or party bureaucrats, reflecting both the liberal civic–national ideology of the decade that shaped its form, and the changes brought by the twentieth and twenty-first centuries.

KÓS KÁROLY TÉR

Kós Károly tér (Károly Kós Square) occupies the centre of the Wekerle negyed (Wekerle quarter), a garden city from the first decade of the twentieth century, with a regular, symmetric plan of orthogonal and diagonal streets (see Figure 10.3). This

scheme would make an octagonal square in the centre of the quarter even more logical here than in downtown Budapest. The power of the 'conceived' is just as strong as in the case of our first example. Yet Kós Károly tér as a 'lived space' is the counterpoint of the Oktogon, being the result of a political programme aiming at social justice and national representation to replace liberal ideals at the end of the nineteenth century. The intention of István Bárczy, democratic representative and the mayor of Budapest between 1906 and 1919, was to create a welfare city at a time of growing dissatisfaction with the housing condition of the lower middle class and the workers. Kindergartens, schools, hospices, homeless shelters, orphanages, social housing blocks and multi-dwelling units were built, and the capital raised substantial loans to finance their construction (Nagy 1994). The Wekerle quarter as a garden city was part of this programme, executed with the exception of the main square between 1909 and 1912, when a new competition for the large square was announced, won by the architect, designer and writer Károly Kós. From 1987, the square was named after him; originally it was simply Főtér (Main Square).

It was Ebenezer Howard, the English pioneer of garden cities, who first formulated the programme of the city relying on social justice. In his 1898 book, *To-morrow: A Peaceful Path to Real Reform*, Howard described the garden city as an alternative to the metropolis, which has modern institutions, but is noisy and unhealthy, and to the village, which is close to nature but backward and underdeveloped (see also Howard 1946 [1902]). He believed that this could be implemented on a cooperative basis, by speculation-free financing. Not only his ideas, but also the schemes for English garden cities left their traces on the plan for the Wekerle quarter. However, the architecture of such models had to be adapted by Károly Kós to suit another of his powerful inspirations, Transylvanian rural architecture. This mountainous region, at that time still part of Hungary, was a mythical topos of Hungarian national romanticism, representing a totality of art and life that was missing in the modern city.

Fig. 10.3   Satellite image of the Wekerle garden city

The Wekerle quarter denied everything that the Oktogon was about, as a centrepiece of the liberal dream of Budapest. It rejected the neo-Renaissance of the Oktogon, as the 'international style' of the West European capitals of the nineteenth century. The form of the Transylvanian village is represented in a transformed, upscaled manner. If the Oktogon's appeal today is first of all atmospheric, Kós Károly tér is occupied by the symbolic: it is all about iconography – using familiar signs for 'rural forms' such as landscaping – with a new attention to detail where landscaping meets architecture.[4] The architects employed materials such as wood and rubble, and used picturesque asymmetries – all familiar to the readers of the popular Hungarian Arts and Crafts journal *Magyar Iparművészet* (*Hungarian Decorative Art*) and other publications of National Romanticism (see Figure 10.4).

The big gates designed by Dezső Zrumeczky and Dénes Györgyi connect buildings on the square, bridging the wide Hungária road to the west and the east, emphasizing the independent urban character of the entire quarter (see Figure 10.5). Such gates would be unimaginable on the Oktogon or on Andrássy út. They are purely symbolic, and the fact that they are not on the limits of the Wekerle quarter but on its main square accentuates the theatricality of the arrangement, the otherness of the quarter, without turning it into a kind of gated community. The garden city as a *heterotopia* demonstrates how the various space concepts can be realized in a given society during the same historic period. While the Oktogon is the centre of representational and commercial functions, the Wekerle quarter is a residential neighbourhood for the lower middle class, based on very clear ideas how they are supposed to live. A look at the map of Budapest suffices to recognize the heterotopic character of the quarter, the self-sufficiency of the fabric, its insular but still connected, penetrable structure. This is the original, medical meaning of heterotopia: the displacement of a tissue from its original position. The centrality of a city, the relationship between the centre and the periphery, is a key aspect of Henri Lefebvre's theory. The centre is the place where political decisions are made, where power, material and intellectual values are concentrated, and the centre tries to connect, to draw certain distant areas closer – like the millennial subway, which connected central areas of Budapest. Conversely, it excluded other areas by marginalizing them.

The marginality of the Wekerle quarter is, however, the result of its programme, to establish a model garden city, a fragment that has the capacity to act as a catalyst of urban change. The spatial organization of the district is closely related to the social programme based on the cooperative model. A general consumer cooperative was founded to operate the quarter's economy independently of the state, owned by the members, and managed democratically; also other consumer cooperatives for public servants were established: a workers' band, a workers' choir and sports clubs were operating. Only one restaurant and no pubs were allowed in the Wekerle quarter. Instead of the impersonal nature of metropolitan relations, the aim was to build a community in a small, self-sufficient town, with no violence or alcoholism. The attempt to achieve specific social and moral goals by means of urban design and architecture called in the Wekerle quarter for the exploration of various modes of dwelling in a new relation with nature, of the production–consumption cycle, or of using leisure time. This is exactly how

Fig. 10.4   The main square of the Wekerle garden city, today's Kós Károly tér

Fig. 10.5   Gate and apartment building on Kós Károly tér

Lefebvre understood the production of social space, as a way to experiment with a range of alternative emancipatory strategies.

According to Michel Foucault, who introduced the notion of heterotopia into architectural theory, the 'garden has been a sort of happy, universalizing heterotopia since the beginnings of antiquity' (Foucault 1986: 26). The heterotopic character, the nostalgic contraction of space in the Wekerle quarter shows – or rather conceals – a major structural shift in the modernization of the city: the attempt of social democracy to regulate the neoliberal management of the building land, with all its spatial and aesthetic consequences. The lower middle class and the petty bourgeoisie lose their status as potential owners of urban land, and the village-craftsman imagery of Howardian or Unwinian origin, the picture-book *Transylvanian Village* disguises the city administration as planner, concealing the pragmatic reduction of the houses to a number of types.

The physical condition of the buildings started to deteriorate as early as during the 1950s, but the Wekerle quarter was declared a protected historic monument only in the 1980s. The privatization of the 1990s, which turned the tenants into owners, presented them with a dilemma. On the website of the social circle (Társaskör) of the quarter a heated exchange is unfolding today: most inhabitants cannot afford the costly materials and solutions that the rules of the building conservation body require when they build new rooms in the attic, change windows or improve thermal insulation.[5] But there is still a sense of community in the Wekerle quarter. It is no accident that the external scenes of the Hungarian television soap *Barátok közt* (*Amongst Friends*) are shot here. The house in the opening titles is standing on Kós Károly tér, called Mátyás király tér (King Matthias Square) in the film. Timea, Miklós and the other inhabitants of the post-socialist global village live comfortably within the walls of the social suburban utopia built a hundred years earlier. The symbolism of the lived space contributes to the *jouissance*, the painful pleasure of living in a neighbourhood-as-community under threat by the metropolitan Other.

II. JÁNOS PÁL PÁPA TÉR

Today's II. János Pál pápa tér (Pope John Paul II Square), as the former Köztársaság tér (Republic Square) has been recently renamed, is the largest green square in Budapest (see Figure 10.6). Its 'conceived' aspects are much weaker than those of the two squares discussed earlier, mainly because of the heterogeneity of the surrounding buildings – it appears like four fields of the urban grid left empty rather than a planned square. The first gasworks of Pest were built here in the middle of the nineteenth century, and the surrounding workers' district was a centre of early labour movements. First it was called Lóvásár tér (Horse Market Square), then Újvásár tér (New Market Square), to be renamed in 1902 after the prime minister Kálmán Tisza, who died in that year. In 1911, the Népopera (People's Opera), today's Erkel Theatre, was built as the only free-standing structure on one side of the square; it hosted the national meeting of councils during the short-lived Communist revolution and its Soviet-style Tanácsköztársaság (Republic of Councils) in March 1919. In 1934–35, an outstanding team of Hungarian avant-garde architects, including Farkas Molnár, József Fischer and Gábor Preisich, designed the apartment house complex of the National Institute for Social Insurance OTI (Országos Társadalombiztosító Intézet), a very important and sizeable example of Hungarian modern architecture on the southern side of the square.

Fig. 10.6   Satellite image of the II. János Pál pápa tér

Comparing the OTI housing with the architecture of the squares already discussed, the way Farkas Molnár and his team opened up the continuous façade line is striking (see Figure 10.7). The six-to-eight-storey building slabs, standing perpendicular to the square, are connected only by a single-storey strip containing shops and services. This was a new, radical idea in urban planning in a downtown environment. Similar solutions were realized only in green areas outside the centre, such as the Dammerstock housing estate in Karlsruhe, designed by Walter Gropius and his team in 1929. The purpose of this scheme was to loosen up the clogged city centres, making the claustrophobic world of speculative blocks and cramped clerks' flats healthier. When air and sunshine were let in, new visual perspectives opened up as well. The photographs of the OTI ensemble made by Tivadar Kozelka in the 1930s attempt to mediate the new ecstasy of space, and the instability of the viewer. Instead of being a void surrounded by walls, space here becomes a limitless expanse, offering new ways of perception – this is how the architects expect the new urban space will be experienced. It is not by chance that the key magazine of new Hungarian architecture was called *Tér és forma* (*Space and Form*). László Moholy-Nagy, the artist associated with members of the designing team of the OTI housing, wrote in his 1929 Bauhaus-book *Von Material zu Architektur* (*From Material to Architecture*): 'The task is not over with the building. We can already see the next phase: it is space, limitless space, spreading in every dimension' (Moholy-Nagy 1929, 1968: 222). He emphasized the beauty of the new world: 'Borders become liquid; space itself is liquefied.' The architects' plan makes it clear: the constructed complex was not meant to be a completed composition; more high slabs should have replaced the existing fabric of smaller houses. It was the seed of a full city transformation. For Molnár and his team, the flat and the house had to fit into the cycle of production and consumption as rationally as steel-tube furniture or cars.

Fig. 10.7   OTI housing ensemble.

While Kós Károly tér realized the social utopia of the early twentieth century, impregnated with national romantic elements, here, the architects and the client, the social-democratic social insurance company OTI, announced a revolutionary transformation. If in the case of the Wekerle quarter we spoke of a contraction of urban space to create a tight-knit neighbourhood, the intention here was spatial extension. Although the OTI complex already reflected the critical, left-wing programme of the international avant-garde, its form was determined by the ideals of capitalist mass production. The dissolution of the traditional city as initiated by Farkas Molnár and his team was first and foremost a change of aesthetic perception, the detachment of the urban 'experience' from the material continuity of built streets and squares. But this 'liquidation' of the urban space was for the architects more important than the socioeconomic goals. This may be why the tenants of these small flats found it difficult to identify themselves with this form, as it represented the rationalized world where they could not feel at home. As a lived space, II. János Pál pápa tér is today much less determined by the modernity of the OTI ensemble than by the political events related to it. From 1940 on the Volksbund, the right-wing cultural and political organization of ethnic Germans in

Hungary, had its headquarters here, turned into offices of the Communist Party in 1945. The square was therefore the site of bloody clashes during the uprising against communism in 1956. The party headquarters on the square was attacked by a crowd on 30 October 1956. They searched for secret prisons using stethoscopes, then tore up the ground with excavators, but found no casemates. When in 2004 the construction of a new metro line started with a station on the square, blogs about underground secrets started to spread – a mixture of historiography, oral history, public memory and urban legends. Monuments and memorial tablets on the square have been unveiled, removed, curtained off or moved to the Memento Park (an open-air museum for statues from the communist period), but Robert Musil's remark about monuments impregnated against attention holds true (Musil 1957: 59–63). The only memorial that seems to resonate with locals is the Jimmy Zámbó Club, run by and for fans of a popular pop singer who committed an unintended, grotesque suicide in his flat here.

The perceived space of the square today has precious little to do with the space Farkas Molnár and his fellow architects conceived. There is a world of difference between the optimism of the dynamic photographs by Tivadar Kozelka expressing a radical spatial opening by modern architecture, and the melancholy of the periphery – today, dog-owners of the neighbouring quarter walk their animals here. The atmosphere of the square as perceived by the novelist Iván Mándy, who lived here, is described in six words by the child-characters of his popular book, *A locsolókocsi* (*Watering Cart*): 'Square, heatwave, rain, bench, doorway, street. That says it all' (Mándy 1965).

In comparison with Kós Károly tér, this is a world impossible to access semiotically by decoding symbols, distinguishing between signifiers. It is opposed to the conceived and is located beyond the lived. Perceptions are tied to the place, to the position of the perceiver in space and time, a position that he himself can never perceive. Again, in the perceived space of the square it is not just reality that figures as the object of perception, but the representations and symbols as well.

NYUGATI TÉR

Nyugati tér (Western Square) is an urban 'square' that is almost formless, if compared with the clear octagonal or quadratic geometries of the three previous squares (see Figure 10.8). It is first of all a traffic hub that spreads out in every direction, over bridges and underpasses. People don't walk on Nyugati tér; they rush to reach the subway, the railway station or to do some shopping. It is dominated by time, the rhythm of subways and trams of the railway network, which connect this place with Hungarian cities and Europe. It is a sign of the importance of the railway station that its iron construction was designed by the engineering office of Gustave Eiffel in Paris. When the square was still called Marx Károly tér (Karl Marx Square) and the plots and buildings were state owned, the construction of the Skála department store and the underpass indicated the new scale of consumer socialism and urban mobility. The present name, Nyugati tér (Western Square), refers both to the

Fig. 10.8   Satellite image of Nyugati tér

geography and perhaps to the reorientation of Hungary on the European map. The large shopping mall WestEnd City Center, opened in 1999, stands as a proof of this reorientation. Its name connects the site on the western edge of the city with a claimed role as a city centre, at least if city centre is understood as a shopping venue.

When the Skála department store was built, the block structure of the section of the grand boulevard facing the railway station was destroyed to create a sunken plaza connected to the subway station. Today, WestEnd, with its 400 shops, is an independent city centre. The middle-class downtown has shifted here, taking consumers from downtown shops on Rákóczi út (Rákóczi Avenue), the Nagykörút (Grand Boulevard) and Váci utca (Váci Street), and it is certainly a huge attraction for shoppers, generating income for the district. While II. János Pál pápa tér was an unsuccessful attempt by modernism to open up space on a large scale, Nyugati tér is the return of a globalized universe to underground spaces. Of course, the Skála department store could not compete with the new mall; part of the building was converted into a popular disco called West Balkan, a telling name – the Balkan starts indeed where the West ends. In January 2011, a fire broke out in the disco and three women died – collective memory found its representation in public rituals in the sunken plaza.

It was clear to the architects from the onset what their clients were expecting the WestEnd City Center to embody. The architects were to use patterns and psychological insights borrowed from well-functioning models in the West and put them to use in the context of the Hungarian reality in the late 1990s. This implied the creation of a space expressive of the striving towards market capitalism: a wish of the would-be consumer to catch up with the world of the movies and television advertisements that he had been exposed to, but had been hitherto unable to attain. In this vein the guiding idea was to place a nucleus of capitalist-consumerist progress into an urban space characterized by late socialist decay (one needs only to tour the crumbling surroundings and derelict housing around the Nyugati railway station to get an idea). In those non-air-conditioned spaces from which we enter the mall, it is easy to find traces of the socialist past, which is like a discarded shell with new inhabitants: coloured ceramics, thick aluminium profiles and mosaic decorations dominate. This space is the amalgamation of global shopping and a global slum, with its petrified relics of the past, its uncovered insulation, anodized aluminium profiles and layers of dirt. To drive home the contrast with the surroundings, whoever enters the mall is greeted with an image of purification – a happily splashing waterfall, a present from the state of Canada, to wash the subject clean of the stalls selling cheap clothes just outside the walls. The straight, long 'avenues' cut through to spaces that celebrate the possibilities inherent in the dawn of a new era: they too replicate a mini-city, where both social and private experiences are possible. This implies spaces for socializing (such as a large 'square' of restaurants at the end of the avenues, where families can chat while being observed from the terraced floors above), as well as shopping (including the introduction of social stratification, with rich 'mansions' and lower-class 'houses' – upscale fashion and jewellery stores with bodyguards; the low-cost store, the souvenir store for tourists). The mini-city must also provide for its own organic functioning, with escalator arteries to draw streams of people to and from organs of retention (anchor stores) and of expulsion (restrooms). Ironically, the streets are named after great Hungarians, but the shops are largely foreign-owned. The WestEnd City Center is, therefore, a conceived space – conceived by developers and architects, who followed common models of Western consumerist and psychological theory – and lived space of the subjects, for whom dreams of escape and social ambitions come true, and a powerful monument to capitalist triumph and control.

French anthropologist Marc Augé published his book *Non-Lieux* (*Non-Places*) in 1992, describing the typical places of transit today (Augé 1995). The air-conditioned, controlled spaces of airports, hotels and shopping centres host similar shops and cafés all over the world, and they never aim to make us feel at home, as we only go through them. They lack their own identity, and therefore they are 'non-places'. Nimród Antal's 2003 film, *Kontroll* (*Control*), described well how a classic non-place, an urban space for transit which lacks any identity, can become the site of urban subculture. The film takes place in the underground spaces of the metro, and its title refers to the struggle for urban space. Hip-hop and graffiti culture are also part of this process, as tagging the places with marks of group identity. The abstract, regulated and conceived space of control, where we stand on the right of the escalator and move on the left, turns into a fast and dangerous lived space, questioning and overwriting the 'normal' rhythms and mechanisms of urban life.

The character Gyalogkakukk (Roadrunner), played in Antal's movie by Bence Mátyási, makes use of the given 'hard' space, the underground tunnels. However, the escalator is not a vehicle of rational transport used to get to work, but its sidewall is misused as a slide for our hero to escape from his chasers – a misuse that suits well the programme established by the Situationists of the 1960s. The leading theoretician of the movement, Guy Debord, was in close contact with

Lefebvre (although later their ways parted, as Lefebvre accused the Situationists of abandoning the urban problem for ideological reasons). Debord called the subversion of space *détournement*, by which he meant the derailment of the intended use of a place or site. The British architectural theorist Iain Borden assumes that skateboarders use urban spaces this way. With reference to Lefebvre's notion of differential space, 'in which sociospatial differences are emphasized and celebrated', Borden investigates skateboarding as a critical practice, 'as a kind of unconscious dialectical thought, an engagement with the spatial and temporal rhythms of the city, wherein skateboarders use themselves as reference to rethink the city through its practice' (Borden 2001: 178–98). Antal's movie shows the parallel society of the jobless turn such places into their pleasure ground. However, their skill in staging bravado acts is part of the survival skills of those who need the underground as a kind of *asylum*, who do not and cannot use the escalator to go to work. To celebrate this as the sign of the *jouissance* of a vibrant everyday life that allows subcultural groups to offer alternative readings is therefore problematic, as if participation in the 'production of space' would count as a symbolic compensation for the exclusion from productive labour.

Focusing on four urban 'squares' of Budapest was a decision to investigate only one level of the city's complex scales. The intention behind this decision was to gauge how Lefebvre's spatial triad performs when using it to understand and explain concrete urban squares.

We have seen that Lefebvre's 'conceived space' is neither a physical category, nor tied to visual perception, but denotes the drawings and models that architects make, as well as the representations of space that developers, politicians, citizen groups and other agents produce. But the notion of 'production' in the urban context should be problematized, since the transfer of this category from the economy is far from trivial. The German philosopher Georg Simmel published his important texts 'Die Soziologie des Raumes' ('Sociology of space') and 'Die räumlichen Projektionen socialer Formen' ('On the spatial projections of social forms') in 1903, and included them in revised form in his *Soziologie* (*Sociology*) as a chapter on social space and the spatial orders of society: 'Der Raum und die räumlichen Ordnungen der Gesellschaft' ('Space and the spatial orders of society') (Simmel 1903: 27–71 Simmel 1908, 1922: 460–526). Simmel had already emphasized here the conflictual character of space, and discussed the social and psychological significance of spatial boundaries. In this work, Simmel – unlike Lefebvre – described the notion of endless space as an abstraction, that cannot be (visually) perceived; perceived space is always reified, a *Ding* (thing); that is, it has contents claimed by interests of individuals or social groups and their particular *Blickrichtungen* (directions of viewing). Abstract space, points out Simmel in his *Philosophie des Geldes* (*The Philosophy of Money*), is a product of the modern economy, something that is so endless, distant and devoid of qualities that it eludes any possibile identification (Simmel 1922). But even efforts to identify with real spaces remain futile for the distanced modern subject, always sensing the fragmentary character of what the subject can grasp as real; always in the intersection of different interests, of conflicting calls for spatial identification, always condemned to fail. But Simmel uses in his texts the term 'räumliche Analogie' (spatial analogy), to stress the point that *distancing* – a key notion in his concept of social space – has nothing to do with spatial distances in our physical environment (Simmel 1908, 1922). It is a question of whether such spatial analogies, coming from psychology, survive under the materialist surface of Lefebvre's *Production of Space*.

Christian Schmid refers in his book *Stadt, Raum und Gesellschaft* to Jacques Lacan's 'topology of psychological Being', his three 'registers' of the Imaginary, the Symbolic and the Real that could be equated to Lefebvre's three formative principles of social space (Schmid 2010: 241). However, Schmid comments that this relationship, as suggested by Walter Prigge, the 'psychologizing' of Lefebvre's materialism, can be questioned (Prigge 1991: 99–112). Still, there are correspondences between the elements of the two triads, if not necessarily ones that Prigge seeks to establish. Such shifts are possible because of the complex mutual relationships between the three poles – the Lefebvrean triad is mirrored within all its elements. As we concluded after comparing the conceived, lived and perceived aspects of the Oktogon, the modality of the perceived includes already the perception of the conceived and lived aspects – not only of the fragile 'mere appearances' and atmospheres that the body is immersed in. Spatial practice includes conscious reflection, the understanding of intentions, programmes, plans, representations and the interpretation of symbols as well. Similarly, lived space also has its perceived and conceived modalities; the space of 'inhabitants', 'users', 'some artists' and 'a few writers and philosophers' would be unimaginable without them (Lefebvre 1991 [1974]: 39). And conceived space, the realm of spatial representations, also starts with 'mere phantasies' but includes along with technical plans representations of the lived (for example, types and archetypes in Carl Gustav Jung's sense) and the representations of the perceived (for example, 'artistic' renderings, moodboards, scenarios); we can even assume that the perceived is accessible only through the conceived and/or the lived.

What do we achieve if we subsume the multitude of spatial representations, projected by various actors, as 'conceived space'? Can we assume that there is an urban subject that 'produces' its own counterpart as 'conceived space'? There is, of course, no such subject, only singular actors – politicians, technicians, tourism experts and so on – all producing their 'conceived spaces' based on their respective *Blickrichtungen*, their particular notions of urban identity. Do those add up to one unified 'conceived space' of the city?

The collapse of socialism induced a process of urban fragmentation in Budapest – the particular city districts have their independent administrations, a fact that makes the emergence of a consistent 'vision' for the city almost impossible. Boundaries of residential areas, green zones and commercial uses again demarcate the fronts of the urban struggle. Certainly, the symbolic representations of the various interests and identities can be theorized as occupying a shared 'lived space', but it would be more appropriate to speak of distinct languages, of competing representations. These stages for demonstrations, lectures, graffiti, posters and so on have their respective locations, where they are supported, tolerated or banned. They are territorially segregated, unlike the perceived, that resists symbolization and occupies the large and undifferentiated territory of experience beyond imagination and language. However, our perception of the physical space, constituted by presence, is increasingly disconnected from the idea of a globalized sociocultural space, constructed by informational networks, where 'being in place' has a different meaning.

The spatial turn might appear from the perspective of our urban archaeology as a romantic turn: the spatial analogy, the metaphor of space, has to help out if we lack the instruments to analyse the different scales and levels of the production of the city: its fractured territory, plot structure, social composition, the questions of land ownership and use. But Lefebvre's proposal is useful for recognizing the need for a space of comprehension, where the image production of the urban actors can be accommodated, viewed and compared. The notion of conceived, lived and perceived space is a realm where different projections, desires, images and signs can be negotiated. Lefebvre's spatial analogy stresses the optical aspects of the city, the level where economic, social or political aspects become visible, and even Simmel's notion of the *Blickrichtung* as a criterion of judgement can help us to understand the controversial positions and competing visions in the debate about the city.

NOTES

1   The idea for this chapter rests on a lecture given by the author in the spring of 2011 in the programme 'Mindentudás Egyeteme/Encompass' of Hungarian Television. A revised version of the lecture was published in German by the Center for Humanities, History and Culture of East–Central Europe, Leipzig University: Ákos Moravánszky, *Mitteleuropäische Raum(ge)schichten: Ein Querschnitt durch Budapest* (Leipzig: Leipziger Universitätsverlag, 2013). I wish to thank Arnold Bartetzky, Christian Schmid, Łukasz Stanek and Bertalan Moravánszky for helping me to develop my argument further.

2   Lajos Hevesi, *Karczképek az ország városából* (Budapest: Franklin, 1876), quoted in Gábor 2010: 33.

3   7 November 1917 is the starting date of the Russian Revolution (the 'October Revolution') in the Gregorian calendar, which corresponds to 25 October in the Julian calendar.

4   Atmosphere is used here in the sense of an affective environment experienced by immersion, precluding any symbolism – an interpretation that differs from Lefebvre's understanding of atmospheres.

5   www.wekerletelep.hu, accessed June 2014.

REFERENCES

Augé, M. 1995. *Non-Places: Introduction to an Anthropology of Supermodernity*. Trans. J. Howe. London, New York: Verso.

Borden, I. 2001. 'Another Pavement, Another Beach: Skateboarding and the Performative Critique of Architecture', in *The Unknown City: Contesting Architecture and Social Space*, edited by I. Borden, J. Kerr and J. Rendell. Cambridge, MA: The MIT Press, 178–98.

Brinckmann, A.E. 1908. *Platz und Monument: Untersuchungen zur Geschichte und Ästhetik der Stadtbaukunst in neuerer Zeit*. Berlin: Wasmuth.

Foucault, M. 1986. 'Of Other Spaces', *Diacritics* Spring: 22–27.

Gábor, E. 2010. *Az Andrássy-út körül*. Budapest: Osiris.

Heidegger, M. 1977. 'Building Dwelling Thinking', in *Martin Heidegger: Basic Writings*, edited by D.F. Krell. San Francisco: Harper & Row, 343–364.

Hevesi, L. 1876. *Karczképek az ország városából*. Budapest: Franklin.

Howard, E. 1898. *To-Morrow: A Peaceful Path to Real Reform*. London: Swann Sonnenschein.

Howard, E. 1946 [1902]. *Garden Cities of Tomorrow*. London: Faber and Faber.

Kiss, M. R. 1987. 'Milyen várost, milyen teret?' *Tér és társadalom* 1: 103–9.

Kovács, T. 2009. '"Verbringen Sie die Nacht nicht schlafend!": Urbane Räume und ihre Licht-Bilder: Budapest im 20. Jahrhundert', in *Imaginationen des Urbanen: Konzeption, Reflexion und Fiktion von Stadt in Mittel- und Osteuropa*, edited by A. Bartetzky, M. Dimitrieva and A. Kliems. Berlin: Lukas-Verlag, 222–45.

Lefebvre, H. 1991 [1974]. *The Production of Space*. Trans. D. Nicholson-Smith. Oxford: Basil Blackwell.

Mándy, I. 1965. *A locsolókocsi*. Budapest: Magvető.

Moholy-Nagy, L. 1968. *Von Material zu Architektur*. Munich 1929, reprinted Mainz and Berlin: Florian Kupferberg, 1968.

Moravánszky, Á. 2012. 'The Optical Construction of Urban Space: Hermann Maertens, Camillo Sitte, and the Theories of "Aesthetic Perception"'. *The Journal of Architecture* 17(5): 655–66.

Moravánszky, Á. 2013. *Mitteleuropäische Raum(ge)schichten, Ein Querschnitt durch Budapest*. Leipzig: Leipziger Universitätsverlag.

Moravánszky, Á and Gyöngy, K.M. 2003. *Architekturtheorie im 20. Jahrhundert. Eine kritische Anthologie*. Vienna; New York: Springer, 121–55.

Musil, R. 1957. 'Denkmale', in *Nachlass zu Lebzeiten* by R. Musil. Hamburg: Rowohlt, 59–63.

Nádas, P. 1989. *Évkönyv: Ezerkilencszáznyolcvanhét, eterkilencszáznyolcvannyolc. Esszéregény*. Budapest: Szépirodalmi.

Nagy, G. 1994. *Kertvárosunk, a Wekerle* [Veszprém:] F. Szelényi Ház.

Prigge, W. 1991. 'Die Revolution der Städte lesen', in *Stadt-Räume*, edited by M. Wentz. Frankfurt am Main: Campus, 99–112.

Schmid, C. 2010. *Stadt, Raum und Gesellschaft: Henri Lefebvre und die Theorie der Produktion des Raumes*. Stuttgart: Franz Steiner, p. 241.

Simmel, G. 1903. 'Soziologie des Raumes' in *Jahrbuch für Gesetzgebung, Verwaltung und Volkswirtschaft im Deutschen Reich*, edited by G. Schmoller, Vol. 27, Bd. I. 1903, 27–71.

Simmel, G. 1908. *Soziologie: Untersuchungen über die Formen der Vergesellschaftung*. 2nd edn Munich; Leipzig: Duncker & Humblot, 1922, 460–526.

Simmel, G. 1922. *Philosophie des Geldes*. 4th edn, Munich; Leipzig: Duncker & Humblot.

Sitte, C. 1889. *Der Städte-Bau nach seinen künstlerischen Grundsätzen. Ein Beitrag zur Lösung moderner Fragen der Architektur und monumentalen Plasik unter besonderer Beziehung auf Wien.* Wien: Guido Graeser, 1889. Published in English as 'City Planning According to Aesthetic Principles', in *Camillo Sitte: The Birth of Modern City Planning*, edited by G.R. Collins and C.C. Collins. New York: Random House, 1965.

Zaicz, G. (ed.). 2006. *Etimológiai szótár: Magyar szavak és toldalékok eredete.* Budapest: Tinta.

11

The Archi-texture of Power: An Inquiry into the Spatial Textures of Post-socialist Sarajevo

Mejrema Zatrić

The creation of a city centre demands an act of unmediated political power. When socialist authorities ventured to build a new centre for Sarajevo in the 1950s, they proceeded to impose a novel, ideologically driven vision on the city that had been the object of many previous orchestrated beginnings. Marginal to the counterpoised geopolitical kernels of the early modern era and the first globalization, Sarajevo then formed the frontline of the clash of eastern and western powers as an assemblage of very different, yet coexisting, socio-spatial arrangements (see Figure 11.1).

Positioned on the very verge of the historic core of the city, and destined to become a new centre by the agency of the socialist regime, the Marijin Dvor stands as an urban fragment that has acquired prominence through the fusion of disparate spatial manoeuvres of power in successive ideological eras. From its beginnings as an early modern real estate venture, the precise architectural articulation of this large crossroads started taking shape in the 1930s with the erection of St Joseph's Catholic Church, continued in the 1970s with the Parliament of the Socialist Republic, and is recently being 'complemented' by the addition of a mixed-use mega-structure financed by a real estate development company based in Saudi Arabia.

The Church, the State and the Corporation have thus contributed, across shifting ideological eras, to the spatialization of this conceived centrality. In Henri Lefebvre's view, centrality is what allows the possibility of the urban as the level of social practice (Lefebvre 2007b: 195). Superseding in his work then-prevalent city planning discourses on the urban core, Lefebvre theorized centrality as a unity of the conceived, the perceived and the lived space with different temporalities in the productive process of the ongoing becoming of the city (Stanek 2011: 193). Only when conceived against the backdrop of Lefebvre's theory is the project of the new centre rendered clear in its audacious strangeness and the inherent political gravity that befalls the architectural project, as it relates to the city as a whole.

The political agency of the architectural artefact and its relationship to the city have been relentlessly theorized. The contesting paradigms of criticality,

The 'Iron curtain' 1950s-90s

Ottoman conquests XIV-XIX c.

Arab conquests VII-VIII c.

Fig. 11.1
Historical
frontlines and
the position
of Sarajevo

'projectivity' and, most recently, 'explication' have been defined as responses to the question of whether (and in what way) architecture aspires to become part of, and effectively contribute to the possibility of, the 'whole'. In Henri Lefebvre's view, the political stakes of architecture are asserted through its definition as 'archi-texture', a conceptualization demanding that each building or monument be viewed 'in its surroundings and context, in the populated area and associated networks in which it is set down, as part of a particular production of space' (Lefebvre 1991 [1974]: 118). This relatively obvious statement gains illuminating potency when the concept of 'texture' is comprehended as complementary to Lefebvre's spatial trialectics. To search for the political agency of architecture in the texture and not the text (or a 'thing') implies searching for a political point of gravity in the exact intersection of the three moments of space.

How can the three aforementioned architectural projects, realizing a political statement of power in early capitalist, socialist and post-socialist eras, be understood in terms of Lefebvre's trialectics? Without encumbering Lefebvre's self-sufficient and firmly internally consistent spatial triad with secondary conceptual categories, the concept of texture describes its motion, makes it operative, and thus adds to its epistemic value. If we imagine the texture as the field of mediation between the perceived, the conceived and the lived space, how did the centre of political gravity move in this field, propelled by the changing modalities of representation dictated by power and materialized by architecture? The proposals for a politics of everyday life were, in each one of the three projects, tailored to the dictates of different ideologies, but failed to provide for centrality in three different ways, thus establishing three different kinds of texture.

SMOOTH AND HARD TEXTURES

'Socialism, capitalism, feudalism and remainders of tribal organization are possibly more intertwined' in this country than anywhere else today, noted architects Juraj Neidhardt and Dušan Grabrijan in the summary of their investigative work that preceded Neidhardt's involvement in the project for the new socialist centre of Sarajevo (Grabrijan and Neidhardt 1957: 28). Through the initiative of the emerging nation-state, the Marijin Dvor was marked anew as a focus of importance, transformed through an architectural intervention into a site for the dialectical resolution of all the social–spatial remnants of past ideological constellations (see Figure 11.2).

While it was the site of an unfinished project of an early modern real estate venture, the Marijin Dvor was landmarked by the building of the Church of St Joseph in the 1930s, facing the main urban axis of the city's largely linear structure. Reflecting on the vivid non-synchronicities of Sarajevo, the regime counterpoised the Parliament of the Socialist Republic to the early capitalist urbanity of the Marijin Dvor with forceful determination by erecting a 70-metre tower that overlooked a large ceremonial square right across from the church, from which it was separated by a wide urban motorway.

This act of intended political clarity contrasted with the previous normalization undertaken by Austria-Hungary, which in the aftermath of the Berlin Congress superseded feudal Ottoman rule in the city. The long and narrow valley, within which the oriental town had nestled inertly for centuries, was to become, once and for all, a racetrack of development. Decades before the socialist regime was to cope with unprecedented urban growth, the Austro-Hungarian regime pioneered the firm nexus between systematic urbanization and political aspiration by launching the decisive vector of progress towards the west. The circulation axis that meandered through the valley in an east–west direction and that was primarily used by Ottoman trading caravans was widened, straightened, paved and defined to become the axis of urbanization. The emerging urban administration abandoned the oriental city of the decaying guilds to deteriorate economically and culturally, while promoting its exotic orientalism as a tourist attraction in the vast empire. But this decoupling of the oriental reality from its image, which circulated in postcards accompanied by the benevolent 'Gruss aus Sarajevo', was but a mere beginning of an accelerating process of abstraction. The geometric and the visual formants of what Lefebvre had called abstract space were setting the preconditions for a new kind of texture.

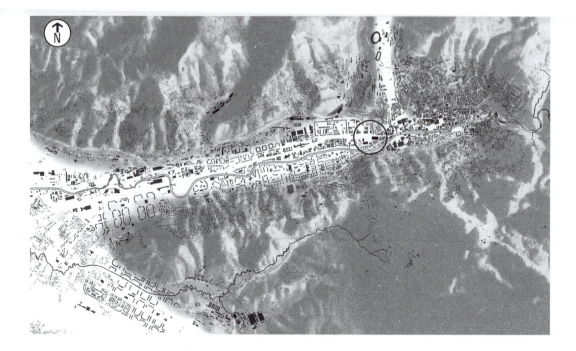

Fig. 11.2   Sarajevo today: the urban structure and the position of Marijin Dvor

Of all Austro-Hungarian spatial arrangements, The Marienhof was the most emblematic of the 'newness' being introduced into the urban development pattern, then arguably idiosyncratic, of the Ottoman city. The Marijin Dvor (Marienhof, or The Court of Mary), which will eventually lend its name to the entire quarter, was initially conceived as the business venture of the city's first real estate developer – August Braun of Vienna. Founded in 1878, his Enterprise for Construction and Building Materials, incorporated as a joint-stock company in 1912, was one of the first agents involved in the inception of the bourgeois city, akin to its Central European counterparts (Spasojević 1999). It is perhaps challenging today to try to imagine the strangeness of the bourgeois residential palace as it must have been perceived when first introduced into the Ottoman-built fabric of Sarajevo. Its vertical layering of functions wrapped in historicist architecture and arranged in a geometrical division of blocks was most certainly distinctly counterposed to the urbanity of the oriental urban core, made of the fine-grained congregations of scarcely decorated, single-function and small-scale buildings.

It was specifically this sort of new architecture, arbitrary in its material manifestation, crudely oblivious to the structures or residents it encountered where it was finally anchored, that lay the foundation for a new kind of everyday life spanning between the oriental city in the east to the Marijin Dvor in the west. This conceived space, homogeneous in its geometric formation of urban blocks, organized itself around the main circulation axis that was now transformed into a wide, embellished boulevard. In this, it effectively connected the clusters of the first civic institutions (seamlessly integrated into the blocks) to the first factories springing up in the urban periphery.

It was in the emerging texture that calcified around the main boulevard that the consensus on the new normality was reached. The spatial representation of geometricized central European urban blocks graced by secessionist and neo-Renaissance façades prefigured the expected response: promenading in the shadows and against the glory of this new architecture, frequenting the cafes and other venues of institutionalized leisure – the citizens of Sarajevo completed the introduction of the new reality.

This revolutionized everyday life, prompted and regulated by the new representation of space established in reference to European urban culture, demanded to be understood on its own terms. The political resolution, unmistakably related to the introduction of a new form of socio-economic organization, namely early capitalism, was acted out between the conceived and the perceived space, thus leaving the lived mired in political mystification.

It is only as part of this smooth texture, which effectively concealed its own politics, that the campaniles of the Church of St Joseph can be properly understood. The idea of erecting a new, large, Catholic church in Sarajevo was conceived, unsurprisingly, in the aftermath of the First World War, when the conclusion of Austro-Hungarian rule actualized the inherent tension developing between the Catholic, Orthodox and Muslim religious communities with new-found freedoms to undisciplined contestation. Among many proposed projects taken into consideration by the then archbishop of Vrhbosnia Archidiocese Ivan Šarić, the proposal by Slovenian architect Jože Plečnik stood out as an 'attempt at the architectural expression of the particularities of culture and architecture of Sarajevo in which the eastern and western influences intertwine' (Dimitrijević 1989: 209). By creatively combining the plastic elements of the early Gothic with those of the Byzantine churches and Ottoman mosques, Plečnik had attempted to symbolically unify the forms constitutive of Sarajevo's specific character (ibid.). The reasons for the rejection of Plečnik's proposal have never been explicitly stated, but the issue gains some clarity in the archbishop's description of the origins of the endorsed proposal, one that he offered in the interview given to the *Jutarnji list* newspaper in December 1939:

> In the year 1935 I was in audience with the late Pope Builder Pius X. In a separate chamber, in front of his working room, he had an entire exhibition of plans and images of churches, which he was building in the negligent periphery of Rome. As I strongly liked one plan, the Pope gave it to me. According to this sketch, mutatis mutandis, the plan was designed for our own votive church. (Jutarnji list 1939, quoted in Dimitrijević 1989: 209)

Since a casual reading of this description could have implied that Pope Pius X himself had designed the church for Sarajevo, the archbishop continued to clarify that architect Karel Pařík employed the Romanesque style, 'which is always convenient and contemporary', to base his project on a 'tested tradition' because 'without tradition comes deterioration! Modernist secession deteriorated because it did not hold on to tradition', the archbishop could not restrain himself from adding (ibid.).

This is how in Marijin Dvor, on the fringes of the early capitalist spatial texture, an unlikely attempt at the unification of the assemblage of contradictions that was Sarajevo anticipated the grand project of the socialist regime. Plečnik's proposed design, which unambiguously referred to the scattered differences that the city still barely managed to contain, demanded the displacement of the centre of political gravity towards lived space and everyday life, however timidly, thus effectively endangering the smoothness of the texture. Instead, and akin to the entire quarter that it now landmarked, the 'conveniently' Romanesque St Joseph's Church preserved the 'normality' established in accordance with the distant reference by searching for the resolution of its political presence in the dialectics between the conceived and the perceived space.

It was specifically this normality that the socialist regime was to challenge as early as the 1950s, with the launch of the anonymous Yugoslavian urban design competition for the concept-design of Marijin Dvor as a new urban centre of Sarajevo, as well as for the architectural concept-design of the future centre's premium 'content' – the Parliament building of the Socialist Republic of Bosnia. This foundational agency of the new socialist government can be understood as an attempt to consolidate what Henri Lefebvre called the 'intermediate level' of social practice into a concise whole (Lefebvre 2007a: 112). In the urban periphery, the problem being posed was organizational, one where economic–social planning employed architecture to ensure rationalization and efficiency. What was at stake in the new centre, however, was political clarity: this was a statement that was to render legible all the painstaking efforts of organization – namely, representation of the proposed relationship between everyday life and power.

For the author of the selected project, Juraj Neidhardt, the core of the solution lay in the 'new reflective emergence of urbanism' (Grabrijan and Neidhardt 1957: 421) that was now constituted by the continuity of open spaces, carefully studied and directed in his proposal.

Entertaining the notion of continuity at the onset of a revolutionary socialist society, however, could have been all but schematic – which obliged the author to embrace the existing city as an assemblage of coexisting textures, continuing to preserve multiple connections between past modes of power and present modes of everyday life. 'We have to investigate everything!' noted Neidhardt in *Architecture of Bosnia and the Way to the Contemporary*, a voluminous manuscript he wrote with his friend and colleague Dušan Grabrijan. Although not published until 1957, this book was the product of at least a decade-long and truly breathtaking attempt at projecting a persistent and attentive analytic gaze at the Ottoman urban germ of Sarajevo (Grabrijan and Neidhardt 1957). As architects, university professors and researchers, the authors were determined in their belief that the sensuality of the oriental, still palpable in the cubical grains of the amphitheatric city-garden, could be married to the dialectic rationality of the socialist Occident to produce a glorious spatial outcome.

The legacy of oriental civilization, they explained, can be metaphorically represented by an accordion player who, in stretching his instrument to its maximal capacity, produces the subtlest and most brutal chords. Similarly, the architecture of the oriental city has been infused with sublimity and brutality, while the indigenous builder has endowed it with honesty and simplicity (Grabrijan and Neidhardt 1957: 316). Le Corbusier, who wrote the preface for the book as a tribute to the accomplishments of his former disciple Neidhardt, evoked these same chords to recognize, in their contemporary echoes, 'a continuity of spirit and continuity of evolution, including also revolutions that may mark the way' (ibid.: 6). But looking for this continuity, and here Neidhardt and Grabrijan undoubtedly agreed, one must not merely succumb to the 'continuity of history', for there were historical episodes in which this spirit had little or no agency, and for that they were worthy of the uttermost contempt. The urban legacy of Austro-Hungarian rule, faithful to and exemplary of Central European bourgeois culture that begins where the Ottoman city ends, and which itself ceases in Marijin Dvor, is therefore not made an object of study for these two authors in their quest to generate a foundational myth for socialist Bosnian architecture. While in the 1950s Le Corbusier's long drift from the capitalist West towards the 'East of possibilities' was definitively fulfilled in his Chandigarh projects, Neidhart and Grabrijan, both self-professed modernists and self-proclaimed believers in progress, were going about the act of dissecting the city's oriental architecture and urbanism with the greatest care. In this labour, in which they arbitrarily disengaged this heritage from the original sin of Turkish conquest, a range of principles was extracted, many of which Neidhardt would fully deploy in his urban design proposal for Marijin Dvor.

While dismissing the historicism of bourgeois architecture as 'pathetic', Neidhardt wrote that every society has its symbols and that the greatest task of socialist society is to understand man, and itself (Grabrijan and Neidhardt 1957: 113). Architecture here was indeed to become instrumental by educating citizens in its own domain, instilling in them a faith and inspiring an awareness of their own values and aesthetics. What was important to grasp in the oriental city was its essence: human relations in architecture and a relationship between man and nature that western man had since long lost and forgotten (ibid.: 112). The proposed project envisioned free-standing structures that were comfortably stationed in the midst of generously scaled urban voids, undisturbed by the logics of land rent, as these vanished in the new socialist organization of the urban economy. But it was not only the mere abolition of the space-as-commodity principle that resulted in Neidhardt's decision to completely shatter the matrix-figure of the bourgeois Marijin Dvor, neatly packed into Central European urban blocks.

To fully understand the twists and turns that the road of the conceived took from Neidhardt's initial ideas about the architecture and social space of the oriental city to the hard texture of the Parliament building tower and the 'great manifestations' square fronting it, we have to re-examine his writings. As *Architecture of Bosnia and the Way to the Contemporary* vividly demonstrates, Neidhardt's search for the essence of centrality ranged between a nation-building, socialist determination at one end, and what he understood to be a warm and intimate 'organic' life in the 'human scale' and in harmony with nature at the other. How could these two impulses be reconciled?

'There is no doubt that the National Parliament should become the monument of our epoch' (Grabrijan and Neidhardt 1957: 416), Neidhardt wrote in explaining his urban-design proposal. Positioned at the epicentre of the centre-in-the-making, at the large crossroads and opposite the Church of St Joseph, the Parliament building was meant to challenge the bourgeois city by its sheer size and the layered meaningfulness of innate principles of design, coded through an unmistakably modernist vocabulary of architectural form. This singularly important architectural project was, indeed, conceived by a transposition of those elements of 'autochthonous urbanism' that the author found to be so symbolic of social life.

But Neidhardt recognized that in order to sublate the smooth texture of the bourgeois city, it did not suffice to dissolve the corridor street into large green voids or to aggregate the institutions of culture and administration, as the competition brief for Marijin Dvor demanded. Here, in the area aspiring to become the centre of the city, what was necessary was political sincerity. To hail the 'eyes that started seeing' (Grabrijan and Neidhardt 1957: 316), power could be neither understood, nor presented, as its own justification. But how could any aspect of everyday life be promoted as comparable with the size and the glory of the State? Struggling with this question, Neidhardt looked back, yet again, to his investigative work on the oriental city, where one recurring motif had been his fascination with the green hills that have squeezed the city into a firm embrace. It was this emblematic trait of Sarajevo that the 'anonymous builder' knew how to approach, encouraged in this undertaking by something Neidhardt could only describe as a 'collective feel'. This is probably why the most prominent cognition he extrapolated from his reflections on this innate wisdom of the 'unknown builder' was the 'unwritten law of the right of unobstructed views': views from the hills to the valley and back again – from the nestled city towards the surrounding hills (Grabrijan and Neidhardt 1957: 257).

In abstracting the importance of 'human relations in architecture' into the view from the manifestations square at the foot of the Parliament building towards the distant hill of Trebević (which was to be preserved at all costs), Neidhardt arrived at nature – that seminal and ultimate justification of any human construct. It was now safe for him to envision the citizens of Sarajevo in their submissive parading on the hard and austere surface of the manifestations square: organic culture and nature merged in the unified view towards the coded forms of the Parliament tower and the hills in the background, excusing, by the same token, the subscription of the regime to unconditional growth and development. The political was now effectively resolved between perceived and lived space, empowering this evolving proposal for the absorption of everyday life into the political and giving rise to the hard texture of the socialist social space.

THE SHATTERING AND THE RE-ASSEMBLING OF TEXTURES

Was it an ironic coincidence that, only a couple of years after this explicit manoeuvre to unify the Old and the New Sarajevo by the founding of a new urban centre, the same hills that Neidhardt evoked in his successful proposal became the site of the first informal settlements in the city (Bublin 2006: 156)? The regime had intended to unify this intermediary level of social space and elevate it to a level of social practice on the scale of one large urban centre. This goal demanded addressing the non-synchronicities of Sarajevo, while the city, almost simultaneously, was slowly starting to become afflicted by contradictions stemming from emerging social geographies of inequality. Intense industrialization in the large urban centres, common to socialist command economies, resulted in an extensive hinterland of deterioration. In Sarajevo, as elsewhere, the regime struggled unsuccessfully to provide adequate housing for the relentless waves of migrants by infilling the valley further towards the west with collective housing schemes. By the 1980s, Sarajevo was a sizeable linear city, the urban structure of which was clearly revealing its historic development. The transportation axis, initially laid out during Austro-Hungarian rule, persisted as the axis of urbanization across different ideological eras. Resembling a timeline of sorts, its constant presence confirmed the vector of urbanization that the variety of shifting regimes preserved.

As if hailing the dawn of the global wreckage of state socialism, the performance of this vector that has, through decades, 'spatialized' the growth-induced contradictions, also rendered null and void the attempts of the regime to single-handedly consolidate the city as a whole in the Marijin Dvor. The unification of Sarajevo at the intermediary level was to arrive, however, very soon and in the most unexpected of ways: through the longest urban siege in modern history.

The remarkable marriage between the urban and natural morphology, one that many medieval chronicles paid homage to while trying to describe the beauties of the city, now turned out to be its decisive weakness: the surrounding hills offered endless privileged vantage points for executioners equipped with sniper rifles. Resembling a stage set of some blood-chilling experiment, everyday life in the valley continued to unfold under sniper fire. The hectic attempts to maintain everyday practices under the perverted circumstances of the war reflected the main preoccupation of Sarajevans: to preserve some form of normality of existence (Maček 2009: 5).

This battle for normal life befell each and every citizen of Sarajevo, and was fought on the frontline of the shattering textures. If spatial texture resembles a meshwork upon space, brought about by mental and social activity (Lefebvre 1991: 117), then the loss of 'normality' meant a profound and sudden alteration of its fabric. The established relationships between the three moments of space were abruptly reconfigured, and the use and the meaning of places changed overnight.

In the Marijin Dvor, the site of that seminal, ongoing, project of representation, the suspension of planning and the inauguration of the reign of destruction became manifest as the Parliament building burned during the first months of the siege. Later denominated by the term 'urbicide' (Bogdanović 1998), the technique of 'the killing of the city' by 'the killing of the monument', reconfirmed the profound interdependence of the architectural artefact and its influences on the texture. By targeting prominent buildings, the 'strong points' of the textural webs (Lefebvre 1991: 222) were endangered and the textures thoroughly destabilized.

As opposed to the manifold intense historical and spatial turns that struck the city as a consequence of those previously discussed ideological shifts, the abnormality of the siege interrupted the prevalent discourses on space without substituting new ones. This temporary demise of the sign and of representation brought about the remarkable circumstances for the manifestation of 'the real'. If reality is contained not in space as a concept but in the spatial and social signifying practice (Lefebvre 1991: 415), then the practices of survival undertaken by Sarajevans on a daily basis wove the textures back into the realm of the perceived, building up informal knowledge in departing fully and solely from the body. This 'going beyond discourse' was also the time of inventions of a formal kind (FAMA Collection 2012a).

The bewildering situation of the sealed city targeted by huntsmen equipped with sniper rifles positioned in the surrounding hills gave rise to a sublimely real lifeworld – a sphere of intimacy marked by the biological essence of the species, in which mediations of language and play of signifiers vanished in blast-induced collisions of 'flesh and stone', triggering a proliferation of the imaginative appropriations of urban space.

It was the emergence of that new texture of survival that unified the city on all levels of reality, consolidating it as a true level of social practice. For the global intellectual community, this unprecedented and forceful unification turned Sarajevo into a real 'subject of history'.

For Jean Baudrillard, the horrors of the besieged city provided a glimpse of the real. In his bitter interpretation of the political 'architecture' of the Bosnian 'historical incident' published in *Liberation* in January 1994, he directed a stinging critique towards the files of compassionate western intellectuals who perpetuated a Eurocentric rationality by frequenting the city as part of humanitarian cultural missions. While the westerners compensated for the loss of strength and sense of reality by 'doing something just because one cannot do nothing', the people of Sarajevo, being where they were, were 'in the absolute need to do what they do, to do the right thing'. In Baudrillard's words, this was 'what it means to be really existing, to exist within reality' (Baudrillard 1994).

It was in this emergent 'reality beyond discourse' that the Marijin Dvor truly engaged with the entirety of Sarajevo – no longer as a 'place of discourse', but as one of the strong points of the new unified texture of the besieged city.

According to the FAMA collection, a bank of accumulated Sarajevian knowledge of survival, urban clearings in particular, such as crossroads and bridges, exposed persistent everyday life to an ongoing killing spree perpetuated from the surrounding hills (FAMA Collection 2012b). The vast open spaces of the Marijin Dvor were accordingly turned into an execution polygon. Tršćanska Street, which forms the Marijin Dvor crossroads by intersecting with the main city's traffic axis, was where the greatest number of Sarajevians succumbed to sniper fire (FAMA Collection 2012c).

As the Parliament building burned and the hard textures shattered, other formal elements gained prominence as strongholds of the social imaginary. As the citizens themselves testified: 'on the whole, throughout the war the people did not go into Tršćanska Street, because they knew what it was' (FAMA Collection 2012c). By becoming a 'strong point' of this new spatial texture of Sarajevo under siege, the once-marginal Tršćanska Street provided a new common node of the lived spaces of the citizens, as is illustrated by the following account by the Sarajevian actress Amina Begović:

> *Everywhere around it was gray, the town was destroyed, everything burnt, the Unis building had been burnt, it looked very ugly. Suddenly in that grayness, on the other side of Tršćanska Street, in front of the Unis building I saw beautiful roses. The roses somebody had planted when there was peace and when it was supposed to look like that. Those roses went somewhat wild during the war. Nobody cut them watered them or whatnot. However, now it was in all that grayness. Meaning, at a time when nobody could clean up Tršćanska Street. When nobody dared to go out, to take a broom and clean up all that glass, suddenly the roses sprang up from all that. My feelings were that beauty couldn't be described, the happiness I felt. I dressed and went across Tršćanska, you know, one sets one's teeth and runs as fast as one can, because it was a clear day. And I took some scissors and I cut those roses and brought them back into my room. Later people asked me: Where did you get those roses? I said: From in front of the Unis buildings. They said, it was impossible. You didn't cross Tršćanska Street because of the roses did you? I did, I said. (FAMA Collection 2012d)*

The years of the siege of Sarajevo were marked by the textures in fast-paced flux. As the monumental architectural artefacts lost their usual status of the strong points of spatial textures, the body produced space, undisciplined by the eloquence of discourse. As the normality of peace took hold, however, the hierarchy of places was recovered and the Marijin Dvor came into its own again. Soon all the forms – the scorched buildings, the wide and narrow streets and the roses – were to be restructured and reassembled to constitute the new spatial texture through the recasting of the social space in accordance with the late capitalist mode of production.

VIRTUAL TEXTURES

The unchanging direction of development, the ever-expanding informal housing on the hills and the desire to complete the unfinished project of the new city centre in Marijin Dvor are the only continuities that link the urbanization dynamics of socialist and post-socialist Sarajevo. If abstraction by rationalization and organization was set in motion in the early capitalist era and intensified during the socialist era, the primary shift that concretized post-socialism in the realm of urbanization was what Lefebvre understood as the ultimate dimension of abstraction – the trading of spatial volumes as commodities (Lefebvre 1991: 337). This relatively new possibility revolutionized the economy of space, of which the economy of things was now becoming a function. The global level of space, long cut off by the state-socialist economic experiment, was now a new arena of political possibility, for local authorities and citizens alike.

That the referent 'normality' of the socialist transition was determined by a very concrete model of perceived space came to be fully clear in Marijin Dvor, which was now judged in the global context and expected to establish 'the international ID of the entire country' (*Oslobodjenje* 2007). Accordingly, the stakes of making the city a consolidated whole were defined by the imperative of it becoming presentable to the world. The currency in which this intended exchange was to be transacted was the projects that were *of* the world – a recognizable value that could be weighed and traded, without confusion, on the global market.

While in the early capitalist era the new conceived space proposed a new type of architecture in the form of the Secessionist residential palace with a commercial ground floor (pursuing the goal of the apparent 'normalization' of the oriental city of the guilds), the late capitalist era performed another 'normalization' of the socialist city by the introduction of the hybrid mixed-use building – a combination of offices, retail and leisure wrapped into one single envelope.

In the smooth texture of early capitalism the social organization and architectural intervention merged seamlessly. In post-socialism, however, the political discourse that followed the inception of these new mega-structures, which in the course of the last decade sprang up one by one along the main city axis, signalled the emergence of a new kind of texture.

When in 2007 the amendments introduced to the Master Plan of the Marijin Dvor were announced, criticism in the press was directed at one particular detail: the 'manifestations square', envisioned by the original urban project of the new socialist centre in the 1950s, now vanished under the enormous footprint of a new mixed-use building marked by a 70-metre tower. When asked to comment on these controversial changes introduced into the planning documentation, the mayor of Sarajevo of the time noted: 'We were not counting square meters but searched with the urban designers for the best visual solutions for the central zone' (*Dnevni Avaz* 2008).

What this, almost sympathy-inspiring, statement left out of the picture was the agency of one new actor – real estate developers were crucial in the process of conceiving this new artefact of normalization that was now to enter into an 'architectural dialogue' with the socialist Parliament building by the mere fact that it matched its height. Sulaiman Al-Shiddi, a Saudi developer, assuming a professional lineage to the city's first entrepreneur of space – August Braun of Vienna – had already entered the fledgling post-socialist real estate market of Sarajevo in 2004.

His company Al-Shiddi Group, based in Saudi Arabia, purchased the formerly publicly owned company Magros and thus inherited its possessions, the most noteworthy of which was the urban lot located in the south-eastern quadrant of the Marijin Dvor crossroads (*Oslobodjenje* 2006). A year later, directives were issued and endorsed to make amendments to the original Master Plan, which was 'corrected' to accommodate the ambitions of the new owner: instead of the two separate buildings that were intially planned with 12 and 4 floors, the new document more than doubled the buildable foot-print by providing for a mega-structure of 18 and 4 floors accommodating 69,000 square metres of commercial space (Institute for Planning of Development of the Sarajevo Canton 2007).

The article, 'The Citizens Against the Master Plan', and published by the daily newspaper *Oslobodjenje*, reported on the general dismay of locals in the Marijin Dvor area, provoked by the changes introduced into their neighbourhood:

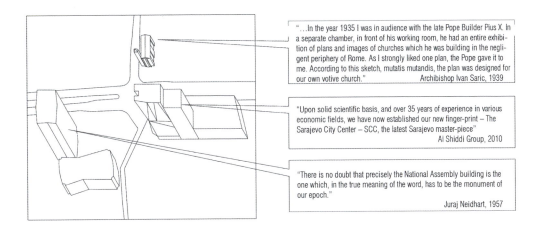

"...In the year 1935 I was in audience with the late Pope Builder Pius X. In a separate chamber, in front of his working room, he had an entire exhibition of plans and images of churches which he was building in the negligent periphery of Rome. As I strongly liked one plan, the Pope gave it to me. According to this sketch, mutatis mutandis, the plan was designed for our own votive church."   Archibishop Ivan Saric, 1939

"Upon solid scientific basis, and over 35 years of experience in various economic fields, we have now established our new finger-print – The Sarajevo City Center – SCC, the latest Sarajevo master-piece"
                                                                    Al Shiddi Group, 2010

"There is no doubt that precisely the National Assembly building is the one which, in the true meaning of the word, has to be the monument of our epoch."
                                                                       Juraj Neidhart, 1957

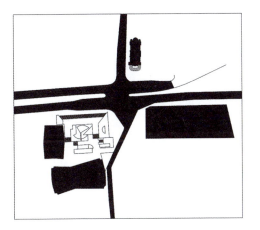

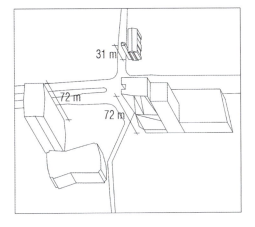

they mostly objected [to] the vanishing of the green spaces and 'the superfluous building of different kinds of office buildings from which they personally will not benefit whatsoever.' They concluded that through the acceptance of this master plan, the degradation of the citizens of Sarajevo is confirmed, taking into account that they did not partake in its production and were never asked for an opinion. (Oslobodjenje 2007)

Fig. 11.3   Marijin Dvor: some features of its spatial textures

These voices of opposition, notably coming from those few who lived in or near the Marijin Dvor area, were soon to be contested by an affirmative uproar on many internet forums, where the as-yet-non-existent building gained life already in 2008, as the visualizations of the project in the form of computer renderings and animations were circulated in the media. Besides occasional comments on the details of architectural design, those interested citizens mostly expressed their thrill about the emerging 'skyline'. The concept of 'the skyline' (used as a word borrowed from English) obviously signalled one shared feature of the transformed lived space of Marijin Dvor. 'Best Skylines in Eastern Europe', to take a more global example, is the title of an internet discussion forum on which users exchange and comment on the images of the emerging 'central business districts' of their post-socialist cities, as seen from a distance (Skyscrapercity 2012a). 'The Sarajevo skyline is taking shape!' is an enthusiastic statement posted by one of the discussants, reacting to the image showing the latest Marijin Dvor tower under construction (Skyscrapercity 2012b). This architecture, contemplated from afar, added to the idea of the central business district skyline, thus obviously becomes a true excess of real over its corporeal cause.

Shared between the citizens of Sarajevo and exchanged with other architectures and other skylines in the form of images, this conceived space articulates the political in relation to the lived on the global level, superseding the details of the perceived that provided the initial impetus for the entire process. In this, it thus establishes the virtual texture of social space.

THE ARCHI-TEXTURES AS THE POLITICS OF EVERYDAY LIFE

Textures are symbolic–material nexuses and, notably, they are wholes (Lefebvre 1991: 132). In accordance with Lefebvre's focus on the production of space (rather than interpretation of its ontological factuality), the texture should be understood as a process. It emerges for the sake of a particular action that simultaneously engages materiality, symbolism and emotion. The texture is thus conceivable as a mediator that integrates the three moments of space at any given moment of time, with the subject as the centre (ibid.).

As an effect of a 'real' action, embraced or rejected by the physicality of space, the texture releases a meaning. While they emerge on the level of habitation, the ways in which these meanings can be 'fed back' into what Lefebvre called an 'intermediary level' determine the prospects of the consolidation of the city as a level of social practice.

It is by contributing to this enterprise that architecture becomes political. As the site of various and unfinished projects of radical normalization through history, Sarajevo is a city in which different ideological political regimes attempted a consolidation of the urban level by means of architecture. The organizational efforts of different regimes that unfolded in the urban periphery crystallized into a political clarity in the conceived centre of the city. If the city is to be understood as the greatest political partnership (Aristotle 1985), this was the point where a prevailing power proposed the resolution of the political by means of architectural form. At the conceived central point, architecture was called upon to excuse the manoeuvring of power by answering a clear question – for which reason were the forces of production concentrated? What was the rationale for the partnership to be established? Understanding architecture as archi-texture, as a medium between conceived, perceived and lived space, provides a determination of the various political gravities that were constituted by means of architectural artefacts in different ideological eras and that produced various types of texture.

If politics was covertly resolved between conceived and perceived space in the form of the Secessionist residential palace in early capitalism, and imposingly resolved between the perceived and the lived through the 'sincere' modernist forms of the State House and its square in socialism, then in post-socialism the political point of gravity shifted towards the dialectics between the conceived and the lived, where the abstracted materiality of the mixed-use tower now became a recognizable commodity that, for authorities and citizens alike, consolidated the city as a whole on the global level of social space. Descending to an intermediate level, one that Lefebvre deemed 'properly urban', we encounter a hole, gaping in-between the selvedges of these smooth, hard and virtual textures assembled around the conceived central point (see Figure 11.3). Is it a coincidence that in the Marijin Dvor, in the concrete physical projection of this imagined hole, we find a wide and heavily trafficked urban motorway – the only constant that stood the test of time and unified all the contesting ideological arrangements in their shared 'will to growth'?

Is architecture 'the missing link between the community of humans and the community of things as political entities' (Zaera-Paolo 2008: 79)? Or is it rather the internal political linkage of the community of humans via the community of things? The assemblage of powers in the Marijin Dvor points to the latter. The image of the corporate building towering over a background of distant slums nestled in the hills has become a redundant disciplinary trope, one that for some indexes the normality of the 'wild reality' of the city. In Sarajevo, however, these different archi-textures denaturalize each other. They testify to the flexibility and mobility of the political centre of gravity, and to the indispensability of architecture for any change to occur.

REFERENCES

Aristotle. 1985. *Politics*. Chicago, IL: University of Chicago Press.

Al Shiddi International Group. 2008. SCC 3D Presentation (online: SCC). Available at http://www.sarajevocitycenter.com/sccbih/gallery.html (accessed 27 April 2012).

Baudrillard, J. 1994. 'No Reprieve for Sarajevo', trans. Patrice Riemens. *Liberation*, 8 January (online: The European Graduate School). Available at http://www.egs.edu/faculty/jean-baudrillard/articles/no-reprieve-for-sarajevo/ (accessed 28 October 2012).

Bogdanović, B. 1998. 'The City and Death', in *Blakan Blues: Writing out of Yugoslavia*, edited by J. Labon. Evanston, IL: Northwestern University Press, 37–73.

Bublin, M. 2006. *Sarajevo u istoriji – od neolitskog naselja do metropolisa*. Sarajevo: Buybook.

Dimitrijević, B. 1989. 'Arhitekt Karlo Paržik (Karel Parik)', PhD thesis, University of Zagreb.

Dnevni Avaz. 2008. 'Urgencije za "Al Shiddi" išle preko članova SBiH'. *Dnevni Avaz* 9 September: 4.

FAMA Collection. 2012a. *Siege of Sarajevo 92–96* (online: FAMA Collection), http://www.famacollection.org/index.php/conceptualindex/search/tag/inventions (accessed 10 April 2013).

FAMA Collection. 2012b. *Siege of Sarajevo 92–96* (online: FAMA Collection). Available at http://www.famacollection.org/index.php/tb-eng/TB-231 (accessed 10 April 2013).

FAMA Collection. 2012c. *Siege of Sarajevo 92–96* (online: FAMA Collection). Available at http://www.famacollection.org/index.php/tb-eng/TB-349 (accessed 10 April 2013).

FAMA Collection. 2012d. *Siege of Sarajevo 92–96* (online: FAMA Collection). Available at http://www.famacollection.org/index.php/tb-eng/TB-822 (accessed 10 April 2013).

Grabrijan, D. and Neidhardt, J. 1957. *Arhitektura Bosne i put u savremeno*. Ljubljana: CZP.

Institute for Planning of Development of the Sarajevo Canton. 2007. *Amendment to the Master Plan City Centre 'Marijin Dvor' II phase* (online: Institute for Planning of Development of the Sarajevo Canton). Available at http://zpr.ks.gov.ba/sites/zpr. ks.gov.ba/files/Izmjena%20i%20dopuna%20Regulacionog%20plana%20gradski%20 centar%20-Marijin%20dvor-%20II%20faza.pdf (accessed 9 January 2013).

Lefebvre, H. 1991 [1974]. *The Production of Space*. Oxford: Blackwell Publishers.

Lefebvre, H. 2007a. 'Levels of Reality and Analysis', in *Writings on Cities*, edited by E. Kofman and E. Lebas. Oxford: Blackwell Publishers, 111–17.

Lefebvre, H. 2007b. 'Space and Politics', in *Writings on Cities*, edited by E. Kofman and E. Lebas. Oxford: Blackwell Publishers, 183–202.

Maček, I. 2009. *Sarajevo under Siege: Anthropology in Wartime*. Pennsylvania, PA: University of Pennsylvania Press.

Oslobodjenje. 2006. 'Korekcije Master plana nisu još gotove'. *Oslobodjenje* 12 June: 18.

Oslobodjenje. 2007. 'Nisu svi investitori isti'. *Oslobodjenje* 29 December: 4.

Skyscrapercity. 2012a. *The Best Skylines of Eastern Europe* (online: Skyscrapercity). Available at http://www.skyscrapercity.com/showthread.php?t=597483 (accessed 9 January 2013).

Skyscrapercity. 2012b. *Sarajevo City Center Development News* (online: Skyscrapercity). Available at http://www.skyscrapercity.com/showthread.php?t=770442&page=7 (accessed 9 January 2013).

Spasojević, B. 1999. *Arhitektura stambenih palata Austro-ugarskog perioda u Sarajevu*. Sarajevo: Rabic.

Stanek, Ł. 2011. *Henri Lefebvre on Space. Architecture, Urban Research and the Production of Theory*. Minneapolis, MN: University of Minnesota Press.

Zaera-Paolo, A. 2008. 'The Politics of the Envelope. A Political Critique of Materialism'. *Volume* 17: 76–105.

12

For Difference 'in and through' São Paulo: The Regressive-Progressive Method

Fraya Frehse

How can one produce conceptual explanations about urban space that are sensitive to empirically given social processes that contribute to making cities differ from one another, amid and despite the vigour of the current global urbanization trend? This theoretical issue, which has been mobilizing sociologists in various academic contexts in the US and Europe (for example, Sassen 1991, 2008, Berking and Löw 2008, Löw 2009), is of special interest to me as a Brazilian sociologist and anthropologist living in and doing research on São Paulo. Although Brazilian urban contexts are experienced in practice as being different from Paris, London, Chicago, Los Angeles or New York, these cities often inspire, empirically speaking, the sociological city notions that present-day Brazilian research relies upon to explain, in theoretical terms, this country's urban space. Notions such as fragmentation, gentrification, global cities and segregation underpin the Brazilian debate (Frehse and Leite 2010). They bring to the interpretive forefront what is mutual among urban contexts amid and despite the elements that make them differ from each other. Empirical differences become (in)voluntarily subject to similarities. In extreme cases, difference entirely disappears from the conceptual agenda (Frehse 2012).

My aim here is to show that Lefebvre's regressive-progressive method plays a *unique* role in changing this state of affairs, which applies not only to the Brazilian academic context. There is a definite 'international division of the academic labour model' in urban studies: research centres outside 'the core countries in Northern Europe and North America' have been 'pushed towards the provision of empirical, but not of theoretical or methodological knowledge' (Fortuna 2012: 138). Instead of addressing the theoretical contributions of Lefebvre's approach to current urban studies in Latin America and abroad (Frehse 2013a, 2013b), I consider this book appropriate for a more radical statement. It does not matter that Lefebvre is usually associated with urban studies of the so-called North: the approach is unparalleled for conceptualizing empirically given differences in definite urban contexts as difference in the production of space *beyond* this region, notably 'in and through' São Paulo – by considering that social relations only exist 'in and through space'

(Lefebvre 2000 [1974]: 465), and that difference is both a (logical) concept and a (factual) content historically produced in the wake of the 'reciprocal, conflictive and appeased relationships' between the 'qualities' of the 'particularities' that 'survived' these encounters (Lefebvre 1970a: 65).[1]

The thesis of the method's uniqueness becomes evident when one addresses a specific dimension of Lefebvre's approach. My sub-thesis is that the method's exclusiveness derives from the conceptual object that it helps the urban researcher to evidence in analytical terms: the mediating role of historicity in the space produced by the mediation of the everyday uses of definite empirically given spaces in various urban contexts, regardless of whether these uses range from fleeting bodily movements to urbanistic conceptions of space. One has only to accept Lefebvre's methodological standpoint regarding the (metaphilosophical) dialectical relation between theory and practice, concept and 'practical reality' (1975: 132): his concern with the transductive identification of historical possibilities contained in empirically given realities, even urban ones (Lefebvre 2009 [1968]: 99–100).[2] From this angle, space, as a 'set of relationships', is a mediation of praxis, thus also a mediation of (bodily) perceptions, of (symbolic) experiences and of (rational and scientific) conceptions: of 'the perceived', 'the lived', and 'the conceived' (Lefebvre 2000: xx–xxi, 48–50). Historicity, in turn, refers to the entanglement of historical times; or, better stated, 'of the temporalities of history concerning the past, the present and "the possible"'.[3]

This chapter elucidates the argument in three steps. First I bring to the fore the specificity of my sub-thesis by both elucidating what the regressive-progressive method is about, and by locating my interest in it in the recent academic debate about its use. Then the analytical demonstration of the method's uniqueness in the search for difference in and through space beyond the North can start. In the second section, I articulate the approach with Lefebvre's space triad and apply this tool set to data related to my investigations into the everyday past and present uses of São Paulo's cathedral square by pedestrians. Scrutinized respectively in descriptive, in analytical-regressive and in historical-genetic terms, Praça da Sé reveals two specific historical contradictions which, finally, evidence São Paulo as a *different* urban space, and hence three factors that ensure the method's exclusiveness, when the issue is difference.

(NON-)USES OF THE REGRESSIVE-PROGRESSIVE METHOD IN URBAN RESEARCH

Lefebvre presented his approach for the first time in an article in the *Cahiers Internationaux de Sociologie*, four years after a paper on the 'problems of rural sociology' published there in 1949 (Lefebvre 2001a). Based on findings of one recent piece of empirical research on a 'peasant community' of the Pyrenean region of Campan, the first article critically focused on 'city-dwellers, intellectuals and even historians or sociologists' that ignore the 'complex organization' of 'our rural villages' (2001a: 21). Inspired by Lenin's law of uneven development, which reveals the 'different degrees and modes of dissolution or reconstitution of the peasant community', Lefebvre then stressed the presence of an unnoticed past in current villages and cities; in fact the persistence and action of 'the historical' upon 'the actual' everywhere (2001a: 39, 22).

In turn, by 1953 the time had come for proposing 'perspectives' for rural sociology (Lefebvre 2001b); hence the regressive-progressive method. This set of empirical research procedures aimed to identify the dialectical interplay between the 'horizontal' (synchronic) and the 'vertical' (diachronic) complexity of peasant reality, so that 'the possible' there might be disclosed (2001b: 65–6). In this sense, whether the approach resulted from Lefebvre's reading of Marx's interpretation method exposed in *Capital* and in *Grundrisse* (Hess 1988: 181), from Lenin's ponderings on the Marxian 'economic-social formation' notion (Martins 1996a: 15–20), or from Lefebvre's contact with Marc Bloch's 'regressive method' (Stanek 2011: 159–60), it operationalized a definite methodological perspective on social reality. On the one hand, 'Agrarian formations and structures' with the same 'historical date' present 'essential differences' and, on the other, the 'rural world' offers 'the coexistence of formations *of different ages and dates*' for 'observation and analysis' (Lefebvre 2001b: 65–6).

Based on these concerns, the regressive-progressive method holds both an operational and an interpretive dimension that become manifest in three main research steps that Lefebvre terms 'moments', which are 'attempt[s] aiming at the total accomplishment of a possibility' (Lefebvre 1961: 348). Based on participant observation and on interviews, surveys and statistics, the researcher 'describes', in the 'descriptive moment', the empirically given 'field' (Lefebvre 2001b: 73); or, more precisely, that which an analyst termed 'social life' or 'social relations', and the 'elements of material and spiritual culture' (Martins 1996a: 21). Thus the horizontal complexity of social reality in the field can be disclosed, putting its vertical complexity at stake. Its 'analytical-regressive' assessment involves the attempt to identify the 'exact' dates of the previously described 'reality' (Lefebvre 2001b: 74). Then, both complexities can be dialectically linked to each other: in the third 'historical-genetic moment', the 'transformations' of the previously dated elements are 'elucidated and understood' against the background of 'the further (internal or external) development', and of these elements' 'subordination to the overall structures', to the 'overall processes'. The effort is 'to return to the previously described actual, in order to meet the present again', but this time an '*explained*' present (ibid.). The coexistence of things, social relations and representations of different ages in the actual – of society, of the individual – brings to the fore contradictions between the research-field elements that historically changed and those that did not – from the methodological viewpoint of other, already accomplished historical possibilities embedded in the contradictory overall process.

Thus the regressive-progressive approach reveals what is historically possible in *any* researched social reality – an aspect Jean-Paul Sartre (1960: 41–2, n. 1) quickly recognized. The coexistence of elements from different historical times turns each one, as opposed to the others, into an indication that a possibility lies 'ahead of the real and of what has been accomplished' (Martins 1996a: 22). This is due to the (Marxian) 'radical needs' embedded in the 'residua' of praxis, in conceptions and relations that, uncaptured by power, remain subterraneous in social life (Lefebvre 1965: 20, Martins 1996a: 22-3). Radical needs cannot be satisfied without changes in society (ibid.).

Given these characteristics, there is, however, more at play in the method – and a departing point for my statement: a set of procedures to evidence in analytical terms how the entanglement of historical times empirically interferes with *space*; or, better stated, with its transformations, as space is a product. Although the approach's first explicit demonstration occurred within a specific spatial context, Lefebvre applied it to various empirical research fields thereafter: from specific cities to the 'field of representations' (Lefebvre 1970b: 69, 2000: *passim*, 1980: 136–7).

Still, present-day empirical urban research rarely takes into consideration both the operational and interpretive roles of the method regarding the link between (historical) time and (urban) space. By doing research in Iberian and Latin American online journals (Frehse 2013b), and in Portuguese, German, French and British university libraries, I found out that the regressive-progressive approach is just about absent from urban research, except for Brazilian urban investigations, and for French institutional analyses. The proliferation of empirical studies on the production of space with the aid of Lefebvre's space triad as of the 1980s (Harvey 1989, Soja 1989, Schmid 2005, Löw 2005, Urban Research 2009) has not changed this situation, even though Lefebvre himself thoroughly dated spatial practice, the space of representations and the representations of space in his analyses, aware that 'all reality in space is exposed and explained by a *genesis* in time' (2000: 51, 53, 56–8, 136).

Brazil's peculiarity in this context is due to the history of sociology there, which is tied to the foundation of the country's first university, in 1934. The first sociologists educated at the University of São Paulo (USP) 'learned to reflect ... on Brazil largely in terms of the past' (Candido 1993: xxxix). This emphasis on history certainly lies at the root of the great receptiveness for the Marxian dialectic method among USP's first generations of sociologists (for example, Fernandes 1959, Cardoso 1962, Martins 1975). A major concern was the 'social obstacles to development' in Brazil, due to the active presence of social practices inherited from its colonial and slavery past (Martins 1998). One can thus understand precisely why Lefebvre's method drove the first attempt to study his works in depth there (Martins 1996b). The regressive-progressive approach became the target of methodological reflections (Martins 1996a, Frehse 2001, 2013b) and of empirical urban research (Martins 1992, 2008, Frehse 2005, 2011, 2013a).

It is to this lineage of studies that this chapter belongs. Its peculiarity derives from its aim: to demonstrate step by step, by applying the method to a definite empirical reality in São Paulo, that the focus of this approach on the relationship between historicity and space makes it unique in present-day urban studies, as regards difference in urban space amid the global urbanization trend.

To this end, nothing is better than strictly 'returning to Lefebvre'; that is, to his methodological concerns with the production of space, and hence with articulating the method with the space triad. This is no easy task, as it implies unfolding methodological aspects Lefebvre himself did not explicitly address when mobilizing both tool sets in his reflections on the relationship between historicity and space.

DIFFERENCE IN SÃO PAULO THROUGH HISTORICITY

A fruitful starting point is to remember that in searching for difference Lefebvre heightened the methodological relevance of 'the formation "in the field" of a differential time-space', of 'differential space' (Lefebvre 1970a: 129, 2000: 407–60). This concerns the relations of juxtaposition, superposition, connection, interference and competition among 'locations, situations and local qualities', of which 'those that resist turn into *differences* in urban time-space' (Lefebvre 1970a: 129).

The historical novelty of postwar capitalism is 'the idea of a dialectic centrality or of a dialectics of centrality', characterized by 'movements based on the inclusion-exclusion spatially provoked by a definite cause: the centre gathers only by spurring distance and dispersion' (Lefebvre 2000: 382, 445). This dialectical movement's central role is played by 'abstract space', which is underscored by the forms and quantities that drive the functioning of capitalism (ibid.: 61). Against this background, differential space points to the possible amid the contradictory centrality of abstract space (ibid.: 64–5, 407–60). This is due to the contradictions from which it emerged: the coexistence of the (historically old) 'contradictions *in* space' (embedded in history, especially class conflicts) and the (historically new) 'contradictions *of* space'; for example, the 'dialectic movement of centrality' besides the 'contradiction between the past and possible abundance, and the factual scarcity' (ibid.: 382, 384–5).

Based on these ponderings, the research question becomes what one should focus on, empirically speaking, to synthetically grasp the formation of a possibility of differential space, at least. Given the limitations of this chapter, one alternative lies in the regressive-progressive exploration of what Lefebvre called a monumental space or monument: a 'spatial *oeuvre*' (2000: 253, 255). Rich in symbols, the monument holds 'an inexhaustible sense' (Lefebvre 2001c [1960]: 93). This is what turns it into 'the memory and figuration of the past' of the city, into 'the active nodes of its current everyday life, into the forecast of its future' (Lefebvre 1961: 308). By condensing various historical times, this space goes 'beyond itself, its façade (if it has one), its internal space', while also being underpinned by dialectics analogous to that of centrality: 'everywhere *monumentality* disseminates, irradiates, condenses, concentrates itself' (Lefebvre 1970b: 57). These traits assure the monument's methodological relevance in analyses of space production in postwar capitalism: it is an 'epistemic tool' (Stanek 2011: 196).

Hence my option to focus on Praça da Sé (see Figure 12.1), whose past and present uses by pedestrians I have moreover studied for years (Frehse 1997, 2005, 2011, 2013a, 2013b).

The cathedral's dates and centrality also impregnate in symbolic terms the square in which this monument was erected. Thus Praça da Sé becomes a mediation that may reveal how historicity interferes with São Paulo's urban space.

Fig. 12.1
Southern view of
Praça da Sé with
the cathedral
(February 2012)

And it *synthetically* discloses this link, as illustrated by the data I have collected on this square.

Therefore it is now only necessary to select the empirical elements of the square for assessment in regressive-progressive terms. After all, there is a great deal to observe in this polygonal forecourt (see Figure 12.2) of some 37,500 square metres (Milanesi 2002: 161).

Praça da Sé is the biggest square on São Paulo's so-called historical hill, where this city of 11.2 million inhabitants in 2010 (19.7 million in its Metropolitan Region) was founded in 1554 as a hinterland Jesuit settlement of the Portuguese colony named Brazil. The plaza's major building is the Roman Catholic Metropolitan Cathedral of São Paulo, a gothic temple 11 metres long and 46 metres wide, with 92-metre towers and a 30-metre cupola (Milanesi 2002: 85), and capable of holding 8,000 people (Porto 1996: 184).

In favour of selection criteria, I kept in mind that the square is a 'place', a 'local space-time' to which a spatial practice corresponds. As this one concerns the (qualitative) use of space that produces this space, being thus mediated by the

Fig. 12.2
Southern
bird's-eye view
of Praça da Sé
(February 2012)

perceived, the lived and the conceived, *the body* is the analytical reference for 'understanding social space in three moments' (Lefebvre 2000: 21, 23–4, 48–50).

This caused me to focus respectively on elements of *the conceived*, *the perceived* and *the lived* Praça da Sé that touched me the most in visual and audio terms during my fieldwork there on weekdays (2–6 pm) between April 2007 and February 2012. This decision, in turn, led me to concentrate on the western third of the immense polygon, a physically circumscribed area that holds pedestrians only sparsely observable in the plaza's eastern two-thirds. As, moreover, the selected area is currently the plaza's historically oldest spot, I termed it Praça da Sé for analytical purposes.

Last but not least, I choose, from now on, to tackle in descriptive, analytical-regressive and historical-genetic terms three elements of the conceived, the perceived and the lived plaza, respectively: urbanistic representations of it; patterns of pedestrian body behaviour there; and verbal images of the square by some of its users.

Descriptive Moment

Given that I usually started my field observations in the square's southern end, and advanced from there to the north, this is also the geographical direction I adopt in this description. Moreover I make use of the present tense for the sake of fluency.

Last, I address only the physical references and pedestrian types that may help to make the selected empirical elements intelligible in the framework of this chapter. Thus I devised the following sketch that, viewed from the bottom to top (in line with my fieldwork's south-north orientation), represents the most usual locations of some of the urban equipments and pedestrian types I most regularly noticed on Praça da Sé (see Figure 12.3).

The plaza's cathedral is built alongside the south of a pedestrianized rectangular cement forecourt without seats, whose east and west sides are dotted with two lines of imperial palms surrounded by (empty) flowerbeds, while the centre holds an art-nouveau piece of rock in the middle of a compass rose. This is Marco Zero, from which all geographical distances in São Paulo are measured. On the forecourt's east side, low walls physically separate this rectangle from the garden area that I do not consider here, and which is covered with flowerbeds and low trees, park benches, water mirrors, abstract art sculptures and the entrances to São Paulo's main underground junction station, named Sé. The rectangular area's west side, in turn, is bordered by a street dotted with commercial buildings, whereas further north one glimpses a statue about three metres high (pedestal included) of the apostle Paul, as well as flagpoles (see Figure 12.1).

This equipment visually separates the plaza's almost shadeless rectangular area from its pedestrianized continuation further north. With broad shade-giving trees also surrounded by empty flowerbeds, this seatless second rectangle holds a statue some 10 metres high of one of São Paulo's founders, the Jesuit José de Anchieta. This segment's east side, in turn, is bordered by a police station, by commercial establishments, and a court leading to two underground entrances. Its west side ends in the aforementioned street. On the north, this area is physically limited by another street. By crossing it, one arrives at the square's last pedestrianized segment: a seatless triangle with some shade-giving trees surrounded by empty flowerbeds.

Underscored by these and other physical traits related to spatial practice, Praça da Sé evidences the coexistence of at least three urbanistic representations of space – that is, 'dominant' space 'conceptions' developed by 'experts, planners and urbanists, by "fragmenting" and "agencing" technocrats, and by artists close to scientificity: they all identify what is experienced and perceived with what is conceived' (Lefebvre 2000: 48). First, there is the conception that bishops' sees must lie in the geographical centre of a city; moreover, the representation that a cathedral square must hold large human gatherings; and finally, the conception that a cathedral square must be the main junction of a city's underground system.

But Praça da Sé is more than a space conceived in urbanistic terms. By considering that the perceived refers to the use of the body through hands, limbs, sensitivity and gesture (2000: 50), one dimension of it surfaces in particular when one pays attention to the pedestrian types that gather there. I mean the patterns involved in how (in Maussian terms) 'human beings make use of their bodies' in specific (Lefebvrean) 'rhythms'. This is what I termed 'modes of body behaviour' (Frehse 2011: 46): 'body techniques' (Mauss 1997: 365) employed in certain sequences of repetitions that induce 'manners' (Lefebvre 1992: 55). The perceived plaza cathedral

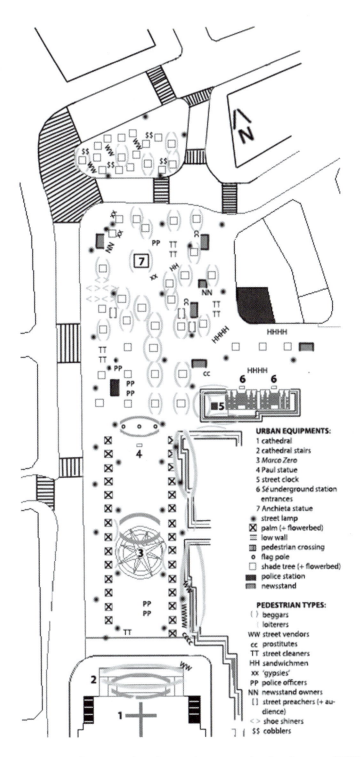

URBAN EQUIPMENTS:
1 cathedral
2 cathedral stairs
3 *Marco Zero*
4 Paul statue
5 street clock
6 *Sé* underground station
  entrances
7 Anchieta statue
  street lamp
☒ palm (+ flowerbed)
≡ low wall
▥ pedestrian crossing
o flag pole
□ shade tree (+ flowerbed)
▦ police station
▤ newsstand

PEDESTRIAN TYPES:
( ) beggars
[loiterers
WW street vendors
cc prostitutes
TT street cleaners
HH sandwichmen
xx 'gypsies'
PP police officers
NN newsstand owners
[] street preachers (+ audience)
< > shoe shiners
$$ cobblers

Fig. 12.3   Location of some regular urban equipments and pedestrian types (2007–12)

square is, on the one hand, the setting for the *regular coming and going* of *passers-by* (see Figure 12.4): of men, women and children that stand out for the physical behaviour of regularly crossing public spaces such as streets and squares (Frehse 2011: 45).

On the other hand, the plaza is enlivened by one mode of body behaviour that I termed the 'regular physical permanence' of pedestrians in São Paulo streets and squares – *whether to perform manual labour, or for sociability purposes* (ibid.: 89). This is why I use to call them *non-passers-by* (Frehse 2013a): indeed, they differ from the passers-by in that they regularly stay in the square (see Figure 12.5).

However, the socioeconomic and gender profiles of these non-passers-by vary, as does their location (see Figure 12.3). On the cathedral stairs and around the low walls, street vendors, prostitutes and loiterers, many of them unemployed and/or homeless, some of them drunk or drugged people, most of them men, few women, illegally sell and exchange food, drugs and alcoholic beverages. The low walls near the stairs, in particular, hold a discrete clandestine fair where (sometimes stolen) apparel, footwear, perfume, mobile phones, among other items, are bartered. The almost shadeless rectangle also holds regular beggars. All these informal non-passers-by lie or sit on the square's ground, on its low walls, on the cathedral stairs or the trees' flowerbeds. There they share the space with a few formal non-passers-by: police officers, street cleaners – that is, state employees engaged in maintaining the square's function as a place of transit and of merely momentary shelter.

Being easily observable in the imperial palm rectangle, all these non-passers-by also appear in the site's other two segments. There they coexist with others that must also be addressed in descriptive terms. In the central part of the shade-giving tree rectangle, street preachers of the most diverse religions loudly argue in front of attentive audiences of (non-)passers-by about gods and devils, while police officers gather inside and around the two police stations nearby. Further northwest is the shoeshiners' workplace. Their activities and those of the newspaper and magazine vendors in the square's many newsstands are the only legally registered street businesses on the plaza. In front of these stands, a few relatively invisible prostitutes gather, whereas next to the Anchieta statue, women in gypsy garb read the fortunes of passers-by. Sandwichmen, in turn, advertise 'I buy gold', mostly near the underground entrances. Last, the non-passers-by of the shade-giving tree triangle are much less variegated in social terms: few loiterers and street vendors share the space with legally registered cobblers who also polish shoes.

What might one say, finally, of the lived Praça da Sé? One must address the 'images and symbols' through which space is bodily lived by its 'inhabitants' and 'users', its artists and writers (Lefebvre 2000: 50). None of these types could be identified as such. Indeed, at least since 1990, there are more people living *on* the streets and squares of São Paulo's historical hill than *in* its surrounding buildings (Sposati 2000). Thus I searched for images of the square verbalized to me by five non-passers-by who had been spending their weekday afternoons there for five or more years, and who agreed to be interviewed during their work or while loitering there.

In search for semiotic and symbolic forms of representations located in 'the sensitive aspects' that link past individual and group emotions to the present as well

Fig. 12.4   Northern view of the plaza's imperial palm forecourt (April 2011)

Fig. 12.5   Northeastern view of the plaza's shaded rectangle (February 2012)

as to the future (Lefebvre 1961: 288, 1980: 240), I was faced with peculiar images. For the 55-year-old homeless Pedro,[4] who had been living in the cathedral square for five years (in February 2012), the site was essentially 'a street vending market where you can even find paperclips', a discreet allusion to its clandestine fair. In turn, the 28-year-old homeless Roberto, in the square for 15 years (in November 2008), described Praça da Sé as 'my home, my third mother', after his mother died and his aunt sent him to a remand home. If both these images are idiosyncratic, the third was shared by three of the square's daily workers in February 2012. The plaza is exclusively a workplace for both the 42-year-old Marco and the 70-year-old José, shoeshiners there for ten and 40 years respectively, and for the 58-year-old newspaper seller João, whose stand there is 20 years old. The cathedral is totally absent from these images. It does not matter that the bishop's see, Sé, gave the square its name, and that all the interviewees stated that they had been raised as Roman Catholics – though not all of them currently practise this religion.

Analytical-regressive Moment

In order to date the aforementioned urbanistic representations of space, the best starting point is the cathedral. Although its external appearance paraphrases a definite Gothic past, it was built between 1912 and 1960, its latest ornaments dating from 2004. Its construction by a German immigrant followed the demolition of a previous cathedral that had been constructed as of 1745, in colonial Portuguese style, in the central-north side of the square's currently shaded rectangle (where, since 1954, the Anchieta statue has stood), when the economically poor hinterland town of São Paulo became a diocese of colonial Brazil (see Figure 12.6).

Although the current cathedral's architecture is totally divorced from this long social history, it reveals traits of São Paulo's modernity in the early twentieth century: its 'cultural uprooting' after centuries of strong Iberian references (Martins 1999: 2–3). The only remainder of the colonial Sé is the ground plan of the square's triangular area, which roughly corresponds to the former Largo da Sé. The word *largo* alludes to the triangular widening of the streets that, since the Middle Ages, usually emerged in front of churches in the villages or cities colonized by Portugal (Teixeira 2001a: 11).

Whereas the cathedral's external appearance stems in historical terms from the German medieval period, when Brazil had not yet come into being, Praça da Sé results from a representation of space that dates back to the Portuguese Middle Ages. The positive evaluation of Catholic sees in the geographical centre of settlements dates from the last decades of the fifteenth century (Teixeira 2001a: 14, 2001b: 75, 78). This conception, which spread worldwide thanks to Portugal's colonizing endeavours, also reached São Paulo. The construction of the first Sé dragged on from the last decade of the sixteenth century to the mid-seventeenth century, in a small Indian–Portuguese settlement that was promoted to 'village' in 1560, becoming a 'city' only in 1711.

The rectangular square, in particular, constructed after the demolition of the colonial cathedral and of three blocks of houses on the south of today's Praça da Sé,

Fig. 12.6
Southeastern
view of the former
cathedral (1862)

results from the urbanistic representation that a cathedral square should be a 'civic square'. This conception became notorious in São Paulo in the 1910s (Sevcenko 1992: 103). It was a novelty in a city with little more than 409,000 inhabitants (1910), a colossal figure relative to the 65,000 people or so of 20 years earlier, and the roughly 32,000 that lived in the still rural and provincial São Paulo by 1872 (Frehse 2011).

Then, during the country's last military dictatorship (1964–85), the 'civic square' representation was merged with the notion that Praça da Sé should become the main junction of the São Paulo underground lines, the construction of which began in 1968 (Milanesi 2002: 118, 142–60). The square was conceived as a place primarily for pedestrian and passenger traffic. In the 1970s, it lost many of its surrounding monumental buildings in favour of the wide pedestrianized area, the compass rose around the 1934 *Marco Zero*, and the eastern garden sector.

In my view, this representation has been reiterated recently, this time under democracy. At least since the latest renovation of Praça da Sé (2006–07), benches have been absent from the area under consideration here. The seating possibilities are now the ground, the cathedral stairs, flower beds, low walls or private chairs (see Figures 12.1, 12.3–12.5).

For all these reasons, the conceived Praça da Sé dates mainly from the twentieth century. The date of the perceived square, in turn, is far harder to establish. Nevertheless, the analytical-regressive perspective enables one to discern that the body behaviour of the square's passers-by dates back to the last third of the nineteenth century and that regular permanence is even older. Regular walking along streets and squares became common in downtown São Paulo in the late

1800s (Frehse 2005, 2011). By the end of the African slavery age (1888), places such as Praça da Sé harboured the regular permanence almost exclusively of pedestrians involved in manual labour (street vending, loitering, begging, animal husbandry, prostitution) and/or with the sociability connections that evolved mainly among poor (ex-)slaves or freemen in these occasions. As a rule, men and women of high social standing left home only on exceptional and ceremonial occasions, such as festivals and religious processions, or to visit relatives. Passers-by were an absolute exception. However, in the wake of the many socioeconomic, demographic and political transformations of the late 1800s, these pedestrians became the new protagonists of regular to-and-fro movements within São Paulo's central streets and squares, thus displaying a body behaviour to which especially the members of the then nascent middle classes were fated. Indeed, they practised the routines of the (few) salaried or self-employed workers in a city marked by slavery.

From this standpoint, the perceived Praça da Sé is much older than the conceived one. The nineteenth century in particular becomes evident every time the square's hard ground, its low walls or the cathedral stairs cease to be passageways and the site of a brief stay, tacitly to become the physical supports of the body to relax or to socialize. An analysis of photographs of downtown São Paulo in the nineteenth century (Frehse 2011: 204, 490–97) reveals body techniques surprisingly similar to today's ones, although the square's current pedestrians are obviously very different from those of the former Largo da Sé.

In turn, the lived Praça da Sé gives one the impression of no historicity at all. The cathedral-square images show virtually no ties with the past, the present or the future – let alone with the possible. Their prevailing time is the present, as indicated by the prompt association of Praça da Sé with a workplace for some, with a place of consumption for others, or with a timeless place of affection and of yearning for affection, those irreducible 'residues' of praxis (Lefebvre 1967: 68–9).

To grasp what this peculiar coexistence of times reveals about difference in and through São Paulo, one must, finally, link the previously dated structures with the 'overall' ones, evaluating their modifications.

Historical-genetic Moment

As in this case the structures are the moments of Praça da Sé that, in a way, mediate the production of space both in present-day urban Brazil and abroad, why not evaluate their modifications in relation to the overall process comprised by the current trend toward global urbanization?

The physical appearance of Praça da Sé indicates that after 40 years this space is still architecturally and urbanistically conceived as a place for pedestrian and passenger traffic. This representation turns the square into an exemplary manifestation of Lefebvrean abstract space. The functionalist and quantitatively oriented character of the architectural 'party' of the 1970s (Milanesi 2002: 161) strongly contributed to the square's beginning, just like abstract space, to 'function negatively' concerning 'historical, religious and political aspects' and differential space-time, while 'functioning positively regarding its implications: techniques, applied sciences, and knowledge tied to power' (Lefebvre 2000: 62). Thus it comes as no surprise that the conceived Praça da Sé disregards the urbanistic representation that the monumentality of the square derives from the presence of a cathedral there.

This suggests to what extent the São Paulo urban space is 'modern', the characteristics of the 'space of "modernity"' being its 'homogeneity–fragmentation– hierarchisation' (ibid.: xxiii). Thus what Praça da Sé pedestrians share with passers- by of postwar abstract space comes to the analytic fore: 'a tacit agreement, a non- aggression pact, a non-violence agreement in everyday life, almost' (ibid.: 70).

Yet, at the same time, everything is different at the heart of the dialectics of centrality. One has only to focus on two revealing contradictions of space embedded in the lived Praça da Sé.

The images provided by the five non-passers-by suggest, on the one hand, that the lived square seems totally dominated by the rationale of abstract space, with its own temporal contradiction: the time that cannot be reduced appears, at best, through the homeless Roberto, as 'intimacy, interiority, subjectivity' (Lefebvre 2000: 452). On the other hand, the images show that, if for the interviewees the square is a 'space of consumption', of exchange made feasible by everyday work, which applies to the 'historical places of the accumulation of capital', this relation with space does not imply its contradiction, the 'unproductive consumption of space' by means of leisure. When asked if they would go to the square outside their working hours, the interviewees responded with a scathing 'no'. Not even the cathedral would be worthy of a visit. Only João said he had gone in there 'sometimes – incredibly seldom, given that I work here'.

What is fundamental here is that neither contradiction is due to the disappearance of time (of history), which applies to the space of modernity, but to the active presence of historicity, particularly of the past! In the wake of an urbanization process that allocated to the historical city centre the urbanistic role of a main public transport junction, while the districts further away became the favourite residential areas of the socially and economically most privileged segments of society, Praça da Sé turned into an epicentre of the process that the specialized bibliography refers to as the 'popularization of the São Paulo city centre' (for example, José 2010). It became the favoured place of residence and of work of the poor, who also tend to concentrate in the city's outskirts, its so-called periphery (Kowarick 1979, Martins 2008), given the very high prices of urban property, largely controlled by the real estate market since the 1930s and especially since the 1970s.

These densely historical processes appear as mediations in the production of a plaza that is lived as if it were atemporal, of a cathedral square devoid of the cathedral's monumentality, of a space of consumption unworthy of the consumption of space. Thus one notices a first contradiction *of* space due to contradictions *in* space, to the way in which the past transpires in and through the perceived and lived square. Less than a centre that attracts while expelling, Praça da Sé is a centre that expels the very centre while – and because – it attracts the periphery.

Still, this very same periphery also differs from the one that haunts the centrality that dialectizes abstract space. It is defined less by the geographical origin and social condition of the non-passers-by than by the historicity of their body behaviour.

Viewed from this angle, this square's monumentality lies less in the materiality of the cathedral than in the bodies of the square's non-passers-by. This is a second contradiction of space due to contradictions in space: the city's memory – a monument – is constituted by the body's unworried gestures, as it insists upon staying in the square despite the pressures of traffic, of the 'silence of the "users"' (Lefebvre 2000: 69). It does not matter that this memory and this past are not lived as such daily.

In sum, if viewed through the operational and the interpretive lenses of the regressive-progressive approach, Praça da Sé is a *peripheral centre whose monumentality is embedded in its pedestrians' bodies*. And it becomes revealing of a conceptually different São Paulo.

THE METHOD'S UNIQUENESS IN URBAN STUDIES

Given that cathedral squares, as a rule, stand out in a great variety of cities, at least in the Western world, due to the long-standing symbolic relevance of cathedrals (Pastro 2010: 262), Praça da Sé offers the urban researcher two sociospatial traits that provide, in conceptual terms, uniquely revealing comparisons with other (at least Western) present-day urban contexts. I know that a comparative exercise of this kind is impossible here. Nevertheless, the results of a recent analysis of mine, particularly of the pedestrian use of space in the Lisbon and São Paulo Praças da Sé (Frehse 2013a), make it possible to propose as a hypothesis for further research that cathedral squares underscored by both aforementioned characteristics are definitely *not* usual in present-day Western metropolises, but mainly in the Northern ones that strongly inspire Brazilian urban studies.

Less than the empirical relevance of this hypothesis, what matters here is that a conceptual possibility as such derives from the application of Lefebvre's method to Praça da Sé. The regressive-progressive angle brings to the analytical forefront historical contradictions of the production of (urban) space that inevitably turn the empirically researched field into a mediation that reveals the *possibility* of socially and culturally *specific* processes of space production.

Hence there is difference at play. A possibility *is* difference (Lefebvre 1970a: 79). Indeed, although the Praça da Sé contradictions are perhaps incapable of turning present-day urban space in São Paulo into a differential space, they are mediations that, at least in conceptual terms, reveal it as a *different* space amid the current historical process. They suggest that, notably in part of urban Brazil, the past continues to provide decisive mediation of the production of space. If the dialectics of centrality is crucial in current urbanization, contradictions in space can be so active amid the vigour of the contradictions of space that the centre becomes a periphery, and the pedestrian's body a monument.

By fostering this kind of conceptualization, the method enables one, finally, to address the three aspects that, for me, ensure its uniqueness in urban studies today.

In fact, it is not the only approach to investigating, at present, the role of historicity in the search for differences between present-day cities. For example, in the contemporary sociological debate, methodologies that underpin concepts such as habitus, identity, path dependence and doxa are often employed to explain how past social practices interfere with sociospatial processes that make it possible to conceptually distinguish cities from each other.[5] However, based on different conceptions of historicity and space, the regressive-progressive method is, first, unique in its way of articulating both notions. Conceived in dialectical terms, both time and space become revealing mediations of each other's specificities in definite modes of production. Thus historical times, especially, become free, on the one hand, of any causal determination, and therefore from the subtle linearity implicit in the use that is made of history in the contemporary path-dependence perspective. The historical, after all, is simultaneously the past, the present and the possible. On the other hand, historicity does not exclusively concern routinized, reproductive events believed to structure social practices, as in approaches to the habitus, the identity and the 'intrinsic logic' of cities. Indeed, historicity *mediates* the (re)production of space, which in turn is a mediation of the (re)production of society, thus of the latter's – and of mankind's – historicity.

This methodological aspect of theoretical nature leads one to a second uniqueness factor of the Lefebvrean method in present-day urban studies. It helps the urban researcher to evidence in analytical terms *how* historicity in and through space mediates between everyday life and the so-called grand historical processes of an economic and social nature. Sometimes, as the Praça da Sé example shows, the past remains actively present in human, rather than in architectural, bodies – an aspect I have developed conceptually elsewhere (Frehse 2013b). However, this is a dimension of Lefebvre's ponderings on space that is entirely absent from current Lefebvre-oriented empirical analyses of the production of space. In analytical terms, these tend to focus *either* on the micro *or* on the macro levels of social practice, thus overlooking Lefebvre's own concern with what mediates between both: time and space; and, in postwar capitalism, particularly historicity in and through urban space. In my view, the regressive-progressive method was developed to cope simultaneously, in operational and interpretive terms, with the relationship between time and space as crucial mediations of a second relationship: that between everyday life and history in and through space.

And thus I arrive at the last uniqueness factor to be stressed. By comprising description, analysis and explanation, the approach mediates between both types of methods that have historically underpinned sociological research: those based on investigation and those based on interpretation (Fernandes 1959: 13–14). This is the peculiarity of Lefebvre's approach: it *mediates* between empirical and theoretical research. Hence it operationalizes a concern that can already be found in Marx's methodological writings, despite remaining a rare undertaking in sociology, not to speak of urban research in general.

Underscored by all these characteristics, it is not difficult to recognize, finally, why the scope of the regressive-progressive method inevitably transcends Northern cities and academic contexts. For as long as there is space for one to scrutinize in analytical and conceptual terms, there will be time and, in the capitalist mode of production, historicity to understand – and this despite the vigour of space, or, better stated, precisely because of it.

NOTES

1   All translations from languages other than English are my own.

2   The transduction 'builds a virtual object with information as the starting point', by reaching from 'the (given) real [*le réel (donné)*] to the possible [*le possible*]' (Lefebvre 1961: 121).

3   'The past becomes (again) present as a function of the realization of the possibilities objectively implied in this past. It unfolds and updates itself with them' (Lefebvre 1965: 36).

4   The names of the interviewees are changed for privacy purposes.

5   For a recent review of the literature see Löw (2009: 92–5).

REFERENCES

Berking, H. and Löw, M. (eds) 2008. *Die Eigenlogik der Städte*. Frankfurt a.M.; New York: Campus.

Candido, A. 1993. 'O significado de Raízes do Brasil' (Preface), in *Raízes do Brasil*, edited by S.B. Holanda. Rio de Janeiro: João Olympio, xxxix–l.

Cardoso, F.H. 1962. *Capitalismo e Escravidão no Brasil Meridional*. São Paulo: Difel.

Fernandes, F. 1959. *Fundamentos Empíricos da Explicação Sociológica*. São Paulo: Companhia Editora Nacional.

Fortuna, C. 2012. 'In Praise of Other Views: The World of Cities and the Social Sciences'. *Iberoamericana* 12(45): 137–53.

Frehse, F. 1997. 'Entre Largo e Praça, Matriz e Catedral: A Sé dos Cartões Postais Paulistanos'. *Cadernos de Campo* 5(5–6): 117–55.

Frehse, F. 2001. 'Potencialidades do Método Regressivo-Progressivo: Pensar a Cidade, Pensar a História'. *Tempo Social* 13(2): 169–84.

Frehse, F. 2005. *O Tempo das Ruas na São Paulo de Fins do Império*. São Paulo: Edusp.

Frehse, F. 2011. *Ô da Rua! O Transeunte e o Advento da Modernidade em São Paulo*. São Paulo: Edusp.

Frehse, F. 2012. 'A Recent Sociological Utopia of Urban Space in Brazil'. *Iberoamericana* 12(45): 103–17.

Frehse, F. 2013a. 'Os tempos (diferentes) do uso das Praças da Sé em Lisboa e em São Paulo', in *Diálogos Urbanos: Territórios, Culturas, Patrimónios*, edited by C. Fortuna and R.P. Leite. Coimbra: Almedina, 124–73.

Frehse, F. 2013b. 'Zeiten im Körper: Der Beitrag der Lefebvreschen Methode für die (lateinamerikanische) Stadtforschung', in *Lo urbano: Positionen aktueller Stadtforschung aus Lateinamerika*, edited by A. Huffschmid and K. Wildner. Bielefeld: transcript, 145–69.

Frehse, F. and Leite, R.P. 2010. 'Espaço Urbano no Brasil', in *Horizontes das Ciências Sociais no Brasil: Sociologia*, edited by H.T.S. Martins. São Paulo: ANPOCS, 203–51.

Harvey, D. 1989. *The Condition of Postmodernity*. Oxford; Cambridge, MA: Blackwell.

Hess, R. 1988. *Henri Lefebvre et l'aventure du siècle*. Paris: A.M. Métailié.

José, B.K. 2010. *A Popularização do Centro de São Paulo*. PhD thesis in Architecture and Urbanism. São Paulo: Universidade de São Paulo.

Kowarick, L. 1979. *A Espoliação Urbana*. Rio de Janeiro: Paz e Terra.

Lefebvre, H. 1961. *Critique de la vie quotidienne*. Vol. 2. Paris: L'Arche Éditeur.

Lefebvre, H. 1965. *La proclamation de la Commune*. Paris: Gallimard.

Lefebvre, H. 1967 [1965]. *Metafilosofia*. Trans. R. Corbisier. Rio de Janeiro: Civilização Brasileira.

Lefebvre, H. 1970a. *La révolution urbaine*. Paris: Gallimard.

Lefebvre, H. 1970b. *Le manifeste différentialiste*. Paris: Gallimard.

Lefebvre, H. 1975. *Le temps des méprises*. Paris: Stock.

Lefebvre, H. 1980. *La présence et l'absence*. Paris: Casterman.

Lefebvre, H. 1992. *Eléments de rythmanalyse*. Paris: Syllepse.

Lefebvre, H. 2000 [1974]. *La production de l'espace*. Paris: Anthropos.

Lefebvre, H. 2001a [1949]. 'Problèmes de sociologie rurale', in *Du rural à l'urbain* by H. Lefebvre. Paris: Anthropos, 21–40.

Lefebvre, H. 2001b [1953]. 'Perspectives de la sociologie rurale', in *Du rural à l'urbain* by H. Lefebvre. Paris: Anthropos, 63–78.

Lefebvre, H. 2001c [1960]. 'Introduction à la psycho-sociologie de la vie quotidienne', in *Du rural à l'urbain* by H. Lefebvre. Paris: Anthropos, 89–107.

Lefebvre, H. 2009 [1968]. *Le droit à la ville*. 3rd edn. Paris: Anthropos.

Löw, M. 2005. 'Die Rache des Körpers über den Raum? Über Henri Lefèbvres Utopie und Geschlechterverhältnisse am Strand', in *Soziologie des Körpers*, edited by M. Schroer. Frankfurt a.M.: Suhrkamp, 241–70.

Löw, M. 2009. *Soziologie der Städte*. Frankfurt a.M.: Suhrkamp.

Martins, J.S. 1975. *Capitalismo e Tradicionalismo*. São Paulo: Livraria Pioneira Editora.

Martins, J.S. 1992. *Subúrbio*. São Paulo; São Caetano do Sul: Hucitec/Prefeitura de São Caetano do Sul.

Martins, J.S. 1996a. 'As temporalidades da história na dialética de Lefebvre', in *Henri Lefebvre e o Retorno à Dialética*, edited by J.S. Martins. São Paulo: Hucitec, 13–23.

Martins, J.S. 1996b. *Henri Lefebvre e o Retorno à Dialética*. São Paulo: Hucitec.

Martins, J.S. 1998. *Florestan: Sociologia e Consciência Social no Brasil*. São Paulo: Edusp.

Martins, J.S. 1999. *Tombamento da Catedral da Sé de São Paulo/Parecer*. São Paulo: Condephaat.

Martins, J.S. 2008. *A Aparição do Demônio na Fábrica*. São Paulo: Editora, 34.

Mauss, M. 1997. 'Les techniques du corps', in *Sociologie et anthropologie* by M. Mauss. Paris: Quadrige/Puf, 363–86.

Milanesi, R. 2002. *Evolução Urbana e Espaço Público*. BA dissertation in Architecture and Urbanism. São Paulo: Universidade de São Paulo.

Pastro, C. 2010. *A Arte no Cristianismo*. São Paulo: Paulus.

Porto, A.R. 1996. *História da Cidade de São Paulo Através de Suas Ruas*. São Paulo: Carthago Editorial.

Sartre, J.-P. 1960. *Critique de la raison dialectique*. Vol. 1. Paris: Gallimard.

Sassen, S. 1991. *The Global City*. Thousand Oaks, CA: Pine Forge Press.

Sassen, S. 2008. 'As Diferentes Especializações das Cidades Globais', in *Cidades Sul-Americanas: Assegurando um Futuro Urbano*, edited by Urban Age. São Paulo: Imprensa Oficial, 4–6.

Schmid, C. 2005. *Stadt, Raum und Gesellschaft*. München: Franz Steiner Verlag.

Sevcenko, N. 1992. *Orfeu Extático na Metrópole*. São Paulo: Companhia das Letras.

Soja, E. 1989. *Postmodern Geographies*. London; New York: Verso.

Sposati, A. 2000. *Mapa da Exclusão/Inclusão Social da Cidade de São Paulo/2000*. CD-ROM. São Paulo: Pólis/INPE/PUC-SP.

Stanek, Ł. 2011. *Henri Lefebvre on Space*. Minneapolis, MN; London: University of Minnesota Press.

Teixeira, M.C. 2001a. 'Introdução', in *A Praça na Cidade Portuguesa*, edited by M.C. Teixeira. Lisboa: Livros Horizonte, 9–16.

Teixeira, M.C. 2001b. 'As Praças Urbanas Portuguesas Quinhentistas', in *A Praça na Cidade Portuguesa*, ed. M.C. Teixeira. Lisboa: Livros Horizonte, 69–89.

Urban Research and Architecture: Beyond Henri Lefebvre 2009. *Program and Abstracts*. Zürich: 24–26 November.

PART IV
Urban Society and Its Projects

Architectural Project and the Agency of Representation: The Case of Nowa Huta, Poland

Łukasz Stanek

Henri Lefebvre's theorizing of space addresses the conjunctures between material environments, their representations, and their ways of use and experience: the three 'moments' of space discussed in *The Production of Space* as spatial practices, representations of space and spaces of representation (Lefebvre 1991, Stanek 2011).[1] Rather than positing an ontology of space that would explain the relationship between its moments; or normalizing this relationship within an ethics or aesthetics of space, Lefebvre described the moments of space as related to each other from within a social practice, governed by an open-ended 'spatial dialectics'. In other words, the production of space always-already implies aggregating its moments, and in this chapter I argue that an architectural project is to be defined by the labour of such aggregation (Stanek 2012).

Architects are 'producers of space', wrote Lefebvre, but never the only ones (Lefebvre in Sturge-Moore 1972: 4). More specifically, they are producers of representations of space and hence Lefebvre writes half seriously, half ironically that their specific space is 'a sheet of white paper' (ibid.). Architects produce drawings and models, but in so doing they respond to representations of space produced by other agents, from individual desires and embodied memories to institutionalized images and collectively shared symbols. Whether theorized as 'collective unconsciousness', 'habitus', 'way of life' or 'cultural model', the two last concepts examined by Lefebvre's collaborators at the Institut de sociologie urbaine in the course of the 1960s (Stanek 2011), these shared representations are reference points, negative or positive, for the social processes of production of space and for the design practices themselves.

In what follows, I discuss how representations of space intervene in the dynamics of space production in a specific geographical and historical conjuncture: that of Nowa Huta, the 'first socialist city in Poland' constructed by the post-war socialist regime near Kraków from the late 1940s. Since the foundation of this city, representations have been the defining factor of the development of Nowa Huta and continue to play this role: at the end what gathers together five districts of

Kraków referred to by the name 'Nowa Huta' is a set of representations strongly embedded in various social practices, rather than an administrative or a spatial whole. (Following these representations, in this chapter, I will refer to Nowa Huta as a 'city', in spite of the fact that it ceased to be an independent administrative entity already in 1951.) In this way, Lefebvre's stress on representations as a necessary part of the processes of space production, rather than their reflection, result or effect, offers a promising starting point for discussing the urban space in Nowa Huta.

This chapter focuses on the representations of Nowa Huta between the end of the Soviet-dependent People's Republic of Poland (1989) and the entry of Poland into the European Union (2004). It is based on a study of printed mass media, in particular local ones, such as the weekly magazine *Głos Nowej Huty* (*The Voice of Nowa Huta*), changed in 1991 to *Głos Tygodnik Nowohucki* (*The Voice. The Weekly of Nowa Huta*), which was established in 1957 as *Budujemy Socjalizm* (*We Are Building Socialism*). All issues of *Głos* between 1988 and 2003 were reviewed, thus enabling quantitative comparisons. Other sources were the Kraków dailies *Gazeta Krakowska* and *Dziennik Polski* (both existed during the socialist period), and dailies that were set up after 1989: *Czas Krakowski* and *Gazeta w Krakowie* (the Kraków edition of the national newspaper, *Gazeta Wyborcza*). These periodicals were confronted with other regional and professional journals, such as *Suplement*, as well as the national daily *Rzeczpospolita* and some articles in the national weekly magazines *Przekrój* and *Polityka*.

This chapter contributes to a larger debate on 'representational cities' developed in ethnographic and anthropological research towards a reading of cities as reservoirs of messages deciphered and reinterpreted by inhabitants and visitors (Jacobs 1993). Hence, for example, in his ethnography of Brasília, James Holston (1989) shows the negotiation between the utopian image of the city and its everyday reality. While several authors stressed the active role of inhabitants in deciphering these urban messages, architects are often opposed to inhabitants and seen as producers of 'dominant' representations, resisted by inhabitants and their narratives. Against this bipolar image, which replaces the heroic narrative of an architect by that of an inhabitant, often equally heroic, I will theorize this negotiation of representations as multipolar and heterogenous. Looking at Nowa Huta with Lefebvre's theory allows not only a better understanding of what architects do when they draw up a design, but also a broader rethinking of architectural practices within the processes of space production (Awan et al. 2011, Stanek 2014).

CONTESTED REPRESENTATIONS IN NOWA HUTA

Located 10 km from Kraków, the historical capital of Poland, Nowa Huta ('new steelworks') was founded as an independent industrial city for the workers of the steel production plant being developed nearby, but it became a district of Kraków as early as 1951. After the administrative reform in 1991, Nowa Huta was divided into five smaller districts which today count 220,000 inhabitants, with Kraków's total population reaching nearly 760,000. The urban plan of the city was based on the concept of the neighbourhood unit, which regulated the distribution of housing and social facilities. The architectural idiom of socialist realism, with numerous quotations from Kraków Renaissance, was abandoned in the early 1960s for modernism, which became sadly impoverished in the years that followed (Irion and Sieverts 1991, Juchnowicz 2002). The city witnessed much political unrest and in the 1980s Nowa Huta was one of the most important centres of popular protest against the regime in Poland. After the political transition in the year 1989, the steelworks were privatized and restructured by their new owner, Mittal Steel, and workers encouraged to leave with comparatively generous compensation were not replaced. At the time the Nowa Huta districts came to be associated with criminality and unemployment. Since the official statistics do not support this association,[2] sociologists studying the transformation of the city in the course of the 1990s feared a 'self-fulfilling prophecy of social crisis' (Bukowski 2003).

This hiatus between the representations of Nowa Huta and its material reality was, in fact, specific to the city from its beginnings. This started with its 'foundation myth' depicting a young man who is lured to the 'first socialist city in Poland' only to discover that the city has not been yet built, and who decides to stay in order to contribute to the construction of Nowa Huta. Omnipresent in the state-controlled press in the 1950s and repeated since then, this narrative introduced mass media representations as the primary framework for the experience of Nowa Huta and the desire to catch up with these representations as the subtext of the city's development.

State socialism was all about 'catching up' and 'taking over', and Nowa Huta was at the forefront. Renata Siemieńska, whose 1969 book *Nowe życie w nowym mieście* [*A New Life in a New City*] included the first systematic investigation of the mass media representations of Nowa Huta, pointed out that the claim of Nowa Huta as 'not yet a socialist city, but a socialist city in becoming' can be found in the mass media articles as early as the 1950s (Siemieńska 1969: 48). The distinction between the project of the city and its dynamic development also appears in a 1952 article by Tadeusz Ptaszycki, the head designer of Nowa Huta, who wrote that 'the designers of the city of Nowa Huta see in their work two forms of the city: a prospective form and a form of the city under construction with all the pressures of the living conditions; a city which is "not there yet" but which lives and which builds itself' (Ptaszycki 1952: 10).

After 1989, this narrative of 'catching up' with the socialist city was replaced, almost overnight, by that of 'moving beyond' it. The most important change in the discourse about the city after the end of socialism was its pluralization. The official discourse on the 'socialist city' did not disappear but rather clashed in the local mass media with other, competing representations, all supported by historians' discourses, personal recollections, private archives and photographic sources. These discussions, often politically motivated, were characterized by a clash between the local discourse, supported by Nowa Huta's local media, and narratives in Kraków's press and the majority of the national press. These two were joined by professional discourses (architectural, sociological, historical, geographical) that permeated the mass media and by discourses tied to particular institutions (the steelworks and the district authorities, but also various cultural centres and organizations, including those of tenants). Orientation points for the discussion on Nowa Huta were provided by some of the most active participants of these debates, including Stanisław Juchnowicz (a member of the Tadeusz Ptaszycki team of designers of Nowa Huta and professor at the Technical University Kraków), Maciej Miezian (the director of the Nowa Huta Museum), Jan Franczyk (the editor-in-chief of the local weekly *Głos Tygodnik Nowohucki*), Mieczysław Gil (one of the leaders of anti-socialist opposition in Nowa Huta), and Niward Karsznia (a sociologist and rector of one of the parishes in Nowa Huta).

In the course of the 1990s, the modalities of the representation of Nowa Huta as a 'socialist city' were nuanced: some claimed that Nowa Huta was planned to be a socialist city but failed,[3] while others attributed such status to its past[4] and even to its present.[5] The political motivations of the city's construction were considered sufficient to call it 'socialist', followed by the supposed attachment of the population to the former regime, motivated either by nostalgia for the social facilities and the communitarian atmosphere in the city, or by political convictions.[6] The latter were manifested during the municipal elections of 2002, when the left-wing candidate, Jacek Majchrowski, received strong support in Nowa Huta. Election results show, however, that inhabitants rather than voting left tend to vote extreme: both the far left and the far right political parties have many supporters. The architecture of socialist realism in the central part of the city led to its numerous comparisons with an 'outdoor museum', an 'experiment', and a 'theme park'.[7] In fact a theme park called 'Socland', which simulated the socialist reality, was temporarily opened in Nowa Huta, while the peculiarity of the city has been exploited as a touristic asset (Stenning 2001, Stanek 2007).[8] Yet at the same time, the representation of Nowa Huta as 'socialist' was challenged by a very strong and homogeneous representation of the city as one of the most important centres of opposition to the regime in Poland: the city of strikes, riots and rebellions.[9]

Starting with the opposition between a socialist and a rebel city, the contradictory representations of Nowa Huta proliferated during the 1990s. They included, first, the contradiction between an 'atheistic' city, designed and built without churches, and the supposed centre of coalescence between labour and religion, which was strengthened by the struggles around the construction of a church in Nowa Huta, and the symbolic visit of John Paul II (1979) (Karnasiewicz 2003). The local priest and sociologist Nirward Karsznia claimed that the socialist – atheist – ideology brought about 'antisocial and immoral behaviors' and 'some marriages were broken due to the laxity of morals triggered by the new environment' (Karsznia 1994: 35); he added that it did not improve much after the end of socialism and the dominance of capitalist 'ideology of consumerism' (Karsznia 1997: 12).

Another opposition was that between Nowa Huta and Kraków: while some described the relationship between them as a 'crusade', others called for a 'reconciliation'.[10] This antagonism was a favourite trope of the official narrative of the 1950s and 1960s, which presented Nowa Huta as a 'young' city where social facilities were evenly distributed and favourably compared to those of Kraków, the 'old' metropolis as based on feudal domination, real-estate speculation and social segregation (Ostrowski 1952: 1). After the political change, these evaluations were reversed, and Nowa Huta was by then characterized as 'deprived of tradition' and 'criminal'. This contrast was further strengthened by the assumption that the main explanation for the social reality of Nowa Huta lay in the incongruence between the migrants from the countryside and the emerging urban reality. The interference of both urban and rural rhythms – the industrial shifts on the steelworks employing 80 per cent of the inhabitants and the habits of the population of whom 74 per cent were of rural origin (according to a 1979 survey) – has traditionally been considered a specific feature of the city, even after 1989 when the workers' population significantly shrunk (Siemieńska 1969, Bukowski 2003). Yet another contrasting pair of images was that of Nowa Huta as a site of ecological catastrophe, with the steelworks harming both the people and the ancient monuments of Kraków, and the vision of a green city, a city of parks.

Most of these contradictions were present in the media before 1989, but the official narrative forced them either into the scheme of evolution (the transformation from peasants to workers) or into a reductive version of Marxist dialectics, according to which the peasants change the material conditions of their life by taking up work in the steelworks and can thus overcome the contradiction between the city and the countryside by creating a new socialist society (Wereksiej 1976). After the end of socialism in Poland both schemes became obsolete. Deprived of a metanarrative that would allow subsuming the contradictions into a single argument, the commentators accept the impossibility of interrelating the representations of Nowa Huta and frame it as a 'city of paradoxes' (Stenning 2001). This suspends the discussion about the city by reducing its descriptions to a collection of contradictory, yet equally justifiable, representations. This crisis of representation is often treated as a symptom of the general failure of Nowa Huta as a city; and speaking shortly after the political change in 1989, one commentator claimed that 'Nowa Huta and its paradoxes testify against programming the future in the name of any intellectual idea, despite the fact that these ideas might be considered today, here and now, correct'.[11]

INSTRUMENTALITY OF REPRESENTATIONS: THE HOUSING QUESTION IN NOWA HUTA

Rather than accepting the stasis implied by the discourse on the 'city of paradoxes', Lefebvre's theory requires interrogating the agency of these contradictory representations of Nowa Huta that are constantly renegotiated and frequently changing hands. In what follows, these negotiations will be shown as vessels for a collective experience in which the production of material enclosures and shared subjectivities go hand in hand. The hints are taken from Lefebvre's analysis of Mourenx (1960), a new town in south-western France, where he discerned a conflict between the imagination of the community built up around the factory, and the urban sphere about to replace the factory in its role as the site of socialization, production and struggle. Speculating about the end of Fordism in post-war Europe, Lefebvre registered a conflict between alternative collective imaginations, which not only reflected the changes in the production of space in Mourenx, but also revealed possible crystallization points for political coalitions (Lefebvre 1960, for discussion, see Stanek 2011).

The representations of Nowa Huta intervene in the struggles over what was one of the most contested issues in the city after 1989: the housing question. Post-socialist liberalization of the real estate market undermined the main urban promise of Nowa Huta: the availability of housing.[12] In the face of the commercialization of the housing cooperatives, which owned the vast majority of the housing stock in the city, and the dramatic rise of rents, local leaders argued for the necessity of defending their rights to the apartments and supported individual ownership of real property.[13] The fact that the housing cooperatives had roots in the socialist system enabled framing those opposing the rapid privatization as supporters of the old regime.[14] These demands were endorsed by new legislation allowing the members of housing cooperatives to buy their flats for a fraction of their market value, and paralleled by the policy of privatization of communal real estate.

By becoming owners, the inhabitants were given the right to organize themselves into what the Polish law calls an 'inhabitants' community', where each owner of an individual flat has a share in the common areas of the property and co-manages it. In this way, the real estate landscape in Nowa Huta after 1989 has been to a large extent defined by frictions between the inhabitants' communities and the housing cooperatives, which were transformed into 'companies' providing 'services' and competing with other 'companies' on the market.[15]

The inhabitants' communities often originated from a protest of the inhabitants of a single block of flats against the housing cooperatives: the neighbourhood bond among the members and the informal ties with other inhabitants' communities facilitated flexible alliances when facing the service providers and politicians. In this way, the creation of inhabitants' communities was fuelled by the appeal to communal ties, embedded in the image of Nowa Huta before 1989, with neighbours growing up together and helping each other out.[16] This was a pervasive theme in the official representation of socialist Nowa Huta, with the stress on the shared experience of work and leisure. Yet the strong neighbourhood ties, and social networks in general, outlived socialism and became important assets for the population struggling with the relegation of the provision of services from the state to the market. This included a range of activities that are trivial but often crucial for the subsistence of many households in Nowa Huta: lending and borrowing food and small items (such as light bulbs, painkillers) and small amounts of money, helping out with repairs and watching over vacant flats. As a recent study showed, the frequency of contact in the neighbourhoods built since the 1960s (Dywizjonu 303 and Oświecenia) is lower than in older ones (Willowe and Górali). This is linked, according to the authors, with the large number of pensioners in the older neighbourhoods who have more sustainable ties to their neighbours. But architectural typologies play a role as well; in particular the two-to-three-storey blocks surrounded by green space in Willowe neighbourhood encourage social contacts (Rochovská et al. n.d.: 9–10, Rochovská et al. 2010).

In this sense, the reorganization of the housing stock reveals flexible references to the representations of Nowa Huta, embodied and remembered by the inhabitants, in particular to the representation of the 'socialist city'. The experience of socialist collectivism and of rebellions against the regime are selectively called upon by members of inhabitants' communities and mobilized in their confrontation with housing cooperatives transformed into commercial providers of services. However, the very same collective experience of Nowa Huta is referred to by several activists who blame the inhabitants' communities for blocking new initiatives and preventing the introduction of new functions that could activate the centre of the city. To be sure, this critique of the communities as privatized islands in the urban fabric cannot apply to all of them: for example the inhabitants' community in the Teatralne neighbourhood was not only cooperating with other communities in order to receive European funding for the renovation of the public spaces, but also co-organized cultural events.[17]

The negotiation between competing imaginations of collective bonds in Nowa Huta defines to a large extent the social spaces of several cultural institutions in the city, including the Nowa Huta Museum (since 2005) and Klub 1949 (2006–10). Through image campaigns and exhibitions, both institutions merged the sympathy for the quotidian experience of the past socialist city with the image of a new, future-oriented community. A similar sympathy for the city's tumultuous history permeates the activities of Łaźnia Nowa, a theatre and a cultural centre that was established in 2004 in the former workshops of the vocational technical high school for mechanics. Łaźnia started with the attempt to combine artistic relevance with a social mission and, according to Bartosz Szydłowski, Łaźnia's director and himself raised in Nowa Huta, argued that its location in the city is a part of the 'stuff' the theatre works with. This guides to a large extent the choice of plays that confront the everyday in Nowa Huta; they are often written by local authors (see Figure 13.1). The theatre programmatically avoids any convention that would signify the distance from its locale and displace the artist beyond the community; thus neither irony nor sarcasm is allowed. 'We don't want to be critical,' said Szydłowski in the interview, and he proudly mentioned that the priests in Nowa Huta include the Łaźnia newsletter in the announcements after Sunday mass. He admitted that, when facing an opposition between artistic quality and the relevance for the community, he does not hesitate to choose the second; at the same time he stressed that the theatre is not an amateur troupe.[18]

Łaźnia sees itself as producer of space of Nowa Huta: both by giving a positive reinterpretation of the city's identity ('we want people to recognize the spirit of the place') and by initiating projects that transform the public space.[19] This included the event 'The Alley of Hope', which, by projecting iconic masterpieces of European painting on to the buildings in the centre of Nowa Huta, linked the badly connoted socialist realist architecture to its Renaissance 'origins' or 'originals'. Łaźnia also launched a programme of social works to tidy up the nearby garden. These events relate the opening towards the community of inhabitants and an appeal to the socialist imaginary – most obviously present in the tradition of socialist work for the community – with the demand of responsibility and professionalism (the inhabitants who participate in the theatre are paid), alongside the entrepreneurial subjectivity endorsed by the EU-funded programmes (Projekt PIW 2006).

Fig. 13.1   'I Live Here': a production in Łaźnia Nowa (2004)

The locations of Klub 1949, the Nowa Huta Museum and Łaźnia facilitate these institutions' production of social space in the city (see Figure 13.2). The positioning of the theatre within the fabric of the Szkolne neighbourhood became the starting point for several projects: the theatre garden is used on a daily basis by the inhabitants living nearby; its cafeteria, with an entrance independent from that of the theatre, becomes a meeting point for youth; and the building in front of the theatre is often included in the spectacles to which its inhabitants contribute. Similarly, the museum and the club are located on the ground floors of blocks of flats, in contrast to older cultural institutions in Nowa Huta, housed in tailor-made, isolated, often monumental buildings designed in the idiom of socialist realism. With the museum grafted on to the former scouts' storeroom and the club in the old second-hand shop, these institutions inherited big shop windows, which ensured constant contact between the street and the interior. Both institutions became members of inhabitants' communities of their respective buildings, which made it necessary for them to negotiate constantly about their activities with the other owners; it is in the course of these, often difficult, negotiations that the use of the spaces of the museum and the club was worked out.

ALLEY OF ROSES: THE AGENCY OF AN ARCHITECTURAL PROJECT

In three volumes of *Critique of Everyday Life* (2002 [1961], 2006 [1981], 2008 [1947]) Lefebvre described how representations of space penetrate everyday practices, the

Fig. 13.2   Klub 1949 in 2008

quotidian language, ways to use spaces, and their experiences. In *The Production of Space* (1991 [1974]) this approach was developed into a more general questioning of the ways in which representations of space are mobilized in the processes of space production.

Nowa Huta's recent history reveals a variety of such roles. The representations inherited from the socialist period were referred to as arguments in the discussion on the investments in the district and municipal credit guarantees for the steelworks.[20] The opponents of such help argued that Nowa Huta was founded as a 'revenge of Stalin' and 'hostile to Kraków'; this is why its interests are supposedly divergent from those of the old royal capital.[21] This proved to be a successful argument: the first decision on financial guarantees for the steelworks was negative.[22] The leaders of the community of Nowa Huta opposed this representation with the image of a rebel city that 'resisted the communist indoctrination'.[23] On top of these polemics, mass media representations of Nowa Huta became reservoirs of new street names: those referring to socialist heroes, institutions and events were more often than not renamed after 1989.

The representations also provided reference points for the architectural and urban design competitions in Nowa Huta. For example, the narrative of a city that 'expressed' the socialist ideology was the starting point for the 2002 Kraków IX International Biennale of Architecture, held in Nowa Huta under the slogan: 'Less Ideology – More Geometry'. The introductory text claimed that the city was built as an entity uniting 'ideology' and 'geometry'; the ideology has come to pass whereas the geometry has not been completed (Kozłowski 2002). To 'complete' the city was hence the aim of the Biennale, taken up by the majority of the designs submitted to the competition. More generally, representations of space constitute an important part of the architectural context both for public buildings, such as churches, and residential complexes, including the postmodern housing complex Centrum E, which was claimed by the designer to be a 'protest against the architecture of socialist realism' (see Figure 13.3).[24]

This close relationship between the representations of space and urban design can be traced in the Alley of Roses, located at the central axis of Nowa Huta, where before 1989 the Lenin monument stood: a broad passage closed to vehicles that connects the Central Square (Plac Centralny) with the City Hall Square (Plac Ratuszowy). This site was not designed as an urban square and it hardly was one: the buildings surrounding the site are exclusively blocks of flats and the only entrances accessible from the site lead to staircases connecting apartments. Following the original masterplan, a rose garden was created in front of them, shown in a photograph published in 1959 (Ptaszycki 1959; see Figure 13.4). The layout was symmetrical with the main axis of the ensemble, but the position of paths and seats stressed the direction perpendicular to the axis. These transversal paths were directed towards the entrances to the blocks of flats, making the rose garden easily accessible to the inhabitants. Thus the rose garden was designed as a calm spot between two spaces to be enclosed by monumental buildings, which were never constructed: the planned theatre for the Central Square on the one side and, on the other, the city hall, which was no longer needed after Nowa Huta ceased to be an independent city.

In response to the need for a symbolic site suitable for political celebrations in the city, in 1973 the site was redecorated and the monument of Lenin was built on the axis of the ensemble (Miezian 2004: 85ff.). The roses were removed and the area covered with stone slabs. The rhythm of the site changed: the slow pace of the rose garden was replaced by the supervised void (a sentry box was built nearby) interrupted by official mass demonstrations and occasional riots. By removing the transversal paths and placing the monument on the axis, the site was given a new direction. At the same time, since the theatre and the city hall were not built, this site was the only place in the centre of the city that was completed in terms of urban design (see Figure 13.5).

The monument was attacked several times by anti-government protesters and once even with a bomb that amputated one foot of the Soviet leader. Shortly after the first non-socialist government was formed (1989), the monument was defaced with paint by demonstrators, who demanded its removal. Under this pressure, the municipal authorities reluctantly decided to remove the monument. (It is a historical irony that the former leaders of the democratic opposition defended the Lenin monument, trying to avoid one more irritation to the Russian authorities whose troops were still deployed in Poland.[25]) The monument was sold to the highest bidder, who happened to be the owner of a theme park in Sweden. The Lenin monument, however, dominated the popular imagination about Nowa Huta; the poet and musician Marcin Świetlicki confessed in 1997: 'when I think about

Fig. 13.3
Romuald Loegler
and team, Centrum
E housing complex
(1988–95), as seen
from behind the
Lenin monument

Fig. 13.4   Alley
of Roses in 1950s

Fig. 13.5   The Lenin monument in the Alley of Roses, after 1973

Nowa Huta I see the monument of Lenin, although it is no longer there'.[26] With the removal of the monument, the site was deprived of an element that gave it its name; it has since been known colloquially as 'the square after Lenin', or the 'void after Lenin'. This name not only shows the branding power of the monument, but also demonstrates that the site was accepted as a 'square' in spite of the lack of commercial, cultural or administrative functions that could generate urban activity (for a period of time at least one of the staircases in an adjacent block of flats was used as a temporary shop).

In yet one more attempt to 'complete' Nowa Huta, in the course of the 1990s the inhabitants and the local press called for a redecoration of this site.[27] The discussion about future development encompassed all competing representations of the city. The context of this demand was a broader discussion in the late 1990s about the future of Nowa Huta, when the local press registered the rapid degradation of the city, accelerated by insufficient municipal investment that many argued was unjust (according to an article from 1999, Nowa Huta districts provided 35 per cent of the municipal income of Kraków, while the municipality invested only 10 per cent of the available money in these districts).[28] Thus the feeling of discrimination was widely expressed in the local press and the discussion was dominated by the old antagonism between Nowa Huta and Kraków.

What followed was a new design commissioned by the city council and delivered by a Kraków-based architectural office, Aarcada. The design, realized in 2001, suggested lowering the inner part of the square by three steps, and flanking this depression by two rows of stone socles. In the depression, in the place where the Lenin monument used to stand, an elevated flower-bed for roses was constructed, continuing to preserve this geometrically privileged spot as inaccessible to passers-by. Opposite the flower-bed, a podium for 'artistic performances' (as the designers put it) was erected.[29] Thus the gaze of the spectators was redirected: they were supposed to look in the opposite direction to that of the participants in official ceremonies held in front of the Lenin monument. This was the only potentially critical intervention in the design, which closely followed the geometry set by the 1950s masterplan of the site (see Figure 13.6).

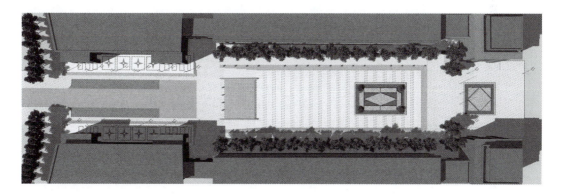

Fig. 13.6   The design of the Alley of Roses (2002) by the architectural office Aarcada

The designers called the new Alley of Roses a 'forum', and have seen it as an attractor for the whole city.[30] Yet while during socialism the inhabitants gathered on this site in order to participate in or, occasionally, protest against the festivities organized by the regime, the new design could not change its character as a pedestrian passage. Hence, in contrast with the official optimism of the members of the district council,[31] many inhabitants of Nowa Huta expressed their disappointment with the realized design[32] and argued that more greenery, and in particular more roses, were necessary.[33] Some stated that the best solution would be a return to the square as it had been before the erection of the Lenin monument.[34]

This particularly strong and unanimous demand for greenery cannot be explained by its lack in the immediate vicinity of the site. The blocks of flats flanking the Alley of Roses have generous garden-like courtyards, and there are two parks in the immediate neighbourhood, while Centralny Square faces the Vistula meadow with a unique and protected ecosystem. Rather than by a 'need' for greenery in what was perhaps the only urban place in the whole city, the disagreement with the design can be better understood by referring to Lefebvre's concept of 'space

W oczach mieszkańców

PLAC CZY KLEPISKO?

Do naszej redakcji dotarł list od stałego Czytelnika, mieszkańca jednego z osiedli położonych w sąsiedztwie placu Centralnego. List zawiera wiele pytań dotyczących otoczenia reprezentacyjnego placu Nowej Huty. Kierujemy je – jak zrobił to nasz Czytelnik – do Tomasza Urynowicza przewodniczącego Rady Dzielnicy XVIII, mając nadzieję, że tym razem wiele problemów, które poruszaliśmy również w naszych publikacjach, znajdzie odpowiedź i pozytywne rozwiązanie.

Koniec lat sześćdziesiątych: różany kobierzec w al. Róż.

(CIĄG DALSZY NA STR. 9)

of representation'. For Lefebvre, such space refers to an 'elsewhere' that becomes embodied in the everyday experience; space of representation is 'directly *lived* through its associated images and symbols' (Lefebvre 1991: 39). The Alley of Roses is such a space of representation where, during the socialist regime, the visitor was confronted with the ruling representation of Nowa Huta: that of a socialist city. In this sense, the main change in the Alley of Roses after 1989 was not its material transformation, not even the removal of the Lenin statue, but, rather, the end of one dominant representation of space and the unleashing of a competition between various representations of Nowa Huta.

Spaces of representation were described by Lefebvre as not having a 'signified' but a '*horizon of meaning*: a specific or indefinite multiplicity of meanings, a shifting hierarchy in which now one, now another meaning comes momentarily to the fore, by means of – and for the sake of – a particular action' (Lefebvre 1991: 222). The voices of the inhabitants' concerning the site, both before the new design was presented, and after the project was realized, convey an expectation of an architectural design to negotiate between these various 'meanings'. Their critique of the realized project can be seen as a demand for putting aside one particular representation of Nowa Huta – that of a city caught in the ideological opposition between socialism and anti-socialism – by means of 'putting to the fore' another influential representation, that of a 'green city'. The mass media representations were central in the formulation of these demands, and this can be illustrated by one of the articles that criticized the new design by reproducing a picture of the rose garden taken in the 1960s, that is before the erection of the monument[35] (see Figure 13.7 above). In this sense, the choice of the park rather than of an urban square is, perhaps, a response to an instrumental understanding of urbanity before 1989, whether associated with the discourse on modernization controlled by the state, or with urban tactics chosen by the protesters. The desire for a park, the wish to avoid a monument in the Alley of Roses[36] and the rejection of the design as a 'parade square'[37] can be seen less as an anti-urban sentiment than a protest against the restriction of 'the urban' to ideological dichotomies entrenched in the post-socialist discourse, and hence as an attempt to open up the urban everyday in Nowa Huta to a new multiplicity of meanings .

NOTES

1   This is a development of my paper 'The Instrumental Use of Representations of Space in the Practices of Production of Space in a Postcommunist City', in *De-/signing the Urban. Technogenesis and the Urban Image*, ed. P. Healy and G. Bruyns. Rotterdam: 010 Publishers, 2006, 284–301.

2   *Dziennik Polski/Nowa Huta* 2004 (151): 2; *Gazeta w Krakowie* 2004 (106): 12. Because of their large number, the references to newspaper articles will be given in footnotes in an abbreviated form: title, year, issue number, page number.

3   *Głos Nowej Huty* 1989 (1693): 6, 7, 8; *Dziennik Polski* 1993 (288): 10; *Polityka* 1999 (30): 92–7.

4   *Głos Tygodnik Nowohucki* 1996 (275): 7; 1997 (350): 4; *Przekrój* 2001 (38): 30–31.

5   *Gazeta Krakowska* 1996 (207): 10–11; *Przekrój* 2001 (38): 30–31.

6   *Głos Nowej Huty* 1989 (17–18): 8, 9; *Głos Tygodnik Nowohucki* 1998 (373): 1, 10; *Gazeta w Krakowie/Gazeta Wyborcza* 1999 (131): 6, 7; *Gazeta w Krakowie/Gazeta Wyborcza* 2000 (211): 1; *Gazeta Krakowska* 2000 (77): 12; *Dziennik Polski* 2001 (172): III.

7   *Dziennik Polski* 2000 (11): 37; comp. *Gazeta w Krakowie/Gazeta Wyborcza* 1999 (131): 6, 7.

8   *Głos Tygodnik Nowohucki* 1995 (224): 7; *Dziennik Polski* 1997 (124): 45; *Polityka* 1999 (30): 92–7; *Dziennik Polski* 1999 (260): 13; *Przekrój* 2001 (38): 30–31.

9   *Głos Nowej Huty* 1989 (1693): 6, 7, 8; *Tygodnik Małopolska* 1991 (18): 10; *Czas Krakowski* 1991 (83): 6; *Rzeczpospolita* 2000 (99): 6; *Głos Tygodnik Nowohucki* 2001 (553): n.p.

10   *Głos Nowej Huty* 1990 (1706): 1, 3; *Głos Tygodnik Nowohucki* 1991 (1769): 1, 2.

11   *Głos Nowej Huty* 40 (1693): 7.

12   *Głos Nowej Huty* 1989 (1677): 1, 8; 1989 (1695): 5; 1989 (1697): 5; 1990 (1706): 3.

13   *Głos Nowej Huty* 1990 (1707): 3; 1990 (1708): 3; 1990 (1709): 1, 3; 1990 (1710): 1, 3; 1990 (1711): 1, 2, 4, 5; 1990 (1712): 2; 1990 (1713): 2; 1990 (1714): 5; 1990 (1717–18): 7; 1990 (1719): 5; 1990 (1729): 4; 1990 (1730): 1; 1990 (1732): 9–10; 1990 (1741): 6–7.

14   Interviews with M. Lorenc, interview with K. Wąchal, interview with P. Wolak, interview with P. Adamczyk; interview with M. Miezian (Kraków, December 2006).

15   Interview with M. Lorenc, interview with P. Wolak (Kraków, December 2006).

16   Interview with K. Wąchal, interview with P. Wolak (Kraków, December 2006).

17   Interview with K. Wąchal, interview with P. Wolak, interview with P. Adamczyk, interview with M. Miezian (Kraków, December 2006).

18   Interview with B. Szydłowski (Kraków, December 2006).

19   Ibid.

20   *Głos Tygodnik Nowohucki* 1992 (73): 1, 2; 1999 (449); 2000 (457): 1, 9.

21   *Głos Tygodnik Nowohucki* 1993 (123): 3; 1993 (124): 1, 4.

22   *Głos Tygodnik Nowohucki* 1991 (1766): 6, 7; 1991 (1768): 3.

23   *Głos Tygodnik Nowohucki* 1992 (45): 3; 1992 (46): 3; 1991 (50): 3.

24   *Magazyn Gazety Wyborczej* 1994 (292): 16–18.

25   *Polityka* 1989 (50): 7.

26   *Gazeta Wyborcza* 1997 (307): 20–21.

27   *Polityka* (18): 30–31.

28   *Gazeta w Krakowie/Gazeta Wyborcza* 1999 (13): 2.

29   *Głos Tygodnik Nowohucki* 2000 (491): 1, 9; 2000 (462): 1–2.

30   *Głos Tygodnik Nowohucki* 2000 (491): 1, 9.

31   *Głos Tygodnik Nowohucki* 2001 (550): 12.

32   *Głos Tygodnik Nowohucki* 2001 (550): 12; 2002 (584): 16; (598), 1, 16; interview with J. Franczyk (Nowa Huta, May 2003).

33   *Głos Tygodnik Nowohucki* 2001 (550): 12; 2002 (584): 16.

34   *Głos Tygodnik Nowohucki* 2001 (550): 12.

35   *Głos Tygodnik Nowohucki* 2002 (594): 1, 9.

36   *Polityka* 1996 (18): 30–31.

37   *Głos Tygodnik Nowohucki* 2002 (584): 16.

REFERENCES

Awan, N., Till, J., and Schneider, T. 2011. *Spatial Agency: Other Ways of Doing Architecture*. London: Routledge.

Bukowski, A. 2003. 'The Diagnosis of Social Situation in Nowa Huta in the Context of Socio-therapy Centers Establishing', 5th Transnational Meeting: Demos – improving local democracy (Kraków, 15–17 May).

Holston, J. 1989. *The Modernist City: An Anthropological Critique of Brasília*. Chicago, IL: University of Chicago Press.

Irion, I. and Sieverts, T. 1991. *Neue Städte. Experimentierfelder der Moderne*. Stuttgart: Deutsche Verlags-Anstalt.

Jacobs J.M. 1993. 'The City Unbound: Qualitative Approaches to the City'. *Urban Studies* 30 (4/5): 827–48.

Juchnowicz, S. 2002. 'Nowa Huta, a Relict of the Past or a Chance for Cracow', in *IX International Biennale of Architecture*. Kraków.

Karnasiewicz, J. 2003. *Nowa Huta: Okruchy życia i meandry historii*. Kraków: Wydawnictwo Towarzystwa Słowaków w Polsce.

Karsznia, N. 1994. *Powstanie parafii i budowa kościoła Matki Bożej Częstochowskiej w Nowej Hucie*. Kraków: Sponsor.

Karsznia, N. 1997. *Życie rodzinne w Nowej Hucie. Obserwacje i rozwiązania*. Kraków: Sponsor.

Kozłowski, D. 2002. 'Less Ideology – More Geometry', in *IX International Biennale of Architecture*. Kraków: MBA, 14–23.

Lefebvre H. 1960. 'Les nouveaux ensembles urbains (un cas concret: Lacq–Mourenx et les problèmes urbains de la nouvelle classe ouvrière)'. *La Revue française de sociologie* 1 (1–2): 186–201.

Lefebvre, H. 1991 [1974]. *The Production of Space*. Oxford: Blackwell.

Lefebvre, H. 2002 [1961]. *Critique of Everyday Life Volume 2. Foundations for a Sociology of the Everyday*. New York: Verso.

Lefebvre, H. 2006 [1981]. *Critique of Everyday Life Volume 3. From Modernity to Modernism (Towards a Metaphilosophy of Daily Life)*. New York: Verso.

Lefebvre, H. 2008 [1947]. *Critique of Everyday Life Volume 1: Introduction*. New York: Verso.

Miezian, M. 2004. *Nowa Huta. Socjalistyczna w formie, fascynująca w treści*. Kraków: Bezdroża.

Ostrowski, W. 1952. 'Kształtowanie przestrzenne miasta socjalistycznego'. *Miasto* 15(1/III): 1–4.

Projekt PIW Equal w Polsce realizowany przez Partnerstwo Inicjatyw Nowohuckich. Nowa Huta–Nowa Szansa. 2006. Leaflet.

Ptaszycki, T. 1952. 'Fundamenty nowego miasta'. *Miasto* 15(1/III): 8–11.

Ptaszycki, T. (ed.) 1959, *Nowa Huta*. Kraków: Miastoprojekt.

Rochovská, A., Smith, A., Stenning, A. and Świątek, D. n.d. 'Social Exclusion and Household Economic Practices in Nowa Huta', www.geog.qmul.ac.uk, accessed December 2012.

Rochovská, A., Smith, A., Stenning, A. and Świątek, D. 2010. *Domesticating Neo-Liberalism: Spaces of Economic Practice and Social Reproduction in Post-Socialist Cities*. London: Wiley-Blackwell.

Siemieńska, R. 1969. *Nowe życie w nowym mieście*. Warszawa: Wiedza Powszechna.

Stanek, Ł. 2007. 'Simulation or Hospitality: Beyond the Crisis of Representation in Nowa Huta', in *Visual and Material Performances in the City*, edited by L. Frers and L. Meier. Aldershot: Ashgate, 135–53.

Stanek, Ł. 2011. *Henri Lefebvre on Space. Architecture, Urban Research, and the Production of Theory*. Minneapolis, MN: University of Minnesota Press.

Stanek, Ł. 2012. 'Architecture as Space, Again? Notes on the "Spatial Turn"'. *Spéciale'Z* 4: 48–53.

Stanek, Ł. 2014. 'A Manuscript Found in Saragossa: Toward an Architecture', introduction to *Toward an Architecture of Enjoyment* by Henri Lefebvre, edited by L. Stanek. Minneapolis: University of Minnesota Press, xi–lxi, 155–171.

Stenning, A. (2001), 'Representing Transformations/Transforming Representations: Remaking Life and Work in Nowa Huta, Poland', www.nowahuta.info, accessed 7 March 2006.

Sturge-Moore, L. (ed.) 1972. 'Architecture et sciences sociales'. Seminaire annuel 22–26 juin, 1972, Port Grimaud. Compte rendu des communications et des interventions. Paris: Centre de recherche sur l'habitat.

Wereksiej, F.Z. 1976. 'Jubileuszowe obrachunki'. *WTK Tygodnik Katolicki* 35: 1, 8.

14

The Debate about Berlin Tempelhof Airport, or: A Lefebvrean Critique of Recent Debates about Affect in Geography

Ulrich Best

On 30 October 2008, Berlin Tempelhof Airport was closed and ceased to be an operational airport; it became – at least temporarily – a park. The closure was preceded by a long and heated argument culminating in a referendum in April 2008, which managed to mobilize considerable support, but not enough for a valid referendum. Since then, debates about the use and accessibility of the space have not abated. The new park has seen an 'occupy'-like movement that opposed a fence around it; it has seen successful guerrilla gardening, debates about future construction on the area and has become a well-used place of leisure, even a destination for tourism. In this chapter, I shall investigate the politics and discourses around the closure of the airport, in the media and in the neighbourhood. This debate is of interest not only for an analysis of local politics in Berlin. It is relevant also because it addresses a current theme in urban and cultural geography: a turn towards memory and affect. Berlin has taken a central role in this theme, and the debate about Tempelhof Airport presents an opportunity to link these ideas more closely to the social and political geography of the city. In order to do so, this chapter will bring some concepts of Henri Lefebvre into conversation with these more recent contributions in urban studies.

The campaign 'For Tempelhof' from 2007 to 2008 was rich in constructions of affect and memory.[1] Initially, the closure of the airport had already been decided in 1996, because it might jeopardize the future of the proposed Berlin Brandenburg International Airport at Schönefeld near Berlin. Nevertheless, a referendum was brought about mainly through a coalition of the conservative party (CDU) and business elites. The city government, at the time a centre-left coalition of SPD and DIE LINKE, the Green Party and environmental citizens' associations campaigned for the closure of the airport, using financial, environmental and safety arguments. The main line of campaigning by the supporters of the further operation of the airport focused on the 'meaning' of Tempelhof for the people – Tempelhof as a monument to the Berlin Air Lift that was necessarily linked with its current function as an airport. It also had, however, an underpinning of economic discourse, playing with the promise of possible future jobs near the airport and Tempelhof as a gateway for business. There are two lines of enquiry that I will follow in this chapter: first, affect as a resource that can be influenced and mobilized in urban struggles by the elite; second, affect as an element of the production of space that also incorporates visions of the city at the neighbourhood level. This is where I argue that a conceptualization applying Lefebvre becomes important. First, it allows us not only to interpret affect as a dimension of a struggle, but also to connect this dimension with the other dimensions of social space – 'spatial practice' and 'representations of space', in Lefebvre's terms. Second, it becomes possible to incorporate the analysis of more abstract constructions of affect into an analysis of how, at the everyday level, an entirely different 'spatial politics of affect' was enacted: one that tied the debate about Tempelhof into the wider symbolic geographies of inclusion and exclusion in Berlin. Bringing in Lefebvre's dialectics also helps to problematize the celebration of affect in recent cultural geography. *Espace vécu* (literally 'lived space'), the space of affect, is not only a potential space of freedom; it is also, as I shall argue, a potential space of control.

The first part of the chapter briefly sketches the background of current theories of affect in geography, how they have been applied to Berlin, and a critique of these concepts using Lefebvre's approach to the production of space. The following sections outline two levels of the conflict about Tempelhof: first, city-scale political and planning debates; and second, the scale of the everyday, drawing on interviews conducted with residents of the adjacent neighbourhoods of Tempelhof and Neukölln. In the final section, the argument about Tempelhof will be linked back to the production of urban space.

GEOGRAPHIES OF AFFECT AND THE CITY

In a much-quoted paper, Nigel Thrift argued for a 'spatial politics of affect'. He singled out the city as the location of 'roiling maelstroms of affect' (Thrift 2004: 57) and indeed as paradigmatic of it. In his plea for increased attention to its role in geography, he complained that it had been ignored as an instance of urban politics, 'even in the case of issues such as identity and belonging which quiver with affective energy' (ibid.). Affect, for Thrift, seemed to be a force for change and transformation. Although Thrift also gave a number of examples showing that there can be an 'engineering of affect' (ibid.: 64), meaning that it can be used instrumentally, he demanded a 'politics of emotional liberty'. In spite of these minor critical tones, his take is a celebration of affect.

Thrift's paper has met with some criticism. The main criticism, voiced for example by Tolia-Kelly, was that the 'literature on affect is particularly inattentive to issues of power' (2006: 213).[2] Thien similarly criticized the protagonists of the debate for 'implying that the emotion of the individual, that is, the realm of "personal" feelings, is distinct from wider (public) agendas and desirably so' (Thien 2005: 450). In spite of these criticisms, the ongoing debates about affect seem to answer to a certain lack in the theoretical debate. However, I would argue that the protagonists themselves produce this lack by a very selective reading of urban theory. This limited perspective must intentionally exclude many tools that critical social theory has provided for the analysis of affect in the wider sense – one might think of Raymond Williams's structures of feeling (1973), Agnes Heller's earlier work (1979) or that of Fredric Jameson (1991), who all combined a Marxist analysis of society and the analysis of feeling, emotions and affect. For them, feelings were related to class constellations and social change, and an analysis of them had to start with society. Regarding urban politics, there is also a well-established legacy of work that addresses related questions, starting with the Frankfurt School's critical cultural theory (see Savage 1995), and including the Chicago School (Cressey 2008 [1932]), humanist geography (Tuan 1979) or Marxist approaches. Lefebvre in particular, as I shall try to show in the following, provides a framework that allows an analysis of power relations, a materialist analysis, and an analysis of the construction of meaning and affect.

FROM THE SPATIAL POLITICS OF AFFECT TO THE DIALECTICS OF AFFECT

In the reception of Lefebvre's theory, it is remarkable that affect, art and sometimes love play a key role. Rob Shields, for example, in his introduction to Lefebvre tellingly entitled *Love and Struggle*, writes that Lefebvre is 'perhaps the only communist – certainly the only political economist – to have dared assert that all he had ever written about was love' (1999: 7). Roberts (2006: 13), with reference to Lefebvre's theory of everyday life and his rethinking of Marxism, writes that '[in] Marx, there is no critique of political economy, no critique of the value-form ... without the collective aesthetic and sensuous reappropriation of everyday experience'. In *Critique of the Everyday Life II*, Lefebvre wrote about the connection of revolution with art and creativity:

> The creative activity of art and the work of art foreshadow joy at its highest. For
> Marx, enjoyment of the world is not limited to consumption of material goods,
> no matter how refined, or to the consumption of goods, no matter how subtle
> ... He imagines a society in which everyone would rediscover the spontaneity of
> natural life and its initial creative drive, and perceive the world through the eyes
> of a painter, the ears of a musician and the language of a poet. Once superseded,
> art would be reabsorbed into an everyday which had been metamorphosed by its
> fusion with what had hitherto been kept external to it. (Lefebvre 2002 [1961]: 64)

Besides these references to utopian socialism, Lefebvre also theorized the question of affect in his concept of social space. Of the three interlinked aspects of the production of space – *espace perçu*, *espace conçu* and *espace vécu* – the third is often the source of a certain lack of clarity in the interpretation of Lefebvre. Soja (1996) interprets it as 'Thirdspace', and it is often associated with symbols or art, but also with 'life', with 'love', or defined as the production of meaning. The root of change is often located in this dimension. On the other hand, Schmid (2005) argues for a three-dimensional dialectics, according to which a transformation of social space should be possible through a shift in any of the aspects. Nevertheless, Schmid, in line with other interpreters of Lefebvre, singles out the *espace vécu*, the 'lived space', as the key to revolutionary change – only if the everyday changes is revolutionary change possible (see also Charnock and Ribera-Fumaz, Chapter 7 in this volume). Lefebvre described this dimension as having an 'affective centre', containing 'places of passion and action' (Lefebvre 1991 [1974]: 42). In this dimension, he places 'works, images and memories' that can be 'sensory, sensual or sexual' (50). He also calls it the dimension that connects physical space with the imagination through marking and symbols – and through affects: 'Symbols, in this view, always imply an emotional investment, an affective charge (fear, attraction, etc.), which is so to speak deposited at a particular place and thereafter "represented" for the benefit of everyone elsewhere' (141). Throughout *The Production of Space*, Lefebvre locates affect in this dimension. However, and this is what I argue here, Lefebvre also locates a contradiction in this dimension – between domination and appropriation. Like the other two dimensions, *espace perçu* (the dimension of social/spatial practice) and *espace conçu* (the dimension of knowledge and concepts), *espace vécu* is open to change, open to appropriation, but can also be a means of domination.

This contradiction contained in the dimension of *espace vécu* becomes clear in Lefebvre's discussion of 'monumentality'. Analysing the character of the street and the monument in *The Urban Revolution*, he contrasts a celebration of the street with a condemnation of it. It is on the one hand a 'meeting place', 'a form of spontaneous theater' (2003 [1970]: 18). 'All the elements of urban life, which are fixed and redundant elsewhere, are free to fill the streets and through the streets flow to the centers, where they meet and interact, torn from their fixed abode. This disorder is alive. It informs. It surprises', Lefebvre writes (ibid.). On the other hand, the street is the site of anonymous superficial encounters, 'an exhibition of objects for sale' (ibid.: 20). In the street, Lefebvre argues, we can observe the '*colonization* of the urban space, which takes place in the street through the image, through publicity, through the spectacle of objects' (ibid.: 21, original italics).

Similarly ambivalent is the character of the monument. 'The monument is essentially repressive. It is the seat of an institution … Any space that is organised around the monument is colonized and oppressed. ' (ibid.: 21). Lefebvre directly links this with the symbolic role of the monument: 'And although the monument is always laden with symbols, it presents them to social awareness and contemplation (passive) just when those symbols, already outdated, are beginning to lose their meaning' (ibid.). On the other hand, he writes that it is 'the only conceivable or imaginable site of collective (social) life' (ibid.), a utopian place. In *The Production of Space*, Lefebvre takes up the discussion of monumentality and outlines how individual bodies and affects are organized and coordinated (1991: 224). Here, he clarifies that monumentality is not defined by consisting of symbols or signs, but by the strict organization of these across the dimensions of social space. Monumentality links the level of affect and the everyday with public discourses and 'rallying cries' (ibid.) – and controls them. 'The affective level – which is to say, the level of the body, bound to symmetries and rhythms – is transformed into a "property" of monumental space, into symbols which are generally intrinsic parts of a politico religious whole, into co-ordinated symbols', Lefebvre writes (ibid.). Just like the other two dimensions of the production of space, the *espace vécu* can be a means of domination or control as much as of freedom and collective appropriation. It is the dimension of 'passion', of affect, of identification. With the three dimensions of the production of space, Lefebvre offers a way to analyse the 'spatial politics of affect', but a way that does not separate this dimension from power – all dimensions are interlinked, all open for change, all potential dimensions of oppression.

THE NEW BERLIN SCHOOL – BERLIN AND AFFECT

Lefebvre's concept, with its discussions of monumentality, is particularly relevant for an analysis of urban politics in Berlin. In much recent English-language literature, Berlin has featured prominently as a showcase of affect, memory, and the connection of built urban space and meaning, so much so that one could speak of a Berlin School (see, for example, Colomb 2007, Costabile-Heming 2005, Ledanff 2003, Neill 1997, 1998).[3] In an early contribution, Peter Marcuse assigned different meanings to some of the new sites of the 'New Berlin':

> The construction of the Regierungsviertel stands for the power and wealth of the German state, while Potsdamer Platz reflects the power and wealth of German business, and Friedrichstraße, at least in design, reflects the enjoyment of the fruits of that power and wealth in consumption. (Marcuse 1998: 337)

We could read this as a mapping of urban affects, and, more specifically, of their construction 'from above' – in Lefebvre's words, a strict organization of signs and symbols, that is, monumentality. Potsdamer Platz and the government buildings are meant to inspire awe; Friedrichstrasse is designed to express enjoyment and consumerism. The design of affect clarifies how affect can work as, and be linked to, mechanisms of rule, an ordering not only of physical urban space and spatial practices, but also of the affective and symbolic geography of the city. Karen Till's work on urban politics in Berlin and the representation of the Holocaust has also been influential. She constructs Berlin as a prime example of a 'haunted place': 'Berlin is a place haunted with landscapes that simultaneously embody presences and absences, voids and ruins, intentional forgetting and painful remembering', referencing the production of symbolic and affective landscapes of Berlin (Till 2005: 8). Similarly, Cochrane characterized Berlin as a city of memorials:

> The making-up of the new Berlin as capital city is dominated by the question of how to reinterpret and re-imagine its history: it is a city of memorials and of deliberate absences; of remembering and of forgetting, or trying to forget; of reshaping the past and of trying to build a new future. (Cochrane 2006: 7)

Cochrane is explicit in recognizing that memory, and the feelings it is meant to evoke, is inextricably linked to power, however.

While there is clearly a wealth of debate on memory in Berlin, very little of it links with the wider social geography of the city. Memory seems to work in an isolated space of meaning, mostly unconnected to other dimensions of urban space. In this chapter, I would like to analyse exactly this nexus: how does the social geography of the city matter in a debate that seems to be about memory and meaning? How does the construction of affect interlink with everyday life and social exclusion in the city? The debate on Berlin has impressively outlined key points: in Berlin, the construction of affect in urban space often involves ideas of the past and their relevance for the present, is often produced in more abstract debates, and has marked specific sites – as sites of memory of the Holocaust, of the Cold War, of the 'New Berlin' and a new 'normalized' Germany, or of consumerism. The affective weight of these places is created in discourses and narratives about them, and memories to which they are linked. They are sites not only of local, but much more of national, if not global, landscapes of affect, and are linked to political projects and power geometries at the scale of the city and the nation. In Lefebvre's sense, they are all monuments in their primary function as domination. The public that is targeted with their constructions of affect is meant to connect them with a feeling – pride, horror, distinctions of good and evil, hope for the future, regret for the past and so on.

The Tempelhof Airport is one such site. In the next section, I shall look at the transformation of the constructions of affect about Tempelhof. However, I would like to add a further perspective. The sites mentioned above are not so much constructed by the people who live around them, but are marked from a distance. The same is true for Tempelhof Airport in the long media debate about it. However, Tempelhof is also subject to different constructions of affect – by the people who live around it and give it a place in their everyday lives.

PRODUCING TEMPELHOF – FROM GERMANIA TO FREEDOM

Tempelhof Airport is both a monument and something like a street – site of exchange, mobility, spectacle and anonymity. Tempelhof became an airport in the late 1920s and was designated Berlin's central airport. In the 1930s, the building was extended under National Socialism in monumental style, adorned with eagles and other nationalist regalia. It was also meant to be a place for mass parades, air shows and other mobilization events (and was also the site of a small concentration camp; see Schilde and Tuchel 1990). After the war, the airport was taken over by the US Air Force, which used it to support the Western orientation of West Berlin during the blockade and the Berlin airlift of 1948/49. A monument commemorating this event was erected in front of the airport as early as 1951, on the renamed 'Airlift Square' (*Platz der Luftbrücke*). After decades of back-and-forth between civilian and military use, in 1993 the airport was returned to the civilian authorities, but flight numbers never really grew. In the course of German unification, discussions about a 'modern new airport' for Berlin started. In 1996, after a lengthy decision-making process, Schönefeld Airport emerged as the winner and was designated 'single airport' of Berlin. At that time, the closure of the other two Berlin airports, Tempelhof and Tegel, was agreed on between the Federal, Brandenburg and Berlin authorities. The driving logic was that Berlin could not sustain three airports, and in order to be successful and profitable, Schönefeld needed to be the single airport. These were the early unification years, and an enormous optimism was connected with the debate about the planned new airport and its site. The Berlin newspaper *Tagesspiegel* wrote after the decision for Schönefeld:

> For Berlin, a new large airport does not only mean a quantum leap in terms
> of transport, but also in terms of urbanism. After all, the time when Berlin had
> an exemplary modern airport is more than 60 years past. Berlin Schönefeld
> will mean the rise of a third 'megaport' in Berlin after Frankfurt and Munich.
> (Tagesspiegel, 18 November 1996, author's translation)

At that moment, Tempelhof was not at the centre of a popular mobilization or any considerable political debate – it seemed to be unsuitable for Berlin's global aspirations. Only the Interessengemeinschaft City-Airport Tempelhof (ICAT), founded in 1995 by the small airlines, which flew from Tempelhof, stressed the importance of the airport for 'business travellers'. While the campaign of 2007/08 picked up on this argument of business travellers, which continued to be pushed by ICAT, it mostly put forward an argument resulting from a very selective reading of the history of the airport: the memory of the Berlin airlift. Although this event had been monumentalized almost instantly (by the monument and the renaming of the airport square as Airlift Square), throughout the decades after 1949, the memory of the airlift surfaced only during anniversaries, most prominently the 15th anniversary of Kennedy's visit to Berlin and the 50th anniversary of the airlift in 1998, when Tempelhof was praised by Bill Clinton as the 'symbol of freedom'. This legacy of Tempelhof was transformed into the most important theme of the debate starting in 2007 and running full steam in 2008. However, while judging from the 2008 debate that the main legacy of Tempelhof Airport might appear to have been its status as a monument, there is a quite different possible legacy from the airport too – and this legacy is a grassroots struggle for open space.

Contesting Tempelhof

Looking at the changing role of Tempelhof, it has become clear that the airport was most often an outdated symbol pointing backwards, a monument used for domination, not liberation. It was presented as a monument during National Socialism, as a different monument during the Cold War, and, in the campaign of 2007/08, as a monument to the memory of the Cold War through the eyes of West Berliners. Looking at the role of the airport in the production of space, these aspects refer to the dimension of affect – *espace vécu*. They are closely linked with spatial practices, like the role of Tempelhof Airport as a military base in the Cold War, and the dimension of *espace conçu*, the spatial divisions of the Cold War.

Concepts of space, however, were also central to alternative movements of Cold War (West) Berlin. Starting with the grassroots urban movements in the 1960s and 1970s, Tempelhof Airport was regularly the focus of alternative and utopian visions for West Berlin. In 1976, the citizens' initiative against the building of an inner-city highway in West Berlin published a plan for a renaturalized Tempelhof Airport (Bürgerinitiative Westtangente 1976). Explicitly public uses for the area were proposed – a senior citizens' and a youth centre, a swimming pool, and recreational areas for West Berliners. This vision was continued in later proposals. In 1986, a citizens' initiative was formed specifically aiming at closure of the airport (Bürgerinitiative Flughafen Tempelhof BIFT 2001, 2006). The plan for 1988 was similar to the 1976 vision, incorporating an aeronautics museum and a centre for solar energy, but aiming mainly at recreational use.

After the decision for a single airport at Schönefeld in 1996, further plans were put forward, now also increasingly by the Berlin city administration and including some residential development of the area, but maintaining the bulk of the area as green and recreational spaces. The future closure of Tempelhof was even the topic of a 'concept workshop' set up by the Berlin Senate, aiming at a post-airport use of the field. A master plan was developed in a further workshop – the Zukunftswerkstatt Tempelhof 2020 (Tempelhof Future Workshop 2020) in 1998. In 2007, the Berlin Senate set up an online forum where individuals could contribute their ideas and plans for the future development of Tempelhof, and an architecture competition for future use was announced in 2009 and decided in mid-2011 (Senatsverwaltung für Stadtentwicklung 2008; see also Figure 14.1). In these recent plans, collective and participatory aspects play a significantly smaller role than in the grassroots plans of the 1970s.

The post-2008 plans clearly refer to the dominant planning discourses. They focus on 'innovative living' in the Columbia neighbourhood at the northern edge of the airfield bordering Kreuzberg, named after the adjacent street; on the 'creative economy' in the envisioned Forum Tempelhof (the former airport building); and 'future technologies' in an area at the southwest of the airport, labelled 'Tempelhof urban neighbourhood'. To the east of the airport area, bordering Neukölln, the plan is for an 'urban neighbourhood' with urban living. This mapping links not only with Berlin's development strategy centred on the 'creative economy', but also links the airport with its neighbouring districts – in the north, where 'innovative living' is to be implemented, the neighbouring area of the Kreuzberg district has undergone significant gentrification and redevelopment. The new Columbia neighbourhood would border on the renamed 'Viktoria neighbourhood', a condominium/loft development marketed as 'fine Kreuzberg living' (Neue Viktoria 2007). In the area bordering poor and (until then) mostly ungentrified Neukölln, 'urban living' can be understood as still almost on the edge of the bourgeois comfort zone.

These plans for Tempelhof Airport highlight the contestation of representations of space: collective plans versus expert plans; planning discourse and formal language versus grassroots mobilization. They also show links to spatial practice in attempts to influence the way people use the area, the role Tempelhof plays in people's everyday lives. The plans place Tempelhof Airport in the social geography of the city, in which the Tempelhof, Kreuzberg and Neukölln districts have different roles – as in Marcuse's mapping of symbolic space in Berlin Mitte, these districts are also located on a map

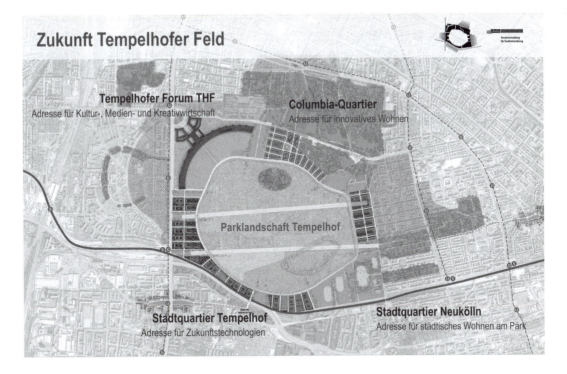

Fig. 14.1   Future Tempelhofer Feld

of symbolic space, as either desirable middle-class (Tempelhof), poor immigrant (Neukölln), or gentrifying areas (Kreuzberg; see Best and Gebhardt 2001b). In these visions, there is also good evidence of their role in social questions: who are the users of the areas going to be? What are they allowed to do? Who should decide about these questions? They are, however, also connected with the third dimension of the production of space – the *espace vécu*, the space of meaning and affect. This dimension became the key site of public debate about Tempelhof, and again it can be broken down into the distinction between the monument and the street: is the former airport to be a space of encounter, grassroots mobilization, collective visions, or in line with the existing discourse about the city, where 'innovative living' means exclusive living, and creativity is reduced to the creative economy? And, most importantly: will the airport be a monument that binds spatial practice through reference to a specific past?

CONSTRUCTING THE 'LEGEND' – THE 2008 REFERENDUM DEBATE

In 2006, ICAT (Interessengemeinschaft City-Airport Tempelhof; see above) started collecting signatures for a referendum on Tempelhof Airport with the aim of keeping it as a functioning airport. The main mobilization took place during the second phase of the referendum process and up to voting day, 27 April 2008. A poster campaign and advertisements by ICAT were accompanied by a strong campaign, particularly in the tabloid press (*BZ* and *Bild*). Also in much of the rest of the press, a preference for a working airport was clear. The CDU and the FDP generally supported and also partly staffed the campaign, with the then leader of the Berlin CDU, Friedbert Pflüger, often heading protest marches. The diversity of arguments used in the media, however, was limited. Combinations of two arguments dominated the public debate: Tempelhof needed to be kept as an airport because of the memory of the airlift; and Tempelhof was necessary to bring business travellers and investors into the city. In the first line of argument, Tempelhof was labelled the 'airport of hearts', the 'Tempelhof legend'. Interviews frequently featured people who stressed that they had an 'emotional' relationship with Tempelhof, that it had 'historical meaning' for them. To give just a few examples: on 7 January 2008, *Bild* published 'love declarations' to Tempelhof by German celebrities. This became an important theme, to be followed up in the next days and weeks by further declarations. The referendum was accompanied by front-page headlines such as 'Yes! Yes! Yes! Already 160,509 votes for Tempelhof' (*Bild*, 26 January 2008). On 24 April 2008, *Bild* listed '100 reasons for the airport of hearts'. *BZ*, the second large Berlin tabloid (owned by the same publisher) also frequently presented lists and declarations by people supporting the continued operation of the airport – on 19 March 2008, for example, *BZ* presented 39 'business captains' speaking out for Tempelhof, often stressing that they 'love' the airport, and on 25 March, a German–American couple described how they met during the airlift, with the title: 'In Tempelhof, our love grew wings'. Even Chancellor Merkel was quoted as saying:

> The continued operation of Tempelhof is significant not only for the economy and jobs; for many and for me personally, the airport with the airlift is a symbol for the history of this city. (Merkel, quoted in BZ, 19 April 2008, author's translation)

In an interview a few days later, she again stressed her commitment to the operation of the airport and underlined the 'strong emotional relation [of the Berliners] to the airport of the airlift' (Merkel, quoted in *Welt*, 24 April 2008, author's translation). She saw, however, the decisive reasons for Tempelhof in the 'future perspectives of the city' and its significance for 'business, the creation of jobs and the development of Berlin in general' (ibid.). Friedbert Pflüger, then head of the Berlin CDU, called Tempelhof 'an airport of opportunities, a landing field for investment and jobs' (Pflüger, 18 April 2008, Press Release, author's translation).

The second aspect of the debate featured the 'investors' who were to fly into Tempelhof and create jobs, as already mentioned by Merkel and Pflüger. The American businessman Ronald S. Lauder was often reported as a potential US$350 million investor interested in building a luxury hospital with a connected airstrip in Tempelhof. In an interview, Lauder also linked this promise of jobs with feelings that Americans had for Tempelhof, just as for the Statue of Liberty:

> When I was working in the Pentagon, I spent much time taking care that Berlin remains a free city, and for this freedom, Tempelhof is the symbol, for Americans almost even more than the Brandenburg Gate. During the airlift, a lot of pilots died – and over here ['bei uns'] we cannot believe that this symbol is to be rejected now. (BZ, 18 March 2008, author's translation)

In the economic discourse, Tempelhof was often characterized as an advantage for Berlin in the global competition with other cities – which were reported to be envious of its central airport or laughing at the decision to close it. Both arguments – Tempelhof's historical meaning and investment potential – were often linked. Throughout the months, these topics remained constant and relatively unvaried. In the run-up to the referendum, the campaign also took a marked anti-SPD/DIE LINKE stance, claiming to fight for the right of citizens to express their opinion against the administration. Posters had slogans such as 'All power to the people', meaning that people should express their power in the referendum by voting for the continued operation of flights.

The arguments brought forward for the closure of the airport came from two sides. The argument by the city administration was the same as in 1996 – Tempelhof needed to be closed so that Schönefeld could be run at a profit. Tempelhof was also seen as a financial liability. The citizens' initiatives argued against the danger, noise and pollution that the airport caused, and for a redevelopment of the area. The poster campaign by the governing parties had slogans such as 'Finance a VIP-airport for rich people? Count me out!'. Echoing this slogan, Gregor Gysi, head of DIE LINKE in the federal parliament and former senator (minister) in Berlin, said:

> Air traffic at Tempelhof is to cease. All else would mean that millions of taxes of either Berliners or of all Germans will be spent on a VIP-airport so that bosses and other rich people can have their private flights to and from Tempelhof. (Gysi 2008, author's translation)

Carola Bluhm, parliamentary head of the Berlin DIE LINKE, argued that CDU and FDP were 'abusing the pain of parting [Abschiedsschmerz] that … Berliners always have' (Abgeordnetenhaus 2008: 2542, author's translation).

In the end, the referendum failed because not enough people voted for the airport to remain open. It did not obtain the required number of votes, although the majority of the votes cast were in favour of the proposal. The airport operation was closed on 31 October 2008. The public debate in the media and parliament was saturated with references to the emotions and feelings attached to Tempelhof. It is quite clear, however, that the stress on these emotions was made with a purpose –Tempelhof was constructed as an emotional symbol, a monument, in order to control, to evoke popular opposition against the city government, and to picture the city government as acting against the interests of the majority population. This engineering of emotional attachment is directly linked with a specific representation of space in a political struggle. However, it is also linked with everyday constructions of Tempelhof, which place the debate about Tempelhof even more clearly in the field of contested urban imaginings and practices.

SITUATING TEMPELHOF AIRPORT IN EVERYDAY LIFE

At the margin of the public debate, one argument surfaced on very few occasions: if Tempelhof Airport was shut down and replaced by a recreational area, it would be overrun by 'criminals' and 'drug dealers' from the neighbouring Kreuzberg and

Neukölln. In their comments on the Senate proposals for a post-airport use, be-4-tempelhof (another organization that had sprung up to argue against the closure of the airport) wrote: 'The adjacent neighbourhoods Neukölln and Kreuzberg are in the top positions of the new Berlin crime atlas, and the neighbouring Hasenheide park is absolutely notorious for its criminality' (be-4-tempelhof 2008, author's translation UB). In the newspapers, this was a relatively rare argument. A small number of articles feature residents of the Tempelhof district who fear criminals crossing the airport from the Neukölln and Kreuzberg districts. On a city-wide scale, this argument was made not out of fear for the middle-class Tempelhof district, but linked to a wider discourse of urban threats and stigmatization. In the years preceding the debate, the northern edge of the Neukölln district had moved to the centre of a new debate on crime, poverty and unemployment, a role that had formerly been assigned mostly to other districts such as Kreuzberg and parts of Wedding (Best and Gebhardt 2001a, 2001b, Lanz 2007). In the context of the wider debate, the Hasenheide park to the north of the Neukölln district, directly bordering on the airport, had become a code for a dangerous area. In the Tempelhof debate, this was made obvious by a remark of the head of the Berlin FDP, Martin Lindner, in the final debate of the Berlin parliament before the referendum. He argued: 'Instead of an airport reasonably supplemented by BBI, the Berliners get a Hasenheide XXL with drug dealers, youth gangs and similar criminals, who will take over there' (Abgeordnetenhaus 2008: 2543, author's translation).

This discourse situates the Tempelhof district in the wider stigma-mapping of Berlin, where it figures as a desirable area with low density, a predominantly non-immigrant population and single-family houses with gardens. Opposed to this idyll are Kreuzberg and Neukölln, districts that are regularly pictured as 'ghettos' that have 'schools without German kids', as high-crime areas, no-go areas for the police and a drug-ridden park (see also Best and Gebhardt 2001b). This discourse on Tempelhof draws a map of fear in which the airport has the role of a protective division between the 'bad areas' and the 'good area'. The views of the residents on two sides of the airport illustrate the different positions in relation to this discourse.[4]

M, 39 years old, married with two children, presents a good example of the contradictions. She works for the federal government and lives on the Tempelhof side of the airport. M considers Tempelhof to be the district best suited for young parents. Her concern is that if the airport is closed and becomes a park or is unused for a while, it becomes like Hasenheide Park, where she feels threatened. If it is to be closed, then she wishes for a fenced-off park that costs a small entry fee, so that it does not become run down. Asked about residential use, M sees two conflicting possibilities – social housing, which to her would mean an extension of the Neukölln population; or terraced houses for young families, which would mean an extension of the Tempelhof district population. She clearly echoes the stigma-mapping of the wider debate. The main question for her is not about memory, but about fear. Similarly, physiotherapist W, 45, also a resident of Tempelhof, is afraid that the airport area will be swamped by drug users from Hasenheide if the airport is shut down. She also pictures a problem with Turkish families if it becomes a park, because she thinks that they do not stick to the rules in public spaces, and bring huge picnic baskets to the parks. In general, however, W can also imagine being happy with the airport being closed – there could be horses, a lake, an adventure playground in the park, she says. The fears of M and W are also reflected by N, 52, who lives in Tempelhof district with his family and is a doctor. He likes the idea of an open green space, with mixed-use buildings at the margins. However, he feels that this area would have to be protected so that it does not become another Hasenheide. There would have to be a fence, a small entrance fee, more control. The drugs and people from Hasenheide should not be allowed to flow into the area. He thinks that the closure of the airport could also improve the quality of life in Tempelhof district; maybe also a leisure park would be good.

Nevertheless, there are also other voices, like that of W, 62, a pensioned teacher who has lived on the Tempelhof side of the airport since the 1970s. He feels very disturbed by the airport noise and the kerosene smell it sometimes produces. He is a member of BIFT (an initiative against the airport) and highly critical of ideas such as the hospital/airstrip – like all ideas by capitalist businessmen, he thinks, this aims only at taking the profits and seeking state support if the project fails. In the case of a closure, he is generally in favour of the idea of new construction at the margins, with a large central open space. W knows from some of his neighbours that they are afraid of Neukölln and Kreuzberg, but he cannot see any danger, only if the new neighbourhoods become slums, but this is not to be expected, he says. He is also in favour of use of the airport building by artists. He thinks the house prices in Tempelhof district will rise after the closure of the airport and the area will become more attractive. While he closely echoes the Berlin government's line, he ties it to the grassroots opposition of the 1970s.

On the Neukölln side, the positions are different. L, 41 years old, unemployed, lives in Neukölln and feels very disturbed by the noise. He cannot enjoy his balcony and is a strong supporter of the closure of the airport. He is not allowed to vote, however, because he does not have German citizenship. L is in favour of sports areas for young people on the airport area. He also likes the idea of a hospital (but is not aware of the idea of the airstrip) – a hospital would be quiet and the people deserve a bit of peace. One other argument in his mind for the closure is that if the airport is closed, there will have to be some new construction, which will also mean jobs on building sites, which is good, in his opinion. A, 25, lives on the Kreuzberg side directly adjacent to the airport. He considers the idea of the airport staying operational as nonsense. Instead, A is in favour of having a park, but thinks that there should be a fee so that the park can be kept up. Just an open space will deteriorate, he says. On the other hand, he says, the park should be freely accessible for everyone, combining two contradictory perspectives. Asked about residential development, A mentions the expensive new developments on the Kreuzberg side and that nobody can afford these anyway, so the houses should be affordable. H, 56, from the Neukölln side of the airport, introduces himself as unemployed and generally uninterested in the debate. He is for a closure, he says, because the airport is no use to him anyway, but he fears that if it is closed, it will only be replaced by expensive shopping malls which will not be accessible for him either. He is also sceptical about whether a park could be managed, pointing out that everything is dirty anyway, and that people do not take away their rubbish from open spaces. H particularly blames this on immigrants.

The interviews show one central concern of the residents on both sides: the question of access. For those against the closure of the airport, the reason is fear of unwanted 'others', of an invasion from lower-class neighbourhoods. For those in favour of the closure, their arguments are almost always connected with visions of greater access for more people, including construction jobs and affordable housing. Sometimes they fear that limited access will not allow them to participate in the redeveloped amenities. The points of reference are clear: those who experience exclusion or ally with the excluded argue for openness, even if these arguments are sometimes made in a contradictory manner. They refer to their experiences of exclusion from expensive developments – also adjacent to the park in a gentrified area – and build on this. The other side of the discourse has the 'ghetto' as a stable point of reference. Neukölln, Kreuzberg and particularly the nearby Hasenheide Park feature prominently in their scenarios. They stand for people whom they wish to exclude from their lives and the spaces they use. Tempelhof district appears as a protected island, with only the airport stopping a threatening flood of drug dealers and criminals. Their wishes for redevelopment – should the airport be closed – reflect this geography of fear. If the airport is closed, the barrier against the 'others' must be kept up with the help of a fence, fees or expensive housing. These positions were, however, not clearly distributed according to the residents – some residents of Tempelhof were also in favour of the closure, and some even like the Hasenheide Park. On the other hand, not all respondents on the Neukölln side were for the closure. Some pointed to the possible deterioration and neglect of a park, but also showed an awareness of the possibility of exclusion from it. Clearly, however, the use of Hasenheide as a negative pivot of the debate is important. Equally, the awareness of strong divisions in the city emerges – with many places that poorer people cannot afford to go to or use, and places to which the better-off do not want poor people to have access. In these discourses of the residents, nostalgia does not play a major role. Their positions revolve around questions of spatial practice in the form of access and affect in the form of fear or longing.

TEMPELHOF IN BERLIN'S SPATIAL POLITICS OF AFFECT

Lefebvre writes that monumentality means the organization of symbols, affects and everyday practices according to a single logic. In the example of the debate about Tempelhof Airport, we can see a complicated picture emerge. On the one hand, the debate can be seen as an attempt to produce a consensus and to tie the electorate of Berlin into this consensus. The tool for the creation of this consensus was memory, a dead memory, a memory of something past that furthermore only speaks for one part of the city – the western part. The campaign run on nostalgia exemplifies this attempt to link the everyday conversations of Berliners with the discourse on Berlin as a whole. Thus Tempelhof Airport was located in the wider symbolic geography of Berlin, next to Friedrichstrasse and Potsdamer Platz, in a large-scale ordering of symbolic space. This symbolic space can be seen as a spectacle, an alienated arrangement of signs and affects. On the other hand, the aspect of monumentality is accompanied by another aspect that shows the interlinking of the different dimensions of social space. In positions drawing on everyday life experiences, two affects matter most: fear of 'others' and a desire for openness and access. The fear of others is again linked with a very distinctive mapping of Berlin and of the role of Tempelhof Airport in this. It links to a wider map of fear that is constructed by the tabloid press, by the police, conservative politicians and other actors. It is this ordering of symbolic space that matters mostly on the neighbourhood scale, even if at the same time it ties in local conversations with city-wide mappings.

The symbolic dimension of urban space matters. It matters much more than the current debate on memory takes into account, because it is not an isolated dimension of life, but linked with all other dimensions. In addition, the political aspect of affect is not only one-sided. Rather than being all about freedom and liberation, affect and *espace vécu* can be a means of control, of oppression. While this can be analysed without reference to Lefebvre, his theory provides an analysis of the interaction of the different dimensions of the production of urban space, rather than isolating them as single elements. Urban fear, for example, connects discourses across the scales, and ties in with a class dimension, with specific spatial practices and locations, and with visions of urban development. Exclusion is at the same time an affect, an element of spatial practice, and deeply connected to questions of planning.

With the final closure of the airport, the space has continued to be contested, and it might still regain its potential as this elusive other side of monumentality – a space of utopia and something like the street, as 'disorder that is alive' and as a place where elements of urban life meet, interact and surprise, without becoming a festival that is directed and organized.

NOTES

1   Note that 'Tempelhof' can refer to the airport, to the former district of Tempelhof, or to the neighbourhood that gave the airport and the former district their names. Since the communal reform in 2001, the former district of Tempelhof (comprising Tempelhof and three other neighbourhoods) is now joined with Schöneberg (as Tempelhof–Schöneberg).

2   Her point here being that it is the geography of emotions that is conscious of power.

3   Note that this school would consist almost exclusively of people not resident in Berlin, but in the UK and North America.

4   The following material is based on in-depth interviews with residents of the two areas of Tempelhof and Neukölln, adjacent to the airport. The interviews took place in the three weeks preceding the referendum.

REFERENCES

Abgeordnetenhaus Berlin 2008. *Plenarprotokoll 16/28 (24 April 2008)*. Berlin: Abgeordnetenhaus.

be-4-tempelhof (2008) *Nachnutzungskonzept des Senats für Tempelhof*, http://www.be-4-tempelhof.de/printable/hintergrund/nachnutzungskonzeptdessenatsfuerempelhof/index.html (accessed on: 25 April 2008).

Best, U. and Gebhardt, D. 2001a. Stigmastadtpläne Berlins, in *Politische Geographie. Handlungsorientierte Ansätze und Critical Geopolitics*, edited by P. Reuber and G. Wolkersdorfer. Heidelberg: Institute of Geography, 217–27.

Best, U. and Gebhardt, D. 2001b. *Ghetto-Diskurse. Geographien der Stigmatisierung in Berlin und Marseille*. Potsdam: University of Potsdam.

Bürgerinitiative Flughafen Tempelhof (BIFT). 2001. *Der Flughafen Tempelhof ist...* Available at: http://www.autofrei-wohnen.de/Berlin/bift-argumente.html (accessed: 25 April 2008).

Bürgerinitiative Flughafen Tempelhof (BIFT). 2006. *Tempelhof endlich schließen! Sechs gute Gründe für eine unverzügliche Stilllegung*. Available at: http://www.autofrei-wohnen.de/Berlin/BIFT.html#top (accessed: 25 April 2008).

Bürgerinitiative Westtangente (eds) 1976. *Stadtautobahnen – ein Schwarzbuch zur Verkehrsplanung*. Berlin: self-published.

Cochrane, A. 2006. 'Making Up Meanings in a Capital City: Power, Memory and Monuments in Berlin'. *European Urban and Regional Studies* 13(1): 21–40.

Colomb, C. 2007. 'Requiem for a Lost Palast. "Revanchist Urban Planning" and "Burdened Landscapes" of the German Democratic Republic in the New Berlin'. *Planning Perspectives* 22(3): 283–323.

Costabile-Heming, C.A. 2005. 'Tracing History Through Berlin's Topography: Historical Memories and Post-1989 Berlin Narratives'. *German Life and Letters* 58(3): 344–56.

Cressey, P.G. 2008 [1932] *The Taxi-Dance Hall: A Sociological Study in Commercialized Recreation and City Life*. Chicago, IL: University of Chicago Press.

Gysi, G. 2008. *Pressemitteilung 18.04.2008 – 16. Wahlperiode – Merkels Parteinahme für VIP-Flughafen Tempelhof ist falsch*. http://www.linksfraktion.de/pressemitteilung.php?artikel=1213782805 (accessed: 25 April 2008).

Heller, A. 1979. A *Theory of Feelings*. Assen: Van Gorcum.

Jameson, F. 1991. *Postmodernism, or, The Cultural Logic of Late Capitalism*. Durham, NC: Duke University Press.

Lanz, S. 2007. *Berlin Aufgemischt: Abendländisch, Multikulturell, Kosmopolitisch? Die Politische Konstruktion einer Einwanderungsstadt*. Bielefeld: Transcript.

Ledanff, S. 2003. 'The Palace of the Republic versus the Stadtschloss: The Dilemmas of Planning in the Heart of Berlin'. *German Politics and Society*, 21(4), 30–73.

Lefebvre, H. 1991 [1974]. *The Production of Space*. Oxford: Basil Blackwell.

Lefebvre, H. 2002 [1961]. *The Critique of Everyday Life, Volume 2*. London: Verso.

Lefebvre, H. 2003 [1970]. *The Urban Revolution*. Minneapolis. MN: University of Minnesota Press.

Marcuse, P. 1998. 'Reflections on Berlin: The Meaning of Construction and the Construction of Meaning'. *International Journal of Urban and Regional Research* 22(2): 331–8.

Neill, W.J.V. 1997. 'Memory, Collective Identity and Urban Design: The Future of Berlin's Palast der Republik'. *Journal of Urban Design* 2(2): 179–92.

Neill, W.J.V. 1998. 'Place Visions and Representational Landscapes: "Reading" Stormont in Belfast and the Palast der Republik in Berlin'. *Planning Practice and Research* 13(4): 389–406.

Neue Viktoria Quartier GmbH & Co. KG. 2007. *Fine Kreuzberg Living.* Available at: http://www. finekreuzbergliving.de (accessed: 25 April 2008).

Pflüger, F. 2008. *Presseerklärung 18.04.2008, Wowereit muss Angebot der Bundesregierung endlich annehmen,* http://www.cdu-fraktion.berlin.de/Aktuelles/Presseerklaerungen/ Bundeskanzlerin-und-Bundesminister-der-Finanzen-unterstuetzen-Chancenflughafen (accessed: 25 April 2008).

Roberts, J. 2006. *Philosophizing the Everyday. Revolutionary Praxis and the Fate of Cultural Theory.* London: Pluto Press.

Savage, M. 1995. 'Walter Benjamin's Urban Thought: A Critical Analysis'. *Environment and Planning D: Society and Space* 13(2): 201–16.

Schilde, K. and Tuchel, J. 1990. *Columbia-Haus. Berliner Konzentrationslager 1933–1936.* Berlin: Edition Hentrich.

Schmid, C. 2005. *Stadt, Raum und Gesellschaft – Henri Lefebvre und die Theorie der Produktion des Raumes.* Stuttgart: Steiner.

Senatsverwaltung für Stadtentwicklung 2008. *Prozessuale Stadtentwicklung Tempelhofer Feld – Columbiaquartier Berlin. Offener städtebaulichlandschaftsplanerischer Ideenwettbewerb. Ausschreibung.* Berlin: Senatsverwaltung.

Shields, R. 1999. *Lefebvre, Love & Struggle: Spatial Dialectics.* New York: Routledge.

Soja, E.W. 1996. *Thirdspace: Journeys to Los Angeles and Other Real-And-Imagined Places.* London: Blackwell.

Thien, D. 2005. 'After or Beyond Feeling? A Consideration of Affect and Emotion in Geography'. *Area* 37(4): 450–54.

Thrift, N. (2004). 'Intensities of Feeling: Towards a Spatial Politics of Affect'. *Geografiska Annaler B* 86(1): 57–78.

Till, K. 2005. *The New Berlin: Memory, Politics, Place.* Minneapolis: University of Minnesota Press.

Tolia-Kelly, D. 2006. 'Affect – An Ethnocentric Encounter? Exploring the "Universalist" Imperative of Emotional/Affectual Geographies'. *Area* 38(2): 213–17.

Tuan, Yi-Fu 1979. *Landscapes of Fear.* New York: Pantheon Books.

Williams, R. 1973. *The Country and the City.* New York: Oxford University Press.

15

Novi Beograd: Reinventing Utopia

Ljiljana Blagojević

Novi Beograd (New Belgrade) is a new city, planned and constructed in the post–Second World War period during socialist rule in the former Yugoslavia. Planned on the principles of modern urbanism and the paradigm of the 'functional city', it developed in an area with no previous settlement on the site of a marshy alluvial plain bordered by the rivers Sava and Danube, between the historical cities of Zemun and Beograd (Belgrade). Over time, the modern urban structure integrated the two previously independent and territorially autonomous centres into the Greater Belgrade metropolis (Blagojević 2004, 2005, 2007, 2012b). The Municipality of Novi Beograd today covers an area of around 4,000 hectares and is inhabited by some 250,000 people. By virtue of its location, modern infrastructure and development potential, Novi Beograd finds itself at the centre of contemporary post-socialist/communist socio-political and economic transition of the metropolis and its region, thus undergoing profound socio-spatial transformations. In this respect, the relationships between the emerging post-socialist urban reality and the extant modern urban landscape of the socialist era continue to be spatially, environmentally and socially contested, while questions about the opportunities of collective and cooperative appropriation of space remain largely unresolved. Pertinent questions concern the relation of new development to the urban structure, architecture and social space of dilapidating and ideologically stigmatized socialist housing. What qualities of socialist architecture but also of its social space need to be recognized and preserved, and where can the new development improve on the inherited urban structure? Some recent studies present the current processes of urban change in the bright and positive light of an eagerly awaited progress towards a market economy, while others see the paramount importance of modernist architectural heritage and the need for its protection and preservation (cf. Waley 2011). Could we argue that the balance between the two is to be found in the complex appreciation of the urban landscape quality of the modern city and in the perspective of ecological urbanism?[1]

Novi Beograd was realized as a city of predominantly socialist mass housing and a city in 'societal ownership' based on the ideological premise of the right to a residence as a universal right for the common public good. The category of societal ownership has been gradually eradicated since the fall of socialism, so that the present Constitution of the Republic of Serbia (2006, Article 86) recognizes only private, cooperative and public property, and stipulates that the remaining societal assets 'shall become private'.[2] Consequent to overarching processes of change during the past two decades of post-socialist transition, the urban space in Novi Beograd has been transformed primarily as a result of privatization, commodification and gentrification. I would contend that the post-socialist processes put into practice the issues raised by Henri Lefebvre (1991 [1974]: 54) back in 1974, about 'the relationship between, on the one hand, the entirety of that space which falls under the sway of "socialist" relations of production and, on the other hand, the world market, generated by the capitalist mode of production'. This chapter looks into this process of change, taking the general viewpoint of Lefebvre's theory on space and focusing on his critique of modern planning explicitly expressed through his direct practical involvement with the urban problematic of Novi Beograd. Taking Lefebvre's theory as a point of departure has consequences not only for the relevance of the issues raised in the above quotation, but for its currency throughout the socialist period and especially in the post-socialist conditions of today. From the late 1950s, Lefebvre's works have been regularly translated, studied and discussed in the former Yugoslavia, and his critique of modern urbanism in capitalism was used as an influential platform for the critique of the socialist city, or rather the auto-critique related to the import of capitalist modern urbanism into socialism.[3] His concept of *autogestion* owes much to intense interest and direct contacts and exchanges with the Yugoslav philosophers and intellectuals of the *Praxis* circle, through his participation in the Korčula Summer School from 1964, and publication of his texts and reviews of his books in the *Praxis* journal. It can be said that Lefebvre's post-PCF[4] years and Yugoslavia's era of self-management were strongly related in the concurrent, if mutually diverging, search for a society with a difference. Finally, in 1986, through collaboration with architects Serge Renaudie and Pierre Guilbaud in submitting an entry to the International Competition for the New Belgrade Urban Structure Improvement, Lefebvre reasserted his concept of the right to the city in direct relation to self-management. The right to the city, the competition text reads, 'comes as a complement, not so much to the rights of man … but to the rights of the <u>citizen</u>' and 'leads to active participation of the <u>citizen-citadin</u> in the control of the territory, and in its management … also to the participation of the citizen-citadin in the social life linked to the urban' (underlined in original; Renaudie et al. 2009 [1986]: 2. Cf. Blagojević 2007, 2009a, Stanek 2011: 233–44). I would argue that the socio-spatial meaning of the right of citizen-citadin as linked to the urban is becoming particularly relevant today, that is, in the post-socialist transition to free market capitalism of the last two decades.

As Lefebvre (1965: 164) noted in the mid 1960s, in what one saw when passing through Yugoslavia and at the same time traversing from European capitalism into Yugoslav socialism, it was not always easy to differentiate what had ensued from industrial development, what from the ancient Mediterranean civilization and what from socialism proper. The analysis, as he says, requires as much concentration as chess or bridge. Similarly, what is seen today when passing through Novi Beograd, itself traversing from Yugoslav socialism into the capitalism of present-day Serbia, ensues as much from the socialist city, modernist urban development and contradictions inherent in it as from the post-socialist socio-economic conundrum and subsequent collapse of the planning system.

FROM SOCIALIST TO POST-SOCIALIST CITY

Following Ivan Szelenyi's (1996: 294–303) theory of socialist 'under-urbanization', we can see the post-war urbanization of Novi Beograd with less spatial concentration of urban population, resulting in physically much less dense urban spatial structure than in cities of market capitalism. Looking further at the character of socialist urbanization as pointed out by Szelenyi, it is safe to say that Novi Beograd offered less diversity and less marginality than its capitalist counterparts, still with a degree of segregation mostly according to occupation and in relation to traditionally marginal social and ethnic groups. Where it differed most was in societal ownership of all urban land and subsequent absence of an urban land market, all development land transactions taking place between actors from the state sector. In sum, in its development, directed more by political will and less by population pressure, socialist Novi Beograd developed with less attention to economizing on space, as a sparsely urbanized landscape in societal ownership, and abundant in green open space. Its development and densification were left entirely to administrative decisions, rather than economic processes and decision making, whereby the state and state subsidiary organizations acted as central subjects of urban and social development in the name and common interest of society and as sole purveyors of public welfare. Characterized also by an underdeveloped urbanity resulting from a reduced tertiary sector, it harboured a void that is now being rapidly filled by the private sector forces operating in the hybrid conditions of post-socialist – proto-capitalist – laissez-faire (cf. Kušić and Blagojević 2013).

One of the changes that most directly affected urban development following the demise of socialism in the 1990s, according to Vujošević and Nedović-Budić (2006: 275, 280), was 'the relinquishing of land development process to market forces and a multiplicity of investors and other participants', while 'an upsurge of new, legitimate private interests paralleled the collapse of many previous, unequivocally public interests'. Moreover, as Petovar and Vujošević (2008) discuss, with the breakdown of former (socialist) public interest, the contradictory relation of individual (partial) and common interests becomes the central issue in the process of urban development, and subsequent pursuit of a contemporary notion of public good and associated rights. The turbulent transition period of the 1990s, in the conditions of war, isolation and internationally imposed sanctions, accommodated explosion of the informal sector of the economy, the black market and illegal construction on an unprecedented scale, ignoring what was left of the largely dismantled former system of planning. From 2000, more recent transitional reforms taking a neoliberal course largely discard 'any relatively ambitious notion of planning, reducing its role to the so called "project-led cum market-based" planning and concomitant ideologies', as phrased by Vujošević and Nedović-Budić (2006: 280). The process of change from socialist to ex-socialist and post-socialist city might best be described as radical transformation of ownership, value and rights of residence. Substitution of state ownership for the former societal ownership replaces the right to a residence by that of occupancy right and, following privatization, by private property rights. With the change of ownership status, the residence use value based on the premise that a place of residence in socialism is not a commodity or not only a commodity is replaced by the commodity exchange value and rising property value with the introduction of the real estate market.

Even though the formalized privatization of urban land has not been undertaken via *sui generis* legislation (property laws and similar), privatization is effectively being introduced. It has been regulated by the provisions of planning and construction acts (and consequent spatial, regional and master planning documents), the most current being the Republic of Serbia Planning and Construction Law (2009), under the jurisdiction of the Ministry of Environment and Spatial Planning. Thus the privatization of urban land is regulated by a law that stipulates a conversion of the leasehold right into a property right (Nedović-Budić et al. 2012). With these substitutions in place and in conditions of what can be termed post-socialist primitive accumulation of capital, what is seen on the site of Novi Beograd is persistent, street-by-street, block-by-block advance of new private development. In the context of eminently ideological anti-socialist/communist discourse in the making, the space of the modern city is reductively seen as the physical residue of a deposed socio-economic and political system or as its ideological monument. Thus ideologically stigmatized, the modern urban structure of a characteristically large percentage of open and green space becomes easy prey to haphazard re-urbanization. Open communal spaces of housing blocks are being parcelled, privatized and developed by programmes deemed to have been lacking in the socialist epoch, namely those of up-market residential, business, retail, leisure, banking, gambling and religion. Simultaneously, not yet conquered by capital, the abandoned landscapes of the unfinished modern plan are being appropriated for informal and transient urbanism of the shanty town and the flea market. The rise of informal spatiality is coupled with the ongoing lack of user/citizen participation and the planning profession's failure to cope with spontaneous practices.[5]

REAL AND EXISTING CITY: SEQUENCES OF NOVI BEOGRAD URBAN LANDSCAPE

In effect, the spatial processes of commercialization, hybridization and commodification play out the extreme criticism of the functional-city concept of Novi Beograd and by extension of the socialist city, which culminated in the postmodernist critique of the 1980s. Yet, where critics of late socialism saw space for development of alternative urban models based on the 'lessons of the past', and aestheticizing and humanizing the modern city (Perović 1985), the capital of the transition period leaves no alternative to its own supreme authority. In the face of the predominant conviction that there is no alternative to capitalism as a system, Fredric Jameson (2007: 232–3) suggests the utopian form of a break itself, the 'future as disruption', as it were.

Maligned and rejected in the process of post-socialist/communist paradigm change, utopia seems to be relegated to dwell in backrooms of socio-political and economic transition. Paradoxically, identification of utopia with communism/socialism gained new currency with the collapse of socialism, even though within socialism proper utopia had been denounced vehemently as idealism and lacking political agency. The word utopia or utopian in titles of histories of socialism, or books about socialist politics, projections and constructs, space and time relations, or about socialist cities and everyday life therein, often directs enquiry towards a utopian remembrance of things past. Rather than this kind of backward-looking vision of utopia, I ask if, in the present, actual and very real city of Novi Beograd, utopia may still be called for to produce a difference. How can Lefebvre's notion of 'different space' be leading the speculation on where in Novi Beograd one could see such 'a counter-space in the sense of an initially utopian alternative to actually existing "real" space' (Lefebvre 1991: 349)? I would argue that the alternative offers itself in the urban landscape quality of Novi Beograd and its rethinking towards a socio-environmentally sustainable future. The actual landscape is far from unproblematic; it is torn apart by all sorts of contradictions, old and new; that is, it is torn between the contradictory legacy of the socialist era and the problematic properties of post-socialist processes at work. My aim is, thus, to look more closely into three concrete sequences of the actually existing real space of Novi Beograd in order to discern what this landscape holds in the present and what it can hope for in the future.

Sequence 1: Landscape of Shifting Centrality

The first sequence concerns the disappearing landscape quality of modern urbanism and subsequent loss of identity intrinsic to Novi Beograd. In the past six decades, the natural landscape before the eyes of the citizens has been persistently transformed from the uninhabitable marshland into the cultural landscape of a modern city. Indeed, from the very outset, the planners emphasized the primacy of landscape and waterscape aspects in Novi Beograd (Blagojević 2007). For instance, in his 1947 Plan, the Slovenian architect Edvard Ravnikar argued for the *Ville Radieuse* concept of *soleil, espace, verdure* (see Figure 15.1), In parallel, the leading Belgrade urbanist Nikola Dobrović proposed a neo-baroque vision of urban landscape in his Outline Plan (1948), with large artificial ponds surrounded by open urban blocks set in abundant greenery (see Figure 15.2). Writing on the significance of Novi Beograd's urban landscape and waterscape, Dobrović (1957: 1770) referred to André Le Nôtre and his waterworks in Versailles, arguing that they were analogous to his own contemporary visions: 'What was once considered one

Fig. 15.1 Radiant Landscape: Novi Beograd Plan, 1947, by Edvard Ravnikar

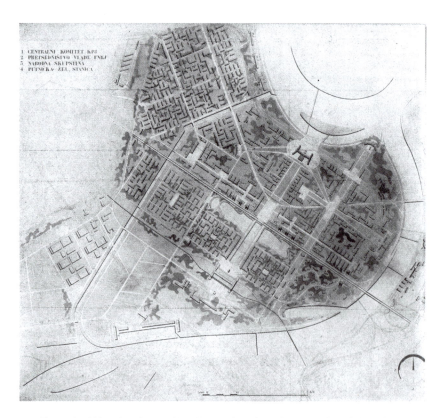

Fig. 15.2 Urban Landscape: Novi Beograd Outline Plan, 1948, by Nikola Dobrović

king's whim, today is becoming a real democratic requirement and possession of the socialist society.'The Belgrade Master Plan enacted in 1950 included a plan for New Belgrade as a 'city on water' criss-crossed with wide 'green avenues' and water features in the centre, while the Novi Beograd Master Plan by the architect Branko Petričić enacted in 1958 embraced *la ville verte* concept (see Figure 15.3).

Still today, when observed from the vantage point of the historical city, Novi Beograd is perceived as a modern urban landscape. For decades, however, at close proximity and in the everyday life of its inhabitants, the under-urbanized modern socialist city, under-equipped with shops and services, has largely been experienced neither as a landscape nor as a city, but as an empty space. It felt continually draughty, the sparseness of its urban structure believed to be a primary cause of alienation and the housing blocks containing tens of thousands of flats perceived as but a huge dormitory. Over a long period of becoming an urban space, the landscape of Novi Beograd posed difficulties for its inhabitants when it came to walking about and getting one's bearings. The discontinuous space of open blocks awaiting the growth of greenery, wide street profiles and excessive length between pedestrian crossings seemed more favourable for driving than for walking. An all but easily graspable logic of house numbering, as well as sheer size of residential buildings with multiple entrances, made it difficult for citizens to orientate themselves, remember the names of streets and find the right house number or entrance (for instance, residential building A-7 in housing block no. 21 is a single 980-metre-long, four-storey meander containing some 800 flats). The logic of walking about and orientation in the historical centre was entirely different from that in the modern urban landscape, and Novi Beograd, it seemed, necessitated the invention of a different logic of tracking the landscape rather than walking the pavement.

Despite the fact that the space in between the blocks has been used for diverse individual and collective activities, from walking, strolling, sports, children's play and neighbourhood meetings, as space open for individual and collective use, critics generally tended to view these spaces as a social and physical void or as an empty field of disjunction. Viewed as a void, the urban landscape quality of Novi Beograd was rendered invisible in many an architect's vision, especially with the onset of postmodernist denunciation of modern urbanism in the 1980s (*Arhitektura Urbanizam* 1986). In one of the most authoritative studies of the period, undertaken by the city's urban planning department, the open areas of Novi Beograd were represented as a blank, white background of figure ground plan, rather like a blind map which is then, in the proposal, filled in with the traditional urban typology of corridor streets, squares and perimeter blocks with pitched roofs forming regulation profiles (Perović 1985: 198–219).

Renaudie, Guilbaud and Lefebvre (2009 [1986]: 7, 11) discard such 'Post-Modern Historicism', as well as its opposite, that is the 'Neo-Rationalism' that maintains, even reinforces, the functional-city concept of zoning. Simply stating that the city is complex and dynamic, they suggest the principles of diversity and imbrication of production, management, appropriation of space as well as of its use, physical structure, rhythms, interaction with, activities and the like. Rather than striving

Fig. 15.3   Green
City: Novi Beograd
Master Plan, 1958,
by Branko Petričić

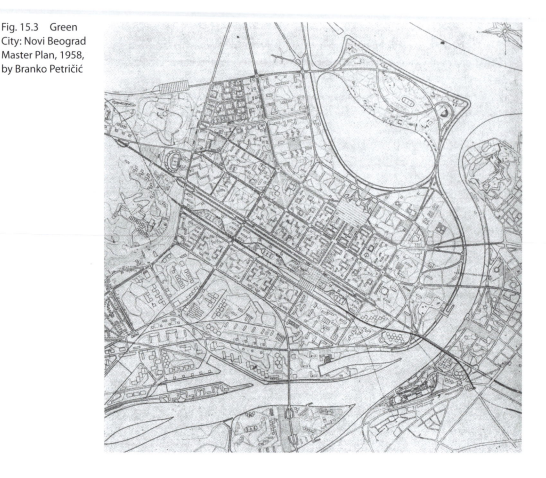

for that kind of dynamic complexity, diversity and imbrication, the current spatial
processes play out the densification scenario by collage of colourful commercial
programmes onto the grey background of a progressively dilapidating socialist
city. As it turns out, metaphorically speaking, the collage works admirably in luring
the citizens from their black-and-white background to consumerism in colour.

In November 2007, over a period of one month, still not finding it easy to
orientate themselves, around 1.2 million people visited a bright new shopping
mall in Novi Beograd called Delta City – city in name if not in content. Since then,
reportedly, more than 50 million visitors found their way there, some 30 new global
brands have been introduced through its 30,000 sq. m. retail space into the Serbian
market, earning it 'The International Council of Shopping Malls Award' in 2009 in
competition with 41 other malls from 19 countries.[6] What had become visible all
of a sudden? Apparently, instead of a change in the logic of walking about Novi
Beograd, the landscape itself was changed. Not at all unexpectedly, the centrality is
reconfigured in the free landscape of the market, that is the free market landscape
(Blagojević 2009b). Even though it is still difficult to orientate oneself on the basis
of the correct address, the name of the street or the house number, there are no
such problems when it comes to finding all those spaces bearing universal place-

names such as cash-and-carry, mega-market, cineplex, city, mall, expo and the like. The products of post-socialist restructuring, all these spaces most certainly do not form enclaves with an emancipatory potential or the seeds of a future city, but a homogenizing realm of a new social order. As a way out, might I suggest *le rappel au paysage* as a form of utopian break, future as disruption of permanent hard construction of ubiquitous consumerist space towards a more flexible way of thinking consumerism, which is learned from ephemeral, nomadic, marginal and informal practices in the landscape. The work of the artist Constant Nieuwenhuys comes to mind, in particular his studies of a gypsy camp as the origin of radical urbanism (Andreotti and Costa 1996: 3, 129).

Sequence 2: Archipelago of Marginality

The second sequence, thus, looks at *differences*, which as Lefebvre (1991: 373) says, 'endure or arise on the margins of the homogenized realm'. In the case of Novi Beograd, differences are to be most readily found in the excluded shanty town in the landscape surrounding new commercial developments. With all planning visions, including those on urban landscape and the like, suspended indefinitely following the fall of socialism, I would ask if and how architects envisage or script the parallel production of mall-and-slum in the post-socialist city. The aforementioned Delta City, for instance, is one in a series of projects by an Israeli firm, MYS Architects,[7] produced for market-orientated commercial development in ex-socialist countries. One lateral detail strikes me while perusing renderings on the architects' website, that is the generic landscape that forms the background to projects from all these disparate places, from Serbia and Romania to Ukraine and beyond. It is a kind of bad rendering executed in what looks like a consciously unskilful manner, representing a neutralizing landscape dotted with generic patches of greenery with pitched red-roofed houses and flat-roofed white apartment blocks (see Figure 15.4 above). It is clear that architects are largely unconcerned with the actual contexts, as their projects of this kind need only fit perfectly into the preordained image of the free market landscape and not the socio-spatial situation of an actually existing real city. The generic city depicted in the renderings effectively neutralizes all economic, socio-cultural and historical differences.

Fig. 15.4   Generic City: background rendering

Lefebvre (1991: 23) asks about neutralization of social and cultural spheres: 'Is this social entropy? Or, is it a monstrous excrescence transformed into normality?' The imposed normality, he continues, makes permanent transgression inevitable. Transgression invisible in the website pictures appears as a duality of Delta City and the surrounding landscape harbouring a permanently shifting space of shanty town.

Half-hidden behind unkempt shrubbery, the modern city harbours an archipelago
of some 15 informal settlements of makeshift huts and open-space dumps used
for the economy of collection and separation of recyclable waste. The settlements
connect fluidly to a chain of informal flea markets, which spread over any available
space with heaps of goods retrieved from rubbish for resale (see Figure 15.5). It
is this fluid landscape of flexible commerce and live-work residential cardboard
typology that also inhabits the modern city since the fall of socialism, its residents of
high 'mobility', with no addresses, streets or house numbers, but with mobile phone
communication.

Lefebvre (1991: 374) was impressed by the modus operandi of vast Latin
American favelas: '[t]heir poverty notwithstanding, these districts sometimes so
effectively order their spaces … *[a]ppropriation* of a remarkably high order is to
be found here', resulting in a '*spatial duality*' – contradiction and conflict on the
ground (emphasis in the original). In Novi Beograd, this conflict is permanent, as
can be seen in the case of the informal settlement that sprang up next to the site
of Delta City and its progeny, Belville, the private residential complex developed
by the same holding company.[8] In order to be used as an athletes' village for the
international sporting event Summer Universiade 2009, Belville was given priority
and fast-tracked through otherwise complex administrative procedures. But three
months before the opening of the event, the administration had no solution for
the shanty town nesting next to its site. The planned demolition and relocation
were halted by the opposition of the inhabitants and ensuing public pressure,
postponing the solution to an indefinite date.[9] After years of conflict, negotiation,

eviction, partial demolition and period of impasse, the site had finally been cleared by the city in 2012 and some 280 families resettled into container accommodation at less exposed peripheral locations. The neighbouring informal flea market was subsequently removed, only to give way to a veritable Potemkin village in its place, that is, a film-set copy of the historical centre of Belgrade erected there as part of the highly questionable propaganda project under the slogan 'Belgradization of Belgrade'. Rather than providing public and leisure space to the housing communities of Novi Beograd, as promised by the promoters, the site stands locked and unused, clearly serving only to reserve space for future commercial use and, more importantly, to pre-empt any thought, let alone action, about the return of the expelled. In the absence of contemporary planning for future inclusion of the expelled, what is being awaited in the Novi Beograd landscape, a mirage or a dream?

Sequence 3: Landscape as a mirage effect

> 'We are in the middle of a desert', says Vera Pavlovna in astonishment. 'Well, in the middle of a former desert. But now, as you can see, this whole expanse of land ... has been transformed into the most fertile fields ... "the land of milk and honey" ... now green and covered with flowers. Throughout the whole area, ... enormous buildings stand three or four versts (old Russian unit of length) apart ... sort of enormous crystal building ... For a considerable distance all around the crystal palace there stand rows of tall, thin pillars; on top of them, high above the entire palace and about half a verst around stretches a white canopy. 'It's continually being sprinkled with water ... Consequently, it's cool to live here.' (Chernyshevsky 1989: 374)

The above passage from Vera Pavlovna's fourth dream is invoked as a reaction to a recent, much-heralded architectural project for the Centre for the Promotion of Science (CFPOS) in Novi Beograd by the Austrian architect Wolfgang Tschapeller (see Figure 15.6). This was the winning project selected from 232 entries at the international architecture competition promoted by the Ministry of Science and Technological Development of the Republic of Serbia and the European Investment Bank, organized in 2010 by the Association of Belgrade Architects under the umbrella of the International Union of Architects. Not too dissimilar from the imagery conjured up in the dream sequence quoted above, the computer-generated renderings show CFPOS as a mirage in Novi Beograd.

CFPOS is a 15,000 sq. m. large perpendicular building lifted up some 20 metres above ground. In computer renderings, it appears floating in the air between other enormous objects visible in the distance, all set in the purity of bluish haze, well cleansed from the contradictory post-socialist reality down on the ground. Out of sight, out of mind: it is an architectural vision of 'an elevated city detached from the ground' levitating above the terrain, itself 'occupied with a multitude of different vegetations, exotic and local plants, waterlines, bike routes, jogging path' (Tschapeller 2010; emphasis added). This project of vegetal multitude, oblivious to the multitude living nearby, has an imperial presence, poised on four gigantic inverted steel tripods. The mirrored surfaces of the building's underside 'reflect all

Fig. 15.6
Wolfgang
Tschapeller, Centre
for the Promotion
of Science in Novi
Beograd, winning
competition
entry, 2010

the movement on the ground as well as the visitor who by entering the centre is penetrating the reflections of the earths [*sic*] surface', deemed by the competition jury to be 'enormously attractive to potential users and visitors' (ibid.). The CFPOS not only narcissistically reflects the space of Novi Beograd rendered abstract as a tabula rasa, but it violently dwarfs the difference produced over time in the living city (cf. Blagojević 2013). Certainly not a utopia, the CFPOS project foresees much the same continuity of the transitional capitalism paradigms and homogeneity of urban space as Delta City. The time and space they project substitute the event and spectacle of late shopping night or the event promoted as the 'Researchers' night in Belgrade', for the rhythms of everyday life.

'This analysis leads back to buildings, the prose of the world', writes Lefebvre (1991: 227) and goes on to say:

> In their pre-eminence, buildings, the homogenous matrix of capitalistic space, successfully combine the object of control by power with the object of commercial exchange. The building effects a brutal condensation of social relationships … embraces, and in so doing reduces, the whole paradigm of space: space of domination/appropriation (where it emphasizes technological domination); space as work and product (where it emphasizes the product); and space as immediacy and mediation (where it emphasizes mediations and mediators, from technical matériel to the financial 'promoters' of construction projects).

From 2005, the bright prospects for Novi Beograd have been saturating the press, the headlines announcing the '*Migration of Business World to Novi Beograd*', '*The Serbian Wall Street Shoots Up*', '*The Most Modern Business Centre in the Heart of Novi Beograd*' and advertisements for new developments reading 'The City of Successful People. Take your place in it now!' In a competition organized in 2006–07 by the *Financial Times*, which selects 'Cities of the Future' in 13 regions of Europe, Beograd was voted Southern European City of the Future. Architects produced designs to

match the media booster and supply dazzling imagery, if not actual buildings. In the long line of glitzy computer renderings, the latest one published in the daily *Danas* (28 October 2011) is an architectural extravaganza of a rotating glass skyscraper with 80 floors named the Dynamic Tower, a generic design by David Fisher. Yet, out of the blue, as abruptly as it was announced, the tower and investment group information disappeared into hot air. By the time I finalized this text all traces of its mention on all related websites had disappeared completely, leaving the newspaper's stub as the only solid piece of evidence it ever was considered. This only demonstrates that, with mediations and mediators in abundance, the whole paradigm of space is being reduced to projected mirage.

Fig. 15.7   Hotel 'Jugoslavija' as billboard, 2007

All the while, the modernist city fades away, stigmatized and marginalized. The silence fell over the final blow delivered in 2005 to modern architecture and its symbolic kudos, when the hotel 'Jugoslavija', one of the first three representative modernist buildings planned and erected in Novi Beograd (1947, 1969), was closed down and turned into a giant billboard for a mobile network operator (see Figure 15.7 above). The bright mirage with images of happy people, and the company's motto 'You've got friends' wrapping around all four façades, instantly transferred the hotel along with its name commemorating a no-longer-existing country into the blind field of society. Pending major renovation and extension, the hotel waits, its rooms depopulated and its minimalist foyer interiors stripped down and refitted into a grand casino. It hosts, among the gamblers, an art form of burlesque, the new meaning of the word itself ushered into the Serbian language with specially flown-in international strip-stars.

Down the Danube from the closed-down hotel stands the exquisite modern building of the Museum of Contemporary Arts (1965), itself shut down and awaiting renovation since 2008, its extraordinary collection of Yugoslav modern art put in storage indefinitely. Not far beyond, vanished from the mind's eye, is what uninvitingly stood as the Central Committee of the Communist Party, a typical modernist tower in the park at the new city's entry point from the historical centre. Guarded and perceived as a forbidden zone for decades, the tower and the park have been depoliticized and transformed in 2009 into a space of mass consumerism – corporate office space and what was advertised as the largest shopping mall in the region – with millions streaming in, the invisible hand making it all happen. With the ease of image production, the new design rendered the past invisible and the symbol of the failed socio-political project is gradually disappearing from public consciousness – a mirage in the changed nature of the modern city.

CONCLUDING REMARKS: LANDSCAPE UTOPIA (REINVENTED)

In the accompanying text submitted with the plans for the 'International Competition for the New Belgrade Urban Structure Improvement' in 1986, Renaudie, Guilbaud and Lefebvre (2009: 4, 6) claimed that the 'planification of Novi Beograd has failed, both in its attempt at global coherence and in the political will to create a city'. Instead, they suggest utopia as a point of departure and an ultimate break with the modern city (ibid.: 6):

> If utopia were allowed us, we would build on the flanks of the plateau and research a development of Novi Beograd towards the hills, hanging onto the slopes as the ancients knew how to do.
>
> The bars and towers, progressively abandoned, would become the ruins of another time, a museum in memory of a former era where individuals were not entitled to be citizens in full measure.

What can be said of this utopia today, 25 years since this proposal proved a prediction, an omen, rather? The bars and towers of the modern city in disrepair, if not abandoned, are literally becoming ruins that can rightly be seen as ruins of another time. The reality of Novi Beograd is, however, far from a picturesque notion of a sublime ruin or a *folie* in the landscape. In order to understand that reality, I will reiterate my statement that Novi Beograd was realized as a city in societal property and extend it to say that it was planned and constructed on a marshland site with no previous urban history, which served for centuries as a no-man's-land between the borders of empires (that is, East and West Roman, Byzantine and Frank or Ottoman and Austrian/Austro-Hungarian). Most of central Novi Beograd territory has no history of private ownership and no history of nationalization and confiscation of private property, and, therefore, there is no restitution of land pending regulation. Today, Novi Beograd is the capital's frontier where leasing state-owned land has no legal strings attached and is thus up for grabs. In the landscape of the unfinished open plan of the modern city, the only disruption to the homogeneity and hegemony of development's unrelenting advance is the archipelago of marginality, both the marginalized socialist housing and the marginalized shanty town. It is in those two that counter-space is inserted into spatial reality of advancing privatization, as Lefebvre (1991: 382) would have it, 'against the Eye and the Gaze, against quantity and homogeneity, against power and the arrogance of power, against the endless expansion of the "private" and of industrial profitability'.

In reinventing utopia, I would suggest an urban counter-landscape where the archipelago of marginality is seen as a space with a perspective of a future as disruption, along the lines of Lefebvre (1991: 381): 'What runs counter to a society founded on exchange is a primacy of *use*.' This means, in my mind, investigating models, including architectural and urban models, of 'primacy of *use*' that are inclusive of informal and autonomous practices of the shanty-town and the flea market. The right to the city understood also as the right to urban landscape comes to mind as an anticipation, which presupposes the democratic concept of socio-spatial justice and its mediation with Novi Beograd's social, environmental and cultural–historical urban reality.

CODA

In the dominant academic discourse of post-socialist Serbia, Lefebvre and his writings as well as the local reflections of his work from the era of self-management socialism have been relegated to the dump of history. It is indicative to note that as the translation of Lefebvre into the Central and East European languages of the Warsaw Pact countries came to an 'abrupt end' after his suspension from the PCF in 1957, as shown by Stanek (2011: 52), in the former Yugoslavia it started only at that point and flourished until the country's own abrupt end, when it came to a grinding halt. When in the course of my research I unearthed an unpublished text on Novi Beograd by Renaudie et al., its partial translation and appraisal in my doctorate (2005) and book on Novi Beograd (Blagojević 2007) and subsequent facsimile publication of the whole document by Bitter and Weber (2009: 1–71), passed by in deadly silence, ignored tacitly even by the committed Lefebvrians from the bygone days of self-management socialism.[10] Discontinuation of translation, termination of public libraries' orders of books and publication by or on Lefebvre and his work leaves a gaping void and a growing time lag of discourse on space and society. Just as I was putting the finishing touches to the final draft of this chapter, I received what might well have been the only copy in Serbia of the study of Lefebvre on space by Łukasz Stanek (2011), the reading of which seemed to me a longed-for dialogue (cf. Blagojević 2012a). A while back, a passing mention of Lefebvre's involvement with the Novi Beograd project in the Introduction to his *Writings on Cities* (Kofman and Lebas 1996: 23) opened a new chapter of research on the topic. Today, so does the awareness of climate change and subsequent reinvention of landscape, sometimes as utopia or myth, sometimes also as a Lefebvrian departure from the real, the given, towards the possible.

NOTES

1   This chapter was realized as a part of the project 'Studying climate change and its influence on the environment: impacts, adaptation and mitigation' (43007), financed by the Ministry of Education and Science of the Republic of Serbia within the framework of integrated and interdisciplinary research for the period 2011–14.

2   Constitution of the Republic of Serbia (online) http://www.srbija.gov.rs/cinjenice_o_srbiji/ustav_odredbe.php?id=219 (accessed 7 April 2013).

3   Up to the collapse of socialism and break-up of the Federation in 1991, translation of Lefebvre's work into Serbo-Croat included about fifteen books, from *Contribution à l'esthétique* (1953), translated in 1957, to translation in 1988 of the whole of *Critique de la vie quotidienne*, that is vol. 1, *Introduction* (1947, first translated into Serbo-Croat in 1958), vol. 2, *Fondements d'une sociologie de la quotidienneté* (1961), and vol. 3, *De la modernité au modernisme: Pour une métaphilosophie du quotidien* (1981). *Urban Revolution* (*La révolution urbaine*, 1970) was translated in 1974, and excerpts from *The Production of Space* from 1975. Cf. Blagojević (2012a).

4   Parti communiste français, French Communist Party.

5   See Diener 2012. Also, in the same edited volume, on more recent transformations, see Topalović 2012, with the proviso that the thesis on change of paradigms and the historical overview of New Belgrade development largely appropriate and restate research by Blagojević (2004, 2005, 2007).

6   As reported by a Belgrade weekly magazine; see 'Šoping molovi: Novi društveni centri', *Vreme*, 1162 (2013), 72–3.

7   'The largest, most prestigious and experienced architecture firm in Israel ... [and] the largest international architectural firm operating in Eastern Europe with projects in Albania, Bosnia, Bulgaria, Croatia, Cyprus, Czech Republic, Georgia, Hungary, Kazakhstan, Montenegro, Poland, Romania, Serbia, Ukraine, Russia and more.' See MYS Architects (online). Available at: http://m-y-s.com/ (accessed 23 October 2011).

8   Belville (online). Available at http://www.belville.rs/ (accessed 25 October 2011).

9   Belleville. 2009. Video, documentation (online). Available at http://www.modukit.com/raedle-jeremic/ (accessed 30 October 2011).

10   I am grateful to the sociologist Ksenija Petovar for presenting me with the text from her personal archive. Subsequently, the text was published as a facsimile in Bitter and Weber (eds) (2009). Integral translation into Serbian is not available.

REFERENCES

Arhitektura Urbanizam (1986). *The Future of New Belgrade: International Competition for the New Belgrade Urban Structure* XXV, special issue (not numbered).

Andreotti, L. and Costa, X. (eds) 1996. *Situationists: Arts, Politics, Urbanism*. Barcelona: Museu d'Art Contemporani and ACTAR.

Bitter, S. and Weber, H. (eds) 2009. *Autogestion, or Henri Lefebvre in New Belgrade*. Vancouver: Fillip Editions; Berlin: Sternberg Press.

Blagojević, Lj. 2004. 'Novi Beograd oder die Hauptstadt von Niemandsland'. *Bauwelt* 36 (*StadtBauwelt* 163): 34–41.

Blagojević, Lj. 2005. 'Back to the Future of New Belgrade: Functional Past of the Modern City'. *Aesop 05 Vienna* (online). Available at http://aesop2005.scix.net/cgi-bin/papers/Show?204 (accessed 9 February 2012).

Blagojević, Lj. 2007. *Novi Beograd: osporeni modernizam*. Beograd: Zavod za udžbenike, Arhitektonski fakultet and Zavod za zaštitu spomenika kulture (Cyrillic).

Blagojević, Lj. 2009a. 'The Problematic of a "New Urban": The Right to New Belgrade', in *Autogestion, or Henri Lefebvre in New Belgrade*, edited by S. Bitter and H. Weber. Vancouver: Fillip Editions; Berlin: Sternberg Press, 119–33.

Blagojević, Lj. 2009b. 'A Free Market Landscape', in *Differentiated Neighbourhoods of New Belgrade*, edited by Z. Erić. Belgrade: Museum of Contemporary Art, 128–33.

Blagojević, Lj. 2012a. 'Book Review: *Henri Lefebvre on Space: Architecture, Urban Research, and the Production of Theory*'. *The Journal of Architecture* 17(5): 807–12.

Blagojević, Lj. 2012b. 'The Residence as a Decisive Factor: Modern Housing in the Central Zone of New Belgrade'. *Architektúra & urbanizmus* 46(3–4): 228–49.

Blagojević, Lj. 2013. 'The Post-Modernist Turn and Spectres of Criticality in Post-Socialist Architecture: 'one:table' at the Venice Biennale 2012'. *The Journal of Architecture* 18(6): 761–780.

Chernyshevsky, N. 1989. *What Is to Be Done?* (1863). Trans. Michael R. Katz. Ithaca, NY: Cornell University Press.

Diener, R. 2012. 'New Belgrade: The Instability of the Collective Form', in *Belgrade Formal In-Formal*, edited by ETH Studio Basel. Zürich: Scheidegger & Spiess, 48–67.

Dobrović, N. 1957. 'Teritorijalne vode Beograda, njihov značaj za osnovu, lik i celokupnu strukturu Novog Beograda i Velikog Beograda'. *Tehnika* XII(11): 1765–71.

ETH Studio Basel Contemporary City Institute (ed.) 2012. *Belgrade Formal In-Formal*. Zürich: Scheidegger & Spiess.

Jameson, F. 2007. *Archaeologies of the Future: The Desire Called Utopia and Other Science Fictions* (2005). London: Verso.

Kofman, E. and Lebas, E. 1996. 'Lost in Transposition: Time, Space and the City', in *Writings on Cities* by Henri Lefebvre, edited by E. Kofman and E. Lebas. Oxford: Blackwell, 3–60.

Kušić, A. and Blagojević, Lj. 2013. 'Patterns of Everyday Spatiality: Belgrade in the 1980s and its Post-Socialist Outcome'. *Český lid: Etnologický časopis* 100(3): 281–303.

Lefebvre, H. 1965. 'Socijalizam za vrijeme ljetnjeg odmora'. Trans. S. Popović-Zadrović. *Praxis*, II(1): 164–6.

Lefebvre, H. 1991 [1974]. *The Production of Space* (1974). Trans. D. Nicholson-Smith. Oxford: Blackwell Publishing.

Nedović-Budić, Z., Zeković, S. and Vujošević, M. 2012. 'Land Privatization and Management in Serbia – Policy in Limbo'. *Journal of Architectural and Planning Research* 29(4): 306–17.

Perović, M.R. (ed.) 1985. *Lessons of the Past*, Belgrade: Institute for Development Planning of the City of Belgrade.

Petovar, K. and Vujošević, M. 2008. 'Koncept javnog interesa i javnog dobra u urbanističkom i prostornom planiranju'. *Sociologija i prostor* 179(1): 24–51.

Renaudie, S., Guilbaud, P. and Lefebvre, H. 2009 [1986]. 'International Competition for the New Belgrade Urban Structure Improvement (1986)', in *Autogestion, or Henri Lefebvre in New Belgrade*, edited by S. Bitter and H. Weber. Vancouver: Fillip Editions; Berlin: Sternberg Press, 1–71.

Stanek, Ł. 2011. *Henri Lefebvre on Space. Architecture, Urban Research, and the Production of Theory*. Minneapolis, MN: University of Minnesota Press.

Szelenyi, I. 1996. 'Cities under Socialism – And After', in *Cities After Socialism: Urban and Regional Change and Conflict in Post-Socialist Societies*, edited by G. Andrusz, M. Harloe and I. Szelenyi. Oxford: Blackwell, 286–317.

Topalović, M. 2012. 'New Belgrade: The Modern City's Unstable Paradigms', in *Belgrade Formal In-Formal*, edited by ETH Studio Basel. Zürich: Scheidegger & Spiess, 128–205.

Tschapeller, W. 2010. *International Architecture Competition for the Centre for Promotion of Science Belgrade 2010* (online). Available at www.blok39.com/index.php?option=com_content&view=article&id=58&Itemid=57 (accessed 19 October 2011).

Vujošević, M. and Nedović-Budić, Z. 2006. 'Planning and Societal Context – The Case of Belgrade, Serbia', in *The Urban Mosaic of Post-Socialist Europe*, edited by S. Tsenkova and Z. Nedović-Budić. Heidelberg; New York: Physica-Verlag, 275–94.

Waley, P. 2011. 'From Modernist to Market Urbanism: The Transformation of New Belgrade'. *Planning Perspectives* 26(2): 209–35.

16

Lefebvrean Vaguenesses: Going Beyond Diversion in the Production of New Spaces

Jan Lilliendahl Larsen

For almost a decade, Supertanker, which started as a grassroots urban laboratory, has studied and participated in informal and creative diversions of industrial wastelands in the harbour of Copenhagen (Larsen 2007). By experimenting with various arenas of urban action research, dialogue and practice, Supertanker has studied and unfolded some of the potentials in Lefebvrean concepts such as the lived, the urban, the moment, the possible, autogestion, appropriation and understanding. Perhaps most importantly, Supertanker has cultivated the small but essential seed Henri Lefebvre laid down for understanding the possibilities of participation through and lived reappropriation of abandoned spaces in the city: *diverted space*.

In this chapter, a conceptual modification of diverted space is developed in four parts. First, Lefebvre's concept of diverted space is introduced in relation to the Parisian context of Les Halles in which it was coined. While Lefebvre presented it as a significant window on to the production of new spaces, it is argued that the concept is stronger in its link to Lefebvre's lived experience than in its clarity. Second, perceived, lived, social and conceived associations in the development of Supertanker in an abandoned space in Copenhagen are presented as different moments in a contemporary example of Lefebvre's diverted space. The experiential resonance with developments in other European cities makes the general case for the urban potentials of diverted spaces. Third, however, it is shown how the diversionary experiments, due to their lack of cultural and conceptual clarity, tend to be reintegrated into more established discourses *for* and *against* creativity in urban planning and development.

In the fourth part, *vagueness* is proposed as an essential conceptualization of the potentials and perils of diverted space – denoting the empty, unclear and discursively weak and yet, or rather therefore, also the openness towards lived experiences and thus the potentials for new productions of space. Lefebvre's conceptual articulation of vacant spaces as diverted spaces is, in its transducive affinity with lived experience and its conceptual indeterminacy, presented as a defining example of vagueness. The concept of *vague space*, which expresses the varying conditions of possibility for participation in and appropriation of an unevenly developed social space through the different moments of association, is thus proposed *both* in order to further develop and anchor Lefebvre's important conceptualization *and*, through this, to give the contemporary discourse of temporary and creative spaces of redevelopment an urban grounding.

LEFEBVRE ON DIVERSION

Henri Lefebvre has argued that we need a new perspective on modern life and society – both in order to critique the contemporary order but, even more so, to emancipate new tendencies hidden not least in the urbanity of the city. According to him, the dominant *industrial*, that is economic and administrative, perspective of modern society makes us blind to the potential of the *urban*, that is a phenomenon in contact with the body, everyday life, lived culture and the city. The critique of the contemporary discursive fields of blindness and the corresponding conceptual disclosure of the possible urban potentials was at the core of Lefebvre's work (Lefebvre 2003).

Perhaps one of the most poignant manifestations of this line in Lefebvre's work comes in Kristin Ross's interview with him in the early 1980s when speaking in retrospect of the new tendencies of revolutionary movements (Lefebvre 2002), which, like the Situationists, 'leave behind classic organizations' (Ross 1997: 76). In a vein similar to his thoughts within political theory on *autogestion* and contemporary radical democratic theory, he states: 'What's beautiful is the voice of small groups having influence' (ibid.). Even though his work was very focused on urban tendencies and their urban context, Lefebvre only sporadically crystallized it in general conceptualizations of the dynamics influencing the conditions of possibility of these voices. One very potent, but alas also very latent, concept, which is especially tuned to the frail and contingent search for the *possible*, is *diversion*. It is unfolded over a few pages in *The Production of Space* (Lefebvre 1991 [1974]) in relation to a period of redevelopment in his local neighbourhood in Paris, Les Halles. Having been one of the initial laboratories for the Situationist *dérives* (Khatib 1958), the abandoned physical structure of the former food market was gradually taken over by young groups in Paris in the late 1960s. For a couple of years, while awaiting the plans for its redevelopment, it was a hotspot of alternative activities never imagined by the architects, planners or politicians.

Living just a couple of streets away from Les Halles, Lefebvre followed the developments with a keen eye to urban *moments* in this metamorphosed 'gathering-place and ... scene of permanent festival ... for the youth of Paris' (Lefebvre 1991 [1974]: 167). Lefebvre had developed dialectical pairs of critically diagnostic concepts like *product* versus *oeuvre*, *industrial* versus *urban* and the philosophically more canonized contradiction of *domination* versus *appropriation*, that is, a sterilized and empty product of technology exemplified by 'a slab of concrete or a motorway' versus a work of social creativity such as '[a]n igloo, an Oriental straw hut or a Japanese house' (Lefebvre 1991 [1974]: 165, 1995 [1962],

2002 [1961]). But in Les Halles of 1969–71, Lefebvre perceived and sought a conceptualization of tendencies of something else, something beyond these dualisms. Lefebvre described Les Halles, neither dominated nor appropriated, as 'vacant, and susceptible of being diverted, reappropriated and put to a use quite different from its initial one' (Lefebvre 1991 [1974]: 167). He thus coined the term *diverted spaces* (the concept of diversion having been used since the early 1950s by the Situationists) and deemed them 'of great significance', since 'they teach us much about the production of new spaces' (ibid.).

With the concepts of the triad, what Lefebvre saw in Les Halles was a certain instance of fragmentary and contradictory balance of the three moments of *spatial practice*, *representations of space* and *spaces of representation*: not the intolerable imbalance of *abstract space* with the systemic representations of space dominating spatial practice and the spaces of representation related to its use; not a space of harmonious balance between three moments reciprocally feeding on and feeding each other – as had arguably been the case in the Renaissance (ibid.: 7). No: a somewhat vacated space, a space with no clear, designated or determining spatial practice or representation. If balanced at all, then a balance marked by the absence of defining or dominating practices and representations, except for the distant shadows of times gone by or frail premonitions of future possibilities, that is, spaces of *symbolic* or *imaginative* representations in a quiet but emergent resonance with a torn spatial practice.

However, despite its 'great significance', and despite his reference elsewhere to political *voids* as conducive of autogestion (Lefebvre 2009: 144), Lefebvre never performs such a conceptual exercise in relation to the triadic moments or to other elaborations, which could further ground the concept of diversion in his work or in the current social space of the city. In fact he merely mentions the concept of diversion sporadically through *The Production of Space*. Lefebvre refers explicitly to the concept only on pages 167–8, where he elaborates dominated, appropriated and this 'something', neither/nor. Here it is defined both negatively (as diverted *away from*) and positively (as in diverted *towards*) defined.

It is an 'almost' concept, which in Lefebvre's political project means that it is either half complete or half failed. Thus, as early as in these pages one is a bit puzzled by its (n)either/(n)or status. This confusion is increased and replicated on a terminological level in other parts of *The Production of Space*. Thus the phenomenon represented through diverted space is also represented through terms such as *co-opted* (Lefebvre 1991 [1974]: 368–9, 383, 422), *counter space* (ibid.: 349, 367, 381–3, 419–20) and *reappropriated* (ibid.: 167), referring exactly to the varying degrees of alignment with potentially new *productions* of space. In a quotation that once again lacks somewhat in terminological, if not conceptual, precision regarding the distinction between *appropriation* and *diversion*, Lefebvre's epitaph for the concept of diverted space reads: 'The goal and meaning of theoretical thinking is production rather than diversion. Diversion is in itself merely appropriation, not creation – reappropriation which can call but a temporary halt to domination' (ibid.: 168).

All in all, diverted space, in all its confusing potency, is a crucial conceptual manifestation of Lefebvre's *transduction* (Lefebvre 2002, 2003) of ever new critical perspectives on the present and, more importantly, of new emancipative urbanities within a contemporary social space of otherwise dominant representations and practices. However, while Lefebvre's articulations of the concept might function as adequate and enlightening expressions of his main project, one is left with a feeling that he might have done well to take in more nuances of this specific, albeit puzzling, phenomenon – and doing so with a larger degree of conceptual clarity, thus bringing the lived experiences of his and his fellow transducers 'into language' (Lefebvre 1988: 80). By treating diversion as a deductive point, a conceptual in-between *vis-à-vis* the dualism of dominated or appropriated spaces, Lefebvre replicates its empirical fuzziness rather than teasing out the emergent dynamics at work in the significant moments of the production of new spaces.

EXPERIENCES IN A CONTEMPORARY DIVERTED SPACE IN COPENHAGEN

Since Lefebvre's days, 'shrinking cities' all over the industrialized world have witnessed an explosion in vacant spaces – and their consequent diversion (Oswalt 2005, Overmeyer 2007). In this process, spatial diversions, just like other subcultural currents, have moved closer to mainstream perceptions of and tendencies in urban development. From a traditional stronghold in squatting movements, the tactical act of diverting unused spaces towards alternative aims has spread to other, less explicitly political, groupings (Dienel and Schophaus 2002). Hence, in Europe alone a large number of diverting experiments have unfolded in a multitude of post-industrialized spaces (Groth and Corijn 2005). Below, I will present the development in Copenhagen of the harbour café, Luftkastellet, and the grassroots urban laboratory, Supertanker, which takes us through four phases and two radically different modes of production of space with several just as different articulations of the potentials of a diverted space. As one step towards my *vague* conceptualization, I will refer to these articulations as different moments of social, perceived, lived and conceived *associations* between urbanites and their sociospatial context.

Wilder's Island: Vacant and Susceptible to Being Diverted

After centuries of constant growth, general processes of globalization and economic restructuring meant that Copenhagen went through decades of painful crisis in the 1970s and 1980s, seeing industrial jobs, inhabitants and tax revenues fleeing to other parts of the country, Europe and the world (Andersen and Jørgensen 1995). A physical consequence of this was that major parts of the capital were laid waste, especially along those means of transportation where industry developed up to the Second World War: the railway and the harbour.

For several centuries maritime communication was the major economic factor in Copenhagen. The central harbour was dotted by several so-called trading places of large mercantile companies. A major one of these was the Greenlandic Trading Place (KGH in Figure 16.1) at Wilder's Island (Wilders Ø) in the historic Christianshavn

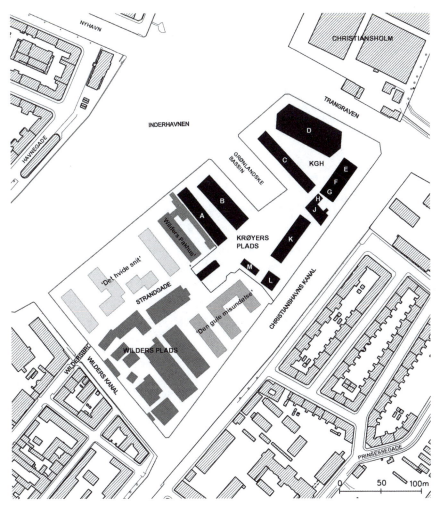

Fig. 16.1   Wilder's Island with Krøyer's Place in the central part of the harbour of Copenhagen

neighbourhood. Having been the hub for trade on the North Atlantic for centuries, the trading company left for a more peripheral location in the mid-1970s, and the historic warehouses became spatial leftovers for the following decades. While locals thus called their beloved island 'The Sleeping Beauty', it was seen ambivalently both as a 'Dead Dog Space' and as a potential 'Golden Egg Goose' by planners and developers of the city. However, in the late 1990s and early 2000s, the real estate market was not ripe for a redevelopment of the site.

Luftkastellet: Intensification of the Perceived, Lived and Social Associations of the Vacant Space

Then, in relation to prospects of a possible film location in early 2001, a group of entrepreneurial people discovered the obvious spatial potentials in the relative emptiness of a spot at Wilders Ø called Krøyer's Place (Krøyers Plads) – on the

Fig. 16.2
Diversion in a
space of vacuity.
Through simple
wood structures
and sand,
warehouse B
is transformed
into an urban
meeting place

quays in the historic harbour area. The idea of a harbour café quickly entered their minds, and in a matter of weeks they got the necessary permissions and turned parts of two empty warehouses (buildings A and B in Figure 16.1) into Luftkastellet (literally the pipe dream), which was characterized by one defining diversion: the landscaping of the quayside as a sandy beach (see Figure 16.2). The plan was just to run the café over the summer, but the informal social arena of this urban sandbox and the historic warehouses made it such a huge success (Café of the Year in 2001) that the temporary lease was prolonged several times (see Figure 16.3). In the meantime, the café encouraged Copenhageners to meet not only over informal and yet expensive cups of latte, but also over different kinds of projects. Gradually, the warehouses were filled with several sorts of entrepreneurs, all making simple and gradual reorganizations of the spaces at hand (Ørskov 1999): fashion designers, graphic designers, video producers, an event bureau, a clothing outlet, a kayak club, a monthly culture magazine and so on. One of the initiators thus described the place as a spot 'where the energy was let loose'.

In this way, Luftkastellet became an icon of another way of redeveloping the harbour (see Figure 16.4), which was otherwise undergoing a commercial redevelopment dominated by large cultural institutions, business headquarters and gradually also housing – all in very debated architectural styles (Desfor and Jørgensen 2004). It was thus heralded by the Lord Mayor of Copenhagen as an example of

Fig. 16.3   'Where the energy was let loose'. Copenhageners participate in the diverting sand beaches of the quayside on the north side of Luftkastellet

Fig. 16.4   Sheep grazing on the roof of warehouse B send a diversionary message to the rest of Copenhagen

informal development making way for a new kind of creative – that is informal, inclusionary, dynamic *and* economically booming – city. In autumn 2002, during a period of heated debate regarding the redevelopment of the harbour, the café was invited to participate in a panel meeting with other influential actors of Copenhagen in order to develop a new and constructive form of dialogue. Here the café crystallized some of the special, neo-tribal energy in burgeoning social associations (Maffesoli 1996) and the gradual intensifications (Ferreri 2009) of perceived and lived associations (the gradual, practical diversion and the concomitant cultural expressions) in the social space of Krøyer's Place. It did so by conceiving itself in terms of a 'milieu breaker' in an otherwise languishing space and a 'communication bridge' between different actors in the city. Despite this fresh input, the meeting turned into a farce of destructive political antagonism through the power of a routine political de- and resubjectivation so symptomatic of the contemporaneous political climate in Copenhagen (Desfor and Jørgensen 2004).

Supertanker: Further Intensifications of Social, Political and Conceptual Associations

However, the meeting not only affirmed once again disbelief in a constructive debate in Copenhagen. Through Luftkastellet's intervention, it also became an essential *moment* in the formation of a new and, in a radically democratic sense, *political* actor in Copenhagen. Thus, from its *serial* identity as fragments of a negatively subjectivated crowd, another social association unfolded, as Supertanker was formed as a Sartrean *group-in-fusion* (Sartre 1976) – united negatively in an endeavour not to replicate the debating climate of Copenhagen in general and the atmosphere of that meeting in particular – but also positively by venturing towards the making of something else.

The group found some space in one of the warehouses (see Figure 16.5) and, after refurbishing the premises during the spring of 2003, started experimenting with new ideas for harbour development and new ways of dialogue – one of the latter being to invite opposing interests to partake in an openly agitating and therefore *agonistic*, but also constructive, arena. One year of experimentation led to Supertanker having a keen eye for the constructive potential of informal urbanity – pursuing 'the *fulfillment* of the positive potential of civil society' (Arato and Cohen 1988: 54) both in the overall urban development through emerging terms about self-made spaces (*selvgroede miljøer*) and regarding the way people interact in dialogue. Simultaneously, as an example of Arato and Cohen's conception of the dual (defensive and offensive) politics of civil society, a gradually clearer critique of the conventional way of planning and debating the contemporaneous development of Copenhagen unfolded. With a new dialogical concept, *Free Trial!* (see Brandt et al. 2008; Figure 16.6), Supertanker thus helped a student organization to organize a large event criticizing and reopening the otherwise antagonistic debate of spring 2004 about the future of the alternative community of Christiania.

Gradually unfolding their perception of the potentials of self-made spaces, Supertanker also became a central part in the debate on creative urban development, which grew in influence in Copenhagen just as in several other post-

Fig. 16.5   The informal atmosphere of Luftkastellet spills into the refurbished Supertanker workspace in warehouse B

Fig. 16.6   Supertanker translated the informal but politically conscious atmosphere of the warehouses into strict public processes of deliberation, for example in staged trials such as *Free Trial!* here at Copenhagen Town Hall

industrial cities all over the world (Lund Hansen et al. 2001, Landry 2000, Florida 2002). Using their own experience from the diverted warehouses and their potential for all kinds of economic, cultural and political projects, Supertanker produced several smaller events and documents on the topic. This culminated in the spring of 2005 in another influential *Free Trial!*, gathering locals, creatives and a great number of people from the urban development industry on the theme of 'Cool Cash and Creativity' (*Kroner og kreativitet*). From the new social association of Supertanker, different, now more conceptualized aspects of the diversionary perspective on urbanity in self-made spaces and in dialogical processes thus started to leap into and challenge other practical and discursive spaces in the general, public domain of Copenhagen. And, as such, Supertanker evolved explicitly political aspects of its voluntary, social association (Arato and Cohen 1988).

Reduction in the Face of the Dominant Mode of Production of Space

However, during spring 2004, four years into the experiments of Luftkastellet and Supertanker and the gradually unfolding social, perceived, lived and conceived associations, a newly booming real estate market caught up with the diverted space at Krøyers Place. A luxury housing project in an expressionistic design was projected for the location. A historically unique situation of agreement between politicians, planners and developers supporting a strong 'Yes' to the proposal quickly and naturally subjectivated the general and especially the local public in the Christianshavn neighbourhood as strong adversaries mobilizing around a just as clear and loud 'No'.

Somewhat taken by surprise, Supertanker and the milieu at Luftkastellet struggled to find a fitting role in a new field of negotiation concerning the future of their own biotope. Instead of backing either one side or the other, Supertanker, based on a local initiative, tried to develop an alternative vision process gathering different interests across yet another slowly but surely developing antagonistic dualism – but to no avail. As the diverted space of Krøyer's Place travelled from the fuzzy margins of planning debate to the discursive centre of a heavily defined and reductively signifying conflict resembling the event that gave birth to Supertanker in the first place, the dialogical message was lost in a traditional battle over the summer of 2004 between pro and contra positions in relation to established planning categories such as building form, height and function. The antagonistic process, in this established and rigid mode of production of space, thus ran to the end of the line, leading to a controversial but final 'No' in the city council in spring 2005.

The new energy of the warehouses also faded, as they were cleared and, later, in summer 2005, torn down (see Figure 16.7), leaving Supertanker with no resonating space in which to further unfold their experiments. To paraphrase Lefebvre: with the lack of 'conjunction with a (spatial and signifying) *social practice*, the [locally diverted] concept of space can [no longer] take on its full meaning' (Lefebvre 1991 [1974]: 137). Today in 2013, ten years after Supertanker's inception, the result of this lack of conjunction reads loud and clear as yet another attempt at

(re)developing the site is spearheaded by several weeks of performances heralding the economic potential in 'bringing life to the in-between using the energies of urban culture' (Dome of Visions 2013) – without reference to the dynamic, sociocultural and political story of the site, but merely performing a discursive and harnessing construction in resonance with the contemporary floating signifiers of Copenhagen.

Fig. 16.7   From diverted space to tabula rasa. The conventional mode of producing space clears the practical and semantic traces of diversion

Still, the essential diversionary experiences with what Groth and Corijn (2005) call 'the reclamation of urbanity' had already produced original practical concepts for public deliberation and generation of visions as well as theoretical concepts for understanding the crucial role of self-made spaces in urban development, such as 'political urbanity' (combining the insights of radical democratic theory and the perceptions of new urban cultures in French sociology; Larsen 2007) and 'fallow zones' (Brandt 2008).

Thus the double, practical and representational, 'spatial and signifying', realization of this urban culture, with its gradual perceived, lived, social and conceptual associations, provides a temporary yet essential example of what Lefebvre refers to as the production of new spaces through the emergence, within a relatively vacant and undefined space, of what he would characterize in the early 1960s as *images* (2002) and later on as *spaces of representation* (1991) – lived expressions and experiences related to spatial practices gradually finding representational bearings. The case also shows both how different and how weak this *diversion* of space is compared to the dominant, established ways of (representing and negotiating) *production*. And, as such, deprived of a resonating or 'conjunctive' spatial practice, the conceptualizing endeavour in the political urbanity at Krøyer's Place may have been called to a temporary halt. However, there is still a great deal of resonance to be found in other diverted spaces in Copenhagen and all over Europe. The essential question is, however, if this resonance echoes the lived experiences and urban potentials of the diverted space or if it constitutes a lethal representational mirror with a signifying coherence that is paradigmatically different.

CONCEPTUAL ARTICULATIONS OF DIVERSIONS IN DISCOURSES OF CREATIVITY

As signifiers of the multitude of diversions unfolded in shrinking cities across the world, a plethora of terms, referring to different facets of the diversionary phenomenon, has been produced on practical or semi-theoretical levels in direct relation to the specific contexts of the diversions. Gil Doron has noted this with a certain wonder, naming but a few of the terms: 'During the last 50 years or so, from after the Second World War, the discourse and practice of architecture and planning has been perplexed with peculiar spaces in the built environment, which have been labeled wastelands, derelict areas, no man's land, dead zones, urban voids, terrain vague etc.' (Doron 2000: 247).

According to the specific context, the phenomenon is labelled in a certain way. This terminological haze, produced in a few decades, shows that something vital is going on, but it also shows that a great many discursive definitions are being produced, including *some* aspects of the diversions while excluding *others*. Two general lines can be drawn through this haze of terms, one focusing on the perils of contemporary urban development, that is the critique of neo-liberalism, the other on the possibilities in the existing mode of spatial production, that is the discourse of creative cities. Paradoxically, or maybe in fact underlining the argument in this chapter, members of both camps integrate references to diversionary phenomena in competing signifying chains – both drawing upon Lefebvre's urban thinking in the process.

Creative Cities

The 'fuzzy' concept of creativity has become a buzzword in urban planning (Kunzmann 2005). The tenets of creative city-making have evolved slowly from the 1970s through the 1990s, more or less dominating urban planning discourse of the last ten years (Landry 2000, Florida 2002). Today, creative city-making has even been canonized by the United Nations as a way to create a better world (UNDP–UNCTAD 2008).

In general, the vantage point has been a regional growth perspective, but recent years have seen it unfolding on an urban scale. Varying experimental interventions in and studies of informal and temporary uses of wastelands in cities such as Helsinki, Amsterdam, Berlin, Naples, Vienna, Rotterdam and Brussels have concluded that a hitherto unnoticed creative potential for urban development exists here (Urban Catalyst 2003, Urban Unlimited et al. 2004). In short, when 'urban pioneers' (Overmeyer 2007), such as small-scale cultural and economic entrepreneurs, unfold their projects on certain dilapidated sites, not only the site but also the immediate surroundings, the general growth potentials in the creative industries of a city and the overall urban development benefit from them.

Through this further tactical elaboration of the otherwise regionally based discourse, the creative-city tenets have developed a firm footing within both urban planning practice and academia. In the context of Copenhagen, this has produced an ever more tangled web of policy documents (Københavns Kommune 2004), advisory reports (Hausenberg 2008) and research reports and articles (Mathiasen et al. 2006, Pløger 2008), that both utilize and contribute to the selective condensation of the dormant potentials of diverted spaces within the established discourse of urban policy. This brings forth some revisions of urban policies, but the question is: What happens to the broad and soft values of the diversionary developments when they become hard currency in the discourse on creative urban development?

Apart from the fact that formal redevelopment often eventually pushes out informal activities, several studies of the creative potentials of temporary uses underline the detrimental effect of what Malcolm Miles calls 'interpretation from above' (2005: 597), when urban governance integrates temporary uses in planning. In the words of Lehtovuori, 'something important, maybe even essential, slips through the net of the current urban planning and realization procedure' (Lehtovuori 2000: 398).

But even in such a sceptical approach to the integration of temporary diversions of vacant wastelands in creative urban planning, a reductive signifying mechanism is activated. The *floating signifier* (Laclau and Mouffe 1985) of creative cities thus gradually integrates the diversionary perspective so that these developments now become the avant-garde of regional growth with a human face (Heyden 2008: 39-40, Moyersoen 2005: 302). The central discursive mechanism is a closed loop of professionals (researchers, consultants, practitioners) that gradually give the diversionary perspective an ever more creatively defined and more or less precise definition according to criteria internal to the *positive knowledge* (Lefebvre 2005) within existing planning, architecture and real estate development.

Critique of Creative Neo-liberalism

The critique of creative approaches to urban development looms large in the general neo-Marxist critique of neo-liberalism. In this perspective the creative-city approach is seen as part of entrepreneurial projects reinventing crisis-ridden cities in order to attract capital. The critique is that the creative-city projects mostly benefit the well-to-do and come at certain social costs (Swyngedouw and Kaïka 2003, Peck 2005).

A well-argued example of this is Lund Hansen et al.'s (2001) critique of 'creative Copenhagen'. In their general critique of neo-liberal tendencies in urban policy and of the housing market, they point out the shallow character of the discourse of creativity, which according to them is nothing but a tactical rhetoric in a general neo-liberal reformulation of an entrepreneurial growth strategy (see also Bayliss 2007). In their view, the negative social effects of the creative strategy make Copenhagen a revanchist rather than a creative city: '[T]he new strategies are embraced with a near absence of critical thought on possible social costs. "All discourses have their silences" … and the blaring silence of the discourse on creative cities is that about social costs' (Lund Hansen et al. 2001: 866).

The denaturalizing strategy in this quotation is more than visible, and if one focuses on the detrimental consequences of creative urban planning, there are several good reasons for such a critique. However, the problem is that this line of critique goes on to signify as creative most of the current, temporary diversions of space on the basis of their surface appearance (cf. Larsen and Lund Hansen 2012: 144). If one perceives it from another angle, let us call it urban, then this critique reduces the significance of the diversionary tendencies. Here, a tension comparable to the one between the critiques of Lefebvre and Castells in the 1970s appears. In the overarching critique of creative neo-liberalism, the broader and politically crucial urban tendencies within diverted spaces are overlooked or denigrated in a signifying chain, which is more critical, but no less reductive than within the creative discourse.

Focusing on the overall effects and core perils of entrepreneurial urban development, this perspective has only hesitantly included the diversionary and basically urban dynamics underlying what have been characterized as creative and temporary uses. When it happens, it is worth noting how the signification works. For example Swyngedouw and Kaïka state, referring in general to Lefebvre and in a vein very close to the energy that runs through many of the current, diversionary experiments, how contemporary visions of a new social order must of necessity be of an urban character and must come from those 'cracks and fissures' that are opened up by 'present-day hyper-modern urbanization' (Swyngedouw and Kaïka 2003: 7).

Swyngedouw and Kaïka praise the experimental practices that have unfolded in Brussels, but they do so with reference to overarching theoretical concepts such as 'Thirdspace', 'utopia' and 'spectacle' (Swyngedouw and Kaïka 2003: 7, 16). Rather than clarifying and further developing the links between the hazes of practical and representational diversions and those concepts of the positive, urban vantage point, that different social forms of association fight for and from, they focus on the potential contribution from these to general, historically and conceptually already established attempts at fighting the dominant, neo-liberalizing tendencies of society: a negative affirmation of current *policy* rather than a positive affirmation of the minute workings and conditions of current *political* tendencies. Whereas Swyngedouw in recent writings has moved closer to these 'minute workings', especially in Brussels, the generalizing character within the critique of neo-liberalism *vis-à-vis* urban diversions persists.

Both in explicitly critical and in pragmatic perceptions of the creative city, the urban potentials of diversions are reduced in instrumental applications either of floating signifiers (creativity) or of signifiers closely related to overarching, critical discourses (Thirdspace, spectacle) in order to articulate a specific perception of the broader implications (negative or positive) of the matter. The links between these, in Lefebvre's words, *industrially* conceived terminologies and the practical and representational (perceived and lived) tendencies at hand are too weak. Hence, instead of changing the city 'after our heart's desire' – in the paraphrase of Robert Park of the Chicago School by one of the most influential contemporary interpreters of Lefebvre's battle cry for the right to the city (Harvey 2003: 939) – one runs the risk of reducing or emptying the *urban* potentials of current diverting desires, instead reproducing the more established discursive significations, the positive knowledge or *savoir* that 'already exists' (Harvey 2003) in the arena where the battle to define the floating signifiers is fought out.

THE VAGUE SIGNIFICANCE OF DIVERTED SPACE

Sometimes it is better to leave those floating signifiers be, 'wandering about their native soil' as they are (Lefebvre 2003: 28), and unfold the implications of the new diversionary and political tendencies through a vocabulary that better resonates with their character, and thus develop an *understanding* of the possible and the urban instead of reproducing an industrial perception of it. What is needed for an urban perspective to be unfolded is a strategic positioning, which resonates with the peculiar character of diverted spaces, and which provides a conceptual grounding for the productive relation between post-industrial emptiness and the creation of new social and political cultures as well as of the susceptibility of these to discursive reduction. Such a resonating vocabulary has already been under way in some of the very enthusiastic interpretations of the diversionary cases and phenomena at hand.

The Vagueness of Diverted Spaces

Perhaps the most potent explication of the theoretical and social potentials of the new political urbanities of diverted spaces has come in an article by the Dutch and Belgian researchers Groth and Corijn. They point to wastelands as hubs for the reclamation of urbanity in times otherwise dominated by commercial developments and abstract planning. They refer to Lefebvre, but perhaps most importantly, they refer to the very peculiar *indeterminate* character of these weak or soft wastelands as the core dynamic in the creation of new social, economic and political cultures and their innovative reclamation of urbanity:

> *In particular, urban residual spaces such as abandoned industrial areas*
> *– i.e. interstitial sites that are weak in spatial terms may – due to their*
> *indeterminate character and a certain degree of 'semantic emptiness*
> *which reigns supreme' – provide opportunities for new, transitional*

reappropriations that are assumed by civil or informal actors coming from
outside the official, institutionalised domain of urban planning and urban
politics. (Borret, in Groth and Corijn 2005: 506)

Several researchers, architects and urbanists refer to these spaces as empty, soft or weak. However, emptiness is but one characteristic of these spaces, which again is only of a relative nature depending on perspective – planning and architecture, according to Doron (2000), being one of the perspectives emptying these spaces. Likewise, 'weak' might allude to the relative powerlessness of these alternative practices and utterances. But this weak quality is an effect rather than the defining characteristic of the spaces. In using the term 'weak', Lehtovuori also alludes to the 'many systems of meaning' as a defining characteristic of these sites (2000: 408). By referring to Vattimo's *weak philosophy*, Lehtovuori goes a long way in providing the diversionary phenomena with a conceptualization fitting their character (Lehtovuori 2005). His line of thought is paralleled in Borret's argumentation:

Contrary to other unclear sites in the dispersed city, the terrain vague
continues to resist straightforward definition, because its semantic
emptiness turns out to have less to do with an absence of codes than with a
multiple presence of codes that are superimposed, that clash, or even destroy
each other … They are not weak in themselves … but express an excessive
number of interpretative codes. (Borret 1999: 240)

Borret's double reference to emptiness and excessiveness points in another conceptual direction worth examining, namely the French term *terrain vague*, which is already in use in everyday language and within certain disciplines. One could thus substitute uses of *vacant*, *empty* or *weak* with *vague* in order to grasp this double reference. Etymologically, *vague* contains references to vagus (vagabonding, living a vague life, being extravagant), as in something having an undetermined, changing, implying transgressing and even provoking character. In the negative allusion to the lack of (clear) meaning or content lies also another important reference to the related word 'vacuum' (void, empty, blank).

Varying disciplinary genealogies of the term provide further layers of its meaning. It has been used among other places in the aesthetic discourse of the Danish sculptor Ørskov in the 1960s (1999) and the Spanish architect Sola-Morales Rubió in the 1990s (1995), who applied terrain vague in describing the new conditions for a current *weak architecture*. In an etymological and aesthetic elaboration, he integrates different aspects of the paradoxical *terrains vagues*: 'The relationship between the absence of use, of activity, and the sense of freedom, of expectancy, is fundamental to understand the evocative potential of the city's *terrain vagues*. Void, absence, yet also promise, the space of the possible, of expectation' (Sola-Morales 1995: 120).

In equally engaged elaborations, Schofield (2003) and Miller (2006) have uncovered the philosophical implications of (re)introducing the concept in sociology and geography respectively. Within philosophy the concept thus holds a special position. In analytical philosophy, *vagueness* is examined in opposition to *precision* in relation to the Sorites paradox ('how many grains of sand can one remove from a heap before it ceases to be a heap?'). But even more closely related to the diversionary phenomenon, exponents of the American pragmatist tradition, especially William James, explicitly treated vagueness as 'a positive, rather than a pejorative, phenomenon' and thus argued for 'the reinstatement of the vague to its proper place in our mental life' (Schofield 2003: 325).

Quoting other contemporaneous Americans, Maliavin relates this endeavour to the American frontier, that is, the civilizational *void*, that furnishes 'a highly sensitive feeling for the riches of experience and … a sense of renewal and local horizon which serves constantly to galvanize energies' (McDermott, in Maliavin n.d.: 107). It is worth noting the proposed relation between this 'vagueness or emptiness, a peculiar in-determination of frontier experience' (ibid.: 115) and the development of a pragmatist concept of vagueness, which is an attempt to counter the reductive predisposition of our 'logical herbarium' to cut up lived experiences into 'dried specimens' (James, in Miller 2006). So, in pragmatist philosophy the vague represents a double character of being strongly related to lived experiences, but only loosely conceptualized: 'In a positive sense, it means fidelity to experience. Negatively, it refers to terms used so loosely that they can accommodate disparate facts and therefore have no predictive value' (Seigfried 1982: 358).

This is the basic defining weakness *and* strength of the vague, which unfolds in contemporary diverted or rather *vague spaces* in, for example, European cities. Enabled by the absence of definitive, dominant practices or representations, new practices and representations are unfolded in lived endeavours into the possible. However, due to the lack of rigid cultural, conceptual and organizational definition, the energy surging from these new productions of space is easily integrated into and signified in accordance with the representations in abstract discourses. In order to enable further development of the new productions of space, one has to heed their vague character as a defining aspect and not jump to overly defined and defining concepts in order to *grasp* it.

The Vagueness of Lefebvre's Diverted Space

The concept of vague space is not only in tune with the internal dynamism of the reclaimed urbanity mentioned by Groth and Corijn, but also holds theoretical coherence, thus making it an important instrument for reflection as well as for *political* critique. Hence there is also a certain homology between the pragmatist endeavour and Lefebvre's critical project. At the end, where should we look for vague conceptualization if not in Lefebvre's work, which he himself presented as a constant endeavour to unfold lived moments of existential clarity but verbal indeterminateness into concepts? This is how he presents one of his central concepts in a late article: '[T]he concept [of everyday life] is not an object constructed according to certain epistemological rules. Nor is it apprehended by the deconstruction of reality. It is lived experience (*le vécu*) elevated to the status of a concept and to language' (Lefebvre 1988: 80).

This conceptual effort perhaps surfaces most clearly in Lefebvre's twelve preludes in his *Introduction to Modernity* (1995 [1962]), but it is also in relation to Lefebvre's concept of diversion as more than an analogical reference to vague phenomena. Lefebvre's concept of diverted space is almost *the* definition of vagueness, both regarding the signified phenomenon and the way it signifies: being the opposite of a floating signifier, it is not a specific word in search of empirical bearings (through discursive struggles). Rather it is a *very* specific and immediately experienced sense in search of a concrete conceptualization – and by concrete I mean the concreteness of Lefebvre's triadic conceptualizations. Diversion might be the first step towards both appropriation and co-optation or domination. If one jumps to conceptual conclusions, like some of the current creative or critical literature on vague spaces, as well as Lefebvre's own thoughts on diversion, the latter will certainly be the case. It is an emerging phenomenon awaiting a mutually productive relation between the perceived, the lived and the conceived, a vertical 'leap' from lived experience to coherent and collective cultural expression, in the words of Nicolas-Le Strat (2007), and not a quick categorization in reference to the buzzwords of contemporary planning, policy or critical theory.

Thus the vague is a conception that can clarify the fragile and fuzzy conceptual associations from within lived experiences of diversion. At the same time, it signifies those perceived, lived and social associations through which new spatial codes can form. When alluding to spaces as 'vacant, and susceptible to diversion', Lefebvre is alluding to vague spaces; when referring to their potential, he underlines the strong relation between the perceived and the lived in vague spaces in the same way as when Schofield elucidates the potentials of the vague: '[T]he vague becomes a site of activity and novelty where alternative possibilities may be contemplated and tried out. In other words, the vague harbours a generative potential that can find expression in any number of ways' (Schofield 2003: 329).

These 'any number of ways' might very well, when it comes to the current industrially blind, reductive co-optations of diversions of wastelands, lean towards creativity. When Lefebvre sees diversion as just yet another step towards domination, he reads the risk of the vague tendencies being usurped by established and strongly defined practices and representations, be they creative or critical, not *understanding* the vague but reducing it in reproducing their own 'native, discursive soil'. But with his aborted attempt at conceptualizing diverted space, Lefebvre himself reproduces this mode of signification (and thus of production of space as such). Just like the diverted spaces whose inevitable co-optation he so laments, his concept of these is itself a mere conceptual diversion, 'which can call but a temporary halt to domination'.

As shown in the case of Luftkastellet and Supertanker, informal reappropriations of urban wastelands act as essential windows to other possible modes of producing space. From situations of teeming vagueness, new perceived, lived and social associations are gradually formed within these vague spaces in conjunction with each other. And through time these associations may develop into more defined sociospatial and political practices as well as lived and conceived representations. The concept of vague space might therefore be not only a way to move Lefebvre's conceptualization yet another step towards production, but also a way forward in understanding and strengthening the direct participation of the 'small groups' of the city.

REFERENCES

Andersen, H.T. and Jørgensen, J. 1995. 'City Profile – Copenhagen'. *City* 12(1): 13–22.

Arato, A. and Cohen, J. 1988. 'Civil Society and Social Theory'. *Thesis Eleven* 21(1): 40–64.

Bayliss, D. 2007. 'The Rise of the Creative City: Culture and Creativity in Copenhagen'. *European Planning Studies* 15(7): 889–903.

Borret, K. 1999. 'The "Void" as a Productive Concept for Urban Public Space', in GUST (ed.), *The Urban Condition*. Rotterdam: 010 Publishers, 236–51.

Brandt, J. 2008. *Urbane brakzoner og trøffelsvin*. Copenhagen: Supertanker.

Brandt, J., Frandsen, F. and Larsen, J.L. 2008. 'Supertanker: In Search of Urbanity'. *Architectural Review Quarterly* 12(2): 173–81.

Desfor, G. and Jørgensen, J. 2004. 'Flexible Urban Governance: The Case of Copenhagen's Recent Waterfront Development'. *European Planning Studies* 12(4): 479–96.

Dienel, H.-L. and Schophaus, M. 2002. 'Temporary Use of Urban Wasteland and the Development of Youth Cultures'. Working paper, Urban Catalysts.

Dome of Visions 2013. 'Spaces-in-Between: The City Becoming' (online). Available at http://domeofvisions.dk/spaces-in-between-the-city-becoming-byens-mellemrum-byens-tilblivelse/ (accessed 20 May 2013).

Doron, G. 2000. 'The Dead Zone and the Architecture of Transgression'. *City* 4(2): 247–63.

Ferreri, M. 2009. 'Self-organized Spatial Practices and Desires in Conflictive Urban Developments' in *Critical Cities*, ed. TINAG. London: Myrtle Press, 40–53.

Florida, R. 2002. *The Rise of the Creative Class – and How It's Transforming Work, Leisure, Community and Everyday Life*. New York: Basic Books.

Groth, J. and Corijn, E. 2005. 'Reclaiming Urbanity'. *Urban Studies*, 42(3): 503–26.

Harvey, D. 2003. 'The Right to the City'. *International Journal of Urban and Regional Research*, 27(4): 939–41.

Hausenberg 2008. *Midlertidige aktiviteter som værktøj i byudviklingen*. Århus: Municipality of Århus.

Heyden, M. 2008 'Evolving Participatory Design: A Report from Berlin, Reaching Beyond'. *field* 2(1): 31–46.

Khatib, A. 1958. 'Attempt at a Psychogeographical Description of Les Halles'. *Internationale Situationniste* 2. Available at: http://www.cddc.vt.edu/sionline/si/leshalles.html (accessed 6 July 2014).

Kunzmann, K.R. 2005. 'Creativity in Planning: A Fuzzy Concept?'. *disP* 162(3): 5–13.

Københavns Kommune 2004. *Fremtidens København og københavnere – Kommuneplanstrategi 2004*. Copenhagen: Municipality of Copenhagen.

Laclau, E. and Mouffe, C. 1985. *Hegemony and Socialist Strategies – Towards a Radical Democratic Politics*. London: Verso.

Landry, C. 2000. *The Creative City: A Toolkit for Urban Innovators*. London: Earthscan.

Larsen, J.L. 2007. *Politisk urbanitet: Projekter, planer, protester og Supertanker på Krøyers Plads*. Ph.D. thesis, Roskilde University.

Larsen, H. G. and Lund Hansen, A. 2012. 'Retten til byen', in *Byen i bevægelse*, edited by J. Andersen, M. Freudendal-Petersen, L. Koefoed and J. Larsen. Frederiksberg: Roskilde Universitetsforlag, 131–47.

Lefebvre, H. 1988. 'Towards a Leftist Cultural Politics', in *Marxism and the Interpretation of Culture*, edited by C. Nelson and L. Grossberg. New York: Macmillan, 75–88.

Lefebvre, H. 1991 [1974]. *The Production of Space*. Oxford: Blackwell.

Lefebvre, H. 1995 [1962]. *Introduction to Modernity*. New York: Verso.

Lefebvre, H. 2002 [1961]. *Critique of Everyday Life, Volume II*. New York: Verso.

Lefebvre, H. 2003 [1970]. *The Urban Revolution*. Minneapolis, MN: University of Minnesota Press.

Lefebvre, H. 2005 [1981]. *Critique of Everyday Life, Volume III: From Modernity to Modernism (Towards a Metaphilosophy of Daily Life)*. New York: Verso.

Lefebvre, H. 2009. 'Theoretical Problems of Autogestion', in *State, Space, World: Selected Essays* by H. Lefebvre, edited by N. Brenner and S. Elden. Minneapolis, MN: University of Minnesota Press, 138–52.

Lehtovuori, P. 2000. 'Weak Places: Thoughts on Strengthening Soft Phenomena'. *City* 4(3): 398–415.

Lehtovuori, P. 2005. *Experience and Conflict*. Ph.D. dissertation, The Technical University of Helsinki.

Lund Hansen, A., Andersen, H.T. and Clark, E. 2001. 'Creative Copenhagen: Globalisation, Urban Governance and Social Change'. *European Planning Studies* 9(7): 851–69.

Maffesoli, M. 1996. *The Time of the Tribes: Decline of Individualism in Mass Society*. London: Sage.

Maliavin, V.V. n.d. 'The Fossilized Void: On America's Compelling Future'. *Tamkang Journal of International Affairs* 8(1): 103–28.

Mathiasen, S.B., Poulsen, C.F. and Lorenzen, M. 2006. 'Rapport 2006 Rammebetingelser for Københavns kreative brancher'. Unpublished research report, imagine … Creative Industries Research, Copenhagen Business School.

Miles, M. 2005. 'Interruptions: Testing the Rhetoric of Culturally Led Urban Development'. *Urban Studies* 42(5/6): 889–911.

Miller, V. 2006. 'The Unmappable: Vagueness and Spatial Experience'. *Space and Culture* 9: 453–67.

Moyersoen, J. 2005 'Self-determined Urban Interventions as Tools for Social Innovation' in *Social Innovation, Governance and Community Building*, edited by F. Moulaert. Research report for the European Commission.

Nicolas-Le Strat, P. 2007. 'Interstitial Multiplicity', in aaa (ed.), *Urban Act*. Paris: aaa–PEPRAV.

Ørskov, W. 1999. '"Terrain-vague" og "simple organiseringer"'. *Samlet*. Copenhagen: Borgen.

Oswalt, P. 2005. 'Introduction', in *Shrinking Cities: Volume 1*, edited by P. Oswalt. Ostfildern-Ruit: Hatje Cantz Verlag, 12–17.

Overmeyer, K. (ed.) 2007. *Urban Pioneers: Temporary Use and Urban Development in Berlin*. Berlin: Jovis Verlag.

Peck, J. 2005. 'Struggling with the Creative Class'. *International Journal of Urban and Regional Research* 29(4): 740–70.

Pløger, J. 2008. 'Midlertidige byrum', in *Byens rum – det fremmede i det kendte*, edited by H. Juul and F. Frost. Copenhagen: Arkitekturforlaget B, 52–61.

Ross, K. 1997. 'Lefebvre on the Situationists'. *October* 79: 69–83.

Sartre, J.-P. 1976. *Critique of Dialectical Reason*. New York: Verso.

Schofield, B. 2003. 'Re-instating the Vague'. *The Sociological Review* 51(3): 321–38.

Seigfried, C.H. 1982. 'Vagueness and the Adequacy of Concepts'. *Philosophy Today* 26(4): 357–67.

Sola-Morales Rubió, I. de 1995. 'Terrain Vague', in *ANYplace*, edited by B. Davidson. Cambridge, MA: MIT Press, 118–23.

Swyngedouw, E. and Kaïka, M. 2003 'The Making of 'Glocal' Urban Modernities – Exploring the Cracks in the Mirror', in *City* 7(1): 5-21.

UNDP–UNCTAD 2008. *Report on the Creative Economy 2008 –The Challenge of Assessing the Creative Economy towards Informed Policy-Making*. New York: United Nations.

Urban Catalyst 2003. 'Urban Catalysts – Synthesis'. Unpublished report.

Urban Unlimited, o2-consult, MUST, dS+V | OBR and VUB 2004. 'The Shadow City'. Unpublished report.

Index

22@Barcelona 161–7

abstract, transformative mediation of 192–3
abstract space 12, 97, 113–26, 158–61, 222–3, 229, 247
affect 15, 283–97
L'Agence Nationale de la Rénovation Urbaine (ANRU) 99, 101
agoraphobia 208
Algeria 94–5
Algiers 98
Allen, John 73
Alpine fallow lands 41
Al-Shiddi, Sulaiman 238
ANRU (L'Agence Nationale de la Rénovation Urbaine) 99, 101
appropriation 321
architects 265
architectural histories 191
architectural modernism 194–7
architecture 8–9, 13–14, 15, 66n22
archi-textures 228, 240–1
Austro-Hungarian Empire 229

Bangladesh 62, 67n41, see also Dhaka
Barcelona 12, 161–7
Barcelona Activa 168n2
Baudrillard, Jean 236
bazar of Dhaka 54–5, 65n16, 65n17
Benjamin, Walter 53, 65n11
Berlin 15
    New Berlin School 287–8
    Tempelhof Airport 283–4, 288–97
Blakely Plan 179–80
blind spots 175, 180
Blue Strip, Havana 42

BNOBC (Bring New Orleans Back Commission) 175–6
Borden, Iain 222
borders 38
bourgeois architecture 233
Brazil 243, see also São Paulo
Bring New Orleans Back Commission (BNOBC) 175–6
BRS (Building Research Station) 199
Budapest 14, 207–21
    János Pál pápa tér 216–19
    Kós Károly tér 212–16
    Nyugati tér 219–21
    Oktogon 209–12
Building Research Station (BRS) 199
bureaucracy 137–9

Can Ricart 166
Canada 98–102
cartographical analysis 39
Castells, Manuel 28
centrality 227, 247, 305–9
Centre for the Promotion of Science (CFPOS) 311–12
Chatterjee, Partha 64n7
chengs 78
China
    agrarian empire 78–81
    Hong Kong 71–88
    land system 79–80
citizens 141
city dwellers 141
clusters 140–1
colonization 10–11, 74–6, 81–8, 93–106
Community Development Block Grants (Louisiana) 185n5
compact city 162–4, 168n3

competitiveness 12, 157–67
complete urbanization 1–2, 9–11, 38–40,
    51–2, 62–3, 72–5
concrete abstraction 33–4
conjunctures 54
contradictions of space 165–7
cooption 321
Copenhagen 15, 322–30
    Krøyer's Place 323–4, 328
    Luftkastellet 324–6
    Wilder's Island 322–3
creative cities 12, 330–3
creative industries 157
creative neo-liberalism 331–3
creativity 330–3
Crescent Riverfront plan (New Orleans)
    181–2
critical urban theory 2–4, 7
Curtis, Barry 195

de Gaulle, Charles 154n7
Debord, Guy 221–2
decentralized concentration 41
Deep Havana 42–3
Delouvrier, Paul 136
desegregation 98
détournement 222
de-urbanized urbanization 136
Dhaka 10, 49–64, 65n20
    bazar 54–5, 65n16, 65n17
Dhaka University 56
Dhanmondi 56–7, 59–60, 61
dialectical logic 159
dialectics 33
dialectics of affect 285–7
difference 7, 11–13, 38, 160
differential space 158–9, 247
differential time 49–51, 54
dimensions 31–2
diversity planning 98–104
diverted space 319–37

Eid 64n2
Ejercito Zapatista de Liberación Nacional
    (EZLN) 117, 122–5
empirical research 4–9, 35–7
encroachment 66n34
epistemology 32–4
EPZs (Export Processing Zones) 66n28
espace vécu 285–6
everyday life 13–14, 30, 95, 158–9, 192,
    230–1, 240–1

Export Processing Zones (EPZs) 66n28
EZLN (Ejercito Zapatista de Liberación
    Nacional) 117, 122–5

Fanon, Frantz 97
faubourgs 98
female spaces 61
fields 32
forgotten spaces 40–3
formalism 162–4
Forty, Adrian 195–6
Fox, Vicente 116–19, 128n14
France 94–6, 102
    Communist Party 94–5
Franciliens 153n4
functionalism 98, 100

general theory of society 31–2
gentrification 93, 98, 100, 101–2
geographies of affect 284–5
German Dialectic 30
global competitiveness 162–4
globalization 30–1
Grand Paris Express 141
grands ensembles 98
Great Britain
    colonialism 81–8
    London, South Bank 194–7
Greater Paris project 133–5, 139–53
ground exploration 197–202
Gulshan 56–8

Les Halles, Paris 320–2
Harvey, David 28
Havana 42–3
heterotopia 215–16
homogenisation 158–9
Hong Kong 10, 71–88
    British Colonialism 81–8
    under the Chinese agrarian empire
        78–81
    urbanization of 76–8
Howard, Ebenezer 213

India 62, 67n41
industrial development 58–9
innovation-mediated production 157
Inter-American Development Bank
    127n2
Islam, Muzharul 66n22

János Pál pápa tér, Budapest 216–19

Kipfer, Stefan 74–5
knowledge 159
knowledge economies 157
Kós Károly tér, Budapest 212–16
Kraków, Poland 268–9
Krøyer's Place, Copenhagen 323–4, 328
kutti 55, 65n18

Lambert Plans 176–7, 185n4
Le Corbusier 233
levels 31, 65n13
lived space 285–6
logic 159
London, South Bank 194–7, 199–202
London blue clay 197, 199
love 285
Lower Ninth Ward, New Orleans 174
Luftkastellet, Copenhagen 324–6
lungi 65n18

maps 39
marginality 309–11
Marijin Dvor, Sarajevo 228–40
Marx, Karl 17, 75, 202
McKinnon, Malcolm 64n7
Mesoamerican Forum 128n12
metaphilosophy 36–7
metaphors 93–4
methods 17
Metropolitan Development Plan (Dhaka)
    66n29
Mexico 116–22, 127n5, 128n14, 128n16
MLF (Mouvement de libération des
    femmes) 106n2
mobility 141–2, 144
modernism 194–7
monumental space 247, 286–7
Morrison, Herbert 201
Mourenx, France 269–70
Mouvement de libération des femmes
    (MLF) 106n2
multidimensional analysis of
    urbanization 3

NAFTA (North American Free Trade
    Agreement) 117
naturalization of the production of space
    137
Neidhardt, Juraj 233–4
Neighborhoods Rebuilding Plan (New
    Orleans) 176–7
neo-avant-garde 192

networks 38
New Berlin School 287–8
New Orleans 12–13, 173–86
new towns 139–40
non-places 221
North American Free Trade Agreement
    (NAFTA) 117
Novi Beograd, Serbia 15, 301–15
    Centre for the Promotion of Science
        311–12
    mirage effect 311–14
    privatization of urban land 304
    under-urbanization 303
    urban landscape 304–15
    urban planning 303–4
    utopia 314–15
Nowa Huta, Poland 14–15, 265–79
    Alley of the Roses 274–9
    cultural institutions 271–2
    housing 269–71
    Lenin monument 274–6
    representations of space 265–79
Nyugati tér, Budapest 219–21

Oktogon, Budapest 209–12
Ontario 101

Paris 11, 12, 30, 97, 98–9, 100, 101,
        133–53
    governance 145–53, 154n8
    Les Halles 320–2
Parliament building, Sarajevo 233–4
PCF (French Communist Party) 94–5
Pevsner, Nikolaus 194–5
photography 53–4
picturesque planning 195
Plan de Constantine 98
Plan Puebla Panama (PPP) 116–22, 125–9
Plan Realidad-Tijuana 122–5
planetary urbanization 40
Poblenou, Barcelona 161–7
Poland see Kraków; Nowa Huta
political ecology 8
political voids 321
politics of everyday life see everyday life
politics of space 160–1
la politique de la ville 99
PPP (Plan Puebla Panama) 116–22, 125–9
Praça da Sé, São Paulo 247–58
privatization of urban land 304
production of space 4–6, 8–9, 16, 27–44,
        74–5, 159, 160, 265

interpretation 28–9
  naturalization of 137
  three-dimensional analysis 37–8
production regimes 196
public housing 98–104, 180–1, 269–71
public transport 141–2, 144
Puigcerdà 127 167
puja 65n19
Pyrenees 30

quiet zones 41

racism 97
reappropriation 321
regeneration schemes 143
Région Île-de-France 153n4
regressive-progressive method 243–60
regressive-progressive procedure 53–4,
  61, 64n9
representations of space 14–15, 40–3, 54,
  265–79
RFH (Royal Festival Hall) 194–7
right to the city 7, 11–13, 104–6, 144,
  173–85
Royal Festival Hall (RFH) 194–7

São Paulo 14, 243–60
Sarajevo 14, 227–41
  Parliament building 233–4
  siege of 235–7
Sarkozy, Nicolas 135, 145–6
Saunders, Doug 65n21
scale 7
Schéma Directeur d'Aménagement et
  d'Urbanisme de la Région Parisienne
  (SDAURP) 135–9
segregation 139–45, 175
SEZs (Special Economic Zones) 66n28
Situationists 221–2
skateboarding 8, 191, 192, 222
social democracy 194–7
social housing 98–104
social mix 94, 98–104
social reality 7, 29–31
social struggle 7
socialist realism 268
Société du Grand Paris 153n3
society, general theory of 31–2
socio-spatial polarization 139–45
soil mechanics 197–202
South Bank, London 194–7, 199–202
space-time 53

space-time dimensions 31–2
space-time fields 32
space-time levels 31
spatial politics of affect 284–5, 296–7
spatial subsumption 193, 223
spatial triad 6–7, 13, 14, 64n1, 223, 228–9
Special Economic Zones (SEZs) 66n28
squatting 60–1, 167
state-space 13, 196–7
strategy of knowledge 34
Supertanker 15, 319, 326–8
Switzerland 38–40, 41–2
symbols 286–7

technical planning 196
techno-bureaucracy 137–9
technology 196
Tejgaon 58
Tempelhof Airport, Berlin 283–4, 288–97
textile industry 58
textures 228–40
theory 16–17, 35–7
three-dimensional dialectics 33, 37–8
Toronto 98, 99–100, 101
town planning 138–9
transdisciplinarity 16, 35–7
transduction 36
transformative mediation of the abstract
  192–3
transit spaces 221
triage 177–8
22@Barcelona 161–7

ULI (Urban Land Institute) 177
under-urbanization 303
Unified New Orleans Plan (UNOP) 178–9
universities 159
UNOP (Unified New Orleans Plan) 178–9
urban, definition of 11, 67n40
urban age 3
urban competitiveness 157–67
urban concentration 137, 143
urban fabric 1–2
urban fragmentation 223–4
urban growth 58–60, 67n41
urban improvement 56–8
Urban Land Institute (ULI) 177
urban landscape 304–15
urban modernization 97–8
urban planning 137–9, 303–4
urban political ecology 8
urban poor 61, 67n42

urban process 2–3
urban revolution 4, 63–4
urban social movements 7
urban society 2, 14–15, 16
urban space 14, 208
urban territories 38–40
urbanization 1–4, 30, 62–3, *see also*
    complete urbanization
urbanization of water 8
urbicide 235
utopia 314–15

vagueness 15, 333–7
violence of abstract space 114–16
virtual textures 237–40

water 8
Wilder's Island, Copenhagen 322–3
World Bank schemes 66n28

xians 78

Zapatista Autonomous Municipalities 117